G000162487

No Man's Land
Women of the
Northern Territory

Barbara James

Collins
Publishers
Australia

FOR MY PARENTS, NORRIS AND DOROTHY JOHNSON,
AND TO THE WOMEN OF THE
NORTHERN TERRITORY.

COLLINS PUBLISHERS AUSTRALIA
First published in 1989 by William Collins Pty Ltd,
55 Clarence Street, Sydney NSW 2000

Copyright © Barbara James 1989

National Library of Australia
Cataloguing-in-Publication data:

James, Barbara
No man's land : the women of the Northern Territory.

Bibliography.
Includes index.
ISBN 0 7322 2473 X.

1. Women - Northern Territory - History. 2 Northern
Territory - History. 2. Northern Territory - Social
conditions. I. Title.
994.29'0088042

Edited by Margo Lanagan
Designed by Steven Dunbar
Typeset in Trump Mediaeval
Printed by Globe Press, Australia

Cover photographs
Top left: Granny Lum Loy, by Clive Hyde
Top right: Jeannie Gunn
Bottom left: Nellie Flynn, courtesy of the Northern Territory State Reference Library
Bottom right: Christina Gordon, courtesy of Les Gordon

CONTENTS

ACKNOWLEDGEMENTS

Many people have become involved in the production of this book and to all of them I say thank you. A special thanks must go to the women of the Territory, past and present, who served as inspiration for this book, and especially to those who have taken the time during their busy lives to record, in words, photographs or both, their accounts of Territory life. On a practical level I am indebted to the Australian Bicentennial Authority and the Northern Territory government for their generous funding of the research stage of this project, without which it would never have been completed.

Librarians and archivists throughout Australia have patiently and with good humour helped me find material, often very obscure, to help tell this story. Thanks to the staffs of the National Library, Australian Archives, Archives of Business and Labour at the Australian National University, South Australian Archives, Mitchell Library, Latrobe Library, Mortlock Library, Royal Australian Historical Society in Sydney, Victorian Historical Society, Red Cross archives in Melbourne, Australian War Memorial archives, Australian Society of Genealogists in Sydney, New South Wales archives, Sydney Morning Herald archives, Northern Territory archives, Darwin Institute of Technology special collection, Northern Territory Conservation Commission and, last but certainly not least, the ever-helpful staff of the Northern Territory State Reference Library in Darwin.

A special thanks must also go to those friends who have become 'discoverers' along with me and carried out valuable research in places outside the Territory - and outside Australia - and those who have provided accommodation during my research trips. So thanks here to Earl and Wendy James, Vern and Jaci O'Brien and Helen Wilson of Darwin, who turned some of their holidays into library and archives excursions, Kathy Leverett and Patsy Adam-Smith of Melbourne, Trish Egan, Shelly Spriggs, Jon and Pat Isaacs, Jenny Rich and Jenny and David Isaacs of Sydney, Ted Street of Darwin and London, Judy Perry, Vicki Chin, Pam and Alan O'Neil and Susan Grainger of Canberra, Elizabeth Giles, Pearl Young and Peter Simon of Adelaide, Peter and Sheila Forrest of Darwin and other friends who have provided help and assistance. Penny Cook, Director of the National Trust (NT), for whom I worked during part of the writing of this book, and Pauline Cummins of the Bicentennial Authority deserve a special mention for their support.

Thanks, too, to all those who have supplied photographs (acknowledged in the photographic credits) and access to their family records. Although there are many who fall into this category, Heather Harris, Les Gordon, Eileen Fitzer, Pam Rixon, Jean and Creed Lovegrove, Clive Hyde, Peg and Jock Nelson, Val and Austin Asche, Peter Spillett, Hilda Tuxworth, Molly Walsh, Dick Kimber, Joy Bruchek and Vern and Jaci O'Brien deserve particular mention.

On the practical side, thanks to Kerry Davies for her very helpful editing in the early stages of the book when I wanted to write the history of the world; to Jane Bowring for her friendly, patient and constructive editing of the final product, ably assisted in the last stages by Margo Lanagan; and to Kent Computerplus for keeping me friendly with my Mac. To Helen Wilson goes my most sincere appreciation, not only for her innovative and thorough research but also for her moral support, her proofreading and her interest.

Finally, very special thanks must go to Gavin Perry for his good humour and patience in 'living with' this book and the many piles of files it created, for his endless hours photographing and re-photographing much of the material that appears here and for always making sure I actually made it to the airport in time. Thanks too to Judy Perry who, more than most, also 'lived with' the book and provided much support during both the highs and lows. And one last thank you to my many friends who, through many special verandah sessions, lunches and telephone calls, have supported and encouraged me and helped me keep my sense of humour throughout.

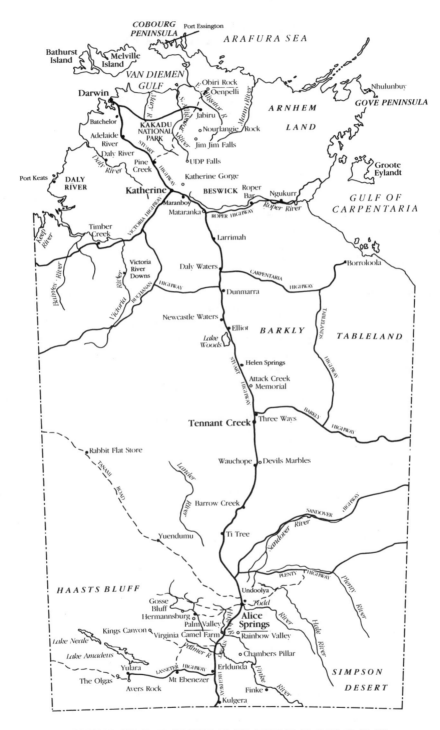

THE NORTHERN TERRITORY

Introduction

'On the woman no less than the man, depends the success of a great venture such as the civilisation and development of the Northern Territory.'
Elsie Masson, Untamed Territory (1915)

This is the story of Australia's Northern Territory and of the women who have been part of it. Although less visible and greatly outnumbered by men for most of its recorded history, women were often the real managers of the Territory, the stabilising influence, the builders of the social structure. They developed and maintained an almost naive faith in the Territory when the challenges they faced and the catastrophes they endured seemed to scream 'Give up!'

This is not to suggest that men did not share that faith or that men did not make their own very significant contribution to the Territory's evolvement. Traditionally, a male, even a macho, image has been associated with the Territory and much of the men's story has been told. For the most part, the story of the women has not yet been told, and this has created an imbalance in the way people have perceived the Territory. This book attempts to redress that situation.

Just as women have helped shape the Territory's destiny, so has the Territory helped shape the women who have shared in that destiny. The Territory's extreme isolation, its vastly contrasting tropical and desert climates, and its cultural and racial diversity have allowed for, and at times demanded, such change. That change may not have been possible, or even necessary, elsewhere.

Although the Territory's isolation and its climate have often given rise amongst the populace to frustration, fear and loneliness, they have also been responsible for a kind of freedom, giving people the chance to expand. Just as the Territory has often been an experimental playground for distant officials and entrepreneurs, it has also been a place where ordinary women and men could experiment with ideas, concepts and characteristics not always possible in more established, rigid societies.

In many ways the Territory can be seen as a microcosm of Australian society, of its problems and its potential. It is a place where extremes and contrasts are often the norm rather than the exception. The Territory's land mass covers one-sixth of the Australian continent while its heavily cosmopolitan population is less than one per cent of the total Australian population. The climate in the Top End is tropical—muggy, moist and monsoonal in the celebrated and often exciting 'wet season', and mild, clear and almost idyllic in the 'dry'. In the arid Centre temperatures during summer can soar well above 40° Celsius while in winter months they drop below freezing. In the Top End too much rain and cyclonic winds can spell disaster of one kind, while in the hot and dry Centre lack of rain can spell disaster of another kind.

Cultural differences, partially influenced by the geography of the two regions, have also developed. For a large proportion of the Top End's formative years under

8

South Australian control, Asians outnumbered its European population, sometimes by several thousands. As well as making their own substantial collective and individual contributions to the Territory, they provided essential labour and 'services'—such as laundry and food—for the Top End's European community, easing the domestic burdens for many women and single men. In earlier days, the scarcity of Asian women in comparison to Asian men led to controversial liaisons with Aboriginal women. In addition to the cultural distinctions, the relative ease with which people could come and go by sea in the Top End meant its population was generally also a relatively transient and cosmopolitan one. Darwin's extreme distance from the various seats of government that controlled Territory affairs—initially the Colonial Office of the British government, through its New South Wales administrations, then the South Australian government and then the commonwealth—did, however, breed a strong parochialism amongst those who stayed for any length of time.

The comparatively small European population of central Australia developed a loyal and parochial attitude towards the Territory, too, but had closer geographical, climatic and social ties with South Australia than did the Top End. This perhaps developed a more stable and traditional population base, though smaller and more scattered. The few European women who shared in the development of this region were generally much more isolated than their Top End counterparts. As there was no real urban centre in the area until the commonwealth took control in 1911 and the Alice Springs population slowly began to grow, these women either lived at one of the few telegraph stations in the area or on pastoral, mining or mission settlements, usually hundreds of miles away from supplies and other female company, with often months between mail deliveries. Although modern communication systems have helped, much of the Territory is still remote and isolated, and its image is still one of a frontier.

Much of the mystery and allure of the Territory is due to its Aboriginal history and people. Certainly part of this story is that of Aboriginal women, of how they were changed by the coming of the Europeans and of how they changed the Europeans who came. One early commonwealth public servant believed that the special qualities that people developed in the Territory were due at least in part to the presence, and help, of those women who had been there longest and knew the land most intimately. He said: 'This land has built up its special type of character, kindness and courage. White women were stronger because they were closer to the ruggedness of Aboriginal women.' They played a significant role, sometimes tragic, sometimes triumphant, in the human evolvement of the Territory.

The first white women to be confronted with the Territory were the few who ventured to the isolated British military and trading establishments at Melville Island, Raffles Bay and Port Essington, between 1824 and 1849. Their stories, although difficult to discover, for records are scarce, are important for the light they shed on the prevailing social attitudes of the day, and the prevailing European ignorance of the tropical climate. The impact of these early European residents on the Aboriginal men and women of the area, and the Aboriginal impact on them, is part of the story.

To better understand the changes that occurred in relation to Territory women in general and certain women in particular, the book is divided into two main sections.

The first seven chapters present, chronologically and thematically, a general social history of the Territory told from a female perspective. They deal with some of the women most closely associated with each administration, with the attitudes and policies about women those administrations perpetrated and with women who were affected by or helped influence those attitudes and policies. These chapters include the colourful, often romantic, observations of women writers. Two of the most prominent were Harriet Daly, daughter of the first South Australian government resident appointed to Darwin, and Elsie Masson, a governess to the family of the controversial commonwealth administrator, Dr John Gilruth. They both wrote books about life in the Territory as they experienced it and their descriptions, though presented from an elitist vantage point, provide excellent first-hand accounts of early Territory lifestyle. Comments in official administration reports and in newspapers, evidence given at Royal Commissions and in court cases, and views presented in diaries and letters about and by women are also used to illustrate aspects of women's lives in the Territory.

The writings encompass an examination of the lives of prostitutes, explorers, nurses, teachers, writers, businesswomen, wives, daughters, and women of many races. The Territory's cultural and racial diversity and the interaction between the races has been perhaps its most intriguing characteristic. The first portion of this book looks at that diversity through a wide range of official and unofficial opinion, relying heavily on newspaper reports of the time to add colour and often conflicting social comment. It concludes with a look at the role of women in the Territory during the Second World War.

Just prior to and after the bombing of Darwin by the Japanese in February 1942, most women resident in Darwin were evacuated to southern states or southern regions of the Territory, to become refugees in their own country. For the women who were allowed to stay, or who were imported through the military to help defend the north, life in a 'war zone' was filled with drama, death, pathos, bravery and often boredom. It was a time when hundreds of women as well as thousands of men were imported to the Territory. Despite the seriousness of their jobs, their stories are often filled with humour, as are those of women who lived 'down the track', and played their own essential role in keeping the Territory and the defence forces functioning. After the war, women returned to the Territory and played a crucial role in re-establishing the social infrastructure necessary for any community to survive and thrive. Their stories are of faith and determination, characteristics shared by most who decide for themselves to make the Territory their home.

Against this general historical background is set the second part of the book, the individual stories of some of the women who shared in the fate, fortunes and frustrations of the Northern Territory, primarily during the pre-war years.

First are the 'urban pioneers', the women who came to Darwin, the only surviving early Territory town of any substantial size, in its formative years. A pivotal figure of this period is the strong and stoic Eliza Tuckwell, a Cockney immigrant who arrived in South Australia in 1855 as a domestic servant and fifteen years later was on the first passenger ship arriving in the Northern Territory. When she died in 1921, she left a diary of sorts about her impressions and her life. She left, too, a family whose descendants today constitute some of the oldest and most faithful of Territory-born-and-bred families.

Some of the most colourful stories come from the women who have run the

Territory's pubs. These women were often substitute figures for the wives, girlfriends and mothers men left behind to venture north in search of fame and fortune or, as often as not, a new identity. They were at the same time 'mates' to the men, hard-nosed, honest and full of humour. As well, they were usually astute and enterprising women who not only recognised where much of the Territory's wealth was to be found, but also contributed a great deal to the financial and social development of the Territory. One of the most significant was Ellen Ryan, who built and managed hotels in the Top End from 1873 to 1915, and who gave the Territory one of its most famous establishments, the Hotel Victoria, which still stands as a monument to her pluck and her faith in the Territory's future.

It was not uncommon to find women in the hotel trade who had started out on the mining fields, intent on making a fortune from the elusive mineral wealth of the Territory. Some became legends in their own time. Perhaps the most notable was the thrice-married May Brown, 'The Wolfram Queen'. She took the hard-won profits she reaped from the wolfram fields of Pine Creek during the First World War and invested in several Top End pubs and business enterprises. She gambled, drank and gave her money away until finally she died, a pauper and alone, in the place of her birth, Sydney. Her story is in many respects the real story of the Northern Territory, symbolic of its long boom-and-bust history.

In the outback too, far away from the towns, women have made their mark—as nurses, missionaries, teachers and sharers of life on the Territory's stations. From these women, the women of Jeannie Gunn's romantic 'Never Never', we learn of a different side of Northern Territory life. The outback was an equaliser by nature. It could be little else; to survive one had to be able to cope, and to innovate. The European women who lived there worked with the land, struggled to reap an existence from it, and came to terms with its isolation. They drove the cattle, raised the children and managed the homesteads, often on their own for months at a time. They knew the Territory as few others did, save the Aboriginal people who knew it best of all.

The book concludes with a brief look at the post-Second World War period, particularly at women involved in various forms of political lobbying, though the results of that lobbying often went unnoticed and unrecognised. Although Territory women, along with their sisters in South Australia, were the first in Australia to get the vote, in 1894, it took more than thirty years for a woman to put herself forward for public office, and half a century before a Territory woman stood for a political position. Nevertheless, it has often been women who have persistently brought attention to the need to improve social conditions in the Territory. This was particularly true during the hardship and reconstruction that followed the Second World War and Darwin's Cyclone Tracy. In both cases women were evacuated from their homes, needed permits to return and then had to face compulsory land acquisitions and replanning authorities.

One of the many post-war Territory women interviewed, who assured me she was 'no women's libber', put it this way: 'Progress is a woman. In the Territory it has more often than not been women who have done the practical, behind-the-scenes work that has ensured that things actually happened, while it has usually been men who have been credited with the achievements.'

As stated at the beginning, this book is not meant to slight the achievements and the significant contributions men have made to the Territory, nor is it meant to stereotype the women who have helped pioneer it. Rather it is meant to present those women in all their diversity and allow at least some of them to come 'out of the shadows' and receive long-overdue credit. Their stories, I hope, will not only reassure modern women that women have indeed played a crucial role in the human evolvement of what has traditionally been described as a man's Territory, but will also provide a solid historical stepping-stone from which women today can take even greater strides forward.

As I discovered when researching and writing this book, it is often as you come to the end of something you have worked long and hard to achieve, that you realise it is only the beginning of something else, some new and more challenging adventure. It is my hope that many others will take up the story which this book has begun and help to fill in the many gaps of which one becomes acutely aware as one attempts to finish such a never-ending story as that of the women of the Northern Territory.

PART ONE

SETTING THE STAGE

Chapter 1

They Also Served (1820s-1849)

*'What of the women and children, the very few of them who came to the north?
They were shadows passing over the pages of the official records.'*
Alan Powell, *Far Country*

When Mary Ann Rycroft was sentenced to death in London in 1824, little did she know that her commuted sentence of transportation to Australia would include what many may well have regarded as a fate worse than death—living as a convict on Melville Island, off Australia's far north coast. And when nineteen-year-old Sophia Hickey married Lieutenant William Hicks in Sydney in 1823, she could hardly have imagined that a mere four years later she would lose a struggle to survive in that same harsh, tropical climate. Neither could the plucky, pregnant and cultured twenty-two-year-old Emma Lambrick have known, when she decided to leave England in 1844 with her baby daughter to accompany her husband, a marine, to Port Essington, that she would never return.

Mary Ann, Sophia and Emma were three of a handful of European women who were destined to be part of the first three attempts by the British to establish a presence on Australia's northern coastline, at Melville Island (1824-29), Raffles Bay (1827-29) and Port Essington (1838-49). The story of their lives that emerges from the jigsaw of obscure records and available observations is a tough, often tragic one, played out on a desperately isolated tropical stage. But it is a story that deserves a place in Australia's collective memory and certainly a place in any social history of the Northern Territory.

This story, like any of the Northern Territory, must begin with the people upon whose land the early Europeans intruded.

According to some Aboriginal ancestral lore, it was a woman who created the people and land of the Cobourg Peninsula, the general region chosen by the British officers for their northern bases. She walked the country, making creeks, hills, animals and plants and populating the region with children. Her children and the Tiwi people of nearby Melville and Bathurst Islands were the first Northern Territory Aborigines to have contact with the outside world when, several centuries ago, people from other countries began reaching Australia's northern shores.

People from Macassar had been fishing for trepang (the much-coveted sea cucumber delicacy) in the Cobourg Peninsula area for several centuries before the British came and Aboriginal men and women had occasionally travelled to parts of Southeast Asia with them, gradually being introduced to other cultures. Not all contact with foreign cultures had been peaceful, however. It is believed that from

1600 to 1800 the Portuguese from Timor raided Melville Island and took the young Tiwi tribesmen as slaves. These acts of aggression probably contributed to the hostile and suspicious attitude the Tiwi took towards some of the early British residents when they made their first official claims on Northern Territory land.

Hoping to establish trade with Southeast Asia and to set up a military deterrent to other countries, especially the French and the Dutch, the British sent Captain Phillip Parker King to carry out extensive surveying and exploration of the coastal area between 1818 and 1822. It was King, as far as we know, who was probably inadvertently responsible for bringing the first white woman to northern shores.

She was Sarah Chambers, a lovestruck teenager who stowed away on the *Bathurst*, the 170-tonne teak vessel King used for his fourth and final survey of northern Australian waters. Several days after the vessel had sailed from Sydney in May 1821, Sarah was discovered among the casks in the ship's hold where she had hidden to accompany her lover, the boatswain, to sea. When she was brought on deck, pitifully weak and filthy after nearly four days of seasickness and confinement in the dark, damp hold, her physical appearance was so altered that she was scarcely recognised by the crew, most of whom had met her before. She confessed that she had stowed away without anyone's knowledge. The ship's botanist, Allan Cunningham, later described her plight:

We pitied the indiscretion and folly of the young female who had scarcely reached her sixteenth year and who could have a very inadequate idea of the barren aridity of the coast over which we would have to pass a miserably long period, in a society by no means calculated to benefit the young and untutored mind and without any clear and certain prospect of touching at any civilized port, where she might introduce herself into a new life with a view to changing her fame and fortune for the better. As we [were] at least 200 miles north of Port Jackson and could not conveniently put back to land this young woman, Captain King reluctantly permitted her to proceed on our expedition, provided the object of her regards would attend to and provide for her; which, being agreed to on the part of the Boatswain, she joined the mess, with perfect content. She therefore became no burden to the vessel—her name not being entered on the books.[1]

King, however, made the cryptic observation that 'in a very short time [she] heartily repented of her imprudence and would gladly have been re-landed, had it been possible'.[2] Without evidence to the contrary, it is presumed that she accompanied the party on its entire 344-day journey which included Goulburn Island in the Northern Territory and various spots along the Western Australian coast. Unfortunately, Sarah's full story may never be known. Apart from her anonymity in official records, it is almost certain she was illiterate so it is unlikely she left behind any written record of her own observations of the history-making trip.

The likelihood that most of the European women who journeyed to the far north shores over the next twenty-five years shared Sarah's uneducated background has served to help mask their identities and personalities. If they are mentioned at all in the official despatches of the day, it is usually as a statistic rather than by name. As the military of the time considered wives to be the responsibility of their husbands, there was usually no need to comment on them in official records at all, unless they died or caused trouble.

Although few in number, the women who were part of these far-flung British outposts also served—usually both the colonial government and the men they accompanied. There are strong indications that women carried out the majority of the domestic chores, wearing clothes suited to the temperate, often cold climate of Britain rather than the stifling, often oven-like climate of the Australian tropics. This in itself is enough to earn them a place in the annals of Territory history.

To capture any sense of the life these women led, it is necessary to place them in the context of events which led to the establishment of the colonial outposts.

MELVILLE ISLAND—FORT DUNDAS (1824-29)

The first British establishment on Australia's north coast was partly the result of intense lobbying by William Barnes, an entrepreneurial trader who had visited the area and wanted a permanent settlement from which to establish regular trading patterns. He spoke glowingly of Port Essington in particular, and convinced several people, including women, to invest in land in the region should it become available. However, when the Colonial Office decided in 1824 that it would establish an outpost on the northern coast of Australia, the main motivation was almost certainly military. It could be argued that the small number of European women permitted or chosen to go to the early isolated outposts indicated that from the beginning the British were never really serious about making them permanent settlements, but saw them instead as temporary 'flag-waving' establishments meant to prevent other foreign powers from getting a stranglehold on the region.

In 1824 the Colonial Office sent Captain James Bremer of the Royal Navy in HMS *Tamar* to Sydney to outfit and direct the expedition north. He was to claim the country for Britain and land supplies and people at Port Essington. Bremer had three ships under his command with detachments of the 3rd Regiment, the marines, convicts and a handful of civilian officers. It is not clear from official records whether or not any women were aboard those first three ships but there is evidence that a few wives and female convicts had arrived by the time Bremer left or shortly thereafter.

Bremer had left his own wife, Harriet, in England to look after their two sons and four daughters. She, like other wives of her time who remained at home in London, Sydney or elsewhere, played her part in the development of a land she never saw, by maintaining the home and family to which Bremer periodically returned. Single parenthood is not the province of the modern generation alone.

Although Port Essington was the site suggested by both Barnes and King, Bremer claimed he was unable to find fresh water there and chose instead a site on Melville Island, which he named Fort Dundas after the First Lord of the Admiralty. Here he had found a permanent freshwater lagoon. Bremer and his company set about clearing the site, which was called Point Barlow in honour of the outpost's first commandant, twenty-six-year-old Captain Maurice Barlow. On the anniversary of Trafalgar, 21 October 1824, they fired a salute and hoisted the flag of the British Empire on these far northern shores.

When Bremer left in mid-November his men had 'explored the country, cleared a considerable piece of land, built a strong fort and magazine, railed in and planted two large gardens, sunk wells, built and covered in twenty comfortable cottages for the troops and convicts, and a commissariat storehouse, capable of containing two years provisions'. Bremer carried with him optimistic reports for the Home Office as to the potential of the place, but it was not long before William

Barnes, who had established a reasonably comfortable house for himself, was describing the place as a 'miserable hole', and he complained that Commandant Barlow was 'just from his mother's apron strings and as ignorant for what purpose the settlement was formed as a child'.

Bremer also carried reports of the first two Northern Territory Aboriginal women he had observed, describing them as having 'small mats of plaited grass or rushes fastened round the body and covering those parts, which decency generally conceals'. This led him to remark that 'if covering of women is general, it is a mark of decency and a step towards Civilization perfectly unknown to the inhabitants of the East Coast'.

One can't help wondering what the local inhabitants thought of the foreign intruders, particularly of the few European women who came to the isolated outpost with so little knowledge of the tropical climate and conditions. They included Catherine Tiernan, widow of one convict and then wife of another; Mary Ann Rycroft, a convict dressmaker serving a life sentence; Jane Richardson, wife of the island's convict gardener; Sophia Hicks, wife of the master of the *Mary Elizabeth*; Marianne Walker, the controversial wife of another ship's master; and Jane Baker, her convict servant. A first-hand description by any one of these pioneer women would probably dispel forever any romantic myth that might linger about life in these frontier outposts. Theirs was a tough, depressing, isolated and lonely existence, where mail took up to two years to reach them, and sometimes never did. They were plagued by mosquitoes, white ants, disease, and frequent attacks by the Aborigines on the cattle, pigs and sheep they had optimistically brought with them. The frequent public floggings of the convicts (who sometimes received up to fifty lashes for such crimes as stealing a pumpkin) could not have made life any more pleasant.

In addition, the outpost suffered three tragedies within the first two years—a ship which had been sent to Timor for more fresh supplies was pirated and all except two men on board were killed; a second ship, the *Lady Nelson*, suffered a similar fate near Baba Island; and in 1826 Julius Campbell, a convict, was brutally speared by Aborigines.

One of the first women mentioned in official records concerning Melville Island was Catherine Tiernan, who was amongst the residents at the fort when Campbell was killed. Catherine had arrived 'free' in Australia from her Liverpool home in 1824 on the female convict ship *Brothers*, along with her three-year-old daughter Bridget. They had come to Australia to join their convict husband and father, Patrick Tiernan, a shoemaker from Lancashire who had been transported in May 1821 for seven years for stealing goods valued at seven shillings. Like many of the other convicts, Patrick had volunteered for a term at Melville Island in the hope of receiving his ticket of leave more quickly, and after months of intense lobbying on his part, Catherine was finally allowed to join him. Sadly, they were reunited only briefly, as Patrick died early in 1826, one of scores who did not survive the rigours of the tropical posting. The following November Catherine married one of his fellow convicts, William Nixon, in what was almost certainly the first wedding performed in the Northern Territory. In the absence of a clergyman, the ceremony was performed by the surgeon, Dr John Gold, in his capacity as a Justice of the Peace. Witnesses were the Fort's gardener, John Richardson, and his wife Jane, one of the few other white women on the Island.

The bridegroom was a cotton spinner, dyer and wheelwright from Manchester, who had been sentenced to death for highway robbery and transported to Australia for life in 1820 when he was only nineteen years old. Like Patrick, he had volunteered to go to Melville Island, where he was put to work as a general labourer. A few months after their marriage, a pregnant Catherine returned to Sydney on the *Isabella* and immediately petitioned the colonial officials to send William to headquarters. The request was refused, but she was told that it would be reconsidered 'when the convenience of the public service permit[ted]'; in other words, when he had served his time.[3]

Although Catherine was given permission to return to William at Melville Island by the next ship, she remained in Sydney, where she gave birth to a daughter, Sarah, in September 1827. By the following September William was invalided off the island and returned to Sydney, where he was granted his promised ticket of leave and took work wherever he could find it in order to support his growing family. William and Catherine had two more daughters before Catherine died in Sydney in 1834. William, after apparently relinquishing their children to the Parramatta Orphanage and listing himself once again as a bachelor, married Maria Harmer in 1835 and raised another family before his death in 1863.

A few months after Catherine Nixon's departure from Fort Dundas, one of the most tragic events events in the Fort's short history occurred. It began with the sudden and unexpected death in November 1827 of Sophia Hicks, the young wife of Lieutenant William Hicks. Sophia had arrived in Australia in 1818 at the age of fourteen with her brothers and sisters on board the female convict ship, *Friendship*,[4] to join their pardoned convict father, John Hickey. Sophia had met William during the journey as he was the ship's first officer. William returned to England for a time, arriving back in Sydney in 1823 with the intention of becoming an agriculturalist. A short time later he and Sophia were married with her father's blessing and settled down on their new 1000-acre (400-hectare) property on the Hunter River near Newcastle, where two years later Sophia gave birth to a son, William Henry. A month before his birth, William and Sophia had suffered a major setback when they were attacked by five armed convicts who plundered their farm of everything worth taking and threatened to shoot Sophia. By June 1826 William had sold part of the property and in March of the following year he was appointed master of the *Mary Elizabeth* and was told to proceed to Melville Island. Sophia, apparently pregnant with a second child, and young William were allowed to accompany him although, as usual, it was made clear that they were his, not the military's, responsibility.

It would have been better for Sophia had permission not been granted. On 2 November 1827 after less than six months at the fever-ridden outpost, Sophia died, aged but twenty-three. The cause of her death is not recorded, but there is some evidence to suggest that whatever condition she may have suffered from was complicated by the difficult birth of a child who did not survive.[5] The day Sophia died, the small population of Fort Dundas gathered to bury her in a grave now long forgotten and obscured by thick tropical growth.

The day's tragedy was not over for Sophia's mourners. When the funeral was over, the Fort's new doctor, John Gold, and the recently appointed storekeeper, John Green, decided to take a stroll in the sunset. A sensitive and cultured man, Gold was not only saddened by Sophia's death, which he had been unable to prevent, he was also troubled by recent news of his mother's ill health and of his two brothers in

Sydney quarrelling over their inheritance. Perhaps he was reflecting on what he had written when he had sailed with his brothers to Australia in 1825, grieving for the lonely mother they had left behind: 'I felt myself...exposed to all the horrors of an angry world, without a home to shield me or a place where to rest my aching head. I almost thought that like Cain I bore a mark about me by which my fate would be known, that awful curse—a fugitive and a vagabond'.[6]

While Gold and Green walked near the Fort, a practice they had been cautioned against, Tiwi men staged a violent surprise attack on them, spearing Gold thirty-one times and Green seventeen. In retrospect it was perhaps not surprising that the attack occurred. Steeped in a background of suspicion toward foreigners, the Tiwi were already agitated by the British taking their best water supply and were probably also concerned about the burial of British people in Aboriginal ground. It may even be that Sophia's burial was the direct catalyst for the attack.

Such reasoning would have been of little comfort to those who found the mutilated bodies of Gold and Green. Their murder cast the darkest cloud yet over the garrison. An inquest and inventory of the dead men's earthly possessions showed Gold to be a cultured man involved with a woman who appears to have been at Fort Dundas but whose background remains a mystery. She was Sarah Fearby, who made up the official list of his jewellery, including a gold keeper and silver waist buckle, which she said she had purchased in Sydney, two wedding rings purchased from a Mr Clayton in Sydney, and earrings, necklaces and a brooch brought from England, indicating that their relationship had spanned a few years. She remains one of the more intriguing mysteries of the period.

As the doctor was the most valued person in any military establishment (his salary was about 380 pounds while that of the commandant was about 300 pounds), Dr Gold was replaced as soon as possible by the well-known Sydney surgeon, Dr William Sherwin, who had recently become the first Australian-born person to achieve the qualification of surgeon. Despite the fate of Sophia and his predecessor, Sherwin's first official request upon arrival at Melville indicated that he believed the women in his life would be better off in the north than faced with an unprotected life in Sydney. Dr Sherwin pleaded with the Colonial Office to allow his sisters, Sarah and Elizabeth, to accompany their brother John, who had applied for a job at Melville. He appealed to the officials to 'take into consideration the anxiety of a brother for the welfare of his sisters, left unprotected in such a colony as New South Wales' and to thus pardon his 'perhaps unprecedented request'. However, when John decided to postpone the trip his sisters remained in New South Wales. No doubt the few European women who were then at Melville would gladly have exchanged places with the Sherwin sisters and taken their chances with the relative civilisation of Sydney.

Certainly that was so with one of Fort Dundas's first female residents, Jane Richardson (née Nelson), who had witnessed Catherine Tiernan's marriage. One incident involving Jane illustrates just how male dominated and orientated the small community was. Jane, who had come free to Australia, had married convict John Richardson in 1824 in Sydney, where he worked as overseer of the government gardens. The following year he was appointed gardener to Fort Dundas, and in November 1825 Jane and their son Matthew were given permission to accompany him. Although Jane was illiterate, she had impressed the Colonial Secretary, Dumaresq, who described her as 'most respectable' and her son as a 'very promising offspring'.[7] John received ten pounds in advance of his twenty-five-pound annual salary to enable him 'to procure the necessary comforts for himself and his family during the voyage'.

The Richardsons arrived at Melville in February 1826 and John set about establishing the gardens at a nearby area which became known as Garden Point. It was the Fort's main vegetable and garden growing centre, meant to combat the debilitating scurvy from which many residents frequently suffered. Despite John's efforts to improve the supply of fresh vegetables, scurvy and fever continued to be a major menace. Some time after their arrival at Melville Island, Jane gave birth to another child, and after the deaths of Sophia Hicks, Dr John Gold and John Green, she became concerned about the health and safety of herself and her children. She asked to be allowed to return to Sydney. The commandant granted her permission to return on the *Amity* and to receive rations during the passage, on the understanding that she might have to reimburse the government in Sydney.

However, while Jane was busy preparing for the journey, her husband was busy committing a common misdemeanour of the day. As is not unusual with the history of the Northern Territory, alcohol was involved. With so little else to amuse them, and seeking relief from the rigours of the climate, the men and women of the garrison were always on the lookout for liquor supplies above and beyond their regular rations. Through some clever and premeditated plotting, Richardson and a soldier had bought sly grog from the *Isabella*, which had arrived in June 1828. They had no trouble in selling it for 100 per cent profit and, according to the commandant, the whole settlement was soon converted into 'one general scene of riot, tumult and intemperance'.

The authorities were not amused, and when Richardson compounded his crime by abusing the marine who had discovered he was one of the culprits, the commandant punished him by 'withdrawing the indulgence of giving his wife a passage to Sydney'. Thus, through no fault of her own, Jane was the one most victimised. She had to spend nearly another year in the outpost before the family was able to return to Sydney. This unjust decision may have cost her her life. Within months of the family returning to Sydney, and shortly after giving birth to her third child, Jane died. She left a distraught and perhaps guilt-stricken John to care for their three children under the age of seven. Soon after, John lost his ticket of leave because of bad conduct and had no means of supporting his family. He wrote to the authorities telling them what a 'serious loss' his wife's death had been to him and pleading for leniency so that he could care for his children.[8] Eventually he was granted a conditional pardon.

While Jane Richardson had been punished because of her husband's conduct, the opposite was the case for another woman who made a brief visit to the northern outpost and provided an assertive role model for any of the women who cared to take note. She was Marianne Walker, wife of Robert Stewart Walker, master of the *Amity*. Marianne and Robert had married in Sydney in 1826, having known each other for several years. Early in 1828 Marianne, along with her young son, Robert Junior, and her convict servant Jane Baker, received permission to accompany her husband to Melville Island on the understanding that she would not cause disruption to the ship's crew. But upon their arrival at Fort Dundas two of the crew immediately lodged complaints, accusing her of 'interfering and annoying conduct' and of being 'a great detriment to the duty on board being conducted in an harmonious and proper manner'. They added that it was Marianne, not her husband, who was the real captain of the *Amity* . They testified that she 'interfered in everything' and that Walker 'was quite under her control...When he doesn't obey, she, whose temper and disposition is most violent, has either taken a fit of the sullens or scolded until he's forced to comply'. They said she had used abusive language, had called one of them a blackguard and a damned fool and had said that she would 'swear her life against him'. Walker and Marianne claimed that the men who complained about her drank heavily, had neglected their duty and continually tried to undermine Walker's authority.

The commandant carried out an investigation and concurred with the view that Marianne was at fault. He ordered her and her female servant, Jane, to disembark and take up accommodation in a 'small and comfortable cottage'. He then suspended Walker, ordering him and his family to remain at Fort Dundas until they could return to Sydney on the *Mary Elizabeth*, under the command of the newly widowed Lieutenant Hicks. In Sydney the Walkers again appealed against their conviction and asked for a full inquiry into the matter. Eventually Walker was given command of other ships, and even returned to north Australia the following year as commander of another vessel. Marianne, who had become pregnant during their trip to Fort Dundas, gave birth to another son in January 1829. The family lived in Sydney until at least 1842.

Marianne's convict servant, Jane Baker, who shared in her mistress's punishment, died shortly after their return to Sydney. It is probable that her health was seriously undermined by her brief sojourn in the tropical north. Jane had been a twenty-six-year-old London housemaid when she had been convicted at the Surrey Quarter in October 1824 of stealing fifteen silver spoons from her employers. When Jane confessed that she had taken the spoons and pawned them for money to give to her sweetheart who had promised to marry her if she would commit the crime, she was transported to Australia for fourteen years. She had been sickly on board the convict vessel *Midas*, and it is reasonable to assume that her state of health was not improved by her time in the tropics. She died in Parramatta in 1829, a convict maid destined never to finish her sentence nor to see her native English shores or her sweetheart again.

While at Fort Dundas Jane Baker had been briefly reunited with another female convict who had been on the *Midas*. This was Mary Ann Rycroft, alias Diana Hughes, who was fated to have a longer life and a longer association with the far north. Mary Ann was a thirty-five-year-old London dressmaker when she had been tried and sentenced to death in December 1824 for stealing two gowns and a shawl from a private dwelling. Although she denied the charge, several women testified against her and she was found guilty and sentenced to death, but when the jury pleaded for mercy, as it was her first offence, her sentence was commuted to transportation to Australia for life. Here she met and married another convict, James Moxham, a gunsmith by trade and six years her junior. He had been sentenced to fourteen years in the colonies for forgery. In late 1827, after attempting to abscond in Sydney, James was sent to Melville, accompanied by Mary Ann, who was also sent as a prisoner and listed under her own name of Rycroft. In February 1829, after serving more than a year at Fort Dundas, James and Mary Ann were among the inhabitants transported to the new British establishment on the nearby mainland, Fort Wellington, Raffles Bay.

The abandonment of Fort Dundas was prompted by sentiments like those of its last commandant, Captain Humphry Hartley, who claimed that Melville could only ever 'prove to the British subjects an infirmary for one portion of its population, a cemetery for the other'.[9] Those who survived left behind the remains of the fort and the temporary settlement, the remains of a herd of buffalo from Timor (later to become a major environmental nuisance in the area), and a small collection of lonely and scattered European graves, including that of Sophia Hicks. Her lonely resting place pays silent testimony to the fact that women also served and sacrificed for this first abortive attempt to establish a British presence in the north.

FORT WELLINGTON, RAFFLES BAY (1827-29)

In mid-1827 Captain James Stirling had been sent from Sydney to establish a second northern outpost, this time on the mainland at Raffles Bay, an area closer to the original Barnes concept and the recommendations of King. He was to build a new fort and thence to proceed to Swan River, Western Australia, where another settlement was to be established. Stirling arrived at Raffles Bay in June, with four ships carrying people and supplies to form the nucleus of the new outpost. He went ashore with Captain Henry Smyth, the first commandant, soldiers from the 39th Regiment, a small group of marines, the naval surgeon, some sailors, a few convicts, two women and five children. Captain Smyth's own wife had died in Sydney the previous September.

Both Fort Dundas and Fort Wellington were suffering simultaneously from an outbreak of illness and from a lack of medical attention. Just prior to Dr Gold's murder on Melville Island, the doctor at Raffles Bay, Surgeon Wood, became desperately ill and, unable to bear the pain any longer, attempted suicide. He died a short time later of fever, still in a suicidal state of mind. The task of looking after his body and belongings was left to the outpost's two marine wives, Jane Millward, who was paid twelve shillings for helping prepare his body for burial, and Mrs George Knott, who was paid five shillings and sixpence for washing his clothes.

Shortly after Dr Wood's untimely death, one of Jane Millward's three children became ill and, in the absence of doctors at both outposts, help was sought from a visiting Malay doctor who successfully treated the child using a traditional method. Interaction with the Malays, and the establishment of regular trading patterns with them, was one of the results hoped for by officials.

But the more immediate needs took priority, such as building accommodation for the marines and soldiers, the Crown prisoners and the few married men with families. Though all the huts were small by today's standards, families at least were given separate dwellings, while the rest of the garrison had to share huts of the same size.

The settlement progressed well under Captain Smyth's command, prompting Stirling to describe him as a 'gentleman of good sense, great zeal and experience'. Immediately after Stirling's departure, however, Smyth embarked on a course of action hardly in keeping with that description.

There had been a number of alarming instances of brazen theft by the Aboriginal people of the area. Following one such incident, in February 1828, when natives had stolen iron and axes from the camp, Smyth decided to take punitive action. Unnerved perhaps by the murders of Dr Gold and Mr Green at Melville Island only a few months earlier, Smyth called for volunteers, offering five pounds for each

Aboriginal person captured, dead or alive. These captives were to serve as an example to other Aborigines who might have ideas about causing trouble. The result was the murder of a defenceless Aboriginal man and woman and one of her two children, during what Governor Darling later described as a 'reprehensible and disgraceful' event.

The full story emerged from evidence given to a board of inquiry at Raffles Bay. A party of three soldiers, two convicts and an interpreter had gone out in search of natives and the promised reward. After following tracks for many hours throughout the night, they eventually came upon a party of about sixty men and women around a camp-fire. They fired at them in order to scare them and take some prisoners. Some of the victims retaliated by throwing spears, the rest retreated into the bush. But the men of the garrison had already wounded a man, a woman and two children who were struggling to reach a canoe at the water's edge. The men pursued them; they were later to claim that they did not at first realise one was a woman because she was so 'large and powerful' and put up such strong and desperate resistance. As she rushed terrified into the water, carrying one of her children and pulling the other alongside her, the pursuing convict James Murray stabbed her with a bayonet, hoping, he said later, to take her prisoner. At this point he began to suspect she was a woman because she showed 'such anxiousness for the children'. But by now it was too late, the wound had been fatal. He watched her swim a little farther out to sea, to sink and then to be 'seen no more'.

The pursuing party dragged the children out of the water, finding one dead and the other wounded. They turned to the wounded man to find that his 'intestines were protruding from his belly' and decided 'it better to put him out of his misery at once and he was accordingly despatched'. Frightened by now of reprisals from the other Aboriginal people, the men picked up an axe, stolen from the settlement weeks before, destroyed the spears, scooped up the wounded child and returned to camp as quickly as possible.

When Governor Darling heard of the encounter, he was furious and ordered a full inquiry, during which Smyth claimed that he had been emphatic in his orders that women and children were not to be hurt and assured the Admiralty that everyone in the camp lamented the event. Although Darling severely reprimanded Smyth and said that nothing could justify his conduct, no more was officially done about the incident. Fortunately, Smyth's replacement, Captain Collett Barker, was a man with great respect for and empathy toward the native population. In fact, his first goal on arriving in September 1828 was to restore good relations with the Aborigines and repair any damage done by his predecessor. Barker also brought more European women to the little camp, including the wife of his servant Mills. The couple received special treatment throughout their stay at the Fort.

Barker, who was single, took a particular interest in the welfare of Mary Raffles, the now motherless Aboriginal child, whose native name was Riveral. She had been put in the care of the wife of a marine, Private John Little, whom Barker at once issued with three yards of dark cotton to make a frock for the frightened but obedient Mary. When, a little while later, Mary became ill and had to be treated with an emetic, Mrs Little reported that she had had a very restless night, continually crying out 'They are coming, they are coming', no doubt reliving the terror of the night she had been robbed of her mother.

Barker got on well with Mary, who appeared to trust him. In his diary for

February 1829, Barker writes: 'Mary very sensible with me this afternoon, talking to me a good deal and loud but she froze into her usual apathy when anyone else came into the room. While we were close, her countenance was sometimes quite animated and her smiles very pleasing. Surely something might be made of her by proper management'.

Barker used his relationship with Mary as a means of liaising with her people, whom he at first found to be, not surprisingly, full of fear and suspicion. Soon he was able to report that he was gaining their trust by 'the kindness with which they have seen the Native girl treated'. He continued:

I had great hopes that our little Native girl would have proved useful as an Interpreter; but she is a timid and rather heavy child, whom it is difficult to get to speak at all and I have been unable hitherto to ascertain whether she remembers her native tongue. She had at first a great repugnance to her countrymen which is not yet worn off. Her father visited us lately for the first time, and shewed much strong feeling on seeing her and I thought gratitude to us for taking such good care of her. They have sometimes expressed a wish to take her into the woods, but on the whole seem satisfied at her being with us.

From Barker's diary, we get a more graphic picture of the encounters between Mary and her father, during which he noted that 'tears poured fast down his cheeks' and observed that she 'gave him her hand and kissed him'.

Barker was concerned not only with Mary's welfare but also with that of the entire garrison, encouraging them with his optimism and enthusiasm about the potential of Raffles Bay. But even he could not stop the sickness and fever that plagued all the early British establishments in tropical Australia.

Only a month after his arrival at Fort Wellington, a serious incidence of scurvy took place there. One to fall from its effects was a Mrs Moon, whose presence at the fort is documented by a single, sad one-line entry in Barker's diary: '10th of October: Mrs Moon died in the course of the day'. She was buried in the now obliterated little graveyard, an unfortunate and virtually unknown victim of decisions made by colonial officials in Sydney and London with little or no idea of what their tropical outpost of the Empire was really like.

But while the heat, humidity and isolation took their toll, there are occasional refreshing glimpses of spirited female assertiveness. For instance, when Mrs Richard Haslem, the wife of a marine private, was faced with a complaint from one of the soldiers, Quinn, that she was washing his clothes only once a week, she promptly replied that the other men she washed for were happy enough with her routine and if he didn't like it he could find someone else. Interestingly, Barker took her at her word and another washerwoman was found. The identity of the unfortunate and probably more timid woman is not known.

Another woman resident of Raffles Bay was Anne Cook, who warranted numerous mentions in Barker's invaluable journal, beginning with a drama that occurred within days of his arrival. In early October Anne's husband, Private John Cook, went missing, pushed too far it seems, by the strict enforcement of rigid military regulations in the sweltering climate. He had been acting strangely for several days and speaking oddly to his child and to himself, but neither Anne nor the rest of the settlement was prepared for his sudden disappearance.

Although he was usually particular and remarkably clean in his appearance, the night before he left Cook had refused to prepare for the day's routine. Instead, Anne had packed his knapsack and rubbed his flintlock for him. At parade the next day, after a dressing-down from the captain, Cook agreed to finish cleaning his flintlock. He returned to his hut and, after a pensive study of the piece of military equipment, put it down, and announced he was never going to clean it again. He then walked off into the bush, never to return.

In desperation Anne dressed herself in her husband's clothes and went off into the bush to search for him. Barker reported that there was 'something wild about her'. No doubt she was wild with grief and anxiety about her future and the future of her child. She later pleaded with Barker that, should her husband not return, she be allowed to stay at the Fort until Barker himself left, as she knew no one in Sydney.

She was allowed to stay, but it was not the end of her trouble. She was often at the centre of controversy, primarily involving the handful of other women at the settlement. The incidents recorded confirm that the climate and isolation these women endured provoked petty bickering and competition more than nobility and tolerance. Anne appears to have developed a particular enemy in Mrs James Emms, whose husband had been demoted from lance corporal to private for 'indulging in liquor on duty' and being 'unfit to be a non commissioned officer' of the 39th. Once, when Anne was dangerously ill, Mrs Emms continued to abuse and disturb her so much that the doctor and Barker decided she was endangering Anne's life. They pleaded with her to desist, but Mrs Emms was adamant. Mrs Cook had insulted her and she did not care if Mrs Cook ever got up from her bed again. She even put her complaint in writing, indicating she was one of the few literate women at the Fort.

Barker had had enough. After the daily military parade, he assembled all the women of the 39th Regiment (except his servant's wife, Mrs Mills) and read them General Order No. 75, warning of his power to stop rations when behaviour warranted it. He ordered Mrs Emms, and presumably her husband, to vacate their hut and promptly moved the whole of the 57th Regiment into it.

In contrast to Mrs Emms's volatility, the female convict Mary Ann Rycroft (or Mrs Moxham, as she was usually referred to by Barker) appears to have kept her slate reasonably clean, probably indicating she was working hard for a ticket of leave. Apart from getting a mention in Barker's journal as being too ill to help look after Anne Cook, one of the few other references to her deals only with her wardrobe. As no clothing was allocated to female prisoners, she received, in lieu, about seven and one-half metres of print, about eight metres of calico and one pair of shoes. She would hardly have had time to put her dressmaking skills to work before fate intervened and Barker received orders from headquarters to 'abandon ship', a decision he accepted with regret, as he had held great hopes for the Fort.

Before their departure, the community experienced one last sad event: Mr Radford, the popular storekeeper, died. As appears to have been the custom, the job of looking after the body was left to the women. Mary Ann washed him and laid him out while Anne Cook made the shroud from one of his sheets. The women of the settlement also took a prominent part in the mourning march at the funeral.

Two more women arrived on the ships bringing the orders to abandon Fort Wellington and remove most of the garrison to the new settlement at Swan River. They were Mrs Hays and Mrs Weston, the wives of the ships' masters, and they brought a little temporary culture to the camp in the form of a piano. Probably the only other luxury the residents had experienced during their stay at Raffles Bay was during the previous Christmas when, as Barker's diary reports, every person at the outpost, including the women, children and the adopted Mary Raffles, had received extra rations of flour, raisins and suet 'so that the tradition of plum pudding [could] be maintained'.

Barker's orders for abandoning the outpost included an instruction to leave Mary Raffles at Fort Wellington, but he defied them, stating it would be 'cruelty to leave her'. He justified his action at the time by claiming that Mary had 'the greatest abhorrence of being left and the natives, so far from wishing it, have asked me to take her and seemed much pleased when I consented, evidently from a feeling that she would be well taken care of and much better off than with them. They kissed and seemed to take leave of her this morning before she went on board. They express much sorrow at our going.'

They were not alone in their regret. Barker was dismayed at having to abandon the settlement, having made progress, he felt, not only with the Aboriginal people but also with the Malays, who had promised to return the next season to settle with their families. In fact the Malay interpreter , William O'Deane, had negotiated a piece of land and had decided to bring his wife and family. He had gone to Sydney to make the arrangements, only to find that his family had already left for Raffles Bay. On discovering the news that the outpost was to be abandoned, O'Deane asked for his old job as watchman in the Sydney dockyards and urged that his wife Evama and children be returned to him as soon as possible, as when he was separated from them his 'feelings [were] wounded beyond conception'.

Barker duly arranged for them to return on the *Lucy Ann* along with Anne Cook and her child. At the last minute, however, Mrs Cook, who had by now probably formed a liaison with one of the other soldiers, was put on board the *Thompson*, as part of the detachment of the 39th Regiment, now bound for Swan River. Also on board were Mary Ann Rycroft, her husband James Moxham, and little Mary Raffles. After a brief sojourn at Swan River, they left for Sydney on the *Governor Phillip*, arriving in January 1830. James Moxham got his ticket of leave in 1831 and Mary Ann got hers a year later, although it was cancelled in 1837 for her alleged drunkenness and disorderly conduct. After serving a sentence of two months in the Parramatta Female Factory, Mary Ann became a household servant and in 1843 finally had her ticket of leave restored as long as she remained in the employ of the woman she served. James died in 1848, and it is believed Mary Ann died in Sydney several years afterwards. The final fate of the displaced and orphaned Aboriginal girl, Mary Raffles, is not known. Presumably the women attached to the 39th left Australia with that regiment when in July 1832 it set sail for its new posting in Madras, and for the most part they passed out of the annals of Australian history.

Captain Collett Barker was ordered to go to King George's Sound and help in its establishment. Unfortunately, he died in 1831 at the hands of Aborigines while swimming alone in the Murray River. Had he lived perhaps he would have had a second chance to prove the potential for settlement of Australia's far north shores. In 1838, six years after his death and influenced by his optimistic reports from Raffles Bay, the British decided to form a settlement at Port Essington, for the purpose of protecting and increasing trade with India and to serve as a refuge for shipwrecked mariners.

PORT ESSINGTON (1838-49)

Once again Harriet Bremer lost her husband to the tropical shores of Australia. Despite his association with the ill-chosen settlement on Melville Island, he was selected in 1838 to command the new outpost. But the woman who would sacrifice her husband longest to this particular British experiment was Mary Ann MacArthur, the long-suffering wife of Captain John MacArthur, the man destined to be in charge of the settlement for most of its eleven-year existence.

John came from a family with strong ties to Australia. He was a nephew of the late John MacArthur of Rum Rebellion fame, and a brother of Hannibal MacArthur, who was about to make a name for himself in New South Wales politics. When John accepted the Port Essington post, he left Mary at home in England with five children between the ages of one and fourteen, having decided that Port Essington was no place to raise a family. The two eldest sons, James and John Junior, accompanied their father to Australia. Despite having single parenthood thrust upon her for so long a period, perhaps Mary took some comfort in the fact that with her husband away, she would escape becoming pregnant yet again.

That was not the case for the women who accompanied their husbands on the journey north. Again there was only a handful of them, the first three being new wives of marines who had served in the HMS *Buffalo*, which arrived in the new colony of South Australia in December 1836. These women were all early South Australian immigrants and had married in some of South Australia's earliest marriage ceremonies. All three were apparently pregnant when married, a situation which no doubt added weight to the view of many South Australians that the marine force was the rowdiest and most ill-behaved sector of the new colony.

The first to be married was Dublin-born Margaret Shines who had arrived on the *Buffalo* as the seventeen-year-old housemaid to the first South Australian colonial chaplain, Reverend Charles Beaumont Howard, and his family. In 1837 she married Corporal Richard Mew. For a short time the newly-weds became pawns in the church versus state power struggle that had developed in the new colony, with Reverend Howard sanctioning the marriage and South Australia's governor, Captain Hindmarsh, refusing his permission. The marriage eventually went ahead, and by the following year the Mews had two daughters. As he wanted to settle in South Australia, Richard tried to buy his discharge from the marines. But he had left his request too late, and in 1838 was ordered to accompany his garrison to the proposed new settlement at Port Essington.

The same fate befell the marine carpenter Private Joseph Davis and his new bride Keziah Teakle, who had married only a few weeks before the order for Port Essington came through. Keziah was a domestic servant who had arrived in the new colony from Gloucestershire as a nineteen-year-old on board the *Katherine Forbes* in June 1837. She was heavily pregnant when the Port Essington instructions arrived. So, too, was twenty-six-year-old Susan Neville, who had arrived with Keziah on *Katherine Forbes* and, within a day of Keziah's marriage to Joseph, had married another marine private, Robert Seagar.

The three women waited with some apprehension for the arrival of their transport, the *Alligator*, and Captain Bremer. They were the only women who were allowed to accompany their husbands to Port Essington. Other marines, who had applied to have their wives and families come out from England, were refused.

Goupil, Etablissement Anglais à Port-Essington, *lithograph, 1846, showing the homes and the store (far right), above which Emma Lambrick and her young family lived.* National Library of Australia/Peter Spillett collection, Northern Territory State Reference Library.

When the contingent sailed for Sydney to meet the second Port Essington-bound vessel, the *Britomart* (which had gone directly from Plymouth to Port Jackson), the South Australian newspapers heralded their departure as a great thing for the colony, claiming that most of the previous two years' disruptions had been caused by the marines.

After making the necessary preparations and ordering their supplies in Sydney, the two ships, in convoy with the transport ship *Orontes,* set sail for Port Essington. On board the *Orontes* was the only other white woman bound for the far north shores, Caroline Short, who was married to the ship's captain, Joseph Short.

Upon arriving at Port Essington, they promptly began carrying out the orders to establish a third northern settlement. Although Bremer's party made haste to develop the townsite as quickly and attractively as possible, erecting, among other buildings, a prefabricated church which the garrison was required to attend every Sunday, the intense and oppressive heat and humidity of the 'pre-wet' build-up must have been almost unbearable for these youthful exiles, particularly the heavilly pregnant Susan and Keziah.

No doubt everyone looked forward to having the population increased so soon after their arrival. Tragedy struck instead. On 10 December Susan gave birth to a son, only to have him die in her arms the following day. Keziah appears to have been no more fortunate. On 12 December she too bore a son but, as there is no record of him leaving the port with the family a few years later, he must have died also. Both infants would have been buried in the little cemetery that would claim nearly a quarter of the population before the experimental settlement was abandoned.

After such a sad start, it must have been with some regret that a few days later the women farewelled Caroline Short, who was to accompany her husband Joseph to India. Within hours of their departure, disaster struck. The *Orontes* hit a reef a few miles north of the entrance to the harbour. Fortunately, Caroline, along with her husband and twenty-eight of the crew, managed to reach shore safely and several hours later they were rescued by members of the garrison from Port Essington. They remained at Victoria, the name Bremer had chosen for the settlement in honour of Britain's new young queen, until 9 February 1839, when finally Caroline and Joseph and five of the crew set sail for India in the *Essington*, which had delivered supplies to the new settlement.

By the time they left, much of the settlement's accommodation, including several prefabricated dwellings, had been erected. As well as MacArthur's home, a dwelling for officers, two barrack rooms, a kitchen, a hospital and a storehouse, and at least twenty-four cottages for the single marines had been built. Each was about 10 feet (3 metres) square with bark or reed-covered walls, a thatched roof, and red clay or beach shell for flooring. Cottages for the three families were also built. These were slightly larger than the single men's quarters but were built of bush materials with small square holes for light and air. An important addition was a semicircular Cornish chimney set against the southern wall of each hut, made of local stone coated with lime plaster, with pieces of timber filling the gaps.

The months passed. Flies, mosquitoes, fever and scurvy were added to the problems of isolation and soon caused the Port Essington inhabitants to grow weary of the daily routine of the men's seemingly senseless military parades and the women's drudging domestic chores. Thus they responded eagerly to the suggestion of the enterprising *Britomart* captain, Owen Stanley, that they cure the ennui by performing a play, a farce called *Cheap Living*. As luck would have it, HMS *Pelorus* arrived the day before the production, swelling the audience until it overflowed the Victoria Theatre, a workshop that had been converted into a theatre for the occasion.

Susan, Margaret and Keziah threw themselves into the spirit of the event and made the flamboyant costumes for the men, who performed all the parts under Stanley's capable direction. On opening night hot muffins, crumpets, gingerbread, mutton pies and oysters were offered for sale outside. All the men and women of the garrison arrived at the gala event dressed in full formal attire and for a few bright, shining hours, civilisation and culture seemed a little nearer. The two men chosen to play the leading ladies gave inspired performances. Of particular amusement to the enthusiastic audience was the spectacle of these two 'ladies' drinking grog, smoking pipes and indulging in non-ladylike conversation behind the backcloth during an interval.

The next event to create a diversion from the domestic routine was not so entertaining. On Monday, 25 November 1839 the *Britomart* was preparing to set sail for Sydney amidst drizzling rain and a growing breeze. By sunset the barometer had begun to drop dramatically and it was clear that a cyclone was imminent. By 10 pm hurricane winds were lashing the little settlement.

The crew of the *Pelorus*, still in port, tried desperately to secure her masts and anchors to steady her against the expected cyclonic onslaught. But all efforts were to no avail: the vessel was tossed and battered all night, and when morning came much of her was submerged under water or mud. Worse still, at least eight men were missing. One by one the bodies of the seamen were found and buried in the lonely cemetery, far from friends and relatives.

The colony itself was devastated and it took months before repairs were completed. Seven of the twenty-one cottages housing the non-commissioned officers and men of the garrison and their families were totally destroyed, and the remainder were unroofed or rendered uninhabitable. Of five private cottages, two were levelled and the others badly damaged. The church and hospital were damaged, the gardens were devastated and the natural vegetation was stripped. The situation was not improved by the intense heat and humidity of the wet season, which moved Stanley to observe: 'The worn out look of the people seems to prove that a place, the mean temperature of which is 81 degrees, will not quite do for European labour.' This was a sentiment which would be repeated and debated many times over the following decades.

The early days of 1841 literally brought new life to Port Essington. In January, Margaret Mew gave birth to her third daughter and Keziah Davis gave birth to a son. Joseph Davis had just been discharged from the settlement, due to illness, a fate that Keziah probably accepted with some relief. In March the Davis family sailed for home, leaving only Margaret Mew, her three daughters and Susan Seagar to represent the white female sex at the settlement for the next three years.

Their presence went unnoticed, however, when a friend of the MacArthur family, Charlotte Waring, included knowledgeable chapters about Port Essington in Australia's first children's book, *A Mother's Offering to Her Children by a Woman Long Resident in New South Wales*, which she published anonymously in 1841, becoming the first Australian woman known to write about what would become the Northern Territory.

Towards the end of 1841, at Port Essington, Margaret Mew and all three of her daughters had gone down with the fever that had already claimed the lives of several of the garrison. Fortunately the Mews survived, but no doubt they wondered how much longer they could continue. Relief finally came three years later when a new marine contingent was sent to replace them, bringing a new group of women, including Emma Lambrick, whose sojourn would end in tragedy.

Lieutenant George Lambrick had been selected to escort the marine guard on the male convict ship *Cadet*, from England and Ireland to Van Diemen's Land, and after leaving the convicts in Hobart he was to proceed to Port Essington to relieve the garrison. He decided to bring his wife and their young daughter with him. George, a veteran of the Carlist wars in Spain, had married twenty-year-old Emma Jane Dillon, a twin daughter of navy lieutenant Edward Dillon and his wife Susan, in Cornwall in November 1842 and the following August their first child, a girl named Emma, was born. His wife was pregnant with her second child when she and her daughter were given permission to accompany George to Port Essington in April 1844.

They were joined by several other women: Mary Ann Clarke, twenty-four, wife of Private James Clarke; the pregnant twenty-seven-year-old Esther Norman, wife of Private William Norman (with their young son); Jane Isaacs, wife of Sergeant Hugh Isaacs; Mary Anne Kirk, wife of Private David Kirk; and Mary Anne Crowden, wife of Private William Crowden, who was allowed to accompany the ship if she paid her own way to Dublin first.

Mary Anne Clarke became ill and was discharged at Kingstown, Ireland, shortly after the expedition left Dublin. Her husband continued on the voyage, however, and did not return to English shores until Port Essington was disbanded in late 1849.

The fate of Esther Norman was more tragic. Heavily pregnant when the *Cadet* set sail, she also became ill soon after embarkation and within the first few days gave birth, one month prematurely. The child lived for a few hours only and was buried at sea. Esther suffered from acute asthma and this, coupled with the unbearable grief of losing her child, took its toll. One day, after she had witnessed the punishment of one of the prisoners at the gangway, as well as the capture of a large shark, she began shrieking and talking 'wildly'. This behaviour continued for days, until finally she joined her infant in a sea grave.

This could hardly have been an optimistic omen for the somewhat fragile Emma. By the time they reached Hobart in August, Lambrick reported that Emma was in 'a most delicate state of health', and he was 'very anxious' about continuing the trip as she would need to be confined. Sail they did, however, and on their way up the Western Australian coast Emma gave birth to George Lambrick Junior.

A short time later they reached Port Essington. After a few weeks of exchanging gossip and news with the new arrivals, the men and women who had been holding the fort for six years departed on the *Cadet*, leaving their replacements to endure their first sweltering wet season. Emma's arrival meant there was now a true 'lady' at the settlement, though this exalted status only ensured that she was socially and psychologically isolated from the other women. The Lambricks moved into a small wooden abode directly over the storekeeper's quarters, while Mary Ann Kirk, Jane Isaacs and Mary Anne Crowden and their husbands moved into the married quarters, as did William Norman and his now motherless son. It was MacArthur's policy to keep the marrieds distinct from the rest of the inhabitants.

Emma's status entitled her to a servant, and since her own servant had not completed the voyage, she 'made do' with a Malay-Aboriginal girl of about ten, who became known as Flash Poll. Emma, with two young children and a third on the way, went about her life on the settlement with apparent good cheer, arousing admiration in those around her. In a letter to a friend, MacArthur described her as a 'truly amiable and sensible woman. How she endures the privations she is exposed to I cannot comprehend. Great equanimity with firmness of purpose appear to be her main characteristics.'[10]

John Sweatman, who spent several weeks at Port Essington with the HMS *Rattlesnake* and lived with the Lambricks in their comparatively comfortable house, painted a slightly different picture. He described Emma as a 'quiet agreeable little woman with unfortunately very bad health and...the only 'lady' and with the exception of 3 of the men's wives, the only Englishwoman in Port Essington. She said she was very happy but I could not fancy it, with no society, no amusement, no one but her husband to speak to, and he constantly occupied with his duties.' However, Sweatman, no doubt reflecting a predominant attitude about the role of women at the time, concluded that at least she had 'an unfortunate baby that was always sick and who, perhaps, served to keep her employed, particularly as she had but one female servant, a Malay girl, whom she could not put much trust in'.[11]

MacArthur had his own views of what the other white women at Victoria should be doing. 'The great evil is want of female domestic servants,' he lamented in a letter to a friend. He reported that he had tried to rectify the situation by putting an ultimatum of 'no song, no supper' to the women who were there, apart from Emma. But he was later forced to adopt a milder attitude. 'They do what they can from things, but washing and ironing in a temperature of 92 degrees...I could never think of enforcing it.' Anyway he had already concluded that 'only one of the three was at all capable of labour'.

The climate was more than an impediment to domestic chores. Tropical fever ran rampant, attacking most of the garrison, including Emma and her son George. He had been sickly from the time of his shipboard birth and finally, in mid-1845, while Emma was again pregnant, he died. A few months later, her second son was born, but he too was sickly and weak.

Then suddenly, in October 1846, only two months after her twenty-fourth birthday, Emma died. A new sense of depression swept through the camp. George Lambrick's grief was intensified when, just a few weeks after Emma's death, her other ailing infant died, leaving only young Emma to comfort her father. In honour of his wife and two sons he had a special monument erected to their memory, with stone brought out from her native England.

In 1913, writer Elsie Masson visited the graveside during an official inspection with the Northern Territory administrator, John Gilruth. She was moved to describe Emma's imagined life and fate:

She came with her little daughter to Port Essington, doubtless expecting to find a comfortable sociable military settlement. A year passed, her baby was born and both she and the child died and were buried in this lonely spot. Not far from the cemetery is a pretty little strip of beach backed by fine tamarind trees. Here the little girl used to play happily in the sand while her mother sat, her hands folded, gazing out on the mournful shores, wondering if she would ever live to pick wild flowers in a cool English forest again...Just as it looked to her eyes, so the harbour looked to ours, utterly lonely and remote, imbued with sadness as if lamenting the lives sacrificed in that premature experiment.[12]

Captain MacArthur, a talented artist, painted a watercolour of the imposing tombstone, which, though weatherworn, still stands to pay silent tribute to Emma's pioneering sacrifice. Painting was one way in which MacArthur sought solace from his own difficulties. Not only had he twice nearly lost his own son from the fever, but he was also losing his sight. After eight years, he was becoming fatigued by his life at Port Essington, made less bearable by a two year lapse of news from his wife. In May 1846 he complained that he had not heard from her since July 1844. 'But I hear of her well being and strive to be patient,' he added in a letter to a friend. He did not realise that she had already been forced to write to the Secretary of State for the Colonies, pleading for an extra allowance on her husband's pay, pointing out that she had five children to keep.

Following Ludwig Leichhardt's successful overland trek to Port Essington in 1845, MacArthur realised anew how weary he had become of his posting and requested six months' leave in Sydney arguing that he had not left the settlement since it had first been established. The request was not granted and he was forced to contend with more deaths in the camp, including that of the learned Roman Catholic priest, Father Angelo Confalioneri. The priest had established himself at nearby Black Point, spreading the gospel to the Aboriginal people of Port Essington. He had become an accomplished linguist during his time at Port Essington and had translated the Lord's Prayer and parts of the Bible into the Aboriginal language. He was highly regarded by the little community, black and white alike, and his death in 1847 was greatly lamented.

In August 1847 MacArthur received word that relief troops were on their way from Sydney, via the *Freak*, bringing with them another woman, Martha Tossell, married to Private James Tossell. In line with his residential policy for married couples, MacArthur had extra accommodation built for them. The ship's arrival was greeted with great joy, not only because it meant the presence of another woman in the male dominated settlement but also because it brought six months' provisions. Unexpectedly, it also brought Surgeon John Irwin Crawford, RM, who took medical charge of the sickly settlement.

In February 1849 the settlement was again besieged by the dreaded fever. This time both Crawford and his assistant Richard Tilston were smitten, along with MacArthur himself. George Lambrick was left to act not only as temporary commandant, but also as supervisor of the hospital and nurse to the sick. He was shocked and distressed when he was unable to save the life of Tilston, who had become well liked and respected in the community. On 4 March the ailing residents of Port Essington dug yet another grave. Had Tilston lived, he would have become the brother-in-law of John MacArthur Junior who later married Richard's sister, Elizabeth.

Despondency descended on the settlement yet again and all that the men and women could think of was when the next ship might arrive to relieve them. They did not have to wait long; the Colonial Office had decided to withdraw the marine force and abandon the settlement altogether.

As another tropical wet season 'build up' began, the *Meander* arrived to help dismantle the settlement. Cabins were constructed on the main deck for the women and children, modifying the comforts to make them more suitable for the journey to Sydney, from where most would return to England. Farewells were made to the Aboriginal people, some of whom had become good friends and servants, and at last the women and children were taken on board and their few belongings brought from the shore. On the morning of 30 November 1849 the *Meander*'s lively band led the farewell march of the men from the town to which they set fire before leaving.

Young Emma Lambrick, now five, was among those watching from the deck as the ship pulled away. She was never to return to the land of her childhood but she did live to a ripe old age, dying in England in March 1925 'a spinster of independent means' as she had been well looked after by her father and two stepbrothers, children of her father's second marriage in England. History does not record what memories she may have had of her childhood home, her mother, or her Aboriginal nursemaid, Flash Poll. But Flash Poll certainly remembered her. She too lived to old age and often repeated stories of the early settlement to anyone who would listen. Her storytelling usually included fluent recitations of the Lord's Prayer, which she no doubt learned from the settlement's chaplain, followed by a string of colourful expletives she had learned from some of the less religious early residents. What a shame her contemporaries did not think to record her remarks in a serious manner, content instead to treat her, albeit affectionately, as a humorous curiosity.[13] Documented more carefully she could have been a valuable source of information about this sad but often courageous human chapter in Territory history.

The value of the three abandoned attempts by the British to settle the north remains a matter of debate. One historian said this about it:

By virtue of its late colonization, Australia provides an excellent area for examining problems of colonialism. The specific value of Port Essington is that it is an extreme example in most respects...The dearth of women at Port Essington ... reflects in exaggerated fashion an Australian colonial problem...[It is] to be seen as a microcosmic example of the situation repeated a hundred times in the early history of Australia and which moulded a new culture from the old, the small, artificial male societies which give rise to the Australian legends of sport, hard drinking and mateship.[14]

Mary Packard (top right), married to surveyor Harrison Packard, was the only woman in the official 1864 photograph of the members of South Australia's second expedition to Escape Cliffs, the fourth aborted attempt to establish a settlement in the far north of the Territory. The men, who had been sent to assist the government resident, B. T. Finniss, dubbed her 'queen of the north'. Mary Packard and Eliza Bauer, married to one of the settlers, were the only two European women to live at the isolated settlement which was abandoned in 1866, a few weeks after Mary gave birth to a daughter. Mortlock Library.

Chapter 2

Of Fantasies and Frontier Dreams (1850s-1867)

Despite the harsh realities of early colonial life on the tropical coast of the Territory, one English lady of the period had a much more utopian vision of what remote central Australia was like. In 1837 she put pen to paper and described her vision in an intriguing piece of fiction entitled *An Account of an Expedition to the Interior of New Holland.*

Lady Mary Fox's fictional plot is set in the vicinity of what is now Newcastle Waters and describes a utopian settlement of between three and four million Southlanders, whose Anglo-German pilgrim parents had sailed in four vessels to the Great South Land to establish a new settlement during the early years of the Protestant Reformation. By the time Port Essington was founded, they had formed a community of eleven states, four of them hereditary monarchies, three elected monarchies and four republics. They lived in a racially mixed society, without conflict and with equal educational opportunities for women and men, low taxes, no foreign policy, the abolition of duelling, and the reform of manners and morals.

In reality, of course, Lady Fox's utopian Territory did not exist, although one point of her portrayal of Southlander society was uncannily accurate—an annual public festival centred on a long beer-drinking ceremony.[1] Alcohol consumption was a problem for the European women who briefly visited the Northern Territory six years after the abandonment of Port Essington. They accompanied the last official British-sponsored expedition to Australia's far north shores. In 1855 Augustus Charles Gregory, who had spent the past thirteen years in Western Australia, was chosen to lead an expedition to the Victoria River region of the Northern Territory. Gregory and his party of seventeen were serviced and supported in the expedition by the coastal schooner *Tom Tough*, captained by David Gourlay, who was accompanied by his wife, their three children and their niece, who served as maid. Along with Gregory's men, the ship's crew and 161 sheep, they spent several weeks sailing up the east coast before reaching their destination at the mouth of the mighty Victoria River, near the aptly named Treachery Bay. The Victoria, with its extreme tidal rise and fall, is one of the most treacherous Territory rivers. They spent six lonely months there, at the height of the sweltering monsoonal season, while Gregory and his men explored the inland area.

The party's twenty-two-year-old surgeon, Joseph Elsey, described the conditions on the schooner: 'The state of things on board was...unfortunate, the Captain and his wife quarreling and drinking, the children crying, and the men grumbling'.[2] By all accounts this was not unusual, Gourlay often being reported as drunk, argumentative and 'openly contemptuous of the members of the expedition...[He] bullied his crew and quarreled with his wife and all the time his children whined and wept'.[3] Given such behaviour, it was probably no wonder that members of the crew described Mrs Gourlay as peevish and the children a nuisance. Although she may have had good reason for being bad tempered, her behaviour caused problems among the crew, such as when she scolded the mate, Riley, with the result that he refused to perform his shipboard duties.

When in July 1856 her husband decided to take the *Tom Tough* to Timor for repairs, Mrs Gourlay finally found some female companionship in the form of the wife of the captain of a British vessel that arrived there at the same time. The expedition's artist, Thomas Baines, wrote that 'now Mrs Gourlay, cordially unloved by all aboard the schooner, also had a friend'.[4] Later, when Baines went to inspect the repairs being done to the schooner, he found that the crewmen also had found some female friends and that the hulk had become 'a floating brothel'. Although Baines was no great admirer of Mrs Gourlay, he did admit that the *Tom Tough* was no longer a fit place for either her or her children. The Gourlays eventually returned to Australia, where the findings of the exploration party were widely publicised.

Gregory's optimistic reports of the broad grasslands of the Victoria River district, combined with John McDouall Stuart's praise of the Top End after his overland exploration in 1862, were instrumental in South Australia's push to extend her boundaries to include the Northern Territory. For a short time some officials lobbied for the Tropic of Capricorn to be made the northern boundary of South Australia, suggesting that the rest of the Territory be given to Queensland. As fate would have it, Queensland declined. South Australia persisted with its claim to the area, however, citing the work of its explorers, and when Victoria and New South Wales showed no interest in the region the colonial office relented. On 6 July 1863 the Northern Territory was annexed to South Australia and, for better or for worse, it would control the affairs of the north for the next forty-eight years.

The first European women credited with coming north as part of South Australia's effort to inhabit the newly acquired Territory were Eliza Bauer, who was married to one of the first would-be settlers, Jacob Bauer, and Mary Packard. Mary was married to Harrison Daniel Packard, surveyor to the second South Australian expedition to the Territory under the command of R.H.Edmunds, who sent his own wife and son to Melbourne to stay with friends for the time he would be away.

The first South Australian expedition had left Adelaide in April 1864 under Boyle Travers Finniss, a newly widowed, one-time British army officer who had been given the unenviable task of serving as the Territory's first government resident. Finniss selected for the settlement site a hard-to-reach, mangrove-infested region near the mouth of the Top End's Adelaide River, called Escape Cliffs. The name certainly reflected the attitude most residents developed towards the place, regarding it as somewhere from which they wished to escape.

That a woman should choose to accompany her husband to such a place attracted the attention of the media. When the Edmunds party left Adelaide to join Finniss in October 1864, the *Advertiser* observed: 'Mr Packard takes his wife with him so that she will be the first European female inhabitant of the new country. It was generally understood that in consideration of her valorous example, the

Government had provided her with an outfit, in addition to granting her a free passage, but we understand such is not the case. Some of the party propose to call her the "'Queen of the North'", a title which she will doubtless bear with becoming dignity.'[5] With Mary was her four-month-old daughter, Edith Mary.

Eliza, on the other hand, was mentioned only in the shipping departure lists as travelling with her husband and their ten-year-old son, Charles. As settlers they were not given the same social recognition as the Packards, although in some ways theirs was the more risky venture.

History does not record whether Eliza and Mary became particularly close friends, although they did join forces at times. As the only two white women in the camp, they were anxious to observe the Aboriginal women in the area at first hand. When the opportunity arose, they spent several days making skirts for the Aboriginal women, who had been, until then, content to be 'dressed in sunshine'.[6] Though they accepted the presents from the white women graciously, they usually tied the skirts around their heads or shoulders, thus thwarting Mary's and Eliza's plan to give them a taste of civilisation.

Soon after this encounter Edmunds made a prophetic observation about the eventual effect of the white South Australian intrusion into Aboriginal land:

Little do these poor savages imagine as they gaze upon us, that they have perhaps seen the harbingers of an approaching revolution in the fortunes of their country, if they did, they would not so easily yield to the advancing movement of the whites and civilization, before which his savage and rude existence, name and race may pass into oblivion as in our southern districts...Where the wilds once resounded with their corroboree...is now the comfortable home of the squatter or farmer, and its former occupant is almost forgotten. I hope these may fare better, they are a finer people than their southern brothers.[7]

Edmunds also had his views on how the alien Escape Cliffs environment was affecting Mary Packard and Eliza Bauer. In July 1865 he wrote that Packard had asked him to see Mary, who was very unwell. 'The woman appears to be suffering from nervous exhaustion...As I am taking beer, I share a small bottle with her just before dinner and send her a little wine at night. Packard is an improvident fellow and provide[s] nothing in the shape of comforts.'[8] Later reports indicate that Mary, in fact, bore the hardships of life at Escape Cliffs with commendable 'pluck and cheerfulness that won for her the admiration of all with whom she came in contact'.[9]

Eliza had problems of her own. One night, when her usually sober husband became violently drunk, she appeared in the camp in her nightdress attempting to persuade him to return to their tent. He grabbed a knife and slit the front of her dress, causing her to beat a hasty retreat.

She apparently found solace in frequent and lengthy talks with the government resident, Finniss, who had, perhaps unwisely, made her his confidante. According to Edmunds she became a pawn in the hands of some of the men. She allegedly repeated in some detail most of what Finniss told her. Edmunds claimed that in order to glean as much information as possible about the increasingly disliked Finniss, the men used to give their 'pretended intentions, sometimes the most ridiculous things to be conveyed through her to the Government Resident'.[10]

But Finniss's days were numbered. He had fallen out with much of the tiny population, including the doctor, John Goldsmith. Mary and Harrison Packard were among the residents who signed a petition supporting Goldsmith against Finniss. Settler Jacob Bauer and two other men had complained to the government about Finniss's choice of site for the settlement, claiming the area near the Victoria River was much more suitable.

By September 1865, after several men from Escape Cliffs had stolen a boat and sailed to Adelaide via Fremantle to report on his incompetence, the government recalled Finniss to Adelaide to face an inquiry, leaving John Manton in charge of Escape Cliffs. Though critical of him, Jacob Bauer may have come to regret Finniss's recall. Under Finniss's jurisdiction, Jacob had been allowed to draw rations as a compensation for keeping meteorological records of the settlement. Manton put a stop to this and informed Bauer that from then on his provisions would be charged to him. When Manton demanded payment, Bauer pleaded to have his credit extended until the next ship arrived. Manton then stopped Bauer's rations altogether 'leaving him, his wife and his child to starve'.[11] It was apparently only through the generosity and compassion of other men in the camp, who shared their rations with the Bauers, that the family survived.

In late 1865, the South Australian government sent explorer John McKinlay to assess the situation at Escape Cliffs and explore new territory. Within weeks of arriving he too was quarrelling with Manton. The tense and unhappy situation was not to last much longer however.

Following a disastrous six-month journey by McKinlay to the mouth of the West Alligator River (during which a man named Ned Tuckwell saved the crew by building a raft out of horsehides) the South Australian government decided to recall the entire Escape Cliffs party.

Unfortunately Jacob Bauer was not among them. He was drowned in mid-October when he fell overboard from a boat that was returning to the camp after a day's journey to the Narrows, a nearby site on the coast. Although attempts were made to rescue him, they were unsuccessful and he sank out of sight, his body never being recovered. Eliza returned to Adelaide a widow with a young son to support. She died in Adelaide in 1885 at the home of her son, who had by then become a popular publican in Stepney. He died two years later, and his widow, Minnie Therese, was able to claim the land in Palmerston that his ill-fated father was entitled to because of purchases made twenty years earlier in the far north of the Territory. She sold the land the same year to assist with finances, and when she died three years later she left most of her estate to her son and Eliza's only grandchild, Jacob.

Mary Packard's continued association with the Territory would be more tangible. In December 1866, just before the entire Escape Cliffs party abandoned the settlement, she gave birth to her second daughter, Eleanor, the first white child born in the Northern Territory while it was under South Australian rule. When the Escape Cliffs residents reached Adelaide on the *Rangatira* in February 1867, the *Advertiser* reported: 'The first thing attracting attention was the remarkable hale and hearty appearance of the party...The ladies and children of the expedition were well; Mrs Packard's infant, born at the Cliffs, being a remarkably fine specimen of babydom.'[12]

Within three years Mary and her family, along with that of Ned Tuckwell, would be back in the Territory, this time as members of the new settlement at Port Darwin, the area which would become the permanent centre of Top End civilisation. There Mary would again make another little mark in history by giving birth to the first white girl to be born in Palmerston (renamed Darwin when the commonwealth took over in 1911).

The only other European woman known to have been in the Territory at the time of the Escape Cliffs experiment was Mrs William Turner Greig, who accompanied her husband to the Lake Nash region in 1866 when Queensland was encouraging pastoral settlement. Greig was in partnership with Francis Nash, who took out several pastoral claims on the Northern Territory-Queensland border. Although little is known of Mrs Greig, who had her young daughter with her, she holds the distinction of being the first European woman known to have lived on the Barkly Tablelands. Eventually other frontier women would follow in her footsteps and become Territory pastoral pioneers in their own right. But before inland settlement of the vast areas of the Territory could take place, the establishment of a permanent urban settlement had to occur. And that was the next chapter in the unfolding story of the Northern Territory in which women would share.

Chapter 3

South Australia Expands Her Territory (1868-1884)

'With regard to women, it may be said that we have never at any time had a very great number of that sex here, but of those we have, a large percentage have lived here for years and years without a change. Some almost born in the Territory and the mothers of families are probably as strong and hearty now as they ever were in their lives, or as they would have been had they put in a similar term of existence in, say, the hot wind and sandstorm regions of South Australia proper.'
Northern Territory Times, 1895.

South Australia was founded on the principle that equal numbers of men and women would provide the most sound and stable social structure, a 'superior society' which could avoid the 'moral degradation' that the principal architect of the scheme, Edward Wakefield, claimed existed in New South Wales. This admirable view was not extended to the Northern Territory, a fact which had repercussions not only for the individual women who ventured there, but also for the frontier society as a whole.

The paucity of white women who went to the Territory during South Australia's reign can be attributed to several factors. One was the patronising concern felt by male decision-makers about whether white women could cope with the tropics. Another may well have been that the men who had gone north and found desirable relationships with Aboriginal women feared that their behaviour would be discovered or monitored. But perhaps the most compelling reason was simply expediency—the desire to get things moving quickly, without having to worry much about the social fabric and physical comforts of the place.

Certainly with one attempt at northern settlement behind them, and a growing group of impatient would-be Northern Territory landowners clamouring at their doors, officials were anxious to get permanent northern settlement underway as quickly as possible. They chose forty-two-year-old Surveyor General George Goyder, appropriately nicknamed 'Little Energy', to head the all-male party that would survey about half a million acres (200 000 hectares) near Port Darwin in less than a year. He proved a highly successful choice.

In December 1868 he set sail for the north in the good ship *Moonta*. The men who accompanied him left wives, daughters, mothers and sisters behind in Adelaide. To compensate, the South Australian government gave some of the wives and girlfriends half-pay during the absence of their husbands and fiancés. For two of the women left behind in Adelaide, the northern expedition brought only grief. Mrs Tom

Bennett lost her son John, who was fatally speared by Aborigines near Fred's Pass in May 1869, and Mrs Richard Hazard lost her husband, one of the camp cooks — he died in August of severe rheumatism and consumption.The only solace for the women was the thoughtfulness of the other men in the expedition. They sent a carefully written letter of condolence to Mr and Mrs Bennett and took up a collection of more than sixty-five pounds for the widow and children of Richard Hazard.

Apart from these two tragedies, the survey and associated work went extraordinarily smoothly and were completed in record time. Four townships were surveyed, and the main streets of the capital, Palmerston, were named in honour of the men who had accomplished the task. It was with a justified feeling of satisfaction that on 28 September 1869 George Goyder sailed out of Frances Bay, named in honour of his wife, and headed back to Adelaide. He left a party of men under the command of the surgeon, Dr Robert Peel, as stewards of the new township until the new government resident and the first settlers arrived.

Goyder returned to professional triumph but personal tragedy. The year before he left for the Territory he had sent his ailing wife and their nine children to England to visit relatives and seek help for an illness Frances had developed. He had been back in Adelaide only a few weeks when he learned of his wife's death in London from an accidental overdose of medicinal opium. Some years later, when new South Australian legislation allowed it, he married his wife's sister, Ellen Smith, and had a second family. (In 1971 one of their granddaughters, Margaret Kerr, wrote the story of her grandfather's work in the Territory in her book *The Surveyors*, written to commemorate the founding of Darwin.)

Within weeks of Goyder's return to Adelaide, the *Kohinoor* left with supplies and passengers, including the acting government resident, Dr John Stokes Millner, the inspector of police, Paul Foelsche, and the first women and children bound for the new northern capital to join their husbands and fathers. They included Escape Cliffs veteran Mary Packard and her two daughters, Eliza Tuckwell and her four children, Emily Hayball and her two children, Ann Devine and her three children, Eliza Edwards and her three children, Mrs Charles Fry and her three children and Mrs Charles Spencley and her child. Mrs Spencley, who was described by one of the male residents of the day as being of 'very low character', stayed only a few months, while the others gradually drifted elsewhere over the next few years. Eliza Tuckwell was the only one whose descendants would remain continuously in the Territory.

The shipload of settlers arrived at Port Darwin on a clear January day in 1870 after a safe but thoroughly uncomfortable journey under conditions described by Eliza as being only 'fit for cattle'. After landing at the Fort Hill camp township, some of the working-class women were able to supplement their family income for a short period by doing the laundry for the men who were about to return to Adelaide on the *Kohinoor*.

A Port Darwin correspondent for the *Advertiser* reported that the women were placed with their husbands in the new huts and appeared to be very comfortable. This view was not upheld by South Australian parliamentarian Thomas Reynolds, who visited Palmerston three years later in 1873 and, after a general criticism of Darwin's makeshift appearance, observed that 'the land officer, Robert Gardiner, and his family were huddled into two rooms built of poles covered with lime, which were exposed to much damp falling from the hill at the back; it is a wonder to me that his young children as well as himself and wife do not suffer more from sickness'.[1]

THE FIRST FAMILY: BLOOMFIELD AND ELLEN DOUGLAS
(1870-73)

In just a few months the Territory's first 'first lady', forty-year-old Ellen Douglas, arrived on the *Gulnare* with her husband, Captain Bloomfield Douglas, the first Northern Territory government resident to serve in Palmerston. With them were their family of five daughters and two sons and their efficient but flirtatious maid, Annie Crerar. 'Class' society had arrived at the tiny frontier settlement.

Elizabeth Sweet, wife of the *Gulnare*'s captain, Samuel Sweet, was on hand to describe the event: 'On arriving at Port Darwin Captain Douglas landed in great state. There were seven guns fired from shore, and returned from the *Gulnare* and troopers and men arranged on the shore as guard of honour. Then the Government party took up their residence on shore, but every morning a boat came with an official letter, requesting some stores for the Government Resident, till our eight months' supplies, which the Government had put on board for our use, were gone.'[2] Although Douglas eventually replaced their rations from some on shore, his actions did not endear him to much of the community. Their dislike of him would increase during the next three years.

There is little to tell us what Ellen, a farmer's daughter who had married Douglas in Northumberland twenty-two years earlier when he was stationed there with the Royal Navy, thought of her new exalted role or her makeshift surroundings. Fortunately, though, her eldest daughter, Harriet, had a great deal to say about those years in her book *Digging, Squatting and Pioneering Life in Northern Australia*. Published in 1887, it is arguably the single most valuable account of the Territory's early European life, although it is written from the elitist and somewhat romanticised vantage point of the privileged middle class.

Harriet's remarks on first seeing her northern home, while perhaps reinforcing the view some had that she and her sisters were snobbish, encapsulate the tyranny-of-distance factor that was to characterise Territory society for much of the next century:

The scene of our exile, for such we deemed it then, though surpassingly beautiful in itself, was, from this very loneliness, hardly inviting...for we were at that time far too strongly attached to the pomps and vanities of this wicked world to appreciate being banished from all we had hitherto enjoyed so keenly...A closer view of the camp did not tend to raise our spirits to any very exalted elevation—a handful of log huts, with crowds of natives looking over our heads; and this tiny settlement literally the only one in the vast tract of Northern Australia.[3]

The question of the 'natives' was one the Adelaide officials had taken into account from the start. Douglas brought clear instructions to Dr Millner, who was Protector of Aborigines as well as the settlement's doctor. He was to see that no alcohol was given to the Aborigines and that the Aboriginal women were not sexually interfered with by the European inhabitants. Millner, and all his successors, failed on both counts. Interestingly, there is some evidence to suggest that Aboriginal men also made some unwelcome demands on the white population. One of the early official letters to Adelaide reported that 'the Woolner Blacks encamped by the stockyard till evening—they were very insolent and demanded white lubras and food'.[4]

The arrival of the government resident's family meant that proper official accommodation had to be built. The first, temporary residency, two log huts with mud floors, was located close to the sea and to one side of the Fort Hill camp. In these primitive conditions the Douglas daughters held court to the community with their piano playing and singing, and brought new life to the tiny community. The community was particularly merry on 23 August 1870 when Anne Devine, wife of the settlement's baker, James Devine, gave birth to the first white baby born in Palmerston.

But the main preoccupation of the few town settlers was to watch the progress of the new government residency. From the time Ellen Douglas performed the honour of laying the first foundation stone to the day the builders put the last stone in place, innovations were necessary, as many materials were not provided by the local environment. As Harriet explains, no lime was available so each day at low tide the residents would go out and collect coral which would then be burned to make lime. Timber was also a problem. Ironbark was plentiful but it was impossible to hand saw, so a search began for an ant-resistant, easy-to-cut timber. Finally a fine supply of cypress pine was found nearby at Bynoe Harbour and transported to Darwin

Picnic outings to the nearby 'jungle' areas of East Point and Fannie Bay were popular with the very early Darwin residents. Here, in 1871, the government resident, Bloomfield Douglas (second from right) and his daughters are escorted by government surveyors and troopers, who were charged with organising target shooting sessions for the Douglas girls. Harriet Douglas (centre) married surveyor Dan Daly (to her immediate right) and in 1887 published what was probably the first social history of the Territory—Digging, Squatting and Pioneering Life in Northern Australia.
Northern Territory State Reference Library.

in the *Gulnare*, although the white ants would make a tasty meal of most of it within a few years. When the building was completed, the lifestyle of the first family improved. There was more privacy for daily ablutions, there was space available for Ellen's beloved geese, ducks and fowls, and there was a flat roof on which the family could sit and watch the tropical sun rise and set over the Arafura Sea.

While Douglas went about the task of trying to administer the settlement, a job undoubtedly hampered by his bouts of excessive drinking and frequent verbal abuse of both the settlers and his staff, Ellen and her two eldest daughters tackled the job of creating social outlets and events for the small population. Described as 'a dignified and gracious woman, with a sweet and plaintive expression of counte- nance',[5] Ellen seems to have been well-suited to playing hostess. Police trooper Catchlove had a less complimentary view of her daughters, complaining that he had to accompany the 'great lumps of daughters [who were] very much stuck up...passably educated...very uncouth and...anything but good looking'.[6]

Douglas, on the other hand, believed the presence of his wife and daughters served a particular purpose. 'The residence of educated women here has been a very great advantage to the settlement, their presence contains the men from irregular and rude habits,' he proclaimed in a letter supporting Police Inspector Foelsche's request (ultimately granted) to bring his own family to the settlement.

If that was true, the women concerned soon had their job cut out for them when scores of men headed for the Territory to take part in South Australia's most momentous and exciting project. At a special ceremony on 15 September 1870, Harriet Douglas was given the honour of officially planting the first telegraph pole of the Overland Telegraph Line, the construction of which would not only boost the population, but also ensure Palmerston's continued existence. Of her part in the historic moment Harriet wrote: 'Amidst a gathering of the whole community, and not without a certain degree of nervousness, for it was my first public ceremony, I declared the pole "well and truly fixed".'

Apart from such official duties, Harriet led an upper-crust life busy with social and sporting activities, primarily in the company of her sisters and selected young men from the elite of the community—police troopers, surveyors and men of the overland telegraph. Their activities included day picnics to Fannie Bay (now an inner city suburb of Darwin), rifle shooting events at which her sister excelled, horse riding, wine and dinner parties, and swimming and fishing expeditions. There were a few less pleasant pastimes, of course. The lack of domestic help available in the embryonic settlement meant that the two elder Douglas daughters had to help their maid Annie with the family washing, a task most certainly foreign to them prior to their sojourn in the north.

Some women had problems of a more serious nature. Late in 1870 Captain Samuel Sweet had been ordered to find the mouth of the Roper River. His wife Elizabeth accompanied him and his second mate on the voyage was a man named Read.

When they were ready to leave the river, Read and three other men were sent to find water fresh enough to drink to fill the tanks for the return trip to Palmerston. As they were leaving, Elizabeth's young son fell down the ship's hold and cut his head, an event Read took to be a bad omen. Before he left to find the water, he gave a small pocket-book to the Sweets and asked that it be given to his wife Margaret in Adelaide if he did not return. He did not, and the three sailors who did sobbed a

Performing the launching ceremony when work began on the Darwin end of the Overland Telegraph in September 1870 was Harriet Douglas (left), eldest daughter of the government resident, Bloomfield Douglas. Other women pictured are (left to right) Mary Packard, Harriet's mother Ellen and Harriet's younger sister Eleanor. Northern Territory State Reference Library.

description of how a crocodile had grabbed Read from the low-lying boat and dragged him, screaming, into the water, never to be seen again. Elizabeth Sweet later passed on their first-hand account to Read's wife.

Suddenly left a widow with five children under the age of ten, Margaret Read pleaded with the government for financial help, a plea supported by seven prominent Adelaide residents, including the Mayor, J. M. Solomon. Her plea was dismissed after investigating officials received a private detective's report that claimed she owned six freehold houses, some of which were let to prostitutes. The report also claimed that both she and her husband had been fined for keeping brothels. In refusing

Margaret's request for help, officials said they hoped that those who recommended that she get assistance were unaware of her character. Her claim for compensation was only one of many that the South Australian government would have to examine over the next forty years, claims that frequently resulted in controversy over what role the husband's status should play in the decision as to whether a woman was entitled to receive financial help and, if so, how much.

Elizabeth and Samuel Sweet had returned to Port Darwin with stores, including some 'liquid comforts', and mail from Adelaide, the only communication the settlement would have from the seat of government for the next eight months. The residents relished the news from family and friends, and Elizabeth Sweet later reported that some of the residents who had over-indulged in the 'comforts' and 'enjoyed themselves right royally' had fallen asleep outside and caught fever and ague, causing sickness in the camp for some time.[7]

In 1871 the population census of the Territory revealed a trend that was to continue for much of its history. Unlike South Australia proper, where, as a result of Wakefield's settlement scheme, the numbers of men and women were nearly equal, the Territory suffered from a huge imbalance of the sexes. There were 172 white men to twenty-nine females, only twelve of whom were adults. This meant that if a Territory girl wanted a husband she could usually get one. Harriet Douglas was no exception. For some time she had been courted by one of Goyder's dashing and talented young surveyors, Dan Daly, a nephew of Sir Dominick Daly, governor of South Australia. In September 1871 she sailed to Adelaide to marry him in the more civilised atmosphere of that city. The newly-weds remained there for nearly a year, taking an active part in Adelaide's social life.

In Palmerston, the Douglas family's popular maid, Annie Crerar, finally said yes to one of her many suitors and in November 1871 married the twenty-four-year-old harbourmaster, William Cook, in the Territory's first recorded marriage under South Australian rule. Four months later, Harriet's nineteen-year-old sister Eleanor became the second Territory-wed bride when she married Enston Squier, cable superintendent of the British-Australian Telegraph Company, at what was Palmerston's first 'society' wedding. The marriage, which took place at the new government residence amidst myriad canon salutes, secured Eleanor's social position in Palmerston among the married women.

The cable staff quickly became the elite of the now bustling township. They were the people who would make Australia's long awaited 'missing link' with the rest of the world operational, and they were thus considered the most essential members of the Territory's populace. The telegraphic officials were not only outside the government resident's area of responsibility, they also had the best accommodation in town with extensive physical comforts provided, including a piano, a library, good furniture and a billiard table.

As well as bringing a new class structure, the construction of the Overland Telegraph brought a new influx of people and activity to the more remote areas of the Territory. This included a few more women, including three who had an unexpected and uncomfortable stay at the Roper River. They came in January 1872 on the barque *Omeo*, along with the Overland Telegraph leader, Charles Todd, who was bringing supplies to the men working at the Roper. Mary Ann Finniss, along with all her furniture, was on her way to join her husband Fred, who was on the staff of the British Cable Company. Newly-wed Ellen Deane was joining her husband George, who later became a well-known Territory stockman. The intrepid Elizabeth Sweet paid thirty pounds for her passage to be reunited with her husband Samuel, who was at the Roper to take a working party up the river. Elizabeth, who had by now borne nine children, had their youngest child and their teenage daughter with her.

The women's sojourn at the Roper lasted ten weeks, during which they lived in tents on the banks of the river at the height of the wet, waiting for a barque to arrive to take them to Port Darwin. It was an uncomfortable wait. It rained almost incessantly and the mighty Roper roared through the landing area, completely surrounding the few acres of high ground on which the party was camped. Clouds of mosquitoes and sand-flies added to the miserable surroundings, and it was with relief that the party greeted the arrival of the *Bengal*, which took them on to Port Darwin. Elizabeth and Samuel eventually returned to Adelaide where Samuel became a well-known photographer. After his death in 1886 Elizabeth took over the business, and for years sold prints of the many excellent photographs he had taken of both the Territory and South Australia.

In August 1872 the overland and submarine telegraph cables were finally completed and the first messages sent. Great celebrations took place simultaneously in Adelaide, London and Palmerston. Years later in London, Harriet Daly lyrically reflected on the significance of the communication link:

I often wonder, when I see Australian telegrams in the London papers, if any of those who read them realise what the work really was that enables us to ascertain during breakfast that there has been a good season and that plentiful rain has fallen almost twenty-four hours ago in a country which twenty years since had only one mail a month from England. I seem to see the message flitting right across the continent, repeated from one station to another through the dry, hot country of the Far North...till at last it reaches the more luxuriantly clothed and well-watered land of Tropical Australia, finally coming into Port Darwin itself, and speeding on its way under water till the message is received in this great city, taking its place amongst the news from every part of the world in our morning and evening papers.[8]

The twelve overland telegraph stations that were built to service the line became the only centres of European civilisation in the Territory's remote regions and the few European women who lived at them sometimes lived for years without seeing another white woman. The rough overland route that linked the stations became known as 'the track', a name many Territorians still use to describe the Territory's north-south road.

Improved communication meant that reports of rich Territory gold discoveries could be tapped out over the lines immediately, and in 1872 and 1873 hundreds of fortune-seekers rushed north, including the newly-wed Harriet and Dan Daly. Harriet at once noticed changes in Darwin, particularly the block of handsome stone dwellings built to house the overland telegraph and cable company. They stood out beside the growing and rather motley collection of bark huts that lined the streets of Palmerston and housed most of the rest of the population.

Harriet and Dan both held mining leases. They named one after their daughter, Anna, who was born in Palmerston in November 1872 in their makeshift Smith Street residence. For much of the time that Dan was out on the fields seeking the family fortune, Harriet remained in Darwin, where her assertive nature drew criticism from some circles. While Dr John Stokes Millner was acting government resident for a spell in late 1872, he complained about Harriet's habit of opening official correspondence addressed to the government resident before Millner had seen it.

Harriet and Dan only remained in the Territory another year, during which time Dan made headlines around Australia when, on a voyage south to purchase mining machinery, he saved the crew and passengers of the *Springbok* by taking command after the barque's drunken captain proved himself incapable of sailing the vessel. Harriet spent five anxious months in Palmerston with her young children before she learned that her husband was not only safe but a national hero. However, a short time later Harriet and Dan decided to give up on their prospecting hopes and they left the Territory, never to return. After a series of adventures and misadventures in Western Australia and Borneo, Dan died in 1889 and Harriet eventually moved to London, where for many years she was a London correspondent for the *Sydney Morning Herald*. Her book, published in 1887, was the first popular history of South Australia's Northern Territory, and as such received due recognition from the critics.

Despite the Dalys' decision to leave the Territory's uncertain fate to others, Harriet concluded her book with an optimistic vision of the future that was to characterise the writing of most women who took up the Territory's cause during the next one hundred years. She told the Territory's British landholders that 'they [had] a possession in that far off land more valuable at the present moment than in their wildest dreams they ever could have imagined'. It was such dreams that, perhaps more than anything, ensured that governments, companies and individuals persisted in their attempts to develop the Territory in the face of consistent disappointments.

By 1873 Harriet's father's reputation for heavy drinking and bad conduct was widespread. This, coupled with the fact that Douglas was perceived to have vested interests in land and mining leases, led to his forced resignation in June. He sent Ellen and their unmarried children back to Adelaide while he remained in the Territory to pursue his mining ventures. A few months later Ellen pleaded to the government for compensation, claiming she had been left destitute with five children, three of them of school age. She was told she would receive nothing until her husband returned to Adelaide, which he did a few weeks later. The matter appears to have been resolved when Douglas was appointed to recruit Chinese men to work the Territory's mines. After arrangements were made ensuring that his wife would receive half his pay while he was gone, Douglas sailed to Singapore in 1874 and returned with the first 186 indentured male Chinese labourers. It became one of the most contentious decisions the South Australians ever made, but it had its positive side for some. As Harriet Daly later observed, the importation of the Chinese, and their eventual employment as cooks, tailors and laundry workers, helped many European women cope better with domestic chores in the dusty, sticky climate.

GEORGE AND CAROLINE SCOTT (1873-76)

A few months prior to Douglas's landing in Darwin with the first of the Chinese, Palmerston welcomed the Territory's new first lady, Caroline Scott (née Ritchie), who had been a governess before she became the wife of civil servant George Byng Scott in 1865. In September 1873, after several others had turned down the job, Scott was offered 1000 pounds to replace Douglas as government resident. He accepted, and in October he, Caroline, their two children and their servant set sail for Port Darwin. Despite a rousing reception on their arrival at Gulnare jetty, Caroline must have wondered what kind of society she had come to when she and her husband were read their official welcome by the town's lawyer, W. Villeneuve Smith, who was dressed in pyjamas (quite common attire in early Darwin), a white jacket, and a pith helmet. Smith urged Scott to rid the community of the 'many evils attendant on a community so remote from the seat of government'.

Scott tried to oblige, and in his first official report speculated on the possible rebellious result of interfering in the public service: 'They consider...their only mission in life is to eat, drink and be merry, do no work, and plunder the government whenever they have the opportunity,' he wrote. 'I have had to weed them out and now I have some very discontented and troublesome people about me.' That discontent remained and grew throughout his three-year term.

The atmosphere of discontent was no doubt exacerbated by the copious quantities of alcohol consumed by many residents. The Territory's first resident minister of religion, the Reverend Archibald Bogle, who arrived during Scott's regime, attempted to address the issue by getting people, including several of the town's women, to sign a no-drink pledge. He despaired when he found his new flock drunk in the streets and pubs a few days later.

The continual ill-health of Bogle's long-suffering wife Hilda did not lighten his burden, and raised the question in his mind as to whether the tropical climate was suitable for women. Not long after their arrival Bogle recorded that 'the least happening affects her. She seems quite unstrung...is irritable and easily moved to tears'.[9] Her illness persisted throughout their stay and he constantly pleaded to be transferred, convinced that a change of climate would restore her health. Although his transfer was not granted until 1877, Hilda survived, and in fact she outlived her husband by many years.

Another family who appeared to suffer from the climate and general atmosphere of Darwin were Escape Cliffs veterans Mary and Harrison Packard. The Packards had started off reasonably well, having been given one of the few iron houses in which to live. Mary Packard was singled out by overland telegraph officer, John Stapleton, as being 'a very nice person' whose two daughters were 'the only clean, well kept children in the community'. However, by May 1874 Mary had become so ill that her husband pleaded with Scott to lobby Adelaide to give her a passage on the first steamer south. '[Her] health is so bad now that the doctors...say that it is absolutely necessary or she will die,' Packard wrote, reminding Scott that she had been 'the first European lady resident in the Territory and [had] undergone all the privations'. He argued that 'so long a residence in a tropical climate necessitate[ed] a change' and that his salary did not allow him 'to send them without excessive inconvenience'.[10] The government relented and allowed Mary and her children to return in June. Unfortunately, the government could not or would not find a job for Packard in Adelaide, and within three months of his family's departure he became extremely ill himself. His condition worsened and in November he died, having only had the comfort of hearing read to him one last affectionate telegram from Mary, who was awaiting his return in Adelaide.

The Adelaide *Advertiser* blamed his death partly on his continuous residence in the Territory: 'Knowing how prostrating the climate in that portion of the colony is there is very little question that its enervating influence hastened the death of Mr Packard. A special recognition of these circumstances on the part of the Government when dealing with the question of compensation would seem to be an act of justice to the family who, we regret to hear, are left unprovided for.' Mary, who received a small pension from the government, survived and lived well into the twentieth century.

Such cases as the Packards' served to highlight the need for improved local medical services, and the building of a hospital was one of the first issues tackled by the Territory's residents. In fact, the first issue of the Territory's long-serving newspaper, the *Northern Territory Times*, which Scott had officially launched in late 1873, devoted many columns to the issue. As was not unusual in the history of Territory social services, it was women who organised many of the fundraising activities, such as concerts and dances in support of the cause. They were encouraged by the generosity of a philanthropic woman living in London, Miss Louisa Da Costa, who donated the first several hundred pounds. She was joined by a Miss Coates, who also gave generously to the fund. Encouraged by their donations, the residents of Palmerston soon raised enough subscriptions through concerts and drives to build a hospital at a seaside site still known appropriately as Doctor's Gully.

Welcome though it was, the new hospital was no help a few months later when the Territory's European community suffered its first great human tragedy. Late in 1874, the South Australian government had sent the first circuit judge, W. E. Wearing, to the Territory to assist the magistrate, Edward Price, to administer justice in the frontier land. Wearing's wife and family had remained in Adelaide, but Price's wife of fourteen years, Minnie, and their five children, had joined him in Palmerston. Accommodation was sparse and Price complained that his family had to be cooped up in a tiny residence next to the courthouse, where they could hear all police court sessions.

After a circuit of a few months, Wearing prepared to rejoin his family and Minnie Price and her children decided to return to Adelaide, expecting that Edward would join them shortly. Along with many other prominent citizens and visitors, they booked passage on the popular steamer *Gothenburg*, which had brought the Scotts to the Territory. The night before they left Wearing had told Scott how delighted he was at the prospect of being reunited with his family.

Having just supplied an immense quantity of beer and spirits to the ever-thirsty settlement of Palmerston the *Gothenburg* sailed from the harbour on 16 February laden with mail, 3000 ounces (85 kg) of gold, the remains from a wrecked ship (the *Enchantress*) and a capacity load of merry passengers and crew. In addition to Wearing and the Price family, there were the retiring colonial surgeon Dr Millner, his second wife, Elizabeth, and the three children of his first marriage, several young girls who were headed for boarding school in the south, the editor of the *Northern Territory Times* , Richard Wells, who was returning to Adelaide to see his wife and child, and the Honourable Thomas Reynolds and his wife, Anne.

Less than a week after she left Darwin, the *Gothenburg* struck a fierce cyclonic storm which rammed her onto part of the Great Barrier Reef near Bowen. Although the vessel remained stranded on the reef for a few hours, heavy winds and seas finally battered it so much that it broke apart and sank. Only twenty-two people, all men, survived. They told how most of the women were placed in a lifeboat but were lost to watery graves when it capsized in the fierce wind and waves. Mr J. Fitzgerald described the last moments of Mrs Osterman who worked for the ES & A Bank in Palmerston: '[she] caught hold of the keel near the stern and struggled bravely and held on until nearly drowned; then she let go and was gone, a few gazing on painfully, unable to assist.' Another survivor, Mr P. Hogan, told of the anguish of watching the final scenes and of the bravery of those who were drowning:

It was something frightful to see men, women and children drowning close to you and be powerless to help them. The men and women met death fearlessly. There was not a murmur from any person on board. When they were struggling in the water they were wishing each other goodbye as if they were leaving for a short time.

Throughout Australia the newspapers heralded the tragedy as one of the nation's most lamentable in recent history and moves began at once to raise money for the relatives of those drowned. Parliament decided to deal with three cases itself and moved to pay the widow and children of Mr Justice Wearing 4000 pounds, of his body servant, Mr C. Lyons, 250 pounds, and of the special crown prosecutor, Mr J. J. Whitby, 1250 pounds. After lengthy debate over the wisdom and fairness of the motion, it was passed. Other widowed families were largely dependent on the voluntary generosity of the Australian people.

Palmerston, which had just lost a significant and prominent sector of its small population, was in deep mourning and gave substantially to the relief fund. Magistrate Edward Price was devastated and successfully applied to Scott for six months' leave on full pay, pleading his case to Scott: 'The recent loss of my whole family has unfitted me to perform duties here properly at present.'

Not the least lamented of the *Gothenburg* victims, particularly by advocates of greater female rights, was the Territory advocate and former South Australian parliamentarian, Thomas Reynolds. As early as 1858 he had raised his voice in favour of greater equality of the sexes, particularly in relation to separation and divorce. He argued that women should be placed on the same footing as men and although his amendments failed at the time, his arguments were used later to change laws.

Changing the law is one thing, changing attitudes is another. Some people blamed a woman for the next tragedy to strike Palmerston—the suspected suicide of the town's new doctor, Frederick George Guy, the son of a well-known English surgeon, Thomas Guy. Significantly, in light of subsequent events and apportioned blame, Guy had signed Reverend Bogle's no-drink pledge shortly after his marriage to seventeen-year-old Fannie Dawson Millett, a stepdaughter of the *Gothenburg's* Captain Pearce. She arrived from Melbourne in September 1875 to marry Guy, an educated man who, because of his knowledge of the Malayan language, had been appointed to accompany Bloomfield Douglas on his mission to collect the Chinese coolies a year earlier. Fannie married Guy within a few days of her arrival.

The following month, after one attempted suicide and several rowdy arguments with his new bride, Guy was found dead in somewhat confusing circumstances. The subsequent inquest failed to prove conclusively whether or not Guy had taken his own life by administering an overdose of a poisonous drug, whether he had died in his sleep, or whether he had died of 'apoplexy brought about by his violent passion'. Several witnesses testified that Guy was of a 'very excitable temperament' and concluded that he had died of the latter.

Reverend Bogle, for one, was convinced that this state of mind had been caused by Fannie. Although Bogle admitted in his meticulous diary that Guy had dragged his new bride home from a party, bashed her about and smashed all the windows in their home, he clearly believed Guy was justified, being 'irritated beyond endurance by the miserable wretch he had married' who allegedly would not perform her 'wifely duties'. Scott, who had been present at the wedding, described her as 'quite a girl of the period, in fact my idea of the advanced Melbourne type. She could smoke a [cigarette], whistle a tune and talk slang with anyone'.[11]

True or not, her marriage to Guy was a disaster in more ways than one. When the inquest was over, Fannie outlined her plight in a neat and carefully written letter to Scott: 'I need scarcely inform you of the peculiar circumstances under which I came here and the position in which I am left by the sudden death of the late colonial surgeon. Not only his furniture and effects but nearly all my own will have to be sold to satisfy the debts left by my husband which will leave me destitute.' Her passage was approved within two days and she gladly left Port Darwin on the next steamer having just been told that Guy's salary had been overpaid and must be refunded. The mystery behind the circumstances of Fannie's short but tragic sojourn in the Territory sailed with her.

She was certainly not the only woman to suffer from alcohol-related marital problems. During her four-year term in Palmerston (1874-78) the Territory's first nurse and assistant to Dr Guy, Alice McGuire, was assaulted both by strangers and by her own hot-tempered Irish-born husband, John, a police trooper. Alice, who had served as a nurse in India where her husband had been with the army for a time, arrived in Darwin from Adelaide in 1874 to take up duties at the new hospital. As the grounds were some distance from the town and the police barracks, where regulations forced her husband to reside, Alice was vulnerable to attack. Despite continual requests for him to be allowed to live with her, the authorities would not allow it. Finally when she was assaulted in her bed by a Malay man, her husband left the police force to stay on the hospital premises with her. However, he soon became the perpetrator of drunken domestic violence himself. Alice became so frightened of his drunken attacks that she gave all her money to Reverend Bogle for safekeeping until finally, during her husband's absence south, she was able to sneak out of town with her two young children and escape to London.

Other women had more luck in their Territory endeavours. By 1875 several had become involved in Port Darwin's commercial life. Ann Kelsey ran a drapery shop, Sarah Bennett managed the Commercial Hotel, and Amelia Traversi ran a Temperance Hotel in Palmerston and then a pub out on the goldfields, as did the indomitable Ellen Ryan (whose life is dealt with in a later chapter). A few women were also making their presence felt in the more remote communities that had sprung up along the overland telegraph, like Jane Murray, who accompanied her station-master husband to Katherine to become the first permanent white female resident there. The Murrays had arrived in Darwin in 1873 and had spent two years at Southport, the nearby township, which had been established largely to service the inland goldmining regions. There, in March 1874, Jane gave birth to the town's first white child, a daughter, Maud Louise. Later the Murrays moved to the Katherine Telegraph Station where Jane gave birth to the first European children born in that centre. The Murrays lived there for nearly twenty years, at a time when few white women ventured into the great unknown of Australia's inland. Throughout their residence there, their hospitality cheered and comforted many lonely travellers.

Meanwhile, Caroline Scott was busy performing the duties of the Territory's official hostess by holding 'at homes' at the residency and occasionally drawing the same criticism as Harriet Daly had for opening official mail in the absence of her husband. As well she was busy as a mother, having given birth to a daughter in mid-1874. Her experience as a governess no doubt helped her be an effective at-home teacher to her other two children. But her time as the Territory's 'first lady' was coming to a close, probably to her relief, as her husband had come under increasing criticism for not achieving enough.

Scott, who had been appointed to his post only after three others had turned the job down, had at times been the target for disenchanted miners and townsfolk. Like many who followed him, he suffered from the difficulties of serving a government far removed from the day-to-day seat of administration. Despite the criticisms, however, he had improved buildings, built roads and bridges to the goldfields, and encouraged the expansion of both Palmerston and Southport. George and Caroline Scott left the Territory in 1876 and went to Mt Gambier, where Scott served as a magistrate until his death in 1886. Caroline died in 1917 at her home in Walkerville at the age of seventy-three .

By the time they left, at least one early male observer—W. B. Wildey, who published his *Australia and the Oceanic Region* in 1876—had voiced the opinion that out of a population of 1700, it was the fifty females who 'seem[ed] to bear the climate better than the men'.

EDWARD PRICE, WIDOWER (1876-84)

The Territory's new government resident was Edward Price, who returned to Port Darwin after he had finally begun to recover from the shock of losing his entire family in the *Gothenburg* tragedy the year before. Just how much this affected his attitude cannot be known, but there is evidence that he was anxious about the difficulties that could arise from his government officers being married men. One day, the junior surveyor of the Territory, David Lindsay, returned to Port Darwin after a trip to the Adelaide River, to find his wife, Annie, very ill. The doctor was not expected back for several days, and Lindsay asked to be allowed to remain with her until the doctor arrived. Price reluctantly agreed, but said he 'did not consider it advisable for the junior surveyor of the Northern Territory to be a married man as it entailed great loss of time...and money'.[12] According to Lindsay, Price refused all his subsequent requests and would barely speak to him or Annie. Lindsay declared he was forced to resign as long as Price was in charge of Territory affairs.[13] For most of Lindsay's later service in the Territory, as an explorer, Annie remained in Adelaide, raising a family of one daughter and four sons. In 1897 Lindsay returned to live in Adelaide, where he and Annie enjoyed social prominence, though he always remained faithful to the Territory and returned many times.

Price also made some contentious decisions affecting women when he acted in his role as magistrate. For instance, in 1877 he became the centre of controversy in Adelaide when he ordered an eleven-year-old girl be sent to the Adelaide Reformatory for four years after being convicted of stealing a concertina. The girl, Mary Grieveson, lived with her mother in Darwin while her father operated a mine on the inland gold reefs and was seldom in town. Her mother was often in court on

Among the first European women to travel outback in the Territory were the few who ventured to the mission station at Hermannsburg, established in 1877. Missionary Liebler and his wife relieved the well-known Strehlow family for a short time in 1910-11. Liebler was strongly criticised for his management of the mission and when the Strehlows returned in April 1911 they were warmly welcomed back. Lutheran Archives, Adelaide.

various charges, and Mary had been accused several times of housebreaking and stealing. After the incident of the concertina, her father came to town and, finding that the child was being brought up to a life of crime, offered to pay all expenses if she could be sent to a reformatory school. Price agreed to this condition and gave the order, stipulating that the mother could no longer associate with her child. The southern press sensationalised the story, accusing Price of 'unpardonable despotism'. The *Northern Territory Times* defended Price, saying that his order had been compassionate and in the interests of the young girl. History does not record what the truth of the situation was, but it does serve to illustrate the lack of support services for women and children in Darwin at the time.

Price kept a paternalistic eye on the behaviour of women out of court as well as in court. At one government resident ball, for instance, he ordered the Chinese coolies not to open any more champagne, 'the ladies present having apparently done ample justice to it'.[14]

The women in central Australia, however, escaped Price's watchful eye. The long distances involved prevented him from monitoring their behaviour quite as closely, although no doubt he would have approved of the temperance of at least two of the pioneer women of the area. They were Dorothea Queckenstedt and Wilhelmine Schultze, who became part of the first mission settlement at Hermannsburg in 1877-78 when they married the first two missionaries, A. H. Kempe and W. F. Schwartz in the first recorded wedding ceremonies performed in central Australia. The two women arrived at Glenelg, South Australia, in October 1877 with a mission party from Hamburg and they set out almost at once on the long, hot and dusty overland journey to Hermannsburg. They were met by Pastor Kempe along the way and at Dalhousie Springs he and Dorothea Queckenstedt were married by Pastor Schwartz. Shortly after the party arrived at Hermannsburg in May 1878, Pastor Kempe married Missionary Schwartz and Wilhelmine Schultze. The Schwartzes remained at Hermannsburg for twelve years, preaching to the nearby Aboriginal people and raising a family. They returned to Adelaide in December 1889 to rehabilitate their health. Dorothea Kempe, who gave birth to four sons and three daughters, was not so fortunate. In November 1891 she died in childbirth and her heartbroken husband, who was recovering from a severe bout of typhoid fever himself, abandoned Hermannsburg with five of his children, leaving the new baby with the family of a lay worker.

Another overland pioneer who came to the Territory during Price's reign was twenty-two-year-old Emily Creaghe, who earned the title of Australia's first woman explorer. She arrived in Palmerston in August 1883 after a six-month journey on horseback with the Ernest Favenc exploration party, which included her husband Harry. The Aboriginal people of the region, most of whom had never seen a white woman before, referred to her as 'the white lubra'. Emily's sojourn in the land of the never never also caused some consternation and excitement among the white men of the area, who rarely had the opportunity to see and speak with a white woman. In fact, when the party left for Powell's Creek, a messenger was sent ahead to warn the men there that a woman was coming, as the 'outback ways in the matter of clothing' were not always considered suitable for a woman's eyes.[15]

Fortunately, in the detailed diary Emily kept during the journey, we have a rare, first-hand insight into her experience, an insight which, because of Emily's innocence of outback life before the trip, contains valuable descriptive accounts of daily bush life and tends in general to give a more human picture than those contained in official reports. Emily's observations of the treatment of Aboriginal women on some stations is particularly telling. She described the procedure of 'bringing in a new, wild black gin' at Carl Creek by first putting 'a rope around her neck and [dragging] her along from horseback'. She was then chained to a tree near the station house with instructions to the station hands not to let her loose until she was thought to be 'tame'.

One of Emily's most disturbing experiences occurred when the party visited Lorne Hill, a property near the Gregory River, where they found 'forty pairs of blacks' ears' nailed around the walls. They had been collected during various raiding parties following losses of cattle for which the station owners blamed Aboriginal spear throwers.[16] Her accounts of such incidents contrast sharply with those of Favenc, who had written articles for Sydney papers claiming that in his experience such atrocities did not happen.[17]

Emily's diary also describes how she became temporarily blind from sandy blight; how the party coped with virtually no water and no food for several days at a time; how depressed the party became when one of the men died during the journey; and how Jane Murray, wife of the station master at Katherine, had wanted to 'keep her' when they arrived there on their way to Darwin. The opportunities for Jane to enjoy European female company were scarce in the remote outback and she wanted to make it last as long as possible. Emily was also warmly welcomed at nearby Springvale Station, where she spent several days with Anne and Alfred Giles. Anne, whose story is told later, had made history of her own, being the first European woman to settle on a Territory property when she arrived as a new bride in 1881. When Emily and Harry left Springvale, Anne Giles travelled with them to Palmerston, where she took a ship to Adelaide for her first holiday since arriving in the Territory.

Having left the Favenc party to continue its exploration south, the Creaghes returned to their southern home, where Emily had her first child. Interestingly, Emily had never mentioned the fact that she was pregnant for much of the trip. Harry was soon back in the Territory, this time travelling overland with a mob of cattle for Hodgson Downs. There he died in 1886, leaving Emily a widow with two young sons. She married again in 1889 and spent the next twenty years as Mrs Joseph Barnett on a cattle station near Rockhampton, where she raised a second family. Australia's first woman explorer finally died in Sydney in 1944.

Emily's observations of the treatment of Aboriginal women had been confined to her experiences in the outback, but their exploitation had also received attention in Palmerston. A front page editorial in the June 1881 issue of the *Northern Territory Times* described the selling of Aboriginal women to the European and Chinese males of Palmerston and caused an uproar amongst some of its readers, several of whom withdrew their subscriptions.

On Monday the 20th instance, the day kept as a public holiday, the blacks from the Adelaide and Alligator rivers, hungering after tobacco and money, arrived on the outskirts of the township. The following morning they were all about anxious to vend their merchandise and to obtain the highest market price. They were free traders certainly, although of a questionable type. They prescribe to the Bright principle of buying in the cheapest market and selling in the dearest. And what do southern Christians, who spend so much money on missionary enterprise, think of their wares, when we tell them that women and children were freely offered...but for the purposes of prostitution in the city? The order of doing business was peculiar.

They were about in lots of twenty and thirty of mixed sexes and no sooner did a European stay to look at their uncouth figures than the salesman of the party stepped forward pointing to the sorted lots.

The old women were offered at sixpence, whilst others ranged in value to one and two shillings, the latter figure being demanded for quite young children under ten years of age. Towards dusk their value had depreciated, lower prices obtained and choice specimens were submitted at a sacrifice. We have written on this subject in a light manner but there is a dark side to the picture; the effects may show after many years.

We obtain almost an annual visitation of these tribes.

Would they come unless they received some remuneration? We think not. The best mode of dealing with them would be to give them a few bags of flour and some tobacco and start them off to their own country. As the country is being rapidly taken up for settlement and their chances of living becomes less, we ask have any portions of the Northern Territory been set apart as aboriginal reserves? The colonial surgeon, their protector, should see to this.

Not all Aboriginal women were reluctant to leave their own cultural environment and enter into relationships with non-Aboriginal men, as is illustrated by an unusual court case. Early in 1884 an Aboriginal girl named Mary Ann charged her brother, Charley, with assault when he tried to take her away from a Malay man with whom she and some of her female relatives were living. In return for being allowed to keep the women, the Malays periodically gave the male Aboriginal relatives gifts of flour, tea, sugar and other sundries. If these were not forthcoming at the right time the blacks would take the women away. But when Charley tried to remove Mary Ann by force, she rebelled. As she wanted to stay where she was, she borrowed enough money to pay for the cost of a summons and took him to court.

The outcome of Mary Ann's determined assertiveness is not clear. When the court asked Charley if he would stay away from his sister if allowed to go free, he told the magistrate, J. G. Knight, it was none of his business. 'What for Malay keep em that girl. That not alright. Suppose I want to beat em that my business,' he told the court. He was allowed to go, with a warning not to repeat the offence. The case was believed to be the first of its kind to go before an Australian court. Although it was described as 'extraordinary' at the time, it does not seem to have set any precedents, other than perhaps to reinforce a male view that men of any race had some right to dictate the future of the women presumed to belong to them.

When Price left the Territory to return to London in 1883 he was given two farewells, which served to emphasise the racial separatism that often existed in the small community. One was conducted by the European population at the newly built town hall and one by the Chinese business community. Price described the Chinese as good, law-abiding citizens. They were, he believed, unfairly treated, particularly in relation to their gambling game of fan-tan, which he believed should be legalised in the same way that European billiards was. 'I have had but few occasions to punish crime among the Chinese,' he said when he left, urging others to show the same tolerance.

The 1881 census figures indicate that the attitude he was advocating was not only philosophically just but practically sensible. Records show there were 3347 men living in the Territory, 2700 of whom were Chinese. The male-to-female ratio was even more marked, with only 104 women listed and only one of those being Chinese. The figures, of course, did not include Aboriginal people or the children of mixed Aboriginal descent, of whom, by now, there were undoubtedly many—a not unsurprising situation given the imbalance of the sexes of other races.

The relations between Chinese men and Aboriginal women in particular began to draw comment, especially the habit of Chinese men 'buying' or 'borrowing' the women with promise of opium, which was both legal and duty free in the early days. Many of the Chinese men had wives and families back in China, but by the early 1880s a few Chinese had begun to bring their wives to the Territory with them. One was Lee Hang Gong, a wealthy businessman from Creswick, Victoria, who had married an Englishwoman, Sarah Bowman. They were amongst the earliest Chinese pioneers to arrive in the Territory, both opening a business and entering into various mining ventures, the most famous being the Wheel of Fortune tin mine. They were certainly part of Territory society by 1881, because in September of that year Sarah wrote to Price asking him to consider employing her two sons, aged fifteen and eighteen, as interpreters as they could both read and write Chinese and English. Sarah, whose granddaughter remembers having to help look after her and in particular clean her clay pipe, remained in Darwin until her death in 1911, having raised a large family, most of whom remained in the Territory or connected with it. One of her daughters, Jane, married George Tye and became one of the most famous and highly respected Territory midwives.

Gradually the percentage of both Chinese and European women would increase, but the imbalance between the sexes remained significant enough during the second half of the period of South Australian control of the Territory for organised prostitution to rear its head along with a growing debate about Aboriginal protection and the issue of whether or not the Territory, particularly the tropics, was suitable for white women. This was despite the fact that by the end of Price's administration women were contributing to nearly every aspect of Territory life—as nurses, midwives, hotel owners, business proprietors, outback dwellers, explorers, miners, missionaries, educators and providers of domestic and social stability.

Chapter 4

Prostitution, 'Protection' and Political Power (1884-1911)

'To give women an interest in political affairs would be to destroy one of the strongest bulwarks of national prosperity and advancement, viz, the home life.'
V.L. Solomon

Although by 1884 women were contributing in a practical way to nearly every facet of Territory life, they did not escape from the largely middle-class public debate dealing with the 'woman question'—what should be women's role in society? In the Territory, this was compounded by officialdom's concern that the tropics, where the majority of people lived during the South Australian period of control, might not be 'suitable' for white women. In both policy and practical terms, this attitude had implications for women of other races, particularly Aboriginal and Asian women, who were considered by Europeans to be able to cope with the climate and the frontier atmosphere, and thus to perform functions that European women supposedly were unable to perform.

Most of the decisions on these questions, of course, were made by men, and evidence suggests that many of the women who actually lived in and became committed to the Territory considered it not only a suitable place for women but a desirable one. This opinion is supported in the surprisingly numerous examples of women's writings, both public and private, which survive from the period.

While the Territory's isolation and the numerical dominance of the male population did mean that Territory women suffered some disadvantages, these factors also meant that they were perhaps freer to expand their own horizons and to make an impact as individuals. They had the added advantage of the same legislative and social reforms as their South Australian sisters, who were the first in Australia to receive the vote and who were subject to reasonably progressive laws in relation to marital and property rights, even though these were still conservative by today's standards. As will be seen in the second half of this book, which deals with the stories of individual women, many of them took advantage of these rights to improve their situations.

Five government residents presided during the last twenty-five years of South Australian control of the Territory, when the 'woman question' and associated issues were being addressed, against a background of major developments—the

Anna Herbert (second from right, top row) served the Territory as first lady from 1905 to 1910. With her husband Charles she hosted many official receptions at government house, such as this one, at which the prominent Chinese businessmen of Darwin met the South Australian governor, George Hunt, and his wife. Anna took an active part in many aspects of Territory life and was living with her two sons on Koolpinyah station when Darwin was bombed in 1942.
Northern Territory State Reference Library.

building of the Darwin to Pine Creek railway, the granting to the Territory of two seats in the South Australian parliament and the granting of the female franchise to South Australian and Northern Territory women, the 1895 Royal Commission into Territory development, the establishment of the newly surveyed townships of Alice Springs (then called Stuart) and Borroloola, a rush to the Arltunga and Tanami goldfields, a cyclone in 1897 that destroyed Darwin, and the transfer of the Territory to commonwealth control.

ATTITUDES AND IMAGES

The first government resident of this period, John Langdon Parsons, arrived in May 1884 with his second wife Marianna, the well-educated daughter of a South Australian school inspector, and their two children. As was common with the women of the upper class, Marianna Parsons made several lengthy trips south with her children during her term as the Territory's first lady. According to some reports, Parsons indulged in heavy bouts of drinking while they were away, an escapist habit still not unusual in the Territory. Perhaps he was influenced by his loneliness, but Parsons had definite views about whether or not European women could cope with the tropics, views which he made public. In his March 1885 report, written a month after the birth of his daughter Ida, Parsons expressed his belief that the tropical climate was 'undeniably healthy' for white women and children, especially as the women were 'freed from the kitchen by Chinese cooks' and thus able to maintain their strength.

Although there is nothing to tell us what Marianna herself thought of her life, a view of life in the Top End is provided by a young Melbourne woman who arrived on the yacht *Cushie Doo* for a five-month stay in the Territory shortly after the Parsons arrived. She was Ada Booty, who was on her way overseas with her cousin, prospective Territory investor W.G. Osmond, the yacht's captain. While he explored the Victoria River area to assess its potential, Ada remained in Palmerston. Through her diary, Ada provides a pleasant picture of her daily Palmerston life, undoubtedly made more enjoyable by the fact that she was one of the very few single women in the community. The fact that she stayed with the more prominent families in town, including the Parsons, clearly gave her an elitist perspective, but it is no less valuable for that.

On her first night in town, she was invited to dine with the Parsons at the residency. 'We were waited on by two Chinamen. On returning to the drawing room there was quite a reception, in fact, I was told, pretty well all Palmerston (there are only about five single girls in the place).'

After settling into the routine of Darwin life, and learning to live with its 'overpoweringly hot' breezes, she wrote:

The days are passing rapidly because so pleasantly. We breakfast at 8. After breakfast I do up the flowers. About 9.30 or 10 the gentlemen go off to their offices and Mrs James and I sit in the veranda, reading or sewing. At 12 Mr McMinn comes in, then Mr James. At 1 p.m. we lunch. We take an after lunch cup of tea on the veranda and soon Mrs James and I retire and discard most of our clothing and sit in her bedroom where there is generally a breeze to be had with three doors open. At 4 p.m. I dress and go for a walk or drive...Generally we have someone in of an evening.[1]

Women who adjusted to and enjoyed tropical living in the Territory soon learned that the verandah was the coolest and most comfortable living area. Isobel Hesketh, who married Overland Telegraph operator and musical entertainer Fred Price in Darwin in 1898, made creative use of tropical plants for decoration. A quarter of a century later Isobel (pictured with Fred and baby Hilda in their Darwin home at the turn of the century) became a pioneer pastoralist of central Australia.
Pearl Powell collection, Northern Territory Conservation Commission.

Ada also describes parties, picnics and balls she attended. After five pleasant months, and after spending Christmas at the residency, Ada recorded that she was leaving Darwin with much regret, the tropical life and people having thoroughly bewitched her.

One of Darwin's earliest European residents, Fred R. Finniss, wrote a letter to his father, Boyle Travers Finniss, in 1886, in which he claimed that, unlike Ada's pleasant view of Darwin's social life, the days were really filled with constant social squabbles that reminded him of his days at Escape Cliffs, except that now they had 'ladies to help intensify the disagreements'. He was also concerned about the absence of Chinese women in the community and advocated a controlled Chinese immigration scheme to help rectify the situation. He believed that a proportionate number of women should accompany Chinese men who came to the Territory and that there was a need for better protection of Chinese women and female children.[2]

The 'Chinese question' was very much in the headlines by the 1880s, which was a period of depression and thus competition for jobs. Because the Chinese were usually prepared to work longer, harder and for lower wages than Europeans, they drew criticism from many quarters. But they had their advocates, including the assertive wife of a doctor resident in Palmerston and the new mining community of Burrundie in 1888-89. She wrote articles in their defence under the pseudonym of Murray Eyre and later published her views in various London and Australian

Chinese women, although greatly outnumbered by Chinese men for most of Darwin's pre-war history, played a vital role in the development of the Top End. In the early years they established the large families that became an integral part of Darwin's cosmopolitan character. This picture, taken in about 1906, shows one young girl (far left) in traditional Chinese costume and with bound feet along with the male members of her family, forebears of many current Darwin families including Chin, Chan, Tang, Moy and Ho.
Photograph courtesy of Ernie Chin.

journals. In one she described the Territory Chinese this way: 'He is shrewd, painstaking, and thrifty, adapting himself readily to the conditions of life of the new country; and the discipline of poverty which has probably confined his ancestors for ages...gives him a love of order, self-control and industry, which adds largely to his value in the pioneer work he has been engaged to do.'[3]

Although the Chinese had first come to the Territory to work on the mines and to establish businesses, the pioneer work she refers to was almost certainly the transcontinental railway, the first section between Darwin and Pine Creek being completed in 1887. In July the entire town of Palmerston turned out to celebrate and congratulate each other on the christening of the first 'full size' locomotive to run in the Territory. The ceremony that took place provides a colourful picture of the social patronage men paid to women a century ago. In the absence of the Parsons family who were holidaying in Adelaide, Emily Pater, wife of the acting government resident, Justice Thomas Kennedy Pater, was given the honour of breaking champagne over the engine and christening it 'Port Darwin'.[4] The 25 July 1887 issue of the *Northern Territory Times* reported:

The ceremony of christening the first locomotive on the Palmerston and Pine Creek railway was performed on the stacking ground last Tuesday by Mrs T.K. Pater in the presence of perhaps the largest crowd that has ever assembled in Palmerston. The engine was drawn up alongside a platform and surrounded with ferns and creepers...At a few minutes past four o'clock, Mrs Pater, accompanied by several ladies, was driven up to the platform and escorted to the side of the locomotive by Mr G. Millar who said: "Mrs Pater, permit me to assure you of the sincere pleasure your presence here today affords me and the very high compliment you pay my firm."

Mrs Pater said that she had a task to perform that was in the highest degree pleasing and satisfactory to her in christening the first locomotive [and] she trusted that the just expectations with regard to it would be fulfilled and that a career of usefulness might await it.

Mr Millar in proposing the health of Mrs Pater said..."I am sure you will all

When the Darwin to Pine Creek railway opened in the late 1880s, the railway sidings became social centres for passengers travelling up and down the 'track'. Here, passengers mingle outside the Brock's Creek siding, where Fannie Haynes ran a popular pub and store for nearly half a century.
Northern Territory State Reference Library.

agree with me that we have just witnessed an important and interesting ceremony. Possibly to some of our fair friends it may not seem quite so attractive as some of the happy little events that occur so frequently and at which they are so pleased to call in the good offices of the Reverend head of their church. But to the more material and less romantic side of humanity today's proceedings will undoubtedly be written on their memory as a red letter day to be chronicled in the annals of this great northern land as the commencement of a new era in its prosperity. I am sure we are all greatly indebted to our fair friend Mrs Pater who has so ably and so charmingly assisted us by christening the first and pioneer engine of the Palmerston and Pine Creek railway and I will call upon you to drink that lady's health in bumpers and with three times three." His Honour Justice Pater responded in suitable terms on behalf of Mrs Pater.

In keeping with tradition, only men were allowed at the celebration banquet that night. Like all good gentlemen of the day, however, they did ask one of their colleagues to pay tribute on their behalf to the ladies. The honour of the toast to 'The Ladies' fell to customs officer Alfred Searcy who claimed he did not have much to say on the subject as he was not a lady's man. He was certain, however, of one thing, 'that without the presence of ladies in Palmerston, the place would not be worth living in,' a comment which drew a hearty round of applause from the gentlemen present.

Apart from this brief moment of glory, Emily Pater had a rather tragic life, which she and others blamed in part on the time the family had had to spend in the Territory. In 1886, two years after their arrival in Darwin, the Paters' nineteen-year-old daughter, Edith, died of an incurable disease. Then, in 1892, two years after their departure from Darwin, Judge Pater died, leaving Emily and their other daughter in 'very necessitous circumstances.' Emily petitioned the government asking for compensation on the grounds that her husband's appointment and subsequent six-year term as the judge of the Northern Territory had diminished his health to such an extent that it eventually led to his death.

Those who argued against the petition pointed out that there were many widowed women of less social standing whose husbands had also given their entire working lives to the public service, but who had never received such compensation. They pointed specifically to the widow and children of a Borroloola trooper who had recently contracted malaria and died, having been a public servant for sixteen years. They argued that she was in greater need than Mrs Pater whose husband had been in a high-paying job most of his life.

Emily's parliamentary friends included John Langdon Parsons, who by then was a Territory representative in the South Australian parliament. Parsons and others argued that Judge Pater had been a long serving and well respected member of the South Australian public service and that, although he had chosen to take up the permanent appointment in the Northern Territory, he had not been responsible for the effect it had on his health, which forced him to relinquish his appointment. Emily, they argued, was an innocent victim of this circumstance and deserved compensation. She eventually received 650 pounds, but when she died in a fire in her Melbourne boarding house in 1901 the *Northern Territory Times* noted that she had 'had to turn to her artistic talents to keep the wolves from the door'. A correspondent of the *Bulletin* noted the contrast between the funeral of her husband, who had the 'largest funeral ever seen in Adelaide', and that of Mrs Pater, 'an estimable woman who had bravely struggled against misfortune—a hearse, a mourning coach with only her daughter and another carriage—empty'.[5]

When Parsons resigned as the Territory's government resident in 1890, South Australian officials chose the versatile John George Knight to take his place. Knight had served in the Territory since 1873 when he was appointed from Melbourne as government secretary. Though his appointment provoked much controversy at the time (many believed a local South Australian should have been selected), it had proved to be one of the wisest decisions the government made. Over the next twenty years Knight not only designed many of Darwin's public buildings, but also became 'mother, father and uncle' to the Territory while his wife and most of his large family remained in Melbourne and, later, London. At the time of his first appointment, his wife, Alice Bertrand, whom he married in Melbourne in 1852, had already born him eight children, so perhaps she had her reasons for not joining him in the Territory. When Knight was appointed government resident, Alice had been living in London for several years receiving a portion of his pay and lobbying hard but unsuccessfully for him to get a job there.

There is no firm evidence to suggest that she ever visited him in Darwin, although several of their children did. Alice did have the opportunity to see her husband, however, during his quite frequent trips to Melbourne, Adelaide and London where he organised Northern Territory exhibits as part of various interstate exhibitions over a number of years. In Darwin, Knight had to rely on other women to play the part of official hostess at government functions. A favourite was Evlampia Holtze, popular and hospitable wife of the talented curator of the botanical gardens, Maurice Holtze. The family had been in Darwin since the 1870s and their home had always been a centre of culture and sociability. Evlampia was described by the *Northern Territory Times* as 'one of [Darwin's] most agreeable ladies' and a woman of dignity, who welcomed everyone. It was thus with considerable regret that Darwin said goodbye to the family in 1891. Maurice became curator of the botanical gardens in Adelaide and his son, Nicholas, became curator in Darwin, where he and his wife Annie continued the Holtze tradition of fine hospitality for the next twenty years.

Knight was well known throughout the Territory and by the time he became government resident, he had served in almost every conceivable official capacity, at one time being paid to hold five different jobs. When he died in January 1892, the whole town of Palmerston, and much of the surrounding district, went into mourning and the entire community attended the funeral.

Chosen to replace Knight as government resident was confirmed bachelor Charles James Dashwood, who arrived in April 1892 with his two younger sisters, Augusta and Millicent. In the absence of a Mrs Dashwood, their role was to help him with his official hospitality duties. After a welcome at the wharf, the party was driven to the newly built two-storey North Australian Hotel owned by enterprising Territory publican Ellen Ryan. Here they remained until repairs had been completed on the residency, which had fallen into disrepair through time, tropical mildew and the ever-active white ants.

Women's rights and responsibilities were very much in the news at the time. The South Australian parliament was debating whether women should get the vote and officialdom was trying to decide whether the tropics were a suitable place for

Ludmilla Holtze poses with a python draped around her neck in Darwin's botanical gardens, which her father established at its present site in the late 1880s. Ludmilla's parents, Maurice and Evlampia Holtze, were extremely popular and her mother turned their gardens home into a centre of culture and society. When the family returned to Adelaide in 1891, Ludmilla's brother Nicholas became curator in Darwin, where he and his wife Annie (née Birkett) continued the Holtze tradition of hospitality. Ludmilla lived to be more than 100 years old. A Darwin suburb has been named in her honour.
Peter Spillett collection, Northern Territory State Reference Library.

white women and, if so, under what circumstances. By 1895 Dashwood, who remained government resident for a record thirteen years, had revealed his views about which sex could better cope with tropical living when he appeared before a royal commission on the Territory and was asked his opinion of it as a place of residence for Europeans:

All I can say is that living in a certain way carefully in the NT I do not think the climate is particularly unhealthy, for the male sex at any rate...but as regards the climate for women and children I do not think it can be called a healthy climate. Children retain their health up to a certain age but feel the climate after that when all sensible people send them away.[6]

The *Northern Territory Times* was quick to respond:

Mr Justice Dashwood's opinion that women cannot live in the Territory is about on a par with what we used to say of cabbages. Twelve or thirteen years ago it was generally believed that it would be quite as easy to grow door knobs as English cabbages. Yet that fallacy was quashed by the production of an article equal to the southern vegetable...With regard to women, it may be said that we have never at any time had a very great number of that sex here, but of those we have, a large percentage have lived here for years and years without a change. Some almost born in the Territory and the mothers of families are probably as strong and hearty now as they ever were in their lives, or as they would have been had they put in a similar term of existence in, say, the hot wind and sandstorm regions of South Australia proper.[7]

Territory businessman and parliamentarian Vaiben L. Solomon, whose own wife had died in Palmerston in 1885, supported Dashwood's view, claiming women were not so healthy in the Territory, wanted a change every three years and spent too much time indoors. One railway official testified that white women and children 'lead an enervated lazy kind of a life', engaging Chinese and Singhalese to carry everything for them. Nicholas Holtze, the new botanical gardens curator, on the other hand, claimed that white women and children could endure the Territory's tropical belts as well as anyone else and said that his family had been there for seventeen years and were still in the best of health. He believed the main reason Europeans suffered from fever and ague was usually due to their own making—because they drank to excess and then slept out in the damp atmosphere.

In 1897 nature interrupted the debate. In the early hours of a January morning a cyclone, similar in strength to Cyclone Tracy, which destroyed Darwin in 1974, devastated the tiny township in just a few hours. The *Melbourne Leader* described the event thus:

The cyclone commenced at midnight on the 6th and reached its height at 3a.m. on the 7th. It continued in full force till 6 a.m. The howling wind blew with terrific force, accompanied by drenching rain which penetrated at once every room of the most substantial building...Some buildings were removed bodily from their foundations; in others, roofs were lifted and deposited on the ground. Corrugated iron and rafters were carried almost incredible distances and thrown over the tops of houses...Some old and infirm persons, unable to face the terrible weather, were forced to remain in their ruined houses till daylight brought relief. An old lady of ninety was in a wrecked house for hours covered by a tarpaulin and attended by her son.

Chinatown is largely a sea of sheet iron, timber, goods and chattels. Only a few double storeyed buildings escaped and the owners of the shattered tenements are burrowing in the piles of debris to construct temporary shelters slightly raised from the ground. The bodies of five Chinese have been found in the ruins and it is expected that more will be recorded later. One Chinaman found in a coffin was fed with rice in that position till he died...The town is a picture of desolation, hundreds of carpenters are necessary to save and restore the property...

In an almost throw-away line the paper added, using the common terminology of the time, that 'Two lubras were found crushed in the ruins of the Catholic Church, having taken refuge on the verandah'.

With the financial help of people all around Australia, and the practical help of imported Chinese carpenters, the town was back on its feet within four months. In particular, repairs to the town's hotels were speedy. The managers, mostly women, were anxious to re-open for business. If the cyclone proved anything, it proved that women could cope every bit as well as men with the tropics and the rigours of Territory life. There is little evidence that women, particularly long-term Territory residents, left because of the cyclone. There is ample evidence, detailed in the second part of this book, that they not only stayed and picked up the pieces, but went on to make major contributions to the Territory's physical and social development.

One of these women was Anna Herbert, married to Justice Charles Herbert, who replaced Dashwood as government resident in 1905. When Charles and Anna and their children arrived in Darwin in April 1905 to take up their posting, the goodwill and support of the people were already secured. Herbert had practised as a lawyer in Darwin in 1896 and the family had lived there for several years. Since 1900 he had represented the Territory in the South Australian parliament and he was highly regarded for displaying 'more than the ordinary ability and courage in honestly and faithfully carrying out his pledges and endeavouring by every means within his power to advance the interests of this settlement'.

These endeavours included actively encouraging women to come and live in the Territory. As a member of parliament, Herbert had attempted to increase the number of women in the Territory by introducing legislation which granted 160 acres (65 hectares) of land to married men with two children.

While Herbert did his best to encourage settlement, others still had doubts about the ability of white women to adjust to the tropics. Bishop White of Carpentaria argued in a speech to the Royal Geographical Society that white women were not hardy enough to survive the heat and isolation of northern Australia and that it was therefore unlikely that permanent white settlement could take place.

As first lady, Anna Herbert took steps to prove that women could not only live in the Territory but could be as capable and creative as women anywhere in Australia. When the first Australian Women's Exhibition was held in Melbourne in 1907 she formed a local committee to organise Territory entries. In supporting her call for participation, the *Northern Territory Times* pointed out that at ordinary exhibits the work of women was usually overshadowed by the handiwork of men and the proposed women's exhibition was important partly because it would bring attention to the talents of women and partly because it might open up avenues of employment for women. After months of encouraging local participants and getting the entries ready for exhibit, Anna accompanied the Territory entries to Melbourne. The work of Aboriginal women from Melville Island was particularly featured, and a 'picturesque fringed hat' drew special comment from the Melbourne press.

Anna's work in this and other areas was clearly appreciated. When the Herberts left for New Guinea in January 1910, where Judge Herbert was to take up a position as deputy chief judicial officer, the women of Darwin gathered at the residence of Edith Somerville to present Anna Herbert with twelve gold sovereigns 'for the purchase of some memento of the many friends she has made in the Territory both as a pleasant and courteous hostess at the Residency and in her more private social relations'.[8]

The family continued to participate in Territory affairs for many years, with Justice Herbert often returning to hear cases and, in 1921, to serve as an acting judge of the Northern Territory. When he died of pneumonia in 1929, Anna and their two sons were left with a Top End property, Koolpinyah. Anna was still living in the Territory when Japanese bombs fell on Darwin in 1942—proof, if any further proof were needed, of the fact that women could handle both the climate and the catastrophes.

WOMEN'S CHOICES

While Anna first went to the Territory because that was where her husband's job took the family, other women chose to go to pursue their own lines of work. They were women who had engaged in the acceptable female professions of nursing or teaching, sometimes combining their work with a religious mission. Although they were generally few in number at any one time, their influence in the community was often quite powerful, as a look at a few of the pioneers reveals.

The first woman teacher appointed to the Territory came after a lobbying campaign from the Port Darwin populace, who claimed in a petition to the government that James Kitchen, who had been holding the position since 1877, was inefficient and should be replaced by a female. In late 1888, twenty-four-year-old Catherine Cooper, newly married to William Pett, was chosen for the job. She was warmly welcomed when she arrived to take up her duties in early 1889, and her devotion to the education and the entertainment of children quickly endeared her to the population. She took a few weeks off in August to have her first child, a son, William Bryan, fondly known locally as 'King' Pett. Sadly, he died of mock croup just before his fifth birthday in 1894; the town offered public condolences. Despite the

The Territory's first woman public schoolteacher, Catherine Pett (right), with her students outside the Darwin public school in 1905. Catherine served as a teacher in the Territory from 1888 to 1910.
Spillett collection, Northern Territory State Reference Library.

tragedy, Catherine continued teaching, while William worked as a gardener, although he appears to have spent a lot of time away from the Territory. During one of his absences Catherine asked permission to take in boarders in order to support herself. When her home, all her furniture, and the school building were destroyed in the 1897 cyclone, she requested and was given a paid return passage to Adelaide and an extended leave on full pay. Two years later she had a second son, Ronald, who survived.

Catherine remained teaching in the Territory for another decade, spending several years as head of the Pine Creek school. During this time she involved herself in much more than just educational issues, and became well-known for organising children's concerts and entertainments. One newspaper article commended her as a 'born organiser' and another praised her for being 'most energetic in getting up dance practices for the children'. When Catherine finally retired and left the Territory in 1910 she was given a grand farewell by the Darwin people, who organised for a visiting brass band to perform in her honour. As was not unusual, the male teacher who took her place was immediately put on a salary fifty pounds higher than hers.

Such discrimination did not seem to deter other women from entering the teaching field. One became the Territory's first travelling teacher. She was Catherine Maude Harrison, who arrived in Port Darwin in September 1905 to open a private school in the upper floor of the substantial, somewhat oriental-looking two-storey home that had been designed and built on Darwin's cliff-top by John Knight. The prospectus she issued offered instruction in French, Latin, music and wood carving, and courses designed to prepare pupils for the Adelaide universities or for civil service or commercial examinations. Her fees per term ranged from one guinea for pupils under ten years of age to three guineas for children over thirteen. The school was welcomed by those parents who had previously sent their children south if they had wanted a higher class education than that they believed was offered in the Darwin public school.

Within a month of launching the private school, Catherine handed the reins over to a Miss Waldron, who remained in charge until 1909. Catherine, meanwhile, had been offered and accepted another job as the Territory's first travelling teacher, working with children who lived in the tiny townships on the Darwin to Pine Creek railway line. She began her travelling classroom in October 1905 at the mining community of Brock's Creek. As there was no schoolroom, classes were held at a private residence, and the project was praised by the *Northern Territory Times* as 'a commendable endeavour to provide a means of education for children living along the railway line'. The system had been successfully practised in sparsely settled districts in the US and Canada. It was very much welcomed by Territory people, who had consistently argued that lack of educational facilities was one of the chief obstacles to the settlement of European families in the outback districts. Catherine Harrison remained the Territory's travelling teacher for two years, and was followed by Minnie Smith and then Helen Carruth, who became a very popular and long-serving teacher in the Pine Creek district.

The other main acceptable profession for women was nursing, and several nurses made names for themselves locally during the period of South Australian control. Miss Isabella Birkett was matron of Palmerston hospital from 1888 to 1892, during which time the Territory's second hospital was established at Burrundie.

During her time as matron, Isabella had the opportunity to learn a great deal about the diagnosis and treatment of leprosy, which was by then beginning to have a significant impact on the Territory's Aboriginal community. She later married telegraphist Walter James Kell, and moved with him to Burrundie, where she became the first woman 'dispenser of drugs'.

Isabella was replaced as matron of Palmerston hospital by Freda Reinhardt, who was replaced four years later by a fellow nursing graduate Marie Davoren. Because of serious financial difficulties, the South Australian government could only pay Marie ninety-six pounds a year, compared to the 144 pounds received by her predecessors. Despite this, and the fact that for much of her time she suffered from a serious illness, Matron Davoren stayed in her job until her death in Darwin in March 1906. The *Northern Territory Times* praised her, saying she had 'won the hearts and affection and sincere respect of a large circle of Territorians'.

One of her nursing assistants during the time of her appointment had been Hannah Wood, who had used her professional nursing skills to make her own living when her husband died shortly after their arrival in the Territory. When Hannah died of a heart attack in 1903, the *Northern Territory Times* told her story, one which reflects the contribution made by, and the fate that befell, more than one woman who chose to make the Territory home:

Mrs Wood was an old resident of the Territory having arrived here to join her husband in 1875 and share with him in many of the rough experiences endured by pioneers in those early days on the goldfields. Her husband died within a year or two of her joining him and since his death she has supported herself by the practice of her old profession of nurse and in this capacity has been brought into more or less intimate contact with nearly every family in the place and by her kindness and attention and skill in cases of sickness had won for herself a no small share of regard and esteem. Like other members of the human family the deceased lady had her failings. She was a woman with strong passions and prejudices, an independent spirit and great determination and she could be a bitter enemy as well as a kindly and staunch friend. But she was cleanly, industrious and skillful and enthusiastic in the practice of her profession. She had a wonderfully clear memory and some of her old time reminiscences, particularly of her early experiences in the settlement, would have made interesting reading if published. She was a woman of great natural intelligence and up to the last took the liveliest interest in everything affecting the welfare of this settlement'.[9]

The paper lamented the fact that only twelve people attended her funeral: 'It might have been expected that so old a resident who from the nature of her calling had been brought into peculiarly intimate relations with so many people would have been more honored on the last occasion.'[10] Like many of the men and women who ventured to the Territory and helped to pioneer their own little patch, she died alone, and virtually anonymous.

Isabella Birkett's sister, Margaret, was also a nurse and won praise not only for her nursing skills but for her composure when, one night, on her way from the hospital to her sleeping quarters, she was attacked by a large and venomous brown snake. The *Northern Territory Times* praised her response, particularly because she was a woman: 'Nurse Birkett who quite alive to the situation and her own danger, cooly met the attack of the reptile with the only weapon she had—a flimsy silk umbrella. She hit the snake but apparently not very effectively for it again advanced and struck out at the nurse viciously. As it did so Nurse Birkett again brought down her umbrella with such force that the reptile's back was broken. This was the more fortunate as the same blow wrecked the umbrella. Nurse Birkett is to be congratulated on displaying such cool presence of mind and pluck in the presence of so unexpected and deadly a peril...Very few women—and how many men for that matter—would have come through so startling an adventure with so much credit.'[11]

WOMEN 'DOWN THE TRACK'

Although most women who went to the Territory ended up residing in Darwin, some were beginning to make their marks in other regions, even though they were usually even more dramatically outnumbered by men than were their Darwin counterparts. One was Jane Murray, who had lived with her family at Katherine Telegraph Station since 1875, a popular and hospitable hostess whose home was a welcome refuge for travellers and country people of the region. The family's pioneering contribution to Territory life came to a sad end in January 1893 when Jane's husband, Robert, who had been poorly for some time and had recently applied for sick leave, became seriously ill while on a visit to Burrundie. Jane was sent for from Katherine and arrived with her son and young daughter just a few hours before he died. His death, and Jane's subsequent departure for Adelaide, was lamented throughout the Top End, as both Robert and Jane had gained the affection and respect of most who had come into contact with them.

One of the very first resident women of the town of Alice Springs (then called Stuart) after it was surveyed in 1888 was Tryphena Benstead, wife of the enterprising Bill Benstead. In the 1870s, at the age of fourteen, Bill ran away from home and became a station hand at Undoolya Station, a few kilometres from the present town of Alice Springs. He returned to Adelaide a few years later to marry his childhood sweetheart, Tryphena Raines, whose sister, Cornelia, had married the Alice Springs Telegraph Station postmaster, Joseph Skinner, in 1886. William had been strongly criticised by his friends when they heard he was planning to bring a wife back to the Territory, but he simply replied with confidence that they didn't know the nature of the woman he had married. He had justified faith in her pioneering spirit.

In 1889 Tryphena and Bill built Alice Springs' first hotel, the Stuart Arms. Two years later their daughter Lucille was born, believed to be the first white girl born in the town, although her cousin, Maud Skinner, had been born at the telegraph station some time earlier. Encouraged by her musically talented mother, Lucille, known as Lulu, showed early signs of having a superior singing voice. After a few years in Alice, the family travelled to various goldfields in Western Australia, where the family, who were all show-orientated, entertained the miners with concerts. Lulu, with her fine clear voice, was the lead singer and soon became known as 'Little Lulu of the Goldfields'. The family recognised Lulu's potential (some music critics were already hailing her as the natural successor to Melba) and in 1911 allowed her to travel to Paris to study voice.

Although Lulu had operatic ambitions, the need for money sidetracked her and she went into the more lucrative area of music hall performances. During the First World War she delighted soldiers throughout Europe with her renditions of the wartime favourites. She later travelled to America, where she became great friends

Atlanta and Thomas Bradshaw and their family and white staff at the Alice Springs Telegraph Station shortly before they left in 1908. As one of the very few European women in the centre at the time, and in the absence of any medical personnel, Atlanta (centre, holding son Allan) became nurse to many in the surrounding district. Her daughter Doris (far left, back row) later wrote a book, Alice on the Line, *about the family's pioneering years at the station.* Bradshaw collection, Northern Territory Conservation Commission.

of movie magnates, Jack and Molly Warner. She returned to England, where she remained until her death in the early 1980s. Though she never again visited the place of her birth, she proudly referred to it in interviews throughout her life and helped put Alice Springs on the map in faraway places.

Another early female resident of the area was Lillian Bloomfield, who arrived in the Centre with her husband, Lewis, early in the century. The family lived for many years at Love's Creek, some four hundred miles north of Oodnadatta, where Lillian used to travel to have her babies, as there was no doctor in the Centre. The family made very few trips into Alice Springs, and when they did it was usually for the races, the one time of the year when the tiny urban population swelled, as she later described:

Alice Springs was then a very small town. There were two general stores, one hotel, several little old shacks and the Post Office and Telegraph Station about two miles distant. Our only amusement was a picnic race meeting held in Alice Springs at

Christmas time. This fixture also depended on the season as all the horses were grass fed. People came from far and near. Bough sheds were made on the course for shelter from the sun and although there was no totalizator or bookmakers, we would have sweeps and everyone would have a very happy time. It was very pleasant to meet again all the old friends whom we had not seen for perhaps twelve months or more. We made our own fun. Most popular was the dancing—on a camp canvas sheet pegged down to the ground very securely and with accordion or gramophone music.[12]

Lillian Bloomfield raised two daughters, Peg and Jean, who both became prominent and permanent Territorians and married into well-known Territory families. Peg married Jock Nelson, whose father had been the first Territory member of federal parliament and who later followed in his father's footsteps as the Territory's sole post-war member of parliament for many years, and Jean married Ted Hayes, whose family had leased Undoolya station since 1884.

Another early resident of the area was Atlanta Bradshaw, married to Thomas Bradshaw, the Alice Springs telegraph operator at the turn of the century. As there was no doctor within hundreds of miles, Atlanta, out of necessity, developed nursing skills and soon became greatly loved and respected by the people in the surrounding district because of the friendly interest she took in those who needed care. On Sundays Atlanta used the telegraph wires to talk to the nurses in Port Darwin, who gave her instructions as to how to deal with the various cases of illness that arose. She was particularly known for her kindness to Aboriginal people, who came into the telegraph station during drought periods for rations and blankets and sometimes in ill health. Because she had no trained medical knowledge she often gave her impromptu patients her invariable prescription of a mixture of ground ginger, sugar and hot water. She comforted herself with the thought that it could do them no harm. When Atlanta died in Adelaide in 1929 at the age of sixty-three, the Adelaide *Advertiser* praised the contribution she had made to life in outback Australia. Years later, her daughter Doris wrote of their life on the telegraph station and in early Alice Springs in a book called *Alice on the Line*.

PROSTITUTION ARRIVES

If white women were scarce in the Territory, Asian women were even scarcer, and this dearth of female companionship inevitably led to the organised establishment of the world's oldest profession.

During Charles Dashwood's term as government resident, the number of Japanese pearlers in the Territory increased and, as most were young and single, they imported their own prostitutes. Most came from Japan through a tightly organised underworld system that distributed women to Darwin, Broome, Cairns and other north Australian centres. In 1888 the Queensland magazine *Boomerang* reported that there were five Japanese brothels in Darwin and twenty-five Japanese prostitutes.

In 1893 the Japanese diet sent a Mr K. Watanabe to Australia to report on the situation. He described the life of the Japanese prostitutes plying their trade in Darwin after gaining experience in Hong Kong and Singapore. Watanabe reported that most were between twenty-four and thirty years of age, but some were as young as seventeen. Although two had been married in Darwin, most were distributed among the brothels with three or four prostitutes living in each. The 1901 census showed there were thirty-nine female Japanese, aged between fifteen and thirty-four, registered as living in the Territory, the majority of them apparently earning their living by prostitution. Watanabe described how the young women were bought in Japan:

The procurer would seek out poor families and make an advance of twenty or thirty yen to the victims. He would then make arrangements with the captain of a foreign ship to smuggle them to Hong Kong or Canton at fifty to sixty yen per head. They would be put aboard from a fishing boat as soon as they were beyond the radius of surveillance by the water police. At Hong Kong the procurer would sell them for about 200 to 300 yen and then return to Japan and repeat the process.[13]

As the prostitutes earned at least four times as much in Australia as they could in Hong Kong, the incentive was strong, although not all of them found the high pay enough compensation, as the *Northern Territory Times* reported:

A Japanese woman essayed the feat of leaping into another world by leaping down a well situated upon the said allotment. She no sooner regained the surface of the water, however, than she repented of her rashness and commenced to sing out lustily for assistance. Fortunately for the woman there are several huts close by the well and her cries being heard by one of the inmates a rope was lowered and she was quickly hauled to the surface. From the top of the well to the surface of the water the distance is nine fathoms or 54 feet [16.5 metres] and it is a rather singular fact that the woman leaped with no more serious injury than a light scratch on one of her hands. It is said the lady had set her mind upon returning to Japan by the *Australian* and being prevented from carrying out her desire, adopted the above unsatisfactory method of expressing her vexation and disgust with things in general.

Sometimes it was the patrons of the prostitutes who became distraught, such as the Japanese diver who fell in love and wanted to marry the girl he had been visiting regularly, offering her nine pounds to do so. When she hesitated, he went wild, armed himself with a sword and pistol, called her outside and shot her in the breast at point-blank range, an attack which she miraculously survived. He then ran off and wrote a suicide letter in large Japanese characters on the surface of the nearby tennis court. On reflection, however, he decided against suicide, gave himself up, and was charged with the young woman's attempted murder. In court the woman concerned pleaded for leniency for him. Judge Dashwood sentenced him to seven years' jail, and took the opportunity to comment in the paper on the problems of allowing 'coloured people' to go about armed.

A previous judge had claimed that the majority of the disturbances in the Japanese brothels were caused by drunken Europeans and said that steps should be taken to close the institutions down. Despite such criticisms, the trade seems to have thrived in the Darwin area until at least 1902, when the Federal Immigration Act curtailed it.

The Japanese prostitution trade was not the only one in the Territory, however. The Darwin newspapers of the period carry occasional references to Chinese prostitutes and to European woman of 'low morals', but the more frequent references are to Aboriginal women being sold or loaned to Asian and European men in return for payment of some kind—usually tobacco, food, or in the case of the Chinese, opium. This led one one resident doctor of the time to complain that Aboriginal women were 'not nearly so useful in houses as they [had] been in previous years; this [he attributed] to the money made by habits of prostitution among the Malays and Chinese'.[14] He believed a few convictions under the Masters and Servants Act would improve the situation.

ABORIGINAL 'PROTECTION'

Others began to take a more critical look at the situation, however, and the treatment of Aboriginal people, particularly of Aboriginal women, increasingly drew the attention of both officials and the southern populace. The era had begun with a controversial event that occurred during the time Ada Booty was staying in Darwin—an event which made headlines around Australia but, revealingly, did not get a mention in Ada's otherwise descriptive diary. In 1884 a group of Aboriginal men attacked and killed three popular miners at the Daly River, and Parsons sanctioned a private punitive expedition, which returned with the so-called culprits. Soon after, reports began filtering back that the party had indiscriminately shot a large number of Aboriginal people, mainly women and children. An official police report of the incident admitted nothing, but officers of a ship anchored in the area reported hearing firearms shooting all night. Such reports stirred up the storm of protest from many people who believed the Aboriginal people concerned had been treated unjustly. The *Northern Territory Times* carried a two-line poem which reflected the attitude of many residents: 'These white men with their loaded guns,/Make black men scarce as married nuns.' A board of inquiry exonerated all the men who had taken part in the vengeful expedition, but the controversy it generated throughout the country about the treatment of Aborigines would continue for a very long time.

Although there had been an Aboriginal protector appointed since the earliest days of South Australian control of the Territory, no laws existed to define what 'protection' was or how it should be administered. One newspaper report of the time confidently claimed that 'The South Australian Government didn't pass an Aboriginal Protection Act because they knew if the women were taken away the inhabitants would leave the country'.[15]

If that was in fact the case, it was not because there were not advocates for such an Act. One of them was Charles Dashwood, who, during his long term of office, gradually changed his views of the way Aboriginal people should be dealt with. He had become particularly dubious about the justice of trying them in a language and under a system that was foreign to them. He became increasingly concerned about their ill treatment, especially the violation of black women by Europeans, and in the late 1890s he wrote a report for the South Australian government supporting changes to the law. He drafted clauses that were incorporated in an Aboriginal Protection Act introduced into parliament in 1899. Pastoralists lobbied against the bill and it failed. Dashwood further angered them by defending Aboriginal people's right to retain access to their traditional hunting ground and watering holes.[16]

Very different views about Aboriginal treatment in the Territory were put during the parliamentary debate on the legislation, particularly a controversial clause which prohibited illicit intercourse by persons with a female Aboriginal or 'halfcaste' who had been employed under certain conditions set out in the bill. One senior official denounced the clause as being a grave moral reflection on the people who lived in the remote regions, claiming 'The keeping of gins for immoral purposes is always the exception, even in bush centres'.[17] But the sub-protector of Aborigines in the Alice Springs area, Thomas Bradshaw, made this counterclaim: 'It is the rule and not the exception for lubras to be used for the purpose specified, as the number of halfcaste children in the country will indicate.'[18]

POLITICAL ADVANCEMENT FOR TERRITORY WOMEN

Although South Australia rejected legislation for Aboriginal protection, an issue which would receive priority attention when the commonwealth took control of the Territory in 1911, in many ways South Australia was the most advanced and reformist of Australian state governments—particularly in relation to women getting the vote.

As a result of the Northern Territory Representation Act, the Territory had been made a single electorate with two members to be elected to the South Australian parliament. In 1890 Parsons retired as government resident to stand successfully for one of the two seats, along with veteran Territory businessman Vaiben L. Solomon, who campaigned by pushing himself around the goldfields on the new rail trolley. Among the emerging issues they had to address was whether women should get the vote.

The official fight for women's suffrage had begun in Adelaide in 1888 but as far back as 1885 a prominent Adelaide University lecturer and MP, Dr Edward Stirling, had begun raising the issue in parliament. By 1893 six men who were pledged to vote for female suffrage were returned to parliament, and support for the appropriate legislation gradually increased.[19]

The Territory's Vaiben L. Solomon made no bones about his opposition to the move. In his second reading speech on the Adult Suffrage bill of 1893, he outlined his position in some detail:

[I have] always been opposed to female suffrage...First, the women of the colony [have] not demanded and [do] not want this vote; secondly, the proposal to give them a vote [is] only being stirred up by small factions of interested persons; and thirdly to give women a vote and mix them up with political work [will] be lowering them instead of raising them.

To give women an interest in political affairs [will] destroy one of the strongest bulwarks of national prosperity and advancement, viz, the home life. [I believe] woman's proper place [is] in the home, and if she [is] to exercise any influence at all upon the politics of a country, that influence [can] be best exercised, not by attending meetings of female agitators, not by leaving her domestic duties or her children, but by inducing her husband, brother or son to adopt the proper course in political questions, and by taking up the cudgels if necessary where the rights of women [require] defence. There [is] nothing to prevent women learning from the press or their husbands the position of any matter connected with the politics of the colony in which they [are] interested.[20]

But his real reason for opposing women's franchise was soon revealed, and was more political than philosophical in its overtones:

In the city, the members of trades unions, with that power of organisation which

[was] shown so clearly at the last elections, [will] see that their wives and daughters [vote], and thus the power of what [is] known as the Labor Party [will] be increased. Surely the members of the Labor Party [are] fully competent to champion the rights of their wives and sisters and [would] see that no injustice was done to them.

Solomon went on to cloak this clear political motivation for opposing the bill with his view of what female franchise would do to home life. He argued that valuable time would be taken away from home duties by political canvassers who would call at the home at all hours to solicit the votes of both the men and the women. Solomon added, however, that should the bill go through, he was confident of winning the vote of his female constituents.

Despite his arguments and those of his conservative colleagues, a bill was finally passed at the end of 1894 that gave South Australian and Northern Territory women over the age of twenty-one the right to vote and the right to stand for election. They were the first women in Australia to be given this privilege and among the first in the Western world, preceded only by the American states of Colorado and Wyoming many years earlier and New Zealand in 1893. When their first opportunity to vote arose in the 1896 election, nearly 60 000 South Australian women and about seventy Northern Territory women turned out to have their say. In the Territory, the two sitting members, Solomon and Griffiths, easily regained their seats. The election, in fact, made little immediate difference to male-dominated life in the Territory.

By the time of Federation in 1901, the Territory's women were themselves embroiled in a renewed debate about their rights. The papers were filled with letters outlining the pros and cons of whether women should engage in politics. One woman, who signed herself 'Antiquarian' advocated that a woman's place was in the home and that husbands did not want to return home after a day's work 'to find his wife either posing as an authoress, which is often a new woman's desire, or gallivanting amongst male legislators at all hours of the day and night endeavouring to obtain the women's franchise'.[21] The writer was soundly condemned by another correspondent signing herself 'New Woman' who claimed that men wanted a woman who was intelligent and politically aware, not someone who could talk of nothing but the home.

Another female correspondent of the day who was disgusted with the people's choice of Samuel Mitchell, an Adelaide resident, in a 1901 by-election, wrote: 'Perhaps [as the people of Palmerston] cannot find a man amongst them good enough for the position they will next June accord their support to Yours, etc.—A Woman. P.S. I wear collars and cuffs and can talk, and so ought to suit.'

By 1905 political candidates were beginning to woo the women's vote. Chief among them was the former critic of female suffrage Vaiben Solomon, who, during his election campaign in that year, inaugurated a special appeal for women's votes. Following a practice adopted in other states after the attainment of women's suffrage, he invited women electors to attend a political lecture at the town hall, promising to make the lecture both instructive and interesting. He argued that since:

women of the state had been granted the privilege of voting for members of both the State and Federal Parliaments, [they] had a duty cast upon them and a grave responsibility to make themselves acquainted with those principal political questions which affect the happiness and prosperity of the whole community as well as of each individual. Sentiment and personal friendship will, of course, influence the way in which the many votes are recorded but the responsibility of returning representatives capable of legislating for the benefit of the whole body politic and with statesmanlike ability is one which should not be clouded by either sentiment or friendship.[22]

But sentiment and friendship would be irrelevant when the commonwealth took control of the Territory and disenfranchised Territorians altogether.

The transition to this new era was presided over by none other than Samuel J. Mitchell and his wife Eliza (later to become grandparents of one of Australia's more famous female legal personalities, Dame Roma Mitchell), who arrived in June 1910 to take up the position of government resident and first lady. They were given a civic reception that, as was common in Darwin, included presentations by both the European and Chinese sections of town. Like Herbert, Mitchell knew the Territory well, having already served since 1901 as the Territory junior and then senior representative in the South Australian parliament, and also as a judge.

The Mitchells served during a transitional period in the Territory. Legislation had been passed by the South Australian and commonwealth parliaments establishing the conditions under which the Territory was to be transferred to the commonwealth, including the still contentious and unfulfilled federal undertaking to complete the railway link between Port Darwin and South Australia.

On 1 January 1911, the Territory was formally handed over to the commonwealth. Mitchell's title became administrator and the capital city became formally known as Darwin. At the ceremony at government house, Eliza Mitchell hoisted the commonwealth flag amid great cheers from the crowd and Mitchell called upon the Territory citizens to exhibit loyalty and patriotism to the new flag. The *Northern Territory Times* hailed the event with an optimistic and patriotic spirit:

We are now the adopted child of six states constituting the Commonwealth, each of which may be expected to take a paternal interest in the development of this backward portion of Australia until that time arrives when it shall have attained a strength and stature entitling it to take its place on the equal footing among the family of states.[23]

Although that strength and stature would be a very long time coming, the Territory wasted no time in establishing a sensational reputation for itself, as the next period in its history illustrates. It was a time when women not only increased in number, but also increased their participation in public affairs—including taking part in the Great War overseas and a political war at home.

Chapter 5

Melting Pot, Boiling Pot (1912-1926)

The first fifteen years of commonwealth responsibility for the Territory were amongst the most dramatic and colourful in Australian history and earned Darwin the title of 'Little Moscow'. They were years of rebellion for much of the white population, of subjugation and 'protection' for much of the black population, and of 'restriction' for much of the Asian population. The 'White Australia' and Aboriginal protection policies contrasted sharply with the realities of many cultures that consisted of several classes living in close proximity in the isolated north. Consequently, the Territory, although very much a multi-racial society, often seemed more like a boiling pot than a melting pot. Adding fuel to the fire was the fact that the transfer of power from South Australia to the commonwealth had resulted in the disenfranchisement of Territorians, who had enjoyed separate representation in the South Australian parliament since 1888.

When the commonwealth took responsibility for the Northern Territory from South Australia, it inherited a region covering some 1 346 800 square kilometres, a public debt of nearly four million pounds, a railway line that still extended only a few hundred kilometres south of Darwin and a population of thousands of Aboriginal people and only 3310 non-Aboriginal people, a third of whom were Chinese. In the Darwin area, where the bulk of the non-Aboriginal population resided, European men outnumbered European women by more than two to one and Chinese men outnumbered Chinese women by almost five to one. It was thus not surprising that it was the men who usually made the headlines during these tumultuous times. However, women were key pieces in the kaleidoscope of characters and events that made their way into those headlines, a fact which can be appreciated by first briefly putting the period into historical context.

Early in 1912 the federal Labor government appointed esteemed Scottish veterinary scientist Dr John Anderson Gilruth as the Territory's first commonwealth Administrator. Although he was extremely talented and respected in his own profession, Gilruth's skill was not in administration and he presided over seven of the most controversial and rebellious years in Territory history, which ended with a section of the townsfolk storming Government House, burning him in effigy and demanding his removal.

He did not have circumstance on his side. His term of office coincided with the rise of a very strong union movement, the outbreak of the First World War, and a time of federal political unrest and national depression. Before his appointment as administrator, Gilruth had been part of the short-lived federal Fisher Labor

The Gilruth family and governess-writer Elsie Masson (behind the elder daughter) inspect the grounds at Government House in Darwin shortly after their arrival in 1912 when John Gilruth took up his appointment as the first commonwealth administrator of the Territory. Elsie later drew on her experiences with the family and on the impressions she gained travelling with Gilruth to write a book on the Territory, giving much attention to the lifestyle as it affected women. Northern Territory Archives.

government's scientific inquiry into the Territory's resources, which resulted in various hopeful schemes for development. Most did not eventuate or, if they did, they were either not completed or not successful, and Gilruth soon became the local focus for much of the discontent.

Throughout his seven-year reign Gilruth received continual and devoted support from Jeannie, the active and competent woman whom he had met and married during a period of study in New Zealand early in the century. He also undoubtedly drew on the strength of character he had observed in his feminist Scottish mother, who not only obtained a university degree at a time when it was most uncommon for women to do so, but also led a fight to improve life for the women workers of the Scottish community in which Gilruth was born in 1872. Another woman who played an important role during Gilruth's early years as Territory administrator was Elsie Masson, a talented and well-educated family friend whom John and Jeannie Gilruth brought with them to Darwin to be governess to their children. Although she spent only the first eighteen months of their administration in the Territory, Elsie travelled with Gilruth on many of his official inspection tours and observed aspects of the Territory's multicultural lifestyle. As well as giving Gilruth her views at the time, Elsie wrote a series of magazine and newspaper articles for the Melbourne and New Zealand press in which she described the Territory's lifestyle and potential and in 1915 she published a hopeful and descriptive book, *Untamed Territory*, which she dedicated to the Gilruths.

By that time, however, Gilruth's popularity and that of his key officials was already very much on the wane. Early confrontation between the Gilruth administration and the Darwin citizenry occurred in 1913 when the popular editor of the *Northern Territory Times*, Charles Kirkland, was brought before the new Northern Territory judge and Gilruth's associate, Judge Bevan, for contempt of court. Catalyst for the event had been Bevan's decision to discount the evidence of a young Russian girl who had bravely charged a local man with assault. Kirkland was disgusted with the verdict, arguing in an editorial that the girl had testified for three hours and not changed her story or broken down, and that her alleged assailant had made some 'shocking admissions'. When Kirkland refused to apologise or pay the subsequent fine for publishing his criticism, Judge Bevan sent him to gaol. Within two hours of his confinement in Fannie Bay prison, the townspeople had collected enough money to pay his fine, marched the three kilometres to the gaol, freed him and escorted him, as if he were royalty, back into the town square.

At about the same time, the first of a series of worker's strikes which were to plague the Territory during the period took place. Members of the newly formed Territory branch of the Australian Workers Union staged a prolonged strike for reinstatement of their wages, which had just been lowered. When they took their grievance to Gilruth he said he could not meet their demands. The union went away and returned with a modified second proposal. This time Gilruth refused to see them and sent a note out with his Government Secretary, H. E. Carey, with a one-word reply—'No'. The AWU members, who to their peril had failed to gain the support of their federal executive and the two other unions then present in the Territory (the engineers and carpenters), were forced to call off the strike and Gilruth revelled in his victory, but not for long.

Gilruth was unfortunate in having as his chief opponent Harold Nelson, a union organiser and a spellbinding orator, who was elected organiser and secretary of the Territory's AWU in 1914. He had arrived in the Territory from Queensland in 1912 with his wife Maud and their five children and was first employed as a railway engine driver in Pine Creek, where the family lived in a modest home. The couple had married in 1904 in Queensland, where Maud, as well as raising a family, had coached Nelson, helping him obtain his engine driver's ticket. When he became a union organiser she also coached him in his speeches, listening and giving advice, although this was an area in which he had clear natural talent. Nelson's forceful oratorical skills, coupled with his natural intelligence and strong background in union organisation, quickly put him at the forefront of both the Territory union movement and the fight with Gilruth. Within a year of being elected union secretary and moving with his family to Darwin, Nelson had massively increased union membership.

As well as enrolling local workers, Nelson signed up scores of unemployed men from southern states and 'new Australians', particularly Greeks, Patagonians and Russians. They had come to the Territory seeking work on the railway (which was being extended), or one of the planned agricultural schemes or with Vesteys, the giant British company that had decided in 1914 to build a huge meatworks facility about two-and-one-half miles from Darwin in an area known locally as Parap. While many of the non-English-speaking immigrants joined the unions, the local Chinese and Aborigines were excluded from membership even though many local residents employed Aboriginal or Chinese servants. This racial discrepancy was the cause of much debate, particularly in the light of the commonwealth government's 'White Australia' policy, and added to the conflict that was intensifying in the community.

One of the most divisive events occurred in 1915 when Gilruth carried out federal government instructions to nationalise the Darwin and Pine Creek pubs and close all others in the Top End. The move was made primarily to fill the government coffers, but Gilruth also wanted to curb the Territory drinking habits, not a popular move in the ever-thirsty and isolated Darwin. The unions organised strikes, public protests and at least two boycotts while several of the Territory's Top End pioneer women, who owned or managed most of the pubs, were forced to fight long battles for compensation. (Two of these battles are described in the stories of Ellen Ryan and Fannie Haynes in the second part of the book.)

Confrontations continued over the next three years, including an accusation in federal parliament that Gilruth had suggested selling the Northern Territory to a large syndicate, presumably Vesteys. The unions lobbied strongly against Gilruth's reappointment when his term came up for renewal in 1917, but the federal government, although concerned about the situation, had too much on its mind with the war abroad to worry about a war at home and it renewed Gilruth's appointment. With this move, the union's resolve to get rid of Gilruth intensified.

The immediate cause of Gilruth's downfall was an incident in late 1918 involving Darwin's barmaids, who asked for a few hours off to join in the celebrations to mark the welcome news that the Great War had ended. The women were all members of the union. Hotel boarders agreed to eat elsewhere to accommodate the request, but Gilruth's hotel supervisor, Callan, refused to grant leave to the women. They took the time off without permission. When they showed up for work the next day, fully expecting a pay dock, they found that Gilruth had locked them out. He insisted on a public apology and a guarantee that they would never stage such a 'strike' again. They refused, and opposition to Gilruth increased.

A short time later hundreds of people met at the Parap meatworks to march on Government House. After a rowdy demonstration outside the gates, during which Gilruth refused to back down, the angry mob burned the stubborn administrator in effigy. A few weeks later, Gilruth realised his predicament was unresolvable and on 20 February 1919 he and his family slipped quietly away in a naval gunboat that had been sent to collect him. A short time later, after the federal government appointed an advisory council under the directorship of Gilruth's former govern-

*Fannie Eliza Bell, who, with her husband, managed Darwin's Club Hotel from
1910 to 1915, treated hotel guests to picnics at Fannie Bay or East Point, driving
them out to the picturesque spots in her stylish sulky. She was usually
accompanied by her children, who helped keep the guests entertained.
Fannie, who first arrived in the Territory with her husband and family in 1907,
lived in Darwin until her death in the 1960s. Not long before she died, she
wrote her reminiscences of life in the Top End and concluded: 'I would never
want to live anywhere else—it's the tropics for me.'
Photograph courtesy of Heather Harris.*

ment secretary H. E. Carey, Harold Nelson, also a member of the council, produced
a letter which implicated Carey and Gilruth in a possible case of corruption and
collusion with Vesteys. The union-led workers again rebelled and marched Gilruth's
three chief colleagues — Judge D. J. Bevan, H. E. Carey and government secretary,
R. J. Evans—onto a visiting steamer and sent them back to Melbourne. A reminder
of Gilruth's tumultuous reign is embodied in the name Gilruth's Neck, given to a
small stretch of curved road which led to Vesteys.

Following Gilruth's downfall, the federal government appointed a Royal
Commission to investigate the affair and an acting administrator to help pacify the
population. They chose a single man, former Western Australian senator Staniforth
Smith, who appears to have tried simply to maintain the status quo during his fifteen
months in the Territory. Most of his duties were far more pleasant than those of his
predecessor. They included welcoming to Darwin Sir Ross and Keith Smith on their

record breaking England to Australia flight in December 1919. The event served as a much-needed tonic for the post-war and post-rebellion population, much of which was by now unemployed. Smith's term also saw the emergence of a second newspaper, the *Northern Standard*, owned by the unions, who used it effectively to propagandise to the public.

One of their targets was Smith's successor, Frederick Charles Urquhart, a former Queensland police commissioner who had gained a controversial reputation for his imposition of European laws on the Aboriginal people of inland Queensland. He was unabashedly anti-union and took a strong, provocative stand, forcing confrontation several times, particularly with Nelson. Despite such conflict, Nelson successfully led demonstrations that kept the 'no taxation without representation' issue before the public, including a period when he and several other leading citizens voluntarily went to gaol for refusing to pay taxes. In 1922 the federal government granted the Territory an elected representative in federal parliament, and Nelson won the seat in a close contest.

Although Nelson had no formal vote in parliament, his oratory made him an effective Territory advocate for many years, the Sydney *Sun* reporting that his maiden speech 'was easily the best...heard in the building for years...By his first speech in the House he stepped into the front ranks of its debaters'. Nelson held the Territory seat until 1936, then returned to the Territory with his family to spend his remaining days in Alice Springs, the base from which, after the Second World War, his son launched a successful bid to regain the Territory seat for Labor.

Urquhart's remaining years as administrator, to 1926, were reasonably peaceful, apart from the strong debate that centred around the 1923 loss of the SS *Douglas Mawson* in a hurricane off the north Australian coast. All on board were reported lost. Reports soon began to circulate, however, that two white women had survived and were living with Aborigines on the Arnhem Land coast. Despite extensive searches and the expenditure of thousands of pounds, the rumours persisted and for many years the matter remained unresolved.

WOMEN BEHIND THE HEADLINES

Ironically, while John Gilruth had been embroiled in his political war at home, Jeannie Gilruth had been doing her part to improve the Territory's image to visitors and to improve the lot of the many Territory boys who had volunteered to fight in the Great War. In 1915 she founded Territory branches of both the Victoria League and the Red Cross.

At the inaugural meeting of the Victoria League the aims and objects were outlined; the great need for putting its principles into practice was emphasised, especially the principle of 'fostering the true imperial spirit'. This was followed by a series of lantern pictures showing the late Queen Victoria, leading members of the royal families of Britain and its allies. Members were told that one of the League's most important duties would be undertaken by the Hospitality Committee, whose job it would be to ensure that visitors to Australia's 'first port of call' received all they needed in the way of advice and hospitality.

The second and more important organisation founded at Jeannie's initiative was the Territory branch of the Red Cross in Darwin, whose members worked endlessly to ensure that the Territory raised more money per capita during the First

Territory women took an active part in the Red Cross during the First World War, raising more money per head of population than any Red Cross group in Australia, and won praise for their efforts from the international office. Among the active workers was Myrtle Styles (second from left), grand-daughter of pioneer Eliza Tuckwell and sister of Walter Styles, the first Territorian to be killed in the Great War.
Photograph courtesy of Heather Harris.

World War than any other part of Australia. Nearly every white woman in the Territory became a member. They spent the first few months making 2767 garments for shipment to Australian troops in Egypt. When all woollen material was exhausted locally, the committee began making direct appeals for money, and through a variety of concerts, card parties, dances, races and other events, they raised more than 11 500 pounds, impressive indeed for the Territory's sparse population. Every newspaper of the time carried lists of subscriptions and of the women who collected the money in each centre. The mayoress, Mona Watts, organised additional public subscriptions and received countless letters of thanks from military officials on behalf of the soldiers.

Proportionally the Territory had sent more men to war than had any other part of Australia. Many never returned, slaughtered on distant battlefields. As the death toll rose, the national debate on conscription intensified. Jeannie Gilruth took a public stand on the issue and was one of several women, including Edith Bell—then co-owner of the influential *Northern Territory Times* —to sign a petition calling for support of conscription. Some who had lost sons and husbands were not so willing to make further sacrifices, and when the second referendum was taken in the Territory, the 'yes's' won by only one vote.

Both Jeannie Gilruth as president and Charlotte Witherden as secretary were commended for their contribution to the Red Cross movement, although Jeannie at one stage was quite maliciously and wrongly accused by some locals of stealing Red Cross funds, a reflection, no doubt, of her husband's increasing unpopularity. Charlotte Witherden made her own bit of history both for the Territory and for Territory women when a few years later she became the first Territory citizen to receive an OBE.

Territory women of the day were also involved in union activities. One member who made sensational headlines for a time was Kate Perreau, the only woman to give evidence before the Royal Commission investigating the Gilruth administration in 1920. Along with her ten children, she travelled to Melbourne for government help and there told the commission her story. She had arrived in Darwin from New Zealand as an intending pastoral settler in 1913 with her husband and eight children. They had two more children in Darwin before Mr Perreau drowned in July 1916, when the youngest child was only six weeks old.

Kate said she had approached Gilruth and argued that as a widow and mother of ten children she considered she was entitled to Government help and had asked for a two-year exemption from payment on her farm. Gilruth refused but said she could have the government cattle with which the farm had been stocked. Kate then joined the union and told Gilruth that in future the union secretary and Gilruth's chief opponent, Harold Nelson, would handle all her dealings with the government.

According to Kate, Gilruth then reclaimed all the cattle except ten young ones and threatened to arrest her when she asked for the cattle back. Kate claimed that once Gilruth learned that the union was providing her with a house near the meatworks, he refused her any government help on the grounds that she had two sons, who at fifteen and thirteen years old could go to work. Kate told the commission that since then she had 'had to work hard driving a team of horses, doing men's work on the roads to earn enough to support [her] children and keep them dressed'.[1] Kate testified that she had been forced to kill a prowler whom she claimed had been sent from 'headquarters' to watch her. She claimed that there had been no inquiry over the killing, strongly implying a government cover-up. Although some questioned the reliability of her evidence, it was given sensational national press coverage and did nothing to help Gilruth's image.

Another woman took an active and public role in the first union elections held after the commission's enquiries. She was 'Billy' Wilson, a talented, middle-aged woman, originally from Western Australia, who had been a continual supporter of Harold Nelson and had organised many fund-raising and charity functions, often using her fine singing voice to enhance the various events. With a strong background in hotel work and organisation she was well suited to stand for the presidency of one of the largest sections of the union, that covering the shop and clerical assistants, hotel and council divisions and the miscellaneous workers. When she won, the *Northern Standard* of August 1921 was quick to commend her achievement:

This journal hastens to be amongst the first to congratulate Miss Wilson on her attainment of such an honorable position...It is the first time in the history of organised labor in the Territory that one of the fair sex has identified themselves officially with any section of the Union. Miss Wilson's brave step marks an epoch in the industrial evolution of the Territory. This paper hopes to see many other women following the good example set by Miss Wilson...This development of women taking a prominent part in administration in the industrial or political field of Labor, although well known in other parts of the world, is new here and marks another step in the progress of the Territory's unionism. We trust that this fearless example of women taking their rightful place with men in an administrative capacity will be emulated by many more of Miss Wilson's sex.

Although there is not much further mention of her either in the newspapers or in the scanty union records of the period, presumably she continued to work with the unions until she left for Singapore in 1923 to establish herself in the hotel trade there.

Another woman who was singled out for her contribution to the union cause was Maud Nelson, who, although she was a very sociable woman and a popular hostess, rather reluctantly shared her husband's limelight. However, her work in the background did not go unnoticed or unappreciated. In November 1917, a group of townsfolk, including mayor Douglas Watts and mayoress Mona Watts, (a grand-daughter of the Territory's first government resident Boyle Travers Finniss), as-sembled at Nelson's house to present Maud with a handsome oak case of cutlery. The presentation, they said, was a token of their esteem, because she had 'always so worthily assisted her husband in his many undertakings and proved so fitting a helpmate.'

Other women publicly supported the union cause in other ways. One was Eleanor Pearse, who ran an Australian Workers Union (AWU) boarding-house for several years, always advertising that she only employed union labour. She proved her devotion to non-capitalistic principles by engaging in such practices as reducing the price of accommodation when boat landing charges were reduced.

Some women also took a vocal role in criticising the unions when they saw fit. One put her views strongly in a letter to the *Northern Territory Times* in May 1919, which she signed 'A Unionist's Wife'. Objecting to a 20 per cent levy unionists were being forced to pay, for a cause she didn't agree with, she called on wives of unionists to organise their own union for the protection of themselves and their children:

It's up to us to go out on strike ourselves and refuse to wash a dish or a shirt or iron a coat, or cook a meal, or sweep a room, but just put on our best and hire some motors and go out for a picnic on our own till we've taught our men to get a bit of backbone and not follow the union boss like a flock of sheep that can't say 'baa!' without the union boss's nod.

NEED FOR WOMEN; WOMEN'S NEEDS

Although overshadowed by the sensational events that took place in the Territory during the twenty-five-year period under scrutiny, the questions of how to settle the place with 'suitable' white women and children and how best to deal with the issue of black women and their interaction with the male society, were very much in the minds of officialdom. One of the first people to raise the profile of Territory women during this time was a woman writer, one of several who became propagandists for the Territory.

If John Gilruth was the wrong man in the wrong place at the wrong time, his children's governess, Elsie Masson, was the right woman in the right place at the right time. She was the daughter of a Melbourne University professor, Sir David Masson, and prominent Melbourne socialite Lady Masson, who were friends of both Baldwin Spencer and John and Jeannie Gilruth. Elsie often accompanied Gilruth on his official inspections of the Territory and wrote prolifically about her impressions and experiences. Her writings appeared first as a series of articles for various newspapers, most prominently the Melbourne *Argus,* and then in a book, *Untamed Territory,* which she published in 1915 and dedicated to the Gilruths. Like Harriet Daly some thirty years earlier, Elsie observed Territory life from a privileged vantage point and waxed lyrical about its potential. Unlike Harriet, however, she paid particular attention to the role and lifestyle of women:

On the woman no less than on the man depends the success of a great venture such as the civilisation and development of the Northern Territory...The prospect of better work or the fascination of life in a more primitive community has drawn him there. The wife, on the other hand, goes because he goes and not because the life appeals especially to her nature. Therefore there is more necessity for her to make up her mind that she will endure discomfort without grumbling, adapt herself to tropical conditions, and set herself to solve the small problems of the home, which are all part of the larger problems in the Territory.[2]

The main domestic problem, to Elsie's mind, was the array of insects one had to combat:

Food cannot be left half an hour on the table before ants swarm on it; cockroaches, sometimes three or four inches long make startling rushes from behind wardrobes; silverfish slither away swiftly when drawers are opened; mosquitoes make life a constant irritation. Each pest has to be combated in a different way. The legs of every table and safe have to be put in tins half filled with water so that the ants cannot get to the food; daily sweeping and dustings hunt the cockroach from his lair and after a wild stampede with the whole family in pursuit, armed with towels and pillows, he is generally caught; the silverfish are baulked by tying in bags of unbleached calico those clothes that are not in constant use...the mosquitoes are also vanquished. Kerosene is poured into the tanks so that the larvae in the water suffocates...[3]

Even Elsie's mother learned at first hand of the insect hazard when she ordered a piano in Melbourne to be sent to Jeannie Gilruth in Darwin and found that she was able to insure it for damage in transport but not against the ravages of white ants.

Elsie was fortunate enough to accompany Gilruth on most of his official trips by motor car, boat or train inspecting various parts of the Territory, and her descriptions provide a valuable insight into the lifestyle of women living in the more remote areas. As well as accompanying Gilruth on the first official motor-car tour of the Territory (to Humpty Doo, a few miles from Darwin), Elsie visited Arnhem

Land, Oenpelli, Port Essington, Pine Creek and several of the new Top End centres that Gilruth had established as experimental farms, hoping to attract more settlers, especially more women, to the Territory.

The scarcity of European women in the more isolated regions was very much evident when Gilruth's official party visited Oenpelli, the isolated Arnhem Land coastal home of buffalo hunter Paddy Cahill. Elsie found she was the first white woman Paddy's wife, Mary, the daughter of a prominent Territory publican family, the Pickfords, and her niece had seen in three years. Elsie found Mary uncomplaining, however, and quite content with her life in the bush. She and her niece were fully engaged with the domestic details of the homestead as well as looking after the newly established dairy, a project for which they were highly commended by Gilruth in his government reports. They worked closely with the Aboriginal women of the area, teaching them domestic skills while Paddy, who was also a protector of Aborigines for the area, taught the men how to build houses, raise stock, grow crops and gardens. This greatly impressed Elsie and she recorded that the Cahills enjoyed tremendous rapport with the Aboriginal people of the area and had great respect for their traditions and knowledge. A few years later when the government proposed a scheme to settle the Oenpelli district, the official government report argued that it 'would be a poor sort of pioneer who could not make good, and a worse one who would feel despondent for long with as neighbours two such cheery and capable optimists as Mr and Mrs Cahill who pioneered the district when the nearest neighbour was many days journey away...they would act as guides and counsellers to newcomers.'

Elsie Masson's book also paid tribute to buffalo shooter Joe Cooper, one of the few European men to actually marry his Aboriginal partner, Alice, whose story is outlined elsewhere. Elsie was undoubtedly influenced in her perceptions and attitude by her family friend and the architect of the Aboriginal protection policy, Baldwin Spencer, who was a great friend of both Cahill and Cooper and relied heavily on them for assistance.

Elsie did not stay in the Territory long enough to witness the turmoil about to descend on both the black and white races or the attempt by the Cahill's faithful Aboriginal helpmate, Romula, to poison the family in 1917. She returned to Melbourne, where she published her book. It was a hopeful, poetic piece of propaganda for the Territory's future:

Fortunes will not be made with ease by the first generation of settlers. Theirs will be the task of breaking in the bush and forcing the country to yield them what it can—a home, a livelihood, a picturesque adventurous life and the prospect of a rich future. Theirs also will be the joy of knowing that the fate of the Territory lies in their hands, that posterity will recognise them as the true pioneers, the makers of a great country.[4]

Baldwin Spencer, who was later to become alienated from Elsie when she married a rival anthropologist Bainslow Malinowski, praised Elsie's work in his review of it for the Melbourne *Argus*:

[She] not only has a keen power of sympathetic observation, but is able to tell us what she has seen and felt and to make us see and feel it also...She touches here upon a question of vital importance...We have heard a good deal about the possibility of white men living in the Territory, but very little about white women and yet from the point of view of settling this empty country the question of whether women and children can live there is the main problem to be solved.

John Gilruth, who publicly acknowledged that he would never have accepted his Territory posting without consulting his wife, who would have to accompany him to what he saw as a rather 'friendless' land, had no doubt that women needed to be part of Territory development. In his first administrator's report he addressed the issue of 'the society of women':

I am convinced this want is more productive (in a subconscious manner it is true) of unrest and fretfullness than any other cause. The change from the populous centres of the south to the monotony of Darwin, with no artificial aids to amusement and few (if any) of the customary means of filling spare time, would be much more endurable were there a social life in which both sexes were fully represented. Is it surprising that in the absence of all recreation to which young men have been accustomed, there should be discontent at the world in general, ready and anxious to focus on anything in particular, due primarily to the starvation of the natural instincts of the gregarious mankind?

Gilruth firmly believed that the north could be developed by white people and was dismissive of the comments that were often put forward by the medical profession that the tropics were not suitable for white women and children, claiming there was no available evidence to support such a view. However, he did believe that in the early stages, the Territory's development was only likely to be accomplished by immigrants who had been accustomed to working for prolonged periods in similar climatic conditions, such as those in the southern parts of Europe. He stipulated that a large percentage should be accompanied by their families so as to encourage permanent settlement in the Territory.

Jeannie Gilruth supported this view, believing it could help solve what she considered a basic problem—the shortage of domestic help for the women of the community: 'If it were possible to have shipments of families who would settle on the land, and if their daughters would settle down to domestic service, it would be an untold blessing to the white women of Darwin,' she told a Melbourne journalist during one of her trips south. By tackling the issue of the need for 'suitable' domestic help, Jeannie was reinforcing a view held by several male officials of the time, including her husband and Sir Baldwin Spencer, who pointed out the conflict with the 'White Australia' policy of using Asian and Aboriginal help. When Sir Josiah Thomas visited Darwin early in 1912 and was met by a women's deputation seeking relief for the domestic service problem, he suggested that a state-owned steam laundry be established, a suggestion that Gilruth did not pursue.

While acknowledging the need for domestic help for women of her status, Jeannie Gilruth did believe that women who lived in Darwin had to make the effort to adjust to the tropical climate and dress accordingly, as she explained to the Melbourne press:

For instance, muslin frocks and open work stockings would be out of the question...The mosquitos have a penchant for ankles and they must not be indulged.

My little girl always wears what you would call a romper. It is a long overall, which comes to the top of long stockings as protectors from the mosquitos and long sleeves are worn.

Jeannie's own dress in the tropics was also based on practicalities rather than fashion. It consisted of a loosely fitting, trabalco frock (worn without corsets), a tropical helmet, and white canvas boots during the day. In the evenings she wore high-necked frocks with cloth-topped boots for protection from mosquitoes.

Another woman who agreed with Jeannie that living in the tropics was a question of attitude and lifestyle, but did not believe in the need for domestic help, was Mrs S. E. Abbott, married to a doctor appointed to Pine Creek in 1910. She had spent some considerable time in tropical and subtropical parts of the world. She put her views strongly in an article in the *Empire Review* of 1912:

My intention in writing this article is simply to let people know that white women can live here, and if they leave the drugs and liquor alone, can rear as healthy a brood of children as one could wish to see...We want sensible practical, clean, healthy-minded women, women who are refined enough to want to take their stand beside their husband and go where he goes, absolutely the helpmate devoid of fear...To be capable is not evidence of unladyhood, but on the contrary is the very reverse; it shows the trained mind, and a trained mind makes a trained hand. All the women in Pine Creek do their own housework, and the same may be said of those in Darwin, and the heat and hardships, and lack of hygienic conditions have not killed any of them off so far.

There were other women who heartily agreed with this view. When Justice Ewing commented during the Royal Commission that he pitied the housewives in the Territory, he got this blast from one of them in *The Bulletin*:

Judge Ewing saw little or nothing of homelife in the NT and the few houses he did visit probably had half-castes and Chinese to do the work, while the missus lay on a lounge and gasped from the heat. But the average everyday woman who does her own housework and cooks her husband's meals and makes her children's clothes and does the family washing doesn't worry about the thermometer. Except for the sake of the children's schooling, the NT contents me...I'd never live south again if I could help it.

Despite such comments from women themselves, the debate continued amongst the male officials. When Sir George Buchanan was asked by the federal government to prepare a report on the development and administration of the Northern Territory in 1925, he commented on how hard he believed life was for women and noted how rapidly white women aged in the Territory. He supported the views of members attending a national Medical Congress who had concluded 'that life [for] many of the women, especially married women, living in the coastal area of northern Queensland and the Northern Territory, [is] little short of deplorable; that without happy, healthy women, permanent settlement is impossible and that a great improvement in the conditions under which the white woman lives is essential'.5

However, in an interview with the *Brisbane Daily Mail* the wife of the administrator, Mrs Frederick Urquhart, reported that despite snakes in Government House roof and a scarcity of fresh milk and vegetables, life in Darwin was not without its compensations. She described her own life in Darwin as consisting of a round of receptions, dances, and garden and dinner parties, the latter being the most difficult to arrange and the longest in duration, lasting until the electric lights were turned out at the regulation time. She said that the Victoria League, of which she was president, was very active in arranging entertainment for visitors who arrived each month by boat. She claimed she had never met so many interesting people in her life as those she came in contact with during her husband's term of office, including Lord and Lady Stradbroke (who bought blocks of land in Alice Springs during their travels), Phillipa Bridges, and Lord and Lady Apsley, who had visited Darwin after travelling incognito to Australia as 'immigrants,' to discover what life was like from that perspective.

Lady Apsley, although she spent only a relatively short time in the Territory, soon formed definite views of life in the north and wrote about them in a book, *Amateur Settlers*, which she co-authored with her husband after their trip to Australia in 1925. The couple arrived in Darwin in July, the middle of the dry season, and from there travelled overland for several weeks. She rejected the view that the Northern Territory was unsuitable for white men and women to inhabit, claiming that recent health statistics of those living there proved conclusively that this was not so.'The trouble is that so few people go there to find out for themselves,' she noted. She practised what she preached and took an overland trip to several stations between Darwin and the Kimberleys, paying tribute to the work and role of the nurses of the Australian Inland Mission (AIM) and to the bush skills of the Aboriginal men and women on the stations they visited.

TERRITORY FLORENCE NIGHTINGALES

While visiting the Graham family at Victoria River Downs Station, Lady Apsley paid particular tribute to the two resident AIM nurses:

[They are] an inestimable boon and an encouragement to white women to follow their husbands and fathers into the Bush. The great difficulty hitherto has been to get women to live in the inland of the Northern Territory and one of the chief reasons up to now has been the entire lack of medical attention, so that the Australian Inland Mission is doing a great practical work for the development of the Northern Territory by making it possible for a married man to take his wife to live on these lonely stations. Moreover the social addition of two charming, unmarried white women fresh from town life is enormously appreciated by every man in the Territory, who sometimes never sees a white woman from one year's end to another.[6]

The AIM was one of the most important projects to be introduced into the Territory in the early years of commonwealth control. It was not, however, a government initiative but rather the brainchild of the Reverend John Flynn, who had been inspired by a letter sent to the church in about 1909 from Territory pioneer Jessie Litchfield who, at the time, lived in the isolated tin mining areas of the Top End and acutely felt the need for both medical and mission services in the outback.

The nurse to pioneer the AIM project in the Territory was Sister Jean

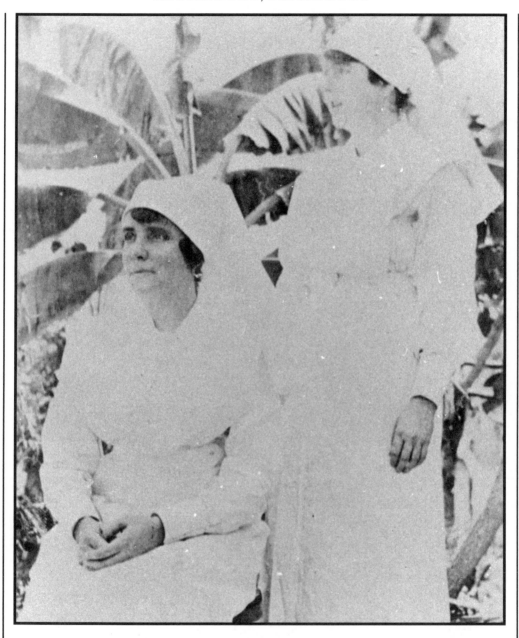

Australian Inland Mission sisters provided a vital service to the people of the Territory's outback. The scheme was first introduced in Alice Springs in 1915 by Jean Finlayson. Among the many AIM sisters to serve the Territory were Doris Dunlop and Jean Herd, who arrived at the mining community of Maranboy in 1920.
Photograph courtesy of Chief Justice Austin Asche and Dr Val Asche.

Finlayson, who had been serving at Oodnadatta in 1914 when a crying child was brought to her from a station near Alice Springs by the desperate parents seeking medical help in Adelaide. Jean travelled by train with the mother as far as Maree and resolved to volunteer for service with the AIM in Alice Springs as soon as possible. She was replaced at Oodnadatta and headed out by horse and buggy for the 530-kilometre journey to Alice, where she arrived in 1915.

For the first few months she stayed with the police sergeant and his wife until long-term Central Australian resident Sam Nicker and a mate established a rough residence for her next to the Nicker home, known as Myrtle Villa. When the Nickers returned to their station property, Myrtle Villa became the first Alice Springs surgery and hospital. Sister Finlayson described the accommodation as 'a slab cabin [with] two small rooms [and] a kitchen a few yards away. My room had a fireplace, the ceiling of calico was full of gaping wounds, the whole interior black with smoke,' she added. For a year Sister Finlayson served the medical needs of the centre within a radius of 150 kilometres from Alice Springs, as well as conducting Sunday School and the town's first regular church services in the prison warden's room at the rear of the gaol. When she left to look after her sick mother in Adelaide it was another ten years before a full-time nursing service and a proper hospital were established in Alice Springs. During that time Sister Finlayson, who had become familiar with the extreme heat, helped John Flynn design a hospital that was, and still is, innovative in having achieved a cool working environment.

Encouraged by the success of Jean Finlayson's work in Alice, AIM nursing sisters were soon sent to test the water in other remote regions of the Territory. They included two sisters at the new Top End mining center of Maranboy in 1917, followed by Sisters Grey and King at Victoria River Downs in 1922, after an outbreak of malaria had affected more than 10 per cent of the staff, highlighting the need for a hospital in the region. Spurred on by consistent lobbying from Sarah Graham, whose husband was station manager, the AIM helped establish the invaluable Wimmera Hospital on the station to serve the entire region.

Years later in her memoirs, Sister Elsie King, a young woman from Gippsland who had decided she wanted to 'do something to help others in life' described a typical incident the sisters had to deal with:

A stockman's wife on Delamere Station, seventy-two miles from Victoria River Downs, sent her husband for me. It took three days for him to come. We set out in a buckboard. Just as we were leaving an [Aboriginal boy] arrived with a note asking us to hurry. The morning her husband left she had an attack of malarial fever and her baby was born. The [Aboriginal boy] had ridden night and day with the news. We started off. In the buckboard there were no springs or cushions. We travelled all night and arrived at Delamere next day at six am. The poor woman was all alone except for an [Aboriginal woman] and her three children and babe. Both mother and infant were absolutely yellow. The mother had fever still and the baby jaundice. I nursed them for four weeks. They were better when I left.

After two years Sister King married one of the local stockmen, Jack Jones. After several years of trying to grow peanuts in the Katherine area, they returned to Victoria River Downs where Sister King resumed nursing. They moved to Alice Springs in 1934 when Jack was appointed superintendent in charge of the 'Half-caste

Home' and Elsie was appointed matron. Two years later, the two took charge of the Leprosarium at Channel Island, where they remained until the bombing of Darwin in February 1942. Sister Jones became very ill and died a month later in Queensland, having given most of her adult life to meeting the medical needs of the Territory outback.

Sister King was not the only AIM sister who ended up marrying and staying in the Territory. Many of her colleagues did the same. One of them was Sister Doris Dunlop, who, along with Sister Jean Herd, took up her duties at Maranboy in 1920. She later married Harold Giles, son of the pioneering Springvale Station family, and together they took up management of Elsey Station. Doris later described her arrival in the Territory as an AIM nurse, and her words highlight the isolation and the good humour of the outback she encountered:

Maranboy is a tin mining field and the nearest railhead was at Emungalen, fifty odd miles away. A bad outbreak of malaria causing the deaths of a small child and several miners resulted in a letter being sent to the Government and the Reverend John Flynn asking for help. The government built the Hospital and AIM supplied the two nurses. The hospital had been built for four years when we arrived.

After a ten day sea trip to Darwin where we waited for the fortnightly train to leave, we set forth on our way outback. Leaping Lena, as the train was called, jerked on starting off at sidings, and nearly threw us off our seats which caused the name I guess. It was a great little old train. The engine was fifty years old.

We spent a night at Pine Creek and then on the next day to the end of the line. We were rather taken aback by the sight of a few small corrugated huts in a dusty street, with bush all round. No one seemed to know who we were, so we walked over and sat on boxes under a small verandah without a floor outside a hut where meals were being served. I said to Jean, 'If this is the railhead, what is it like fifty miles further out?'

The Battery Manager arrived soon after with his battered T-Model Ford, the only car in the Northern Territory outside Darwin. We were lucky to be going by car as most travellers had to go out by the mail coach, a buckboard which took two days to do the trip. We did not pass any sign of habitation on the way after we had crossed the Katherine River and left the Sportsmen's Arms Hotel written about in "We of the Never Never," until we arrived about sundown at Maranboy. The Hospital was a very pleasant surprise. Built on the top of the hill, enclosed with gauze, it looked like a meat safe. It had electric light, water pumped from a spring when the battery was working. We had to depend on a benzine lamp and lanterns if there was not enough tin in to keep the battery working.

Our two years spent there were full of interest. Men from lonely places even further out had come to try their luck on the mine fields. One called Shirtless Charlie had not spoken to a white woman for years. He fled if he saw one of the six or seven women living there. He was painting the kitchen when the first sister arrived earlier than expected, and hid behind the kitchen dresser and fled without meeting her. No one saw him away from his mine until six months later when he was carried in unconscious with malaria. He recovered and it was hard to keep him away after that.

A dramatic incident occurred to the two sisters when Francis Birtles and his travelling companion Roy Fry were badly burned when their car hit a stump and a

Jane Elizabeth Tye was the Top End's leading midwife for nearly forty years until her death in 1934. She inherited her skills from her mother, Sarah Bowman, an Englishwoman who studied midwifery in London. Jane's father was wealthy Chinese businessman Lee Hang Gong. Several women in Darwin in 1988 could still recall how 'Granny Tye' helped them during and after their pregnancies.
Spillett collection, Northern Territory State Reference Library.

drum of benzine caught fire and exploded. With the help of an Aboriginal boy, who got word to the manager of Mataranka Station, the two men were eventually brought into Maranboy, as Doris later wrote:

We found the men in a very bad way. There being only one doctor in the whole of the Territory who never visited the hospital in our time, we spent some very anxious weeks as both men were suffering very badly from shock. Skin was hanging down over their fingers, calico bandages had stuck to the burns and they were badly burned over the chest, face and arms. We treated the burns with salve baths. Birtles was the first to recover and travelled to the railhead on route to Darwin, but it took Roy Fry some months before he was fit to travel.

*Ida Standley (second from right) was ably assisted in her school and at home by
Topsy Smith (second from left), who was born in about 1875 to Mary, an
Aboriginal woman of the Arabana people, and an unknown European, probably
a member of one of the early exploring expeditions. Topsy married a miner, Bill
Smith, and when he died in 1914 she packed up her family and most of their
belongings and drove a dray to Alice Springs. There she got a job helping Ida
Standley care for her students, who included two of her daughters, Emily and
Ada. Ada went on to become one of Alice Springs' most well-loved citizens.
The family's story is told in Dick Kimber's* Man From Arltunga.
Northern Territory Conservation Commission.

The hospitals were actually the social centres for the areas they serviced and
provided facilities other than medical ones. For instance, at Maranboy there was a
well-stocked library, a gramophone and a good supply of records. The nursing staff
spent many evenings sitting outside listening to music and the stories of the
bushmen, most of whom were inveterate storytellers. For some of the bush patients,
a visit to the AIM centre was one of their few brushes with civilisation. Doris
recalled one memorable occasion:

One patient, a teamster, came in with a very bad foot, the big toe hanging. When put
to bed he said it was the first time he had ever slept between sheets. He was as rough
as could be and did not know when he was swearing. The smell of his old pipe packed
with tobacco was horrible. After he was discharged, we were told he had been in gaol

101

for trying to cut a man's throat with a butcher's knife and was known as cut-throat Joe. After his discharge he brought up a horse with a belly cancer and asked us to cut it out. It was the only patient we turned away.[7]

Apart from the AIM sisters and the nurses connected with the Darwin and Pine Creek hospitals, a few other women performed invaluable nursing help as midwives. One of the most loved and well-known was Jane Tye, daughter of Sarah and Lee Hang Gong of local mining fame. She had the reputation of walking anywhere, rain or shine, in order to help with a childbirth. Her skill was such that she is reputed to have never lost a single case either of mother or child. On one occasion she even travelled in a small boat from Darwin to Borroloola on the Macarthur River to bring help to an expectant mother. In the days before motor cars, night calls in nearby areas of Darwin almost invariably meant walking, but Nurse Tye would unfailingly respond to any call. She would usually arrive a few days before the baby was due and stay for several days after, offering advice and passing on her knowledge to the new mothers, many of whom admitted to being extremely naive about the processes of childbirth and post-natal care. When 'Granny Tye' died in 1934 there were many grateful Territory mothers who mourned her loss.

CENTRAL AUSTRALIAN WOMEN

If women in the Top End suffered from isolation, the situation was even more extreme in Alice Springs. One of the most significant changes that occurred after the commonwealth took responsiblity for Territory affairs was in the improvement of services to the Centre. Among the first improvements was the establishment of much-needed educational facilities. In 1914 pioneer teacher Ida Standley was appointed to open the first school in Alice Springs, after Gilruth put forward the idea of offering education to Aboriginal as well as European children of the Alice Springs area. The commonwealth asked the South Australian government to loan them a teacher who might be able to deal with such a situation and Ida Standley, who had been with the education department for twenty years, was recommended. She was hired at an annual salary of 150 pounds which was increased to 170 pounds within a year. As there was no train to Alice at the time, she travelled for fourteen days by horse and buggy from Oodnadatta to reach her new Central Australian home.

She arrived in May 1914, when there were only twelve white children in the town, although later the police occasionally brought more in from bush areas. As was not unusual, with the decision-making hampered by distance, Ida found that no preparations had been made for the school accommodation. The only available place was the police cell, so for two months the prisoners occupied the cells at night and worked outside during the day while the children attended class inside. Eventually a large stone and galvanised-iron hut was built, which Ida called the Bungalow.

She established a cottage home for herself just a few yards away from the school and settled into a routine of teaching white children from 8.30 am to 1 pm and Aboriginal children from 3 pm to 4.30 pm. She spent most of her weekends working with the children in the Bungalow, teaching them to sew their own clothing. During most of her teaching years, the Aboriginal children outnumbered the European children by at least four to one. Ida was concerned about the effect of having the Bungalow so close to the gaol, and after several years of intense lobbying she persuaded the officials to move the Aboriginal accommodation to Jay's Creek.

Ida lost few opportunities to express her concern for Aboriginal women, particularly those of mixed race, reporting in 1914 that:

The halfcaste girl who remains with the tribe anywhere in the vicinity of a civilised settlement has one inevitable destiny, and that the most degraded...she runs the risk when the time and opportunity are favorable of being actually sold by her tribal relatives for prostitution or taken away by forces by some unscrupulous man who keeps her just as long as he cares to do so.

Ida finally retired in 1928, then earning a salary of nearly 300 pounds. During her fifteen years in Alice she had become known as 'Ma' Standley, mother to the Alice Springs community and as such she met most politicians and dignitaries who passed through. Her visitor's book, which has been preserved, is a fascinating and insightful record of attitudes and problems associated with teaching mixed races in the Centre between 1914 and 1928.[8]

The Alice was still not well populated in terms of women. Among the few who did arrive during the period were Isobel Price and family, whose story is told in a later chapter, and Mabel Wilkinson, who first lived at the telegraph station. She later recorded her reminiscences of the Alice:

My father had left Sydney to go to Alice to help his brother George in his general store, he stayed eight months to see if it was suitable for all of us to go there and live for a few years. I was 15 and still going to school in grade seven and learning piano. We had a very comfortable home and my mother had a few regrets about leaving her home but my brother and I thought it would be a great adventure. To get there was a long drawn out affair. The first 700 mile [1127 km] train ride on the Afghan Express from Adelaide to Oodnadatta took three days. The train only travelled during daylight hours and night stopovers were taken at Quorn and Maree. If all was going well the train would arrive at Oodnadatta at 10 oclock at night on the third day. It was necessary to provide our own food on the train and water bags suspended in the rear portion of each carriage were the only liquid refreshments available. Sometimes when the train stopped for more coal and water we would obtain hot water from the engine to make tea. The 300 mile [483 km] trip from Oodnadatta took eleven days by horse and cart. Two horses were used to pull the cart piled high with tents, swags, cooking utensils while another seven pack horses carried extra provisions and feed. Meals were rationed to salted meat, damper and billy tea around the camp fire. Women passengers were accorded the luxury of sleeping in a tent or under a lean-to while the men folk lay out under the stars. Extremely hot conditions and dust storms which prevailed during these times would often make travel impossible, blinding red sand blowing off ranges of sandhills reduced visibility to a few feet and had everyone and the animals huddled together until it blew out.

When I arrived at Stuart I was one of [only a handful of] white women living there. My father and uncle George Wilkinson owned and operated the general stores Wallis and Co. at Alice Springs and Oodnadatta...Ah Hong had his garden on the banks of the Todd River...Charlie Myers had a saddlers shop in Todd Street. The Stuart Arms hotel was run by Mr Brown and his wife Vivian, daughter of Mrs Standley, matron of Bungalow.

Life in the Alice in those days was hard, but pleasant. People were friendly and there was no rush and tear. A camel train brought provisions up from the railhead at Oodnadatta once a month. Very few perishables were transported up from Adelaide. Items like apples would be shrivelled almost beyond recognition and later when the drums of petrol arrived for motor cars [after 1919] evaporation reduced the contents to half. Petrol then cost 10 shillings a gallon.

Yeast for breadmaking was made from dried potatoes—we made butter from goats milk—and nearly everything was kept cool in a Coolgardie Meat Safe. A jelly would take three days to set. Kerosene lamps and lanterns provided lighting and the nearest thing we had to an electric fan was a punkah in one room pulled by Aboriginal staff. During these days there was no hospital, doctor or nurse in the town and when I had my first child, Marie, in 1924, I had to travel to the nearest hospital at Oodnadatta. This was done in relatively luxurious style in a Dodge buckboard. Although I had a fright on the way back when she nearly died in a particularly fierce dust storm...On another occasion before medical help was available in the town an operation was carried out on a man under direction from a doctor in Adelaide relayed to Alice Springs in morse code.

Mabel married the postmaster, Dudley Adamson, and they lived in Alice for many years, raising their family, most of whom remained in the Territory and married into Territory families themselves.

ABORIGINAL PROTECTION

One of the most contentious issues during the Gilruth era, one which had lasting repercussions for the Territorians of Aboriginal descent, was the introduction of the federal government's Aboriginal Protection Act. Elsie Masson had predicted the possible outcome of white intrusion on Aboriginal lifestyle when, after watching an Aboriginal dance on the outskirts of Darwin, she wrote: 'Finally the corroborree music died away altogether drowned by the sound of a neighbouring piano and the strident strains of a gramophone, prophetic, so it seemed to us, of the fate of this primitive people, relic of a bygone era.'[9]

Elsie's friend, Baldwin Spencer, a prominent anthropologist, was the architect of the first and far-reaching Northern Territory Aboriginal Protection policy. He defined particular problems, as he saw them, associated with the treatment of Aboriginal women:

This question is a very serious one and requires careful but, at the same time, firm, treatment. The regulations framed to deal with it must, of necessity, be definite in their nature, but they will have to be carried out with great tact on the part of the Protectors.[10]

The question of who should be appointed protectors was one that evoked much debate for many years, but Spencer spelled out one essential requirement: it was most important that all protectors should be married men. He stated emphatically that no one except a married man should be the superintendent of a reserve or native station or settlement. He was blunt about the reasons for his insistence on married protectors, stating that the absence of any women other than Aboriginal women in outlying districts was the chief reason for so many complaints of the prostitution of Aboriginal women. 'So long as the absence of white women is a

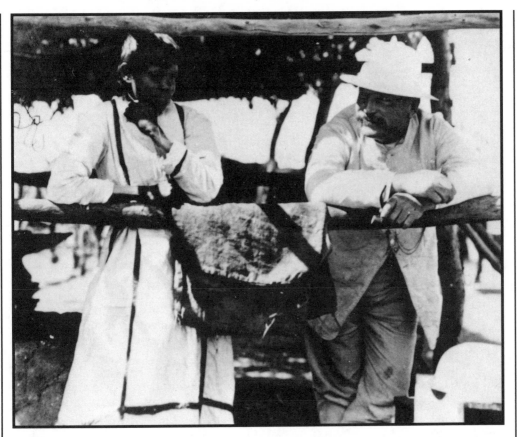

When the commonwealth took responsibility for the Territory, it arranged for several parliamentary parties to make 'official' inspections of the place. This photo, taken at Horseshoe Creek police station during the 1912 trip, seems to demonstrate the interest many men took in the Aboriginal women, who far outnumbered European women in remote Territory areas. This interest caused concern among both black and white populations. Both bitter conflict and some exceptionally successful individual relationships were the result of it.
Northern Territory State Reference Library.

feature of the Territory, so long will it be extremely difficult, if not impossible, to put an end to this serious evil,' he wrote in his 1912 report to Gilruth. His comments were reinforced by the medical officer's report, which dealt with the prevalence of syphilis and gonorrhoea in the Territory. He had no doubt as to the cause and said so in his annual report to Gilruth:

Bushmen, prospectors, and miners roving over the interior cannot indulge their sexual appetite except by intercourse with aboriginal women. The sexual emotions are undoubtedly stimulated by residence in a hot climate. Gratification will be sought and where Aboriginal women are available, will be easily obtained. The black woman contracts syphilis from some white man or Asiatic and the disease is then widely spread.[11]

To help put a stop to the situation, and to have more control over the Aboriginal lifestyle, Spencer advocated a controversial system of Aboriginal reserves, compounds and prohibited areas. Reserves should be established on large areas of land, he said, for Aboriginal people who still wished to live in the traditional ways, and attempts should be made to isolate them from the rest of the population. With regard to those Aborigines who lived around town areas, Spencer recommended that certain areas be declared prohibited to Aborigines and people of partial Aboriginal descent, in particular to lessen their contact with the Asiatics and their addiction to and trafficking in opium. Some Aboriginal people who were employed by Europeans in the town area were to be given special discs that allowed them to enter the prohibited areas when sent on business by their employers.

Spencer decided on a particularly complex and controversial set of policies to deal with Aboriginal people of mixed racial descent. They were to be taken compulsorily from their native camps and placed on stations or in compounds. Spencer attempted to justify the decision by arguing that 'even though it may seem cruel to separate the mother and child it [was] better...when the mother [was] living...in a native camp'.[12] The compounds were to be run by appropriate married couples with the man as superintendent and the woman as matron. It would be the job of the wife to teach the girls domestic skills so that they could be released into the European workforce as servants and nursing aids.

Spencer's policies were largely accepted, and on 19 October 1913 Darwin's Kahlin Compound opened with Frank and Emily Godfrey as superintendent and matron. It covered thirteen acres where sixteen bark huts, a boys' and a girls' dormitory, kitchen, laundry, office, storeroom, coach-house, fowl house and fruit plantation were established. By December there were seventy-six inhabitants, most of them youngsters of part Aboriginal descent. The compound was seen as a resource for the community with the women being trained in domestic skills. Emily Godfrey was commended for rendering 'valuable assistance particularly in regard to teaching the Aboriginal women and children sewing and domestic duties.' Annie Holtze, who was widowed in 1913 when her husband, popular garden curator Nicholas, died, became a teacher at the compound when the first teacher, Mrs Jacobs, resigned because of ill health. Both women were commended for their work and much sadness was felt when Annie, who had been gazetted as an Aboriginal protector and was considered to be a sympathetic and understanding woman, became ill and died in Adelaide in 1917.

According to government reports it was the protector at Pine Creek who had the most difficult job, because of the prominence there of various Asiatic races who were believed to be 'a menace to the betterment of our Aboriginal race,' particularly Aboriginal women, whom they enticed into prohibited areas with offers of opium or some other lure. In 1912 Pine Creek residents complained about the government's failure to enforce the Aboriginal Protection Act, claiming that Aboriginal Department officials often married Aboriginal women to Chinese, Japanese, Malays and whites; that prostitution was rife; and that Aborigines were widely debauched by the opium and cheap liquor sold by Asiatics in order to obtain sexual favours from Aboriginal women.

The treatment of Aboriginal women was also a matter for concern among Aborigines, though not always in the best interests of the women. In the 1916-17 government report, the protector of Aborigines reported a conversation he had overheard on one of the Territory stations. Aboriginal men were complaining that they 'cannot beat our women now, the boss will growl'. The protector's response was probably of limited comfort to Aboriginal women abused by their men: 'No natives are allowed to brutally beat their women. If the woman offends her husband she is brought to me and I get the facts of the case and very often can make peace between them.'

The issue of protecting young Aboriginal girls continued to be raised by several southern organisations, particularly women's groups. In 1920 one of Australia's most well-known and controversial workers among Aborigines, Daisy Bates, asked to be appointed protector of Aborigines in the Territory. She put her argument bluntly:

I am anxious to be of service to Australia in a larger sense and I would suggest the substitution of a woman Chief Protector for the Northern Territory; for the Aborigines question is really a women's question since it is the aboriginal women and children we are called on to protect instead of the men. Native men can take care of themselves at all times but native women and children have never had a chance in the 100 years of Australian settlement.

I will gladly pioneer the change in the Northern Territory and I feel sure the change will rebound to the credit of your Government. Being a gentlewoman I have far more power and influence over the natives and those whites who take advantage of native women and children than any male protector can.[13]

She asked to be appointed for a year's trial but was refused on the grounds that there was no allowance in the budget for such a proposal as the Chief Protector of Aborigines was also Government Secretary. Staniforth Smith assured Miss Bates, however, that the government fully recognised and availed itself 'of the valuable services of white women to ameliorate the conditions of Aboriginal people in the NT'.[14]

That did not prove always to be true. When in 1924 a former Alice Springs resident of eight years, Mrs John Mackay, strongly criticised the treatment of Aboriginal women by white men, she was severely criticised herself. Mrs Mackay, an executive member of the Aborigines' Friends' Association, delivered her remarks before the Women's Non-Party Association in Adelaide. She claimed that Aboriginal women had performed an invaluable part in the development of the Northern Territory and had received little but abandonment from white men in return. Her comments drew an immediate response from another former Territorian, John Dow, who said her allegations 'were not fair to the hundreds of decent and clean-living men in the bush'.[15]

The continuing debate would cause some of the most bitter arguments in and out of the Territory for a very long time. It was not until years later that the stories of some of the women and their families who were the subjects of these protectionist policies would emerge. A few of them are told in the second half of this book.

As the first era of commonwealth control of the Territory came to a close, the federal government decided to experiment with a new policy, not just for Aboriginal residents but for all Territorians. In 1927 it split the Territory into two 'states', North and Central Australia, each with its own administrator. It was not only to become a bureaucratic jungle, but was also to result in even more disillusionment amongst Territorians who had had their hopes dashed by absent policy makers before.

There were some who always kept the faith, however, and the most vocal were women. Perhaps the most vocal and prolific of all was Territory journalist Jessie Litchfield. In 1925 she put the case for the Territory's future in hopeful but challenging terms in a December article she wrote for the *Women's Mirror*:

Altogether the testing in the Territory is severe, but those who have faith may see the vision of the future, when the land shall be spanned with railways and isolation, neglect and misrepresentation shall be things of the past. In the future we shall see the Northern Territory the glory of Australia, the gateway of the North, the mainstay of the Commonwealth; we shall see miles of docks, scores of mines, hundreds of factories and great aviation hangars; we shall see her rivers, waterways of commerce, her manufactures almost inexhaustible, her farms the wonder of the world; and we shall see her land dotted with cities filled with stalwart men, contented women and healthy children in happy homes. These things will come in our day; but we have a share of the work to do. It is our right and our privilege to prepare the foundation on the stability of which the whole structure will depend.

Jessie was one of the growing number of women who would take a more public role in Territory affairs during the next twenty years.

Chapter 6

Time for Change (1927-1941)

'If the Territory was made fit for white women to live there, other problems would solve themselves.'
Rev. H. Griffiths, *Adelaide Advertiser*, 1935.

Although still outnumbered by men by at least three to one, women became more visible in the Territory during the fifteen years prior to the Second World War than they had been previously. This was due partly to the fact that improvements to education, communication, transport and medical services, especially in central Australia, encouraged more women to venture to the Territory. Also, changes to laws and policies affecting Aboriginal women attracted attention to issues that had previously been ignored. And more journalists and writers were coming to the Territory to write about it. As it was still very much considered to be Australia's last frontier, and was perceived to have little in the way of civilised comforts, most people were intrigued by the men and women who made it their home. As usual, government experiments were part of the story.

In 1927 the Bruce-Page government passed the North Australia Act, which divided the Territory into two 'states', North and Central Australia. This split the Territory at the 20th parallel and gave each 'state' its own government resident and first lady and its own advisory committee. In addition, a three-man North Australia Commission was appointed to oversee the entire scheme, creating a bureaucratic nightmare. According to its architect, Senator George Pearce, the main purposes of the act were to establish a sufficient population (particularly of white women and married couples) in northern Australia to bring about its self-government, and to establish one or two new states, a concept in line with the government's 'new state' movement in other parts of Australia. Instead, decision-making became cumbersome and frustrating and the commission became, in the eyes of the many unemployed Territorians, an unnecessary financial sink.

In Darwin the unemployed staged several rowdy public demonstrations, sarcastically claiming that the North Australian Commissioners were doing nothing but drawing substantial salaries and enjoying being the highest paid unemployed people in Australia. Eventually, a group of the demonstrators, led by left-wing union members, erected a tent outside Government House, flew the red flag and cooked stews in four-gallon drums to feed the unemployed. The tense situation eventually erupted into physical confrontation when several demonstrators were arrested and some police and private citizens assaulted. This caused less militant, and perhaps

109

Mrs C. A. Cawood (right) was the first 'first lady' of Central Australia, and Mrs Vic Carrington (centre) was the second. Both women hosted many functions at the government residence, particularly Mrs Carrington, whose husband stayed on for several years as deputy government resident for central Australia when the government dropped the two-state scheme. They are pictured here with school teacher Ida Standley.
Northern Territory Conservation Commission.

less desperate, members of the community to voice their support for constituted authority.

By the time the federal government abandoned the North Australian Act 'for economy measures' in 1931, divisions had deepened in the Darwin community and general frustration was widespread throughout the Territory, although less so in Central Australia than in the Top End. Top End residents felt acutely resentful of the failure of yet another scheme for northern development, particularly as it occurred at a time of economic depression and high unemployment. People in the Centre, on the other hand, had at last been given a taste, however slight, of managing their own affairs and were reluctant to return to the Darwin-based authority. They agreed with the first Central Australian government resident, C. A. Cawood, who had noted in his first report that he had been warmly welcomed by the residents, who were 'imbued with the idea that Central Australia was too far removed from the seat of government in Darwin to receive the attention it requires'.

When the scheme was dropped the government resident of North Australia, Robert Hunter Weddell, became administrator of the geographically re-united Territory and the government resident of Central Australia, Victor Carrington, became deputy administrator, located in Alice Springs. They continued in their posts until 1937, when Charles Lydiard Abbott was appointed Territory administrator and the deputy administrator's position was abolished.

Despite the political frustrations caused by the two-state experiment and its aftermath, the period leading up to Abbott's administration was a time of significant improvements in essential services, particularly in Central Australia, where a boost in population figures had occurred, especially for European women.

MORE WOMEN FOR CENTRAL AUSTRALIA

When the commonwealth took control of the Territory in 1911, the combined population of Alice Springs Telegraph Station and the town of Alice Springs (then Stuart) was eighteen men, five women and seven children—and it had not extended much beyond that by the 1920s. It was hoped that the creation of Central Australia would encourage population growth and development. Growth did occur but for reasons that had little to do with the new-state experiment: the erection of a new school, the establishment of the Australian Inland Mission hospital in Alice Springs, the development of the pedal radio and better mail services, the completion of the railway line between Alice Springs and Adelaide in 1929, and the mining booms of the 1930s at Tanami and Tennant Creek.

When a new school was opened in 1929, the first headmistress was a twenty-eight-year-old teacher from Adelaide, Miss Pearl Burton. By accepting the Central Australian appointment, she increased her annual salary from 310 pounds to 366 pounds, not a small incentive to venture north. Press reports of her appointment indicated that the rest of Australia still saw the Territory as a wild and dubious place for white women to reside. A Melbourne *Herald* article observed:

Few women would look forward to spending twelve months at Alice Springs, particularly if they had to spend their time training the children of that remote region. But Miss Pearl Burton is thrilled at the prospect...part of the journey will be made by train and the rest by motor car. This will be her first excursion so far afield.

When she will arrive at Alice Springs and where she will live when she gets there she does not know. Nor does she care. "It is going to be a wonderful experience," she said today'.[1]

Miss Burton began her new job in May 1929 in a galvanised-iron cottage, where classes were held until the new school building was completed in Hartley Street in October of 1930. A welcome addition to the school, and the community, was a piano, which Miss Burton had brought with her from Adelaide. The authorities built her a residence, specifically constructed for a single woman, which created difficulties in later years.

Although Miss Burton was grateful for the new accommodation, she was not always convinced that women were properly looked after in the Centre. When she returned from a holiday in Adelaide, found there was no one to pick her up at the Finke River railhead, and had to catch a ride into Alice Springs with the mail driver, she let the Minister for Home Affairs know in writing what she thought of the treatment:

I travelled to Adelaide then on to the Finke River, arriving there at Sundown Saturday 8th February, expecting to see the Government car. To my amazement there was nobody to meet me and on making enquiries found that nobody had been sent...I think it an absolute disgrace that a woman should be left at such a place where there are eighty navvies working on the line and these not the best of manhood. If this is how the officials at Alice Springs look after their women employees, especially when instructions had been previously issued, I think some steps should be taken.[2]

Despite the occasional problem, the improved educational services in central Australia were welcomed by the general populace, as was the establishment of a much-needed medical facility, in which women also played a leading role.

In 1926 Alice Springs' first hospital, Adelaide House, opened its doors after nearly eight years of fund-raising in both central Australia and Adelaide. The unique, well-ventilated stone building had been designed by the Reverend John Flynn in consultation with Alice Springs' first AIM nurse, Sister Jean Finlayson, and other inland nursing sisters who had served in such centres as Oodnadatta and were aware of the need to address the problems associated with providing medical services in a hot, arid climate. The first resident nursing sisters, Sister Pope and Sister Small, had to use telegrams to consult with the nearest doctors, who were in Darwin and Port Augusta. Ironically their first patient was a man who had claimed that such services were not needed and were only 'molly-coddling' the populace. When a new hospital was built in Alice Springs in 1939, Adelaide House became a hostel for mothers and children of the outback.

Communication services in central Australia began to improve when the Radio Doctor Service was established between the hospital and Hermannsburg Mission. On 27 July 1926, Pastor and Mrs F. W. Albrecht, newly arrived at the Hermannsburg Mission, received the first radio communication from pedal wireless inventor Alf Traeger in Alice Springs, who, like Flynn, demonstrated resourceful-ness in adapting to rather than fighting the isolation of the Centre. Four years later permanent contact through the pedal wireless was established with several outback areas, and that isolation was relieved considerably.

Pearl Burton, Alice Springs' second schoolteacher, prepares for a sightseeing trip of the surrounding 'red centre'.
National Trust of Australia, Northern Territory Collection.

Isolation was also reduced in 1927, when an overland mail delivery service was launched. The significance of the event was described in the *Northern Territory Times* by young Elsie Bohning of Helen Springs station. Calling herself the 'Little Bush Maid,' Elsie described 8 March as being 'a red letter day for the waybacks' when twenty men and three women (Elsie, her mother and her sister) had gathered at Powells Creek to greet the first overland motor mail, operated by Wallis Fogarty. A transcontinental motor mail service now ran direct from Oodnadatta to Katherine.

An even more significant day for central Australian communications was 6 August 1929, when the first train arrived in Alice Springs on the newly completed railway line from Adelaide. More than 200 people from the surrounding area gathered in town for the event and enjoyed a huge celebration as well as an inspection of the train. One old-timer commented he had never seen so many white people in one place at the same time.

A few days later Elsie Bohning and her mother Esther took charge of the first central Australian trainload of stock to Adelaide, despite the misgivings of Alice Springs rail officials, who doubted that the women could handle the job. They could and did. The Bohning women (whose story is told in a later chapter) were known as the 'Petticoat Drovers' because of their many droving feats over several years. On their arrival in Adelaide, one paper described them as 'true daughters of the bush

Except for women who acted as midwives, medical services in the Centre were virtually nonexistent for nearly half a century after South Australia took responsibility for the Territory. People needing medical help had to make the long, rough journey to Oodnadatta. Thus, when the Australian Inland Mission opened its Alice Springs nursing home, Adelaide House, in August 1926, everyone in central Australia welcomed it. The AIM sisters who arrived to service it, Sisters I. Pope and E. Small, were appreciated for their nursing skills, and for the fact that they were unattached females. Both eventually married local residents.
Northern Territory Conservation Commission.

possessing a thorough knowledge of the cattle industry', and seemed impressed that although this was the first time twenty-year-old Elsie had seen a city larger than Darwin, 'she was by no means awed at what she [had] seen'.[3]

The completion of the railway line to Alice immediately improved the town's economic potential with increased tourism being a major consideration. Special three-week tours were organised for up to sixteen people at a cost of sixty-five pounds each. There was one hitch: the tours were for men only. Officialdom soon got its taste of female assertiveness when an avalanche of letters was received protesting against this sex discrimination. Inspired by Lady Somers, wife of the Governor of Victoria, who had accompanied her husband on a 500 mile [800 km] trip to the MacDonnell Ranges by car, camel and donkey, the potential women tourists of Australia let it be known that they were just as capable of coping with a few uncomfortable conditions on the tour as the men. Eventually, economics, if not some justice, won out and the officials opened the tours to the female populace as well.

Another factor in attracting more women to the central Australian region was the increase in the number of writers who visited and publicised the area. One of several women who wrote prolifically about Territory life at this time, and whose articles and stories had a profound impact on other Australians' view of the place, was Ernestine Hill. She is credited by some as having been largely responsible for the false rush to the Tanami goldfields in the early 1930s. She filed some optimistic, although somewhat misleading, reports about the potential of the area and hundreds flocked there, including the Territory's 'wolfram queen' May Brown, who returned very critical of what she called false 'boom broadcasting' about the fields. However, despite Hill's poetic licence as far as accuracy was concerned, her descriptive literary style captured many people's imagination, and perhaps more than anyone else of her time she made the remote Territory come alive for the rest of Australia.

Several enterprising women were among those who ventured north to take advantage of the Territory mining rushes and to gain more freedom for themselves. One was Alice Springs' first barmaid, the spirited and attractive Mona Minahan, who arrived in 1932 to begin a lifetime of enterprise and good humour as a Territorian. For several years Mona worked for her brother-in-law, Joe Kilgariff, as the only barmaid at the popular Stuart Arms Hotel. She later opened a store opposite the hotel and for a few years joined the influx of people to the Tennant Creek goldfields where she grubstaked many a miner and drover, as she was to do later when she returned to Alice Springs to stay.

Life for the women who went to Tennant Creek in the early 1930s was far from easy—most lived in makeshift tent-homes of hessian and canvas, and put up with the searing heat and persistent attacks from the tiny but stinging spinifex flies which seemed to breed in one's nose and mouth. Clothing and 'home decorating' material was hard to come by, so flour bags, all with the brand name showing, were kept and converted into everything from curtains to shirts and housedresses. The main form of transport for those living outside the bough-shed town was by foot. In August 1936 the Melbourne *Argus* commended the spirit of these women in carrying out their perceived domestic role in the difficult conditions:

Deep in the parched desert of North Central Australia, where many men fear to venture, and comfort is a fantasy of imagination, a band of gallant women are struggling to bring cheer to the home of men who are fighting to win fortune from the ground...They are women to whom honour must be given for the part they have played in pioneering the goldfields of Tennant Creek is historic. Almost insurmountable difficulties have not daunted them in their self-imposed duty of providing help for their husbands, sons and fathers—the men who, without their aid, could not have won 100000 pounds worth of gold from the desert in eighteen months. With the pioneer women of Australia's early settlements and Victoria's gold-rush days these women must be recognised.

Though it cloaked them in a nobility that most of those early women would deny, or at least make light of, the editorial sentiment was valid. Tennant Creek, though much younger than the other three major urban centres in the Territory, did indeed have its pioneer women, not the least of whom was the anonymous Aboriginal woman who is alleged to have found the first gold nugget that began the rush in the early 1930s. Among the first European women to help settle the area were Nora Ford, who arrived with her family in early 1933; Camille Myers, a young bride honeymooning on the Honeymoon Range; Zena Williams who came from Wyndham to open a business in town; Nellie and Norah Sanderson, who worked at the hotel; Mrs Dwyer and Mrs Weaber, whose husbands, along with Jack Noble, discovered Noble's Nob; and Margot Miles, who, not unlike others who found their way to the Territory, ran away from her suburban life in Melbourne to seek adventure in the goldmining town of Tennant in 1934. Margot, who was in her eighties by the bicentennial year, captured much of the colour and excitement of that early life in a series of articles for the *Tennant and District Times*, published in book form, and in interviews with the author. She began with a description of her arrival. After taking the Ghan to Alice, she got a ride with the mailman, Lou Miller, to Tennant Creek:

I alighted from the Old Ghan with my straw suitcase or basket with leather straps to be greeted by Mr Miller, who ascertained if I was the right person, and issued orders all the way up the track. I was to wear my hat at all times as well as my headscarf as he had a certain time to arrive in Tennant. 'Don't talk too much,' and if I wanted to relieve myself I had to put my hand up and 'not take too bloody long about it'.

He frightened the hell out of me and I remained practically speechless during the trip. He had a really terrific sense of humour but I was young and a Prim Miss in those days. The mail van was a touring car with the fabric hood taken off to stack mailbags high. It had running boards with tins of petrol attached with leather straps. The water containers were strapped on the other side and it had a solid glass windscreen in front. When I think of it now it was a daunting experience, with no protection from flying objects.

Eventually, after a very long and bumpy ride, they arrived at their destination, where Margot found work in the one and only hotel.

Barmaids were not allowed to pull beer in Territory hotels, only if they were related to the publican. I always claimed to be Tennant Creek's first barmaid, although I never served a drink. I was always plainfaced but had a good figure, so Alex Scott put me in the bar on Saturday night to wash glasses. Nothing hygienic in those days— bucket of water, cake of soap and piles of tea-towels and work like hell. There was no refrigeration—the beer was packed under the counter and wet bags thrown over it. The barmen were armed with big waddies and if things got too tough, they wielded the sticks. It was rough and tough.

Gambling games were carried on in hessian and bough sheds. The Hop Beer joint was a bough shed and did a thriving business. They brewed hop beer in Beenleigh Rum casks.

Later Sunshine Laundry was built, first of ant bed and iron by a Turkish gentleman who dropped dead of shock after winning a huge amount of money at Heads and Tails. The money was never found. Myself and Flo Bowes leased it. We did dry cleaning, dipped articles in a bucket of petrol and offered to mend socks (no one ever wore them). All washing was done by hand and we ironed with petrol irons illuminated with petrol lights. It's a wonder we didn't blow ourselves to hell, the place reeked of petrol. It had a dirt floor and there was always someone breaking in and digging up the floor looking for the Turk's lost hoard.

When I arrived in Tennant Creek, there were very few white women. We are termed the pioneer women now.[4]

Those who stayed, like those who stayed in other pioneering centres, learned the benefits and the power of collective action when they formed a local Country Women's Association, following the example of women in Rankine River in 1931 and Alice Springs in 1933. Darwin finally formed a branch in 1937, a move which a former Territory journalist and bachelor, Fred Thompson, had advocated since 1927 when he argued in a local editorial that:

The apathy of the menfolk of Darwin wants rousing up and nothing is more likely to bring about this desired consummation than a good example set by the women...Womenfolk can do much in many directions that the menfolk have for years neglected, even to helping primary producers to market their produce and by direct antagonism to any official conspiracy to drive...settlers from their homes in furtherance of any scheme of graft or exploitation by dumb leaseholders.

WOMEN AND LIFESTYLE IN THE TOP END

One of the issues the Darwin CWA became involved in was that of trying to improve facilities. While the women of Darwin had better services than those in central Australia and the remote parts of the Territory, they still endured some rather primitive conditions. When Flora Weddell had first arrived in the mid-1920s when her husband was appointed administrator, she had not found many comforts of domestic life, as she later reflected:

Refrigeration was unknown and ice chests were rare. Fresh vegetables and the mail arrived by the ship once a month. Beef was known as 365 for it was practically the staple diet and we had it every day of the year. We had electric light but it was uncertain and was switched off at midnight.

Despite the discomforts she believed that the idea that white women couldn't live in the tropics was 'entirely erroneous' and made her views clear when she left the Territory in 1937.[5]

There were, in fact, many Top End women making their mark in business and demonstrating a commitment to the place, such as Territory-born Francesca Bleezer, daughter of one of Darwin's most expert botanists. In 1927 she was commended for her initiative by the *Northern Territory Times* when she opened a clothing and fabric business in Darwin: 'It is good to see the younger generation having so much faith in North Australia and launching out in business, thus evidencing a desire to stay in our midst.'

Two years later Jessie Emma Edwards proved that women could run big businesses as efficiently and competently as men. When her husband, Harry Edwards, one of the Territory's pioneer pearlers, died in 1929, she took over the pearling business. She was soon being heralded around Australia as the 'woman pearler of the North'. With the help of her son, Roy, she continued as manager of the business for many years.

As it had in central Australia, the extension of the railway, from Katherine south to Daly Waters, opened opportunities for women in the Top End. Long-term

According to her grand-daughter Pearl Ogden, Sarah Fogarty (centre) was a battler, a very strong woman who didn't like alcohol and who always put her family first—characteristics shared by many of the Territory's women pioneers. In May 1921 she and her husband Ted, with their two children, drove a horse and buggy from Cloncurry, Queensland, across the Barkly Tablelands to Katherine, following the tracks left by early explorers and other travellers. Ted found a job droving. For the birth of their third child, Margaret Mary, Sarah was taken across the Katherine River by punt, then caught the train to Darwin. Her next and last child was born the following year in less comfortable circumstances at Delamere station; Sarah had the baby with no help, as he arrived early, before the AIM sister could get there. Years later when Ted Fogarty died, Sarah moved to Katherine where she purchased a cottage and a few years later married a pastoralist friend of hers and Ted's, George Shaw. She became active in the Katherine CWA, and when the CWA hostel was opened in Katherine in 1956 it was named in her honour. Most of her family have remained in the Territory. Photograph courtesy of Pearl Ogden, who has told Sarah's full story in her family history Leg's More Sweeter Than Tail.

Territory resident Nellie Fisher was praised for establishing a much-needed boarding-house at Mataranka, which Gilruth had once hoped to make the capital of the Territory, and veteran Territory publican Catherine O'Shea was commended for being 'the popular and genial hostess of Katherine's "model little hotel"', the Railway Hotel. Catherine was the daughter of the proprietor of a hotel in Killarney, in the south of Ireland, and had inherited a natural penchant for hospitality which was passed on to her six daughters, all of whom became prominent Territorians in their own right.

Another successful Katherine businesswoman of the period was Kitty Bernhard, who had started her Territory life as a cook at the fencers' camp at Victoria

When aviatrix Amy Johnson landed in Darwin in May 1930, becoming the first woman pilot to fly from London to Australia solo, she was given a rousing reception by the population. The town's Chinese community gave her a special presentation and wrote an open letter to the Northern Territory Times *congratulating her: 'The incident proves that there is a great force in this world...hitherto untried or so hampered in many ways that its best has not come to light. Now we can see that given equal opportunity we can look to women to provide not only the great brain power required in the medical legal political judicial journalist and other fields; but acts of heroism and gallantry...surpassing anything of the kind recorded by either sex in the history of the world.' Photograph courtesy of Alec Fong Lim.*

River Downs in the 1920s. By 1930 she was successfully running Katherine's other major hotel, the Sportsman's Arms. When she was named the 'queen of sports' at a Katherine racing carnival in April of 1930, the papers acknowledged that it was expected and deserved.

Christina Gordon and May Brown, whose lives are outlined in later chapters, became prominent hotel owners in Darwin and Pine Creek, with Christina winning the title of the 'aviators' mother' for playing hostess at the Vic Hotel to most of the male and female aviators who passed through Darwin on their record-breaking flights during the period. They included several women who, although they only passed through the Territory, made their own particular pioneering and inspirational mark on the place. In 1928 Mrs Keith 'Chubbie' Miller arrived in Darwin with Captain Bill Lancaster after five adventure-packed months flying his Avro Avian *Red Rose* from England. When a civic reception was given to them at the town hall, the *Northern Territory Times* reported that 'the ladies turned out in full force to do honour to the first lady to complete the first flight from England to Australia,' an indication of the heroine and role model she had become to other women. Chubbie later lost some of her heroine image when Lancaster shot a journalist with whom she had an affair and she made world headlines of a more sensational kind.

In May of 1930 another aviatrix upheld the heroine image—Amy Johnson, who landed in Darwin during her record-breaking England to Australia solo flight. Darwin's mayor said it was the proudest moment of his life to have the privilege of welcoming Miss Johnson who, he believed, had achieved more than any other living woman. A short time later Miss Eli Beinhorn became the first foreign aviatrix to land on Australian soil at Darwin's Fannie Bay air strip. When journalist Jessie Litchfield asked her if she was nervous flying over the Timor Sea she replied, 'There's no room for fear; one either crosses or one does not—Kismet.' Jessie reported the quote in one of the many stories she wrote for the world press on the feats of the men and women who passed through Darwin in their flying machines.

It was not just women visitors who were winning recognition; Territory women were also gaining honours for themselves and for the Territory. When it was learned that a local female resident, Sister Constance Stone, had been awarded the MBE, local lawyer John Harris had asked her how she'd like to celebrate. 'A night out with the boys,' she decided. The men responded with due compliments concerning her work and toasted her award as 'an honour to all Territorians'. In 1937 two more Territory women, Christina Gordon and Elsie Muriel Jones, received the award for their services to the community. Christina Gordon was recognised for her contribution to business and to charities, both publicly and privately, and Elsie Jones for her services to nursing, particularly as matron at the leper station on Channel Island.

Two other nursing sisters who received MBEs after the Second World War for performing tasks above and beyond the call of duty were Territory born Eileen Styles, grand-daughter of Darwin pioneers Ned and Eliza Tuckwell, and Sister Ruth Heathcock. It was while serving at Borroloola in 1941 that Sister Ruth made the legendary journey that earned her the award for what was later described by some as one of the bravest acts in the Territory's history. She travelled for three days in a dugout canoe with two Aboriginal men, an Aboriginal woman and a Borroloola man, in dangerous floodwaters, to treat a man who had accidentally shot himself. She nursed him for eight days before he finally died, less than two hours before the flying doctor landed at the camp. Although the incident occurred in 1941, because of the focus on the war at the time it was overlooked, until inquest details surfaced in 1946; Sister Ruth was eventually given due recognition in 1961.

Betty Dangerfield was another Territory woman whose bravery was recognised during the period, when she was presented with the Royal Humane Society's certificate for saving a local resident, John Cubillo, from drowning.

WOMEN AND PUBLIC LIFE

Among the most outspoken and passionately parochial woman of the north during the twenties and thirties was Betty's mother, Jessie Litchfield. As well as writing prolifically for both the *Northern Territory Times* and its opponent, the union-run *Northern Standard* (although she fell out of favour with both of them at various times), Jessie was also the first woman to stand for local government office. She campaigned for a seat on the town council in 1927 and 1928 and for a by-election in 1929, but she lost each time.

Jessie wasted no time in publicly pinpointing what she regarded as her main disadvantage:

I consider that I polled very well indeed, considering the circumstances. I had to compete against a handicap that no other competitor suffered with. There are still a few survivors from the Stone Age lingering about Darwin and a large number of these troglodytes absolutely refused to vote for me because I was a woman. They did not declare me debarred on any other grounds and some of them have often enough alluded to the Town Councillors as a crowd of old women, but—simply because I was a woman these ancient survivals of an exploded fetish objected to vote for me.[6]

Both newspapers obliged by confirming a certain sexual prejudice. The *Northern Territory Times* admitted during the June 1928 election that it thought Jessie would make a brilliant member of the council but that a woman's place was in the home and not dodging about attending to other people's business. The *Standard* agreed that the council was no place for women, although it too acknowledged that Jessie had vision, aims and ideals and would undoubtedly do a commendable job.

Jessie Litchfield was not daunted, however, and continued to play a prominent role in the Territory for another quarter of a century, becoming the first female editor of the *Northern Territory Times* in 1930 and publishing a book entitled *Far North Memories*, based on her family's life on the Territory's mining fields between 1908 and 1912. Jessie continued as editor of the *Times* until the *Northern Standard* bought its rival out in mid-1932. She continued to have her say in public affairs, however, both through her articles and at public forums.

In July of 1934, after several years of sometimes violent demonstrations against the government by the unemployed, Jessie attended a public meeting at the town hall to consider a submission to the government for unemployment relief. About 100 people attended, but Jessie Litchfield was the only woman whose contribution to the meeting was reported in the paper, probably indicating that she was the only woman at the meeting who spoke. Jessie spoke in favour of the request for work by the unemployed, saying that she knew something of what unemployment was and what it was to have a family of small children and not sufficient food to feed them. She told the meeting that years earlier her husband had been out of work and she had approached the government to get work, but was only offered a fare out of the place. Jessie said that because the family had faith in the Territory and wanted to remain, they had managed to pull through and progress. She believed the government had a moral responsibility for every child in the Territory and unless it did its share it was putting the fate of those children in jeopardy and was remiss in its duty towards unemployed workers. Jessie was the only woman appointed to the relief committee, which sent a delegation to Administrator Weddell demanding equal opportunities to relief workers to obtain full-time work.

She was not, however, the only woman to face uphill and sometimes lonely fights in her bid for recognition and improved status. Other women had to battle existing prejudices and discrimination, sometimes because they were not European, sometimes because they were women, sometimes because they were both. This was exemplified by what happened to at least one Darwin Chinese woman who was taking a prominent public role in political affairs of the Chinese community. By the mid 1920s, amid much cynical criticism from some sectors of the Darwin community, Lena Lee (Lena Pak Fong before her marriage to Willie Lee in 1924) had become leader of the Territory branch of the Chinese Nationalist Party, Kuo Min Tang, and had represented the Territory at least once at the organisation's national convention. Lena had been educated at Hong Kong University and was a devoted follower of nationalist leader Dr Sun Yat Sen. When she moved to Darwin she became an instructor in the doctrine to Darwin Chinese. After she rose to prominence, a writer in the *Standard*, which disagreed with Kuo Min Tang politics, claimed in an October 1929 editorial that the older conservative Chinese would have nothing to do with a society 'whose chief say-so was a woman'.

The *Northern Territory Times* at once rose to her defence:

No sneering reference can belittle the good done for the Chinese residents by this woman. Believing that the emancipation of her country was imminent, she has fearlessly advocated the absolutely knocking out of foreign capitalists from China. We have lady members of parliament in Australia and the Imperial Parliament possesses nine lady members, including Lady Asquith. Are these women out of place? If not, what is wrong with a Chinese woman emulating her western sisters and trying to assist her lesser educated brethren?

A few months after the newspaper debate about her suitability to be a leader of her people, Lena committed suicide by taking an overdose of opium. She left two notes behind that supported the view that being the centre of such altercations had depressed and exhausted her. One, to the Darwin branch of the Nationalist Party, said she had always tried to serve the party loyally but she was so concerned at the recent disputes that she had decided to depart this life. The other letter, to her mother, said she had grown 'so tired of life' that she was 'compelled' to depart it forever. She left her mother with the several hundred pounds she had saved. She left her enemies to contemplate the effect their criticism had had on her decision to end her earthly life.

CHANGES FOR ABORIGINAL WOMEN

But again it was the treatment and protection of Aboriginal and part-Aboriginal women that caused the most controversy and discussion in the community. Of prime concern, to the authorities at least, was the cohabitation of Aboriginal women and non-Aboriginal men.

One of the more frequent arguments against such sexual liaisons was the claim that they spread venereal disease and leprosy. This led to some controversial practices, such as keeping the women who lived in the Aboriginal compounds confined to their quarters in chains. When the Darwin Council suggested in September of 1927 that the protector, Dr Cecil Cook, should find a more appropriate way of keeping the matter in check, they were strongly criticised by the *Times*, which claimed it was the only effective way. The paper said that Dr Cook deserved the co-operation of the public 'for his efforts in rooting out a horrible disease which [was] rapidly destroying a splendid race of people'.

One woman who drew attention to the plight of some young Aboriginal women and to herself at this time was missionary Annie Lock, who had gone to live alone among central Australian Aborigines at Harding Soak, about 100 miles [160

Missionary Annie Lock worked among the Aboriginal people of central Australia for many years, at times taking strong stands on controversial issues such as the Coniston massacres of the late 1920s. Australian Archives.

km] from Alice Springs. In 1927 Sister Lock, a single woman of about fifty and a member of the Australian Aborigines Society, had gone to Harding Soak to tend to sick Aborigines there. Many white people of the centre believed that an unmarried woman living alone in an Aboriginal camp degraded white women and undermined the whites in general. Annie had been warned by Central Australian government resident Cawood that the government disapproved of her activities and that the chief protector of Aborigines for Central Australia, Robert Stott, described her as a 'crank'.

In late 1928 an event commonly referred to as the 'Coniston Killings' occurred, which brought her work with Aboriginal people to national attention and European attitudes to Aboriginal people under close scrutiny. In August of that year a dingo trapper named Frederick Brookes was killed by Aboriginal men in the Central Australian desert. A few weeks later, a punitive expedition of white settlers led by outback policeman Mounted Constable William George Murray, left at least thirty-one Aboriginal men, women and children dead. In a further attack a few days later at least another fourteen Aboriginal people were killed. The inquiry was set up to discover the circumstances of the killings and decide whether or not they were justified.

Annie would eventually give controversial evidence at the inquiry, but before she did she was involved in her own controversy, which highlighted one of the problems associated with having a North and Central Australia. Most of the Aboriginal people she was tending at Harding Soak had abandoned it because the well had run dry, and when the Methodist missionary of Katherine, the Reverend Athol McGregor, visited the soak in late 1928 Annie decided to travel with him to Katherine to catch a train to Darwin where she wanted the doctor to administer help to two young Aboriginal girls in her care. Annie had been looking after one of the girls for eighteen months and was hopeful of adopting her.

In Darwin Annie was told she had broken the law by taking the girls from Central Australia to North Australia without permission. Annie ignored warnings from officials and did not mince words in the local press about what she described as the woeful conditions of the Aboriginal people in Central Australia. After attending to the medical needs of the two girls in her charge, Annie remained in Darwin for the trial of two Aboriginal prisoners who had been charged with Brookes's murder. A jury found the two men not guilty.

The acquitted men were put on board the train to Katherine. Government officials tried to do the same with Annie's two young Aboriginal girls, but Annie discovered the plan and held both girls in her arms, challenging the officials to tear them from her. After a tense scene, the police saw that a gathering crowd was sympathetic to Annie and let her take them to Katherine, where she remained until receiving a summons to give evidence in Alice Springs before the Board of Inquiry into the Coniston killings.

After a five-week motor journey, she arrived in Alice Springs with the two Aboriginal girls. She had clearly upset some people in positions of power. One particular journalist created sensational headlines by claiming that she wanted to marry an Aboriginal man, with some papers suggesting she had already taken one as a lover. She was treated with jeers and hostility by many of the Alice Springs residents. Her case was not assisted by the evidence of the superintendent of Hermannsburg, who said he disapproved of women missionaries working among blacks because of the nudity of the Aboriginal men and the fact that a woman walking among them would lower herself to their own standards.

Annie Lock countered by telling the inquiry that much of the trouble between whites and blacks was caused by the cohabitation of some white men with Aboriginal women. She also claimed that white men hunted Aboriginal people away from the water-holes, causing unrest and ill-feeling, particularly in the current drought.

After hearing evidence from thirty witnesses, the Board of Inquiry concluded that the shootings of the Aborigines were justified. The Board gave several reasons for the uprising by the Aboriginal people, which was said to have provoked the massacre. Included in the ten reasons was that of 'a woman Missionary living amongst naked blacks, thus lowering their respect for the whites'. The almost complete whitewash of the police killings remains a source of enormous contention in Australia today.[7]

While the police went free, Annie Lock was charged in the Alice Springs court with having taken two Aboriginal children from Central Australia to North Australia without the consent of the protector of Aborigines, Constable Stott. Stott had not only expressed his dislike of Miss Lock on several occasions but had also taken a role in the shootings. She was fined three pounds five shillings and ordered to deliver one of the Aboriginal girls, Dolly, into the custody of the court to be placed in the Aboriginal home at Jay Creek, three miles (seven kilometres) from Alice Springs, where the children from the Bungalow had been moved at Ida Standley's request in 1928. Annie returned with her other girl, Betsy, to Ryan's Well and spent several more years administering help to the Aboriginal people of the Territory.

Meanwhile, a government-appointed inquiry, headed by Mr J. W. Bleakley, Chief Protector of Aborigines for Queensland, was investigating the general status and conditions of Aboriginal people in the Territory. The conclusions were in keeping with the views of the Territory's new protector of Aborigines, Dr Cecil Cook, who wanted to stop white men having sexual relationships with black women. Despite evidence given to Bleakley that the Aboriginal woman was 'one of the greatest pioneers of the Territories, for without her it would have been impossible for white men to have carried on,' he recommended separation of the races.

The issue of Aboriginal-European liaisons was also raised during the building of the north-south rail line. Mrs John McKay, who had pleaded for protection of Aboriginal women in 1924, was again in the forefront of the argument. She and others of the Women's Non-Party Association were concerned that steps be taken to protect Aboriginal women during the construction of the line, when hundreds of single men would be in the region. They suggested that the line be proclaimed a prohibited area to Aborigines and that food depots, managed by two policewomen who would also act as protectors, be established in drought-stricken areas so that Aborigines wouldn't be tempted to go near the construction. The government agreed to the first request and declared a ten-mile (16 km) range on either side of the line as a prohibited area. It did not, however, consider it necessary to send policewomen as female protectors or to establish food depots. What it did do was create institutions and change the law to allow the European officials more control over the behaviour of Aborigines, and to 'breed out the black' in people of part Aboriginal descent. In 1932 administrator Weddell reported that 'half-caste' instutiutions had been established at Darwin, Pine Creek and Jay Creek. In 1933 new legislation required the employers of Aborigines to look after their families and give them a minimum wage. It also specified that Aborigines could not be employed in hotels and could not drink or be in possession of alcohol, and it gave the police power to prosecute any non-Aboriginal who cohabited with Aboriginal women.

Cecil Cook summed up the government policy in his 1933 report:

In the Territory the mating of an aboriginal with any person other than an aboriginal is prohibited. The mating of coloured aliens with any female of part-aboriginal blood is also forbidden. Every endeavour is being made to breed out the colour by elevating female half-castes to the white standard with a view to their absorption by mating into the white population.

In 1934, after further amendments to the law, he stated in his yearly report that the 'undesirable feature associated with the old practice of farming out children on their attaining fourteen years to any person who would take them' had been removed. He claimed that great care was now exercised in the selection of employers and that the employment conditions for female 'half-castes' had been drastically revised. Selection was now made, he said, with a view to permitting their employment only by 'persons prepared to undertake the moral and material welfare of the employee'. Cook claimed that this, coupled with the removal of all unmarried and unemployed female 'half-castes' to institutions, had resulted in an abrupt fall in the illegitimate birthrate and in the incidence of disease amongst those who were under the care of his department.

In 1936, after much controversy and heated debate as to whether 'half-castes' should be given the opportunity for more rights than 'fullblood' Aborigines, the law was changed to authorise the chief protector to exempt certain 'half-castes' from all or any of the provisions of the ordinance. In the first year Cook reported that eleven male 'half-castes' and two females had been granted total exemption and nineteen male 'half-castes' had been granted partial exemption. He added a cautionary note, however, stating that it was not intended that these people should be permitted to abuse the privileges so bestowed on them. He assured the administrator that his department would continue to assist them to attain the status of true citizenship by 'elevating them to the white standard of living'. When he received his first complaints about the conduct of two of the exempted people, he duly warned them that a repetition of their offence would cause a cancellation of their exemption.

In 1937 another lobbying attempt by both Australian and overseas women to have women appointed as Aboriginal protectors in the Northern Territory failed. The issue was discussed by a conference of commonwealth and state Aboriginal authorities in Canberra in April, and the following resolution was passed:

While the use of female protectors or inspectors for the supervision of female natives in populated areas may be desirable, the general appointment of women is not considered practicable because of the very scattered nature of native camps, the difficulties of travel and the isolation.[8]

One of the most strident critics of government policies for Aborigines was Miss Olive Pink, who also demanded that a woman be appointed to help administer the 'native affairs' department. She arrived in Alice Springs in 1930 and applied to the Australian National Research Council to research the social anthropology of Central Australia. The proposal was agreed to, and thus began a lifetime of work, during which Miss Pink became one of the Territory's more colourful identities. Born and educated in Hobart, Olive reached a distinct turning point in her life when her childhood sweetheart, Harold Southern, was killed at Gallipoli in the First World War. Devastated, Olive first sought a career as a tracer with the Public Works Department and later Railways Commission of New South Wales. Eventually she heard of the work of the lone female missionary, Annie Lock, and also visited self-appointed Aboriginal worker Daisy Bates. Inspired by these women, Olive decided to make her own mark in the anthropological world and, after receiving a grant in 1933 to study the organisation of the northern division of the Aranda tribe, she spent more than a year doing just that. The scientific paper that resulted from the work was published in the prestigious *Oceania* in 1936 and very well received.

Although her scientific papers and her skilled botanical sketches drew respect and admiration, her eccentricities and rather prickly personality caused her difficulties at times. Many times, officials who tired of her endless letters, underlined in pink when she wanted to make a particular point, refused to take notice of her pleas to give Aboriginal people the chance to be left alone and live life in their traditional way.

This did not stop Olive Pink continuing her studies or harassing officials until the day she died. Her reams of passionate notes to government ministers and officials, and the often curt replies they evoked, still fill archival shelves around the country, and pay testimony to the more than forty-five years she devoted to studying and defending the Aboriginal way of life, a role she continued during and after the Second World War.

There were, of course, Aboriginal women who broke through the cultural and social barriers within European society and took charge of their own lives. One was Kitty Pon, an Aboriginal woman who was abandoned as a baby in the 1880s during a tribal fight in the McArthur River area. She was discovered and later adopted by the family of William Stretton, then a policeman at Borroloola. She learned to read and write by means of a Bible and later travelled to Darwin with the Strettons when Mr Stretton was transferred there. In 1908 she married Carl Pon, a former Timorese chieftan who was in charge of a pearling fleet for the European firm of Jollys. They lived on the foreshore of Frances Bay, which was known locally as Carl Pon's beach. Kitty soon became a familiar figure, on Sundays carrying tree blossoms and flowers to the Methodist church where she taught Sunday school. As well as raising two sons of her own from her marriage to Carl, in 1930 she was given permission to adopt a tiny Greek girl who had been found abandoned on a vacant Darwin allotment. When the navy threatened to evict her from her home in 1935 because they needed the land for dumping debris, the *Northern Standard* rallied to her defence, saying she had earned the respect of all sections of the Darwin community, having been a Samaritan friend to many unemployed people who were forced to camp on the beach, unable to find jobs or food. Kitty is alleged to have written at least one book about her life, but to date no copy has been found.

Another well-known and respected Aboriginal woman of the period was Alice Cooper of Port Essington, who was married to legendary Territory buffalo shooter Joe Cooper, a European who had come to the Territory in the 1880s with his brother. Joe and Alice had met before the turn of the century, when Alice reputedly saved Joe's life after he had been attacked by other Aborigines. The couple married and lived on Melville Island, where Joe, who learned the local Tiwi language, became a 'king' and Alice became a major figure amongst the Aboriginal people, as well as winning the respect and admiration of the European community. They raised three children, a son and two daughters, whose descendants are now spread throughout the Territory.

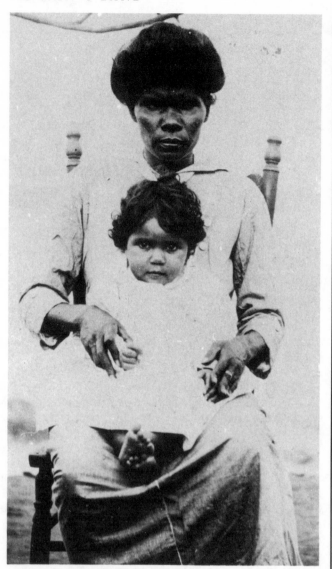

Alice Cooper of Port Essington became a leading figure in her adopted Aboriginal community of Melville Island after she married legendary buffalo shooter Joe Cooper. She is shown here with her son Reuben, who became a famous footballer, as did many of his sons. Alice died in the 1930s, and her descendants are now among the most prominent Territory families of Aboriginal descent.
Donnison Collection, Mitchell Library.

MULTICULTURAL IMAGE

While the attitude and policy which developed during this period towards Aborigines and Aborigines of mixed descent still remains a source of much contention, in many ways the Territory was a racially tolerant, or at least complacent, community. It was certainly multicultural in its make-up. In the 1920s and 1930s Darwin in particular was a hodgepodge of people from all corners of the earth and from all social classes.

The city was divided into cultural sections—Greek town was on the outskirts of the city; Chinatown was in Cavenagh Street; the Aboriginal compound accommodation was in the inner-city area of Larrakeyah and near the prestigious Myilly Point;

and many immigrant workers lived in the inner city suburb of Stuart Park (known as the Police Paddock) or at Frog Hollow, a swamp area a street away from Chinatown. Many lived in humpies or galvanised-iron shacks and struggled to keep their families fed and clothed, women of the household often contributing to the income as well as maintaining the home. A correspondent for the Sydney *Sun* who visited Darwin just prior to the Second World War described the situation of one immigrant mother of four, who, to augment the family income, was taking in washing at the family dwelling in Frog Hollow:

I sat on a humpy bed, looked at a storm wracked sky through a threadbare hessian roof sagging under the weight of tropical rain and listened while a woman, her arms covered in suds from her family washtub philosophically remarked, 'Yes, the rain does come in but,' and with a spread of lean, brown hands, 'It can't be helped. At least it's a roof.'

One person who was especially intrigued by the multicultural aspect of the Territory was author and journalist Ernestine Hill. She captured the atmosphere of Darwin's cosmopolitan community in a feature in the *Adelaide Chronicle* of 21 September 1933:

Five distinct national communities flourish in that vivid patch of Australian tropic bushland. There are the neat attic cottages of the Greeks, incongruous beneath the poinciana trees; the walled campong settlement of the Malays and Islanders; laced bamboo huts of Manilamen, on stilts; and the little bird-cage houses and shops of a village in Tokyo, incredibly clean and bare, with their matting beds, tiny shrines and miniature gardens—to say nothing of the paperbark mias and shacks of the aboriginal compound, where all the tribes of the Territory are summer visitors. In the maze of tin alleys that is Chinatown, where the joss sticks are ever burning before the tiger faced gods of Kwong Sung, and barefooted Oriental tailors bend to their sewing machines, you may lunch—if you have been lucky enough to make friends—upon salted fish roe with soi preserved eggs, spicy with age, boiled bamboo shoots, and sharks fins, dipping your chopsticks in the communal rice with trousered women of the East their faces a smiling mass.

The racial mix was spread throughout the Territory—from Pine Creek, where a particularly large number of Chinese lived, to Katherine and Alice Springs. The Katherine region had an influx of Russians during this period, and several Russian men who had come to the Territory to engage in the potentially promising industry of peanut farming brought Russian wives with them. Alice Springs had a growing Italian community, many of whom had come as whole families to work on the mica fields, and it had its Afghan population, with many of the Afghan men married to Aboriginal women.

THE QUESTION OF WHITE WOMEN IN THE TROPICS

As the numbers of women of many cultures increased in the Territory, the familiar question of whether the tropical Territory was suitable for white women continued to be examined. In 1937 yet another all-male inquiry into Territory land development, this time conducted by William Payne and J. W. Fletcher, concluded that

'Laboratory tests had disclosed an amazingly high percentage of anaemia amongst females in Darwin. In the wake of anaemia came a condition of general malaise, lassitude and discontent.' This was primarily because white women were expected to maintain the 'White Australia' policy and were 'forced to carry out, unaided, all the heavy and enervating duties of household management in a tropical climate not less severe than that of Rabaul.' The report continued:

Most of the women at Darwin do their own housework. The result is that they have all the disadvantages of living in the tropics without any of the usual compensations which tropical countries provide, such as hours of leisure, social intercourse, and labour for household duties. The introduction of a strictly limited number of eastern natives under indenture for domestic duties would, paradoxically as it may seem, help to strengthen the White Australia policy by guarding the health of females on whom the success of that policy depends.

Anyone who has ever visited the Territory and spoken to the women who were there at the time such reports were being compiled could be forgiven for wondering if these usually all-male inquiries ever bothered asking the ordinary woman what her view was. Most would probably smile, look you squarely in the eye and tell you there is no better place on earth. They would be women who participated fully in the life of the place, like Heather Harris, born in Darwin in 1908, the daughter of Fannie and James Bell. Heather, whose parents ran Darwin's Club Hotel and Bell's Tea Rooms during the Gilruth regime, is the self-admitted rogue of the family and took full advantage of the choices Darwin offered.

Heather's earliest memories are reminiscent of scenes from a Somerset Maugham story—Chinese chefs in traditional hairstyles and garb cooking aromatic dishes over wooden stoves; young Aboriginal boys wearing red and white handkerchiefs as pants, their black skin and hair glistening with coconut oil, slowly moving cooling punkahs with their toes; a group of European men clad in tropical whites playing cards and ordering drinks from the hotel's well-stocked bar; and curly-headed Heather herself sneaking behind the counter to pinch a packet of 'My Darling' cigarettes for her brother.

Heather's rebellious and mischievous nature sometimes got her into temporary trouble with her parents—like the time her mother found her on top of the old telegraph pole outside the hotel or the time, at age thirteen, she rode her Harley-Davidson motorcycle at top speed, spraying dust on Judge Mallam while he sat on his usual bench, known locally as the 'seat of knowledge'. Heather, who had childhood and teenage ambitions to be a movie star, was a leader in the local entertainment scene in the 1920s and 1930s. As well as playing the piano for the silent pictures at the open-air Don Theatre and later as part of a local band, she was also an accomplished and extremely acrobatic dancer, which she proved by performing such difficult dances as the 'apache'. Once, when she performed at the old town hall, the deaconess of the church was so outraged she walked out before the number was finished.

Heather's spirited and independent nature came to the fore again when one of her suitors, Tom Harris, finally got a local golf course organised in 1930. Dress regulations stipulated that women players were to wear dresses so Heather turned up in a new pair of shorts, only to be promptly ordered off the course and told to return

One of the Territory's most skilled entertainers was Heather Bell, born in Darwin in 1908 and still lively in 1988. Here she is practising the 'apache dance' with professional dance instructor Dick Ryder with whom she co-produced several shows in the 1930s. Heather also played piano for the town's first silent pictures and later married entertainer extraordinaire Tom Harris, who brought 'talking pictures' to Darwin. Heather was a trendsetter in many areas of Darwin's social life, and always claimed she married Tom Harris because he was the only one of her suitors who was going to stay in Darwin— the only home she ever wanted. She was proud to be present in the Legislative Assembly in the 1980s when her son became the Minister for Education in the Territory's Country Liberal Party Government.
Photograph courtesy of Heather Harris.

The Territory in the 1920s and 1930s was as much in need of entertainment as anywhere else in Australia and women made a major contribution to this aspect of life. Here 'Mrs Green' (left), Darwin's professional dance instructor of the period, performs with four talented local entertainers Phyl Johnson, Myrtle Fawcett, Lilla Bell and Berryl Parer. They performed in countless shows in Darwin and 'down the track', Myrtle Fawcett becoming the only woman in a war-time entertainment troupe that performed throughout the Territory just prior to the bombing of Darwin.
Photo courtesy of Pam Rixon, Myrtle Fawcett's daughter.

when she was suitably attired. This was despite the fact that a friend of hers, Bessie Drysdale, was once playing in a new voile dress when a tropical storm developed and by the time she could run to the club house and escape the rain, the dress had shrunk to such an extent that it was little more than a frill around her waist.

In 1939 Heather married Tom Harris, who had taken over management of the Star Theatre in the early 1930s and had become an entertainer extraordinaire himself. One of the main reasons she married Tom, she confessed, was that he wanted to stay in the Territory—and that's where Heather intended to stay. 'I was in my thirties when we finally got married,' Heather said, 'and I think that's one of the reasons our marriage was so successful. We were both bachelors and we allowed each other the freedom to be ourselves.' For Heather, that freedom to expand her own talents and interests is one of the most appealing aspects of living in the Territory.

Among the Territory's pioneering Chinese businesswomen was Lorna Lim (above left). The family lived in the Katherine region in the 1920s and 30s before moving to Darwin where they operated several businesses for many years. Photo courtesy of Alec Fong Lim.

'There's no other place for me,' she said in 1988 on her eightieth birthday.

Another woman who loved the Territory but was only able to spend about ten years there was Beryl Asche, who lived in Darwin in the late 1920s when her husband, Eric, was appointed Crown Law Officer for both Central and North Australia. Beryl soon entered into the social life of Darwin and quickly learned to love the Territory, despite some major setbacks. In 1933 the family lost most of their possessions when their distinctive two-storey mud-brick home, which had been built overlooking Darwin Harbour in the 1880s by John Knight, was burnt to the ground while they were on holidays. They moved to a home at Myilly Point, which received the main force of the cyclonic winds which ripped through the town in 1937. Remarkably, only one person was killed in that cyclone, an Aboriginal man who was crushed to death by falling timber when a house collapsed. He was carrying his small child, who miraculously escaped harm.

Beryl described the experience in a letter to her parents in Melbourne:

Tonight is Thursday and I'm beginning early so as to tell you of our experiences last night when we had a real cyclone and it is an experience we could well do without. I'm sure it must have made me at least five years older in one night. We at Myilly Point got the full force. Our house and three others got the very worst of it. It was the longest night and the most terrifying I have ever put in...it was pitch black outside and it gave us such a helpless feeling. Between two am and four am there seemed to be at least ten hours and it was raging then at its very utmost...From about ten o'clock on we could hardly hear ourselves speak for the sheets of iron which kept being ripped from the roof and the noise of the blow. It was like a huge roar...The two front doors went first, then first one bit of roof and then another and that dreadful banging went on right up to seven this morning when the complete side of half the house was found to be off, all the copper and kitchen stove piping gone and the bathroom roof and half the other side of the house.

I can't tell you what Eric and I feel like today and if only you could see our house and the desolation everywhere. There are no large trees left out here at all and where from the back verandah we used only to see a peep of Mendil (sic) Beach we can now see it from end to end and all its coconuts and mango trees are gone...We are about the only ones rising our own roof shelter tonight. All the other families have gone to the Hotel.

First a fire and now a cyclone! I think we must have been intended to board.[9]

The Asche family lived in Darwin until the late 1930s when they returned to Melbourne. Eric, a victim of gassing while serving in Europe during the Great War, died in 1940, leaving Beryl with five children. Exhibiting the same pluck that had seen her through some of the more trying times in the Territory, Beryl supported her family by finding employment as assistant secretary and then secretary of the Melbourne Ladies Benevolent Society. Although she never again lived in Darwin, she remained loyal to it, and was fond of saying 'You can leave the Territory but the Territory never leaves you.' For many years she satisfied her longing for Territory days by holding regular 'Territory' parties to which she would invite any ex-Territorians she could find. She would have been pleased to know that her son, Austin, would many years later return to the Territory to serve as its Chief Justice.

At about the time of the cyclone, Charles Lydiard Abbott replaced Colonel Robert Weddell as administrator of the Northern Territory. Although his style of administration and his perceived elitist attitude created controversy and conflict among some sections of the Territory populace, he remained in the position during and after the Second World War, and presided over the period of military build-up in the Top End as the war in Europe progressed.

Many of the down-to-earth Territory residents thought his sense of superiority was shared by his attractive wife, Hilda, who was a creative and prolific writer as well as a skilled furniture designer and painter, designing, among other things, a desk for Government House. However, her many writings, which present a vivid picture of her life in the Territory, are her most valuable legacy. As well as recording her memoirs in an unpublished manuscript entitled *Good Night, All About*, she wrote scores of articles for various newspapers and magazines under the pen name of Haliden Hart while she was serving as the Territory's first lady, helping to put the

Territory on the map. The *Northern Standard*, probably not knowing who she was, once re-printed one of her articles, in which she describes life in Darwin from her elite point of view. It is a romantic picture of a balmy tropical town late in 1941, seemingly oblivious to the war-clouds threatening all around.

But war-clouds were looming. As if in preparation, shortly after her arrival Hilda Abbott had re-formed the defunct Territory branch of the Red Cross, which became increasingly active as the war in Europe heightened. When Pearl Harbour was bombed in December 1941, Australian authorities decided to take definite action. Women and children were compulsorily evacuated from Darwin, leaving the Top End almost devoid of female occupants, a situation which would endure for the next four years, during which time Alice Springs would again become an administrative centre.

The story of those years and of the women who were part of them is one of the most dramatic in Territory history.

Chapter 7

Territory Women at War

'Women of Darwin showed they all had the courage of heroines when Japanese planes launched the first bombing raid on the Australian soil.'
Australian Women's Weekly, March 1942

Darwin was still recovering from the cyclone of 1937, and undergoing a major facelift, when the war broke out in Europe. A top Brisbane city planner was preparing a new town plan; a new hotel, two new banks and a new hospital were under construction; new power and water works were under way; and a road linking Darwin to Alice Springs and the rest of Australia was about to be built.

The advent of war meant that some of this facelift took on a military look and purpose. Construction of the Larrakeyah army barracks complex began in 1937; gun emplacements and soldiers' camps started springing up on the foreshores; an anti-submarine net was being stretched across the harbour; and work had begun on the new RAAF base a few miles out from the city centre.

It was still very much a man's town. When the ships came in the local lads would go down to the wharf and make a bet with any single woman who disembarked and planned on staying. They would bet her that she would be married within three months, and she usually was.

As the war drew closer to Australia, the Darwin population grew larger and more military in nature. Accommodation became scarce. A local resident, Molly Walsh, then a typist with the army, later recorded the atmosphere of those immediate pre-war Darwin days:

It is good that I can visualize best the pleasant things. Sitting out on the steps of our latticed verandah after dinner at night, sipping black coffee from beautiful old fashioned coffee cups, we would watch the distant lightning flash and trace the progress of a storm, or we would admire the delicate tips of the giant bamboos, motionless in the unbreathing air, and etched against the evening sky. One of the lovely things about Darwin is that you can never go far without a view of its lovely beaches edged with verdurous tropical growth and clean white sand, sand that is alive with hermit crabs crawling about in their little spiral shell houses. And I will always remember the little white cottage where I used to buy eggs when there were any to spare. It was set among shady mango trees and untidy pandanus palms. My way there led along a narrow path through bamboos and trees I could not name. In one tree was one of those big nests the pretty green jungle ants make, of leaves cemented together with their own secretions. And the Chinese woman who owned the poultry-farm wore wide Chinese trousers and a tunic and a real coolie hat and could

Between December 1941 and February 1942 hundreds of women and children were evacuated from the Top End to southern cities for the duration of the war, many becoming refugees in their own country. Helping with the evacuation was the USS President Grant, *an American cruise ship diverted to Darwin when the Japanese bombed Manila. Among the evacuees were Molly Walsh (third from left), an army typist who kept a descriptive diary of the events leading up to the evacuation, and Edna Tambling (second from left) whose husband, Ern Tambling, was in charge of the evacuation and thus travelled with the evacuees. Edna and Ern later named their first son Grant; he went on to become the federal member, and later a senator, for the Territory. Both Edna and Molly returned after the war to make their home in Darwin.*
Photograph courtesy of Molly Walsh.

not understand a word I said. But the little nipper, her son, was knowledgeable enough and would quite likely top his class at school over the heads of the white children.

On Friday, 5th December...the first portents of grave events faintly stirred the tropical lethargy of Darwin, land of manana. And it was thus. A number of soldiers were due to go South on annual leave and had already handed in their equipment and gone on board the troopship *Zealandia*, when an order came through cancelling all leave and they were put ashore and returned to their camps. Rumour had it that there would be a riot, the boys would tear the town to pieces and smash the few remaining shop windows. But rumour also said that there was something more behind the cancellation than mere muddleheadedness.

A few days later Molly's husband, Jim, came back for lunch. He brought news: Pearl Harbour had been bombed by the Japanese and the Americans had been caught unawares. That was all—no details were known.

'At such times there is nothing else to do but go on with your ordinary daily program,' Molly wrote. That evening she went to a cocktail party being given by the nurses at the hospital for a friend who was being married the next day. When she reached the hospital area she noticed six strange ships in the harbour. Never before could she remember seeing so many ocean-going ships in the bay at the same time:

While I stood looking out over the dazzling water, along the scrub lined road behind me sped truck after truck taking barbed wire and working parties from Larrakeyah Barracks to strategic positions. The next day when I arrived at work I sensed two things. I received the impression that the war had only just begun. And secondly the feeling was decidedly defensive. We evidently expected to be struck before we had an opportunity to be offensive. The absurdity of having built headquarters and administrative offices in what must be the front line was immediately exposed as soon as action threatened—and plans for their withdrawal had to be made.

My major greeted me with the astounding words, Well, when are you going home? Home? Why this is my home, I replied and so far as I know I'm not going anywhere. You'll be evacuated, he said. The women will all have to go and soldiers' wives will be first. If you are sensible you won't wait for an evacuation order but go straight to town and book a passage, the Major told me. That was the beginning of trouble between the Major and me.

For the next week there was colossal activity. Our men, ordinarily clerks and such, worked like slaves carting sand, filling sand bags, building gun emplacements and learning to be efficient members of lewis gun crews. Only Margaret [a fellow typist] and I were left in the office to carry on as much of the routine work as possible. We were fed on atrocity stories and laughingly devised a scheme of cyanide capsules for women on the death before dishonour principle.

Then on 11 December 1941, an hour before midnight, the stillness of the tropical night was shattered by the high pitched siren of the first air raid warning. It interrupted the revelry of a party at the elegant new Raffles-style Hotel Darwin where soldiers and their girlfriends were drinking. All over town people doused lights and hurried for shelter.

Molly Walsh later reflected on her reaction:

Jim was convinced that it was only a trial blackout but I experienced a curious thrill of anticipation because I thought it could be a real alarm. Jim has been all through the 1914-18 war but after all this was my first taste of this sort of thing and I wanted to get a thrill out of it...Jim was utterly amazed to find on the following day that it had been a genuine alarm and that the hospital patients had been carried down to the beach and some of our friends had spent the night sitting out under trees or in gutters...A nasty shock awaited southern listeners tuning in their shortwave to Germany that morning for Berlin Radio broadcast that Darwin had been wiped off the map. So far as my American friends were concerned Darwin was not yet on the map but Australian listeners would have been startled. In Darwin we could afford to laugh at such a premature announcement.

Molly then penned a prophetic note to her parents. 'After a hectic week here things are settling down a bit and I should think our great danger at present is that we may be lulled into a false security if we don't get a hit of some sort soon. Just one bomb would keep us on our toes.'

EVACUATION

But the male officials had no intention of allowing women and children to share in the waiting game any longer and shortly the administrator, Charles Lydiard Abbott, issued the proclamation demanding their evacuation:

Citizens of Darwin, The Federal War Cabinet has decided that women and children must be compulsorily evacuated from Darwin as soon as possible, except women required for essential services. Arrangements have been completed and the first party will leave within the next forty-eight hours. This party will include sick in hospital, expectant mothers, aged and infirm and women with young children. You have all been issued with printed notices advising you what may be taken and this must be strictly adhered to. Personal effects must not exceed thirty-five pounds. The staff dealing with evacuation is at the Native Affairs Branch in Mitchell Street and will be on duty day and night continuously. The personnel who will make up the first party will be advised during the next few hours and it will be the duty of all citizens to comply at once with the instructions given by responsible authorities...The federal government has made all arrangements for the comfort and welfare of your families in the South. Darwin citizens will greatly assist the war effort by cheerfully carrying out all requests. There will be hardship and sacrifice, but the war situation demands these and I am sure Darwin will set the rest of Australia a magnificent example to follow.

On 15 December 1941 the local school was packed with residents waiting to get the latest information and instructions. 'They were planning to evacuate us overland at first,' recalled Nancy Eddy, who was just recovering from a bout of dengue fever. 'They told all the women to make a calico bag with compartments to hold a plate and cutlery for the trip.'[1]
But the bags were not necessary, as it was decided to evacuate most of the more than 1000 women and 900 children by ship and plane. The bulk of the evacuation took place between mid-December and mid-February and was a mammoth and challenging task for those given responsibility for it. The restriction of only one suitcase per person caused problems and triggered innovations as civilian zone warden Ted D'Ambrosio discovered: 'I remember one lady trying to get away with six hat boxes,' he recalled. 'But the biggest problem was coping with irate husbands who didn't want their wives to go and took it out on us. I had so many bruises by the end of the evacuation it wasn't funny. My own wife went out by plane in early

December, but I had to forcibly shove my way past lines of men who were trying to get away in order to get her a seat.'[2]

A heavily pregnant Christa Roderick went out five days later on a ten-seater plane. She was advised at 7 am that the aircraft would be leaving at 7.30 am the same day. Six weeks after arriving in Perth she gave birth to a son, Marshall, who, forty-seven years later, would become the Territory's chief minister.

Those who left on the *Zealandia* experienced the worst conditions and the troopship well earned the name of 'hell ship'. Jessie Litchfield's daughter-in-law, Gladys Litchfield, was among the 542 women and children who left Darwin Harbour in the *Zealandia* at noon on 20 December 1941, along with 200 troops and 100 crewmen. At Thursday Island they picked up 300 Japanese internees who travelled the rest of the way with them, making conditions on board dangerously over-crowded. Although the commander of the ship reported that food was 'scarce but wholesome' Gladys remembered having only biscuits and water on the journey, except for Christmas, when they were given jelly and ice cream.

Among the other women on board were the first ninety-three Chinese women and children to be evacuated. They were accommodated in hammocks on the deck and were thus more vulnerable in the case of an attack by enemy aircraft. One, Elsie Yuen, was convinced that it was only because of the presence of the Japanese internees on board the ship that enemy planes did not actually drop bombs.[3]

Elsie and her family disembarked in Bowen, Queensland, and then travelled to Longreach, where for much of the war period Elsie supplemented the family income by taking in washing for nearby American troops and making pies to sell outside the town theatre.

Wendy James, only a child at the time of the Darwin evacuation, vividly recalls her mother, Poppy Secrett, refusing to go until the MPs threatened to bodily carry her on board if she did not. She finally went on the *Koolinda*, and when she discovered a room full of boxes she managed to get them put elsewhere and moved herself and three children in. Another *Koolinda* evacuee was Nancy Eddy, who first came to Darwin in 1935.

I had just recovered from a serious bout of the fever. I didn't even know Pearl Harbour had been bombed and my small baby had just contracted the fever as well. I remember my husband, who was a zone warden, coming home on Thursday, December 19 and telling me to pack and be ready to leave in an hour. All I could do was pack baby napkins and a change of clothes for myself, my five year old and my baby. I took the clothes off the line and then realised I had some time before I had to leave so I cooked a leg of lamb I had. All too soon the taxi arrived at our door and we were bundled in and dropped at the wharf. Everywhere there were little groups of women and children and their pathetic thirty-five pound bundles of belongings. The women stood around in unhappy little groups but the small children thought it was a picnic. There were nine people in my cabin and I had to carry my baby in my arms the entire trip as he was so sick with the fever. But I felt especially sorry for the women who had not even seen their husbands before they left—it was very hard on them.

Both Wendy and Nancy remember the tense trip down the Western Australian coast with the ship trying to avoid mines. 'We were told we had air cover for the entire seven day trip but we found out later that wasn't true,' Nancy said.

The women who left on the USS *President Grant* two days before Christmas had a luxurious trip. The cruiser had been attacked when it was in Manila and had received orders to head for the nearest friendly port. The captain chose Darwin, where he was immediately asked to evacuate a group of women and children to Brisbane.

Glad Garton and Kath Finlay were first on board. 'The Americans believed in first come first served and we ended up in the stateroom with a private bath. On Christmas Day we were given a full roast dinner with all the trimmings,' Glad recalled. But she was acutely aware of the seriousness of the trip. Her husband Len had given her a small gun to carry with her at all times. 'I carried it down my brassiere or had it under my pillow. But I was never really sure whether I'd shoot myself or the Japanese if the occasion arose.'

Edna Tambling was one of the few women who had her husband accompanying her, he having been put in charge of the civilians on the *Grant*. 'We were notified at 7 pm that we would leave at eight am the next day,' said Edna. 'I remember we let the chickens out to run loose and then packed a few clothes. The stewards and stewardesses on the ship were tremendous. We had a lot of hospital patients with us and they were wonderful to them. I remember one Greek woman had just given birth that morning and had to get on board with several of her other children in an extremely distressed state.'

Helping to nurse the distressed evacuees was Eileen Fitzer (then Gribbon) a grand-daughter of pioneer Territorians Eliza and Ned Tuckwell, whose story is outlined in the next chapter. A trained nurse, Eileen was accompanying her first husband, Harry Gribbon, who was being sent to Sydney for specialised hospital treatment. 'She was absolutely marvelous; I don't know what we would have done without her,' Edna Tambling said.

Among the last of the women to leave was Audrey Kennon, who worked for Captain Gregory, the pearler, and was responsible for helping take men off the ships and put women on them. As one of the few females around over the Christmas-New Year period, she ended up cooking a Christmas dinner for twelve men. She was finally evacuated by plane just a couple of weeks before the raid.

Another woman who held out until the end was Jessie Litchfield, who had been in the Territory since 1907 and was a press correspondent for many Australian and overseas papers. It was not until they threatened to carry her out in January 1942 that she finally agreed to go. While she accepted that it might be best for pregnant women and those with young children to leave the vulnerable city, she saw no reason why all women should go.

Jessie later reflected on the wisdom of the forced evacuation:

Whether the decision for evacuation was a right or a wrong one is still a debatable question; there is no doubt whatever that the method of such evacuation was crude and cruel in the extreme. Only the barest necessities could be taken by the evacuees; everything else had to be left behind; but no arrangements were ever made for the safe guarding of their possessions. Apparently it was not the business of the Commonwealth Government to protect their own people's belongings, which were left to the looter and the despoiler. The evacuees were crammed into ships with unnecessary haste; in one case, eleven women and children had to share a four berth cabin and that in December, the hottest and worst month of the year. Food on the boats was insufficient, water, whether by accident or design was brackish and almost undrinkable; there was no comfort, no consideration shown to these evacuees, who received less help and less consideration from their own government than did the Japanese men and women who were being interned in the southern states. All of their goods accompanied them to the internment camp. The Australian women and children were the ones who suffered most and were least considered.

Arrived in the southern states, they were left to fend for themselves. Those who had relatives and friends in the south were the fortunate ones, but there were many whose whole lives had been spent in the Territory, and who had known no other home. Their plight was pitiful; can one wonder that some of them gave up the struggle for existence, and simply faded out of life, too sick at heart to carry on any longer?

The last civilian plane left Darwin on 18 February 1942, leaving only about seventy women—engaged in what were considered 'essential' jobs such as postal and hospital work—in the town. A Japanese radio station had already allegedly announced that Japanese forces had landed in Darwin and that a shipload of geisha girls was on the way. Although, as far as we know, this was simply propaganda, the threat of Japanese invasion was very real to most of the residents.

THE BOMBING

Monsoonal rains had been drenching Darwin for days, but on the morning of 19 February 1942, the skies were clear, and when Japanese planes began dropping the first enemy bombs on Australian soil, they could pick and choose their targets. They struck with precision.

They headed straight for the harbour, where they knew a fleet of allied ships was moored, and turned it into a blazing inferno. Minutes later they made a direct hit on the post office, cutting vital communication links with the rest of the world and killing the civilian staff and postal customers, including six women—Freda Stasinowski, Eileen Mullen, Jean Mullen, Emily Young and Alice and Iris Bald. Hurtle Bald, the postmaster, just days earlier had agreed to send the women south and was busy training male telegraphists to take their places. When the bombs struck, the staff had taken shelter in the postmaster's garden, which he believed to be the safest shelter in the area. All were killed instantly when the bombs made a direct hit on the trench in which they sheltered.

Next the enemy planes swarmed in on the RAAF base, crushing allied air resistance. The rest of the city and its people were at their mercy. The hospital ship *Manunda* and the hospital quarters themselves, both with clear Red Cross markings, did not escape the attack. Sister Margaret de Mestre, a *Manunda* staff member from Bellingen, New South Wales, became the first Australian woman to lose her life on Australian shores when she was hit in the back during a raid on the ship. She was twenty-six. Another New South Wales nurse, Sister Lorraine Blow, who had been serving in the Middle East, was seriously injured when flying shrapnel hit her. She spent the following two years in hospital being treated for a fractured spine and perforated abdomen, but she survived and later resumed her nursing career.

Thirty-six hours after the raid the *Manunda* left for Fremantle, carrying 385 wounded. Some were members of the crew, but most were people of all nationalities who had been picked up in the harbour. The medical team worked night and day on the patients, with no let up until all were comfortable. While the doctors worked the nurses gave them sips of hot drinks and put bites of food into their mouths.

The main reason there were so many casualties was that the first bombs were dropping as the air raid sirens began. No one will ever know if the fate of the 243 people who lost their lives that day would have been different had earlier warnings from Bathurst and Melville Island been heeded. For those who survived, many of them Territory residents still, the events of the day are indelibly etched on their memories. Some stories are told in later chapters, but a few brief ones are recorded here.

Lyndall Hadow was typing a letter from her boss asking Melbourne for an extra supply of lighting fuel in case of an emergency due to enemy action. Lyndall had arrived in Darwin to join her husband in 1941 and worked for the land title office until she discovered that only 'essential' women could stay. She offered her services to the OIC of civil aviation. When the bombs began falling she dived into a nearby trench where she sheltered until the planes had gone. She then got up and walked around the civilian area taking photographs, some of which were later published in Melbourne newspapers. With most other women she was forced to evacuate to Melbourne, but within weeks had received permission to return to Katherine as an army typist.

Chrissie Paspalis, married to Greek businessman Michael Paspalis, who would one day be one of the Territory's richest men, was another woman who experienced the bombing at first hand. She and her husband were running Roslyn Court, a boarding-house they had built in Darwin's main street, as well as catering for the Qantas flying boats. The latter was considered an 'essential service' so Chrissie had been allowed to remain in Darwin. When the bombs began to drop, they had only time to lie flat in the gutter of the street outside the boarding-house. The worst part, according to Chrissie, was the fact that the Japanese planes flew so low, sometimes less than thirty feet above the ground, that she could see them machine-gunning the town and the people. Michael and Chrissie managed to negotiate a passage to Sydney with the captain of the Qantas flight the next morning.

Hilda Abbot, the talented first lady of the Territory, was sitting down at her desk to write a cheque for the grocer on the morning of the raid. She was preparing to leave for Alice Springs in two days to help establish the residency there. An accomplished and prolific writer, she later described her own experience in a newspaper feature:

We heard an uncanny thud...we all hurried across the drive and down some steps to below the office. The office and some spare bedrooms were built level with the path but on concrete piles from the slope beneath and here, the Army had agreed, we would be better off than in any of the trenches and safe, except from a direct hit. The hit came at the very moment we were settling to our places...[when] the most deafening, terrifying noise sent us spinning and the whole building came crashing down.

The Russian, Mrs Kampur, and I were blown forward against a vine-covered wire-netting that bulged away from us as every pillar cracked and bent, and then I fell 4 feet[1.2 metres] into a pineapple bed. When I scrambled back I saw my husband emerging from rubble and completely gray with concrete dust. We dragged Elsey from the rubble, but little Daisy, our laundry maid, was nowhere to be seen. I could hear her screaming and Kampur and my husband crawled to where the whole wall had caved in but there was sudden silence and the one little black leg and foot that was visible was still. Poor Daisy was dead.

Hilda and Elsey clung together and lay flat until the raid, which lasted about an hour, was over. They lay helpless and terrified, watching eleven ships slowly sink into Darwin's picturesque harbour.

When we looked out on our so lovely harbour no picture of an inferno could equal what we saw. Black smoke rolled in heavy clouds; flames rose in great tongues to the sky; the water near was covered with black oil. In this water small navy boats were moving, rescuing blackened figures and men were struggling towards our garden where the black water was licking the shore.[4]

Hilda had gone to her room to collect any necessities that may have survived when she and the others were rocked by a gigantic explosion when the *Neptuna*, carrying ammunition and explosives, blew up, scattering debris over the harbour and wharf area. As she prepared to go to the Red Cross headquarters to collect any surviving records and take them to Alice Springs, Hilda was told the news of the lives lost in the post office bombing and reflected sadly that none of the Red Cross aides had been able to get to the posts that the women had spent so many diligent hours preparing in case of such a disaster.

Gwenda Hansen was at her secretarial post in Qantas Airways when the first bomb fell:

We dashed out of our glassfronted office to go to ground [in] the nearest gutter—a very dirty one. We saw a bomb hit the lovely old sandstone post office. During a lull we set out to run there to see if we could help anyone but the planes came over again and we dived flat in the nearest paddock. Several of us from the office lay there for I think about an hour. The planes were so low we could see the rising suns under the wings. As long as I live I shall never forget the awful rat-tat-tat of machine gun fire. As soon as the all clear came we ran to the car and I drove several of our pilots down to the wharf. I shall never forget the sight of men swimming and wading ashore. Some were only half conscious. Most of them, their clothes stripped off by explosions or by themselves to help them to swim, were badly burned...I heard someone call out and saw a man with his arm almost torn off at the shoulder. I know practically nothing about first aid but knew enough to realise that I had to stop the bleeding somehow. I tore up some of my underclothes and made a ligature as best I could. He was almost unconscious and I wondered how on earth I was to get him into the car. A man came along on a bicycle and helped me and I drove the wounded man to the hospital...The nurses were magnificent. When their disorganised day was over they had to set to to evacuate all their patients as we expected more raids the next day. They worked all night to see their charges safely on to the train.

I travelled on the first evacuation trains as far as Katherine. Young nurses, although injured themselves, continually ministered other wounded without thought of themselves. One nurse who had her hip injured when blasted by bombs in a civilian hospital walked among wounded dressing their injuries. The trip of 200 miles [322 km] occupied nearly twenty hours.[5]

Sister Audrey Jaffer, a former Australian Inland Mission nurse from Alice Springs, and Nurse Palfrey were getting ready to help Surgeon Commander Clive James perform an appendix operation in the hospital theatre when they heard the siren and saw the bombs dropping on the harbour. Then the bombs began dropping perilously close to the hospital. The nurses helped get the patients under beds or into shelter of some kind. One nurse held the hand of a dying American soldier throughout the entire bombing raid, giving him comfort and courage in his last moments, without thought of her own safety. Another carried a sick youth from a military hospital under machine-gun fire into the grounds, and remained crouched over him to protect him from bullets.

Within ten minutes of the first bombs dropping, casualties began arriving at the Kahlin hospital, and by the end of the raid the nursing and medical staff were coping with the biggest disaster so far experienced on Australian soil. Most worked for the next forty-eight hours without sleep and in sweltering conditions trying to save and comfort those who had survived. To make matters more difficult, all three hospitals—at Kahlin and Bagot and the new one out of town at Berrimah—had been hit and damaged.

Six RAAF nurses, wearing uniforms treated with khaki dye to help camouflage them in the trenches, were among the staff who witnessed the second raid on the RAAF base at two minutes before midday. One of them later described the attack:

All beds in SSQ were occupied on the day. Patients and staff were all evacuated within ten minutes; the nurses had the best trench in Darwin. One bomb exploded only 10 yards [9 metres] from our trench. We shall never forget the sight that met our eyes. Our home had been strafed, bullet holes were in our uniforms which were hanging in our rooms. When the alarm went again we were ordered to go by truck out bush for two hours and then to the 119th, where we arrived in jeans, tin hats and gas masks.[6]

Perhaps the last white women to leave Darwin were three missionary sisters from Port Keats Mission who had learned of the bombing in a sensational way. They had left their mission station for Darwin late in the afternoon on 18 February and sailed in the mission vessel for nearly two days before reaching Darwin Harbour. As they approached the harbour they found the sea thick and black with oil and they noticed all manner of things floating by them—doors, clothing, pillows, furniture. Then they saw the harbour and realised Darwin had been bombed. The entire wharf was still burning, although the bombs had hit nearly twenty-four hours earlier. One of the sisters observed: 'Poor little Darwin had been taken unawares. For long she had been sleeping lazily in her hot tropical sunshine. Now she was tragically awake and in the grip of great fear. Her blue skies had been darkened with a fleet of bombers which had burst upon her with the swiftness of her own tropic storms.'[7]

After the raids, the administrator had received orders to evacuate all remaining civilian women and children and he organised a special train to get them out, asking his wife Hilda to assist. She drove one group of women in a truck to Adelaide River, where they spent the night running at air raid alarms to a hole in the bank of the river.

'At last we were too exhausted and lay side by side on a tarpaulin under a tree near the house,' she later wrote. 'At 4 am the train arrived and we met up with the twenty-two women who had been kept for essential services, the wounded who were able to be got away, thirty-six Aboriginal children who had been evacuated from Melville Island Mission and arrived in Darwin in time for the bombing, and six Sacred Heart Sisters who were in charge of them.' Along with two long-term Darwin residents, Mrs Annie Herbert and Mrs Roy Edwards, they climbed into a flat tarpaulin-covered truck to begin their southward journey to relative safety. Annie Herbert was the eighty-five-year-old widow of the late Justice Charles Herbert who had served as the Territory's government resident from 1905 to 1910. The Herberts had later purchased Koolpinyah station and Annie had made the Territory her home, staying with her sons who ran the station. Mrs Edwards, better known as 'Ash', a former matron of the Darwin Hospital, had been allowed to stay because her husband owned an aircraft and believed emergency evacuation would be no problem. When the raids were over, and Edwards drove to the civil aerodrome to fly his wife to safety, he found his plane riddled with bullets from Japanese guns.

As the women began their arduous overland journey from Adelaide River, Hilda Abbot recalled that the group of women 'looked out on the grasses and tall straight trees to give us strength of mind and bid us to be brave.' When they arrived at Alice Springs, the mission sisters, along with the Aboriginal children from Melville Island, were sent to Victoria. The children eventually went to a small mission station in South Australia, where they stayed until early 1945, when they were allowed to return to Melville Island.

Margaret Widdup, born in Darwin in 1902, left town just before midnight on 18 February. She had been allowed to stay until then because she had volunteered to be an ambulance driver, but officials finally insisted that she leave. She decided to drive the family vehicle to Alice Springs and stay with her aunt, Isobel Price, whose story is told in Chapter 11. Margaret knew that her husband, a gaoler at Fannie Bay, would eventually end up in Alice Springs, as plans were already under way to transfer prisoners and prison records to the Centre.

However, the army brigadier refused her permission to drive, insisting that the road was flooded and she would never make it. Margaret, who had just returned from an overland trip three weeks earlier, knew this wasn't the case, so she and her husband arranged for a male friend to buy the vehicle and get permission to make the trip with Margaret as a passenger. They loaded the truck onto the back of the train and, when they got to Larrimah unloaded it and headed for Alice. They stopped for the night of 19 February a few miles from the township, unaware of the devastation that had occurred in Darwin just nine hours after they had left.

As the evacuees arrived in Alice Springs, news of loved ones slowly began to filter through; the wait was often very stressful. Among the first to arrive was Margaret Widdup, who had been stranded by floods for three days near Larrimah before being able to continue on to Alice. She was waiting for news of whether her husband and the other men at the jail had survived the bombs when Hilda Abbot's truckload of evacuees arrived. Among the first women she saw was her dear friend Annie Herbert, whom she embraced warmly. It was several weeks before Margaret finally found someone who could tell her that her husband had survived and would arrive in Alice Springs soon to help administer the prison from there.

Hilda Abbot also spent anxious days waiting for news of her husband. 'I did

146

not see or hear from the Administrator for two weeks. There was not any telegraph service, and the only word was from a nursing sister who had seen him at the hospital. She said he was very busy and had taken over the evacuated convent as his headquarters, that many dead were still being washed into our garden beach.'

One of the most remarkable stories of women and war to emerge from the Territory was that of the arduous 3000 mile (5000 kilometre), six-week trek from Croker Island to Sydney made after the bombing by Methodist missionary Margaret Somerville, Miss Jessie March, Sister Olive Peake, Mrs Phil Adams and her then one-week-old baby and ninety-five Aboriginal children from Croker Island. They were first taken from Croker to the mainland on the *Larrpan* and then travelled overland the remainder of the distance, finally reaching Sydney by train, having lost only one life during the perilous journey. Margaret, who was a founder of the Croker Island Mission, later recounted the experience in an intriguing little publication called *They Crossed a Continent*, a small tribute to their courage and fortitude.

After the first two raids on Darwin, the city was evacuated of most civilians and for the next four years it was basically a military town. Although attacked many times, it was never again caught unawares and never again suffered the destruction of 19 February.

Southern headlines were grossly misleading about the number killed in the raids, usually admitting to between fifteen and twenty rather than the more than 240 who in fact lost their lives. One press correspondent did, however, reflect on how Territorians could be expected to respond to the disaster: 'Those very qualities of hardihood, independence and determination in its people which have sometimes made them a centre of conflict should stand them in good stead in this hour of grievous trial.'[8]

WARTIME TERRITORY

The Top End of the Territory became a war zone and only a very few civilians were allowed to remain north of Katherine. One of them was Winnie Sargent, daughter of Harry Sargent, who owned Stapleton Station near Batchelor. Winnie later recorded some of the wartime activity she took part in:

Many [of the evacuees] came to our camp at Stapleton and we fed them and directed them on their way, further toward the inland. Dad and I were still carrying on, slaughtering cattle and supplying the army with beef. The airforce would fly their planes over almost every day and drop orders for beef. The Japs left us alone for awhile, though now and again a reconnaissance plane would fly over for a look-see.

Winnie and her father used to guide and direct units on manoeuvres through the country they knew so well. Because of this, they were granted official free passes to travel anywhere between Katherine and Darwin, a substantial concession, given that most civilians were not allowed north of Larrimah. The Sargents witnessed many bombings and air fights throughout 1942 and 1943. One in particular turned out to be significant to the entire allied forces:

I witnessed the most brilliant bit of fighting I could ever expect to see. One of our Spitfires got above a big Jap bomber; it was like a peewee attacking a hawk. The Jap twisted and turned, then up and down they roared, until they were just specks in the

Principal matron of the army nurses in the Top End for several years was Edith McQuade White, pictured here with Sister Docksey outside her war-time hut. Matron White later wrote a book about her war-time experiences in the Territory, Reminiscences of an Australian Army Nurse.
Northern Territory State Reference Library.

sky; then down they flew again, the Jap bomber howling and roaring, the Spitfire just above him. Then we could hear the rat-tat-tat of machine gun fire as they swept down to tree top level. They sailed right over our camp, still fighting fiercely. Then the Jap bomber turned sharply to the left and crashed. It fell a few chains behind our yard in the paperbark swamps among the logs and rice grass. The Spitfire sailed on.

Dad caught a saddle horse for himself called an old blackboy to accompany him and armed with a rifle each, they rode off to find the Jap bomber. They could not get right up to the plane on horseback so tied the horses to a tree and waded into where the bomber lay in the swamp. Dad counted nine dead Japs at the plane, the pilot having been shot through the heart as well as having other wounds. Dad gathered up all the papers, books, maps, etc that he could find and spread them out on a tarpaulin to dry. There were maps and logbooks and papers galore. In fact he filled two sugar bags with all he was able to collect from the plane. The airforce sent us very warm thanks for the way we helped them out. Some of the air officers said it was the information they were able to gather from the papers which had really turned the tide of the battle.[9]

Sisters Lorna Laffer and Eileen Quinlan were the first nurses to be placed in charge of the Territory's ambulance train, 'Leaping Lena', so called because of its tendency to leap the tracks from time to time. The nurses sometimes found themselves tending to the train as well as the wounded soldiers.
Laffer Collection, Northern Territory State Reference Library.

But Winnie was an exception. The removal of most civilians from the Top End meant that the majority of women who were left were either military or nursing staff. A few were engaged in one of the most interesting jobs of the war — being nurses on the Territory's ambulance train. The train, which became an official war-time hospital in mid 1943, was a converted cattle-truck popularly known as 'Leaping Lena' due to its propensity to jump off the narrow gauge track from time to time.

Two Adelaide women, Lorna Laffer and Sister Eileen Quinlan, were the first nursing sisters to be appointed to the ambulance train run. Years later Lorna wrote about her experiences in a colourful article entitled 'I worked on a Hospital Train'.[10]

Despite the unreliable iron horses which drew her, gasping and grunting on slippery rails, or careering down inclines at what seemed breakneck speed, we grew fond of this rattling contraption, as it swayed its uncertain way from Adelaide River to the

Katherine, evacuating sick soldiers. To these boys, we were as Mother Confessors, the recipients of private secrets and the latest furphies, and the greatest gazers on of photos of wives and children.

Originally, the train comprised four carriages, later increased to seven, and was made up of one car as a kitchen and the others as ward cars. Painted white outside and liberally adorned with red crosses on roof and sides, each one had a storage water tank and latrine. A small burner made water hot, but like the Tilly lamps, was affected by the motion of the train; whilst it greatly improved the kero refrigerator, provided the ice set before the water slopped out of the trays...The couplings didn't always fit and we became quite deft at stepping over the twelve inch gap [between carriages].

The trip to the Katherine where there was a big base hospital, took hours and hours, though it was only a little over 100 miles [160 km] and we made the return journey twice a week....I wonder now if any other woman ever drove that train, or if I was the only one? The permanent way with its undulating rails on the iron sleepers, had previously been used twice a week, and at the time we were on it was feeling the strain of five or six trains a day, carrying guns or butter to the troops.

We never got used to the cars running off the line, and I guarantee that this will strike fear into the heart of even the most intrepid traveller. Getting her back on the line took anything up to twenty-four hours....sometimes we wandered off down the track and in the loneliness of that great waste, removed our uniforms and sat on a boulder for as long as that sun scorched hardness would permit, in such flimsy attire, to say nothing of those little black flies.

We had our times of sadness too. On one trip to Darwin the train—a fair target in the station yard—was hit by bomb fragments and one car was splintered, injuring one young orderly, who later died of his wounds.[11]

The ambulance train operated until late October 1944 with at least six other nursing sisters appointed at various times to carry on the task pioneered by Sisters Quinlan and Laffer. During its sixteen months of service it made 104 trips, covered 23 917 miles (38 500 kilometres) and carried 6050 patients.

The matron in charge of the 119th Australian General Hospital, which in fact covered several different locations in the far north area, was Edith McQuade White who had been serving in the Northern Territory Medical Service since 1937. She later praised the nurses for their untiring efforts in caring for the wounded in the immediate aftermath of the two raids. Matron White was particularly proud of having rendered first aid to the American airman who shot down the first Japanese plane in Australia. He was the only one of the Kittyhawk pilots to survive.

Matron White later described the scene that met the nurses when they went to the aid of the *Manunda* staff:

Loading of the wounded was most difficult and was carried out with great dexterity on the part of the officers and members of the crew...The wharf was still burning on the afternoon of the 20th February and as I waited with four Sisters from the 119th A.G.H. who had volunteered to help the staff of the *Manunda* nurses, the whole scene was one of devastation; bodies were washed up on the beaches. Men were collecting the dead and placing them on barges for burial at sea. It was very sad to see so many ships smouldering.[12]

The stationary hospitals were also scenes of intense activity during the war. In March 1941, after a patient was killed while sheltering under a hospital bed in Darwin, the authorities moved most of Matron White's hospital units at Kahlin, Bagot and Berrimah to Adelaide River. Tents were set up on the south side of the river and were soon accommodating up to 600 patients. Furniture and appliances belonging to the Adelaide River hotel were handed over to Matron White by the hotel's proprietress, Eileen Gribbon (later Fitzer), who had been given permission to return to the area for a month in order to settle the hotel business matters. Eventually tin huts replaced the tents, and a recreation hut was built, as well as a separate mess for the sisters. Matron White served with the 119th AGH until May 1943.

She paid tribute not only to her nursing staff but also to the members of the Territory Country Women's Association, especially those at Tennant Creek. These women had converted a small rest centre into a canteen to help feed the troops and the civilian road crews who travelled daily between Alice Springs and the far north. Many days they fed up to 300 military personnel and seventy-five drivers, baking 2000 scones, and brewing tea in four kerosene tins at a time. Of their efforts Matron White later wrote:

It is truly amazing that such a small band of women, never more than a dozen, and often less, should have been able to maintain such a sustained effort over the long period of their activities. It was their claim that they were able to feed approximately 100 men for one pound.[13]

Red Cross workers, both civilian and military, were amongst the most appreciated group of women in the Territory during the war. Hilda Abbott had re-opened the Darwin Red Cross in 1937, but when evacuation was ordered the decision was made to disband the Darwin group and transfer the records to Alice Springs. No single Red Cross unit anywhere in the world covered such a vast area as was allotted to the Northern Territory Field Force.

They had set up a depot at Alice Springs just before the first raids, and for days after the raids hundreds of evacuees passed through the town. In one day, there arrived fifty-two women, eighty-nine children of all sorts and sizes and seventy-seven aged males. Red Cross members put a box of comforts in every train going south. Three Red Cross women went through every carriage, took telegrams and messages from evacuees, and sent them on. On the small overland convoys they handed out cigarettes to the evacuees.[14]

As the war progressed Red Cross women did the mending and laundry for hospitals, kept the books in order, visited the wounded soldiers, donated vegetables and other produce, and raised funds. They made jam from fruit in their own orchards, sold it to their neighbours and gave the proceeds to the society. They sewed garments for sending abroad and their work was said to be among the neatest and best tailored that ever left Australia. One of their most important services was to supply first aid medical chests to all outback stations. Some 150 of these were distributed throughout the 1 350 000 square kilometres of the Territory, thus laying the foundations for a valuable post-war service.

When some of the station women were allowed to return to their homes they continued to work for the Red Cross. They took fruit, vegetables and cake to the camp hospitals. Women at some stations, such as at Elsey and Tipperary, kept open house for tired nursing sisters in need of some rest and relaxation. Many station owners also lent horses so that race meetings could be held in aid of the Prisoner of War Fund. After one of these meetings the Red Cross was presented with a cheque for over 2000 pounds from the people of the outback.

The workers at a Red Cross centre set up at the Adelaide River Hospital faced one of their biggest tasks when hundreds of women and children refugees from Timor arrived after being evacuated from their homes following Japanese attacks. Language difficulties slowed up the tedious process of recording particulars and weary children became truculent, but Red Cross sweets worked wonders. 'The Portuguese had been kind to Australian soldiers and everyone at the hospital wished to reciprocate as far as possible,' a Red Cross officer wrote.

Most nurses who served in the Top End during the war were attached to the military, the most prominent unit being the Australian Women's Army Service (AWAS). The AWAS women who were posted to the Territory had to comply with very particular conditions: they had to be either volunteers, spinsters, widows, divorcees, wives of POWs or wives of missing members of Defence Forces; they had to be without dependants under sixteen years of age; and they had to be over the age of twenty-one.

Despite all these stipulations, however, there were still problems — often due to the overabundance of men. The male service personnel in the Northern Territory outnumbered the female personnel by approximately 700 to one. One official AWAS report noted that:

Many male members had had no contact with women for up to two years, and this, in itself was a problem. Mixed entertainments were numerous with the result that the AWAS were inundated with invitations—sometimes two and three a night. The effect of this was to throw some members off their balance—particularly the younger members who gained a "swollen head" complex, and became difficult to handle. Women best suited to combat this were those at least twenty four years of age or over who were mentally and morally sound. Highly strung women were useless, and usually became more highly strung under such conditions. They must also be well disciplined, as rules and regulations have to be many and strictly adhered to.[15]

After the bombing raids on the Top End ceased in November 1943, some AWAS women were gradually moved to Darwin. Although regulations were still strict, the women were actually encouraged to invite male friends to dances at the AWAS barracks and as visitors in the evening. The men were entertained in or near the recreation hut. All units and barracks were out of bounds to all males except those on duty and visitors who had been 'properly invited'. AWAS members could attend dances at the sergeant's and officers' messes, if such invitations were issued by the commanding officer of AWAS Barracks. They were also allowed in mixed parties to the pictures and to picnics if there were two AWAS women or more in the party.

Marriage was allowed, but living together as man and wife for more than a week was not tolerated. The bridal couple could spend seven days at a specially built 'honeymoon cottage' next to the Red Cross Recreation Centre and then the bride was

*These nurses, being transported in style to their wards, were among the many
stationed with hospital units in the Top End during the Second World War.
Although they were heard to complain of the heat, the flies, the mosquitoes, the
'fever', the 'build-up', and the army regulations, when it came time for them to
leave the Territory, many found they had developed an affection for the place
that would remain with them for the rest of their lives.*
Laffer Collection, Northern Territory State Reference Library.

posted south. Some were sent south for other reasons, including being under twenty-
one, being emotionally unstable, being medically unfit for the Northern Territory,
being unsuited to their posting, and for disciplinary reasons. Officials also reported
that:

women who were too old and settled in their general attitude were a problem as they
could not readily readjust themselves to the different life. They became, quite often,
full of complaints, annoying to their companions and to people working with them
and sometimes nervous cases.

Another group of women attached to the AWAS were those associated with
the Young Women's Christian Association. There were two YWCA representatives
attached to the AWAS Territory force, one in Alice and one in Adelaide River, later
in Darwin. They arranged picnics and trips and encouraged and helped soldiers and
staff with handicrafts, helping to relieve both tension and boredom. All recreation
rooms were mainly furnished by the YWCA. In northern areas, the YWCA supplied

all members of the AWAS with a canvas chair which they took to pictures, and concerts, as permanent seating was not available.

Although church attendance was not particularly good in the Territory during the war years, the AWAS did produce a nativity play in 1945 called 'The Cradle King' which ran for two consecutive nights in Winnellie Camp with approximately 1800 male soldiers attending.

Aboriginal women played a significant, though often not terribly glamorous, role in war-torn Darwin — as they did throughout the Territory, particularly on stations. In Darwin they were housed at nearby Aboriginal compounds and were transported to the AWAS barracks daily from 9 am to 4.30 pm. They were paid five shillings per week, and given rations by the army. According to AWAS reports, their main work consisted of cleaning ablutions blocks, cleaning officers' quarters, ironing officers' outer garments and keeping the barracks areas tidy. Aboriginal women were also employed in gardening and other maintenance tasks and they served as hospital orderlies and personal maids to the matrons. The Army provided food, housing and clothing for the dependants of all Aboriginal men and women it employed, with the result that many thousands of Aboriginal people had contact with the military during the war. This undoubtedly changed the perceptions of both groups about each other.

Many Territory women and girls of mixed Aboriginal descent were sent south, including those who had been living at the 'half-caste' home in Alice Springs. Many went to Balaclava, a small country community out of Adelaide, where the government established a school under the charge of a former Pine Creek teacher. Most lived in uncomfortable and makeshift accommodation at the racecourse, although some managed to get enough money together from child endowments and support benefits to find independent residence elsewhere. Although many were anxious for the war to end so they could receive permission to return to the Territory, others found the move out of the Territory a freeing experience, and when they did return to their Territory homes, some joined in the reform movements that emerged to gain greater rights for their people.

While the Top End of the Territory had seen the only active military engagement during the war, the Centre had played its role in the war effort as well and Alice Springs in particular took on a new significance. The administration had moved there following the bombing of Darwin, the Abbotts moved into the residency there and the town soon became a giant service centre for the 'camp cities' that sprang up, populated at one time by up to 7000 people. Most troops were located in the immediate vicinity of Alice and permits were needed to cross certain sections of town and some pastoral properties.

One woman who had a great deal to do with the military during the war was the stunningly attractive and spirited Mona Minahan. 'Everyone swarmed to Alice Springs after Darwin was bombed,' she recalled. 'Some of the Chinese who arrived had bolts of fabric and white shirts which I bought up and sold in my shop.' Mona ran a drapery shop and general store during the war period and, partly because of her special relationship with the fiery local army commander Colonel Noel Loutit, did a roaring trade. She became part of a local controversy when Abbott, who resented Loutit's military authority and his use of it to interfere in civilian issues, produced evidence that Loutit was obtaining civilian liquor supplies through Mona's shop and using them to supplement his own stocks. Nevertheless Loutit remained until the end of 1944 and Mona continued to run a profitable shop.

One of the issues over which Loutit ran foul of the locals and Abbott was his refusing or delaying permission for some married government and army officers to bring their wives to Alice. While most still managed to get their wives to the Centre, the army had a controversy over one of its married officers that made headlines around the country. A local girl, Beryl Gregory, had married an army transport officer, Captain G.D. Duncan in Melbourne in 1943, and when he was posted back to Alice Springs a few weeks later Beryl defied army regulations and joined him there, intending to stay with her family if problems arose. She was arrested and sent to Adelaide, where the case immediately hit the headlines. Encouraged by public sympathy, the Duncans took the case to the High Court, where the judge harshly criticised the army's actions.

Despite this, there were at least four weddings and several engagements between army hospital nursing sisters and servicemen stationed in Alice Springs between 1942 and 1944. They all followed a similar format, with the receptions held at the former AIM hostel, which had been converted into quarters for the AANS during the war, and the honeymoons spent at nearby Undoolya station managed by the pioneer Hayes family.

WAR'S END

As the war drew to a close, one of the main activities for the Red Cross workers in Darwin was to meet the ships with baskets full of sweets and cigarettes. They would also meet all arriving planes and see off all planes departing, often in the early hours of the morning. Among the first recovered personnel met were the sisters and civilians flown by Liberator from Manila. These women had been taken prisoner at Rabaul and interned in Japan.

In September 1945 came the great influx of released prisoners of war and civilian internees from the Far East, and, as Darwin was used as a staging centre, the work of the women who were serving as hospital visitors increased tremendously. A reception centre was established at Winnellie where Army and Red Cross women were on hand at all hours to meet the incoming returned prisoners and military personnel.

Although the centre provided two billiard tables and other games, what most of the visitors wanted was someone to talk to, someone to listen. Red Cross women were particularly encouraged to allow prisoners of war to talk to them and get things off their chests. One Red Cross girl wrote:

The day is spent in dusting and tidying up, preparing iced drinks, bournvita, coffee and interminable pots of tea—the nicest the boys have tasted in four years. We prepare and alter their clothes, handle trunk calls for them and contact relatives and friends in Darwin anxious to see them. Hampers are despatched and hundreds of sandwiches...the rest of the time we devote to chatting to the boys, who are all anxious for a good listener. Their experiences are incredible, and one never tires of hearing about them and inspecting the various souvenirs they have brought back with them. They have become very tolerant. Their main worries seem to be matrimonial and the emotion of greeting their people. Any small problem had magnified itself during their years of imprisonment. Nearly every man who has passed through here has experienced the relief of letting off steam about his experiences.

As hostilities ceased the women, too, looked forward to returning to their homes, though some left with regret. As nursing sister Grace Trott (Fordham) has written: 'For two and a half years...Even as frustrations grew and everyone felt he or she had been forgotten by the Powers that be, the Northern Territory was weaving a spell over all. Now, as we look back across the years we all know that we left a little of ourselves behind.'

Some who had served in the Territory during the war received due recognition for their contribution. Matron Clare Shumack of the *Manunda* was awarded the Royal Red Cross medal for her courage and bravery during the bombing of that ship, in which one of the sisters in her charge was killed and Matron Dutton was given a citation for 'her increasing devotion to duty under the most trying active service conditions outstanding'. The citation stated that:

Her energy, powers of organisation have been mainly responsible for smooth operation of the unit and her efficiency, example and tireless efforts have been an inspiration to the Hospital staff. Under primitive conditions and in an area which have been subjected to many enemy bombing raids she have worked unceasingly for the comfort of the sick and wounded and her unselfishness and cheerful personality have had a splendid effect on patients and staff alike.

But there was another group of women who deserved medals for their war-time experiences —those who had been forced to leave their homes and live as refugees elsewhere. Many of these women and the men were determined to return and rebuild their homes and their lives. With the war finally over, Darwin residents were gradually given permission to return to their war-torn home, though for many months permits were required. When the expatriate Darwinians began to straggle home, what they found was mass destruction, their homes often destroyed and the government threatening to compulsorily acquire them. Jessie Litchfield, a prolific collector, found she had lost countless books of press-cuttings, autographed copies of books and much of her various other collections. The material had been destroyed not by enemy bombs but by post-bomb looting. It was a common experience.

As she and the other women began rebuilding their city and their lives, they needed the same pioneering spirit that the women who had helped open the land had displayed. Some of their stories are told in the final chapter of this book.

PART TWO

PIONEERING PROFILES

Eliza's daughter, Eliza Sarah Tuckwell - a photograph probably taken during the 1880s when she was working as housemaid for Victor Voules Brown. Eliza and Victor were later married and had eleven children of their own, the last born in 1910, several months after Victor died. Eliza died in 1925 in a tragic buggy accident with her good friend Lilly Byers, daughter of another Territory pioneer, Susannah Mansfield. Photograph courtesy of Jenny Rich, a descendant of the Brown family.

Chapter 8

Eliza Tuckwell

SERVANT GIRL FROM LONDON TOWN
AND OTHER URBAN MATRIARCHS

'It is not so much heroism on a large scale that is wanted, but bravery in small things, courage to take reverses cheerfully and to look onto a successful future while battling with the hardships of the present...Those who are not prepared for a struggle need not come to the Northern Territory.'
Elsie Masson, Untamed Territory

It was probably no accident that pioneer Territorian Eliza Tuckwell named the boarding-house she opened in Darwin in 1882 'Resolution Villa'. Throughout her life she needed all the resolve she could muster. Her working-class life is a study of what pioneering Australia's far north urban Territory was all about, as are the lives of women of other races and cultures who chose to remain in the Territory and raise families who also made the Territory home. Their descendants form the multicultural mix which is at the core of Territory urban life today. Although there are now many urban centres in the Territory reflecting that cosmopolitan community spirit, during the period of South Australian control there was really only one substantial town—Port Darwin. With the exception of Pine Creek, the other population centres which now flourish, such as Alice Springs, Katherine and Tennant Creek, were then only overland telegraph centres, where usually the only resident women were the wives and daughters of the station master and policeman. Some of their stories are told elsewhere in this book. But for a cross-section picture of urban pioneering in the Territory one would be hard pressed to start with a better example than Eliza Tuckwell.

She was born Eliza Sarah Hemmings in 1836, within the sound of London's Bow Bells and at the time Colonel William Light was laying out Adelaide. She had to learn to fend for herself at an early age. Her father was a soldier who died early in Eliza's life, leaving his wife with a young family. Eliza was sent to live with her aunt, who struggled as best she could to raise her, but times were lean and as soon as she was old enough Eliza had to earn her own living. She found work as a domestic servant, but, like many young English girls of the time, she wanted to improve both her employment and marriage prospects.

England at the time had a surplus of single women, while Australia was suffering from the opposite problem. South Australia, under Edward Wakefield's colonisation scheme, was looking for both single and married women to emigrate to the new colony so that there would be an equal representation of the sexes there, unlike the mother colony of New South Wales. Moreover, the planners were looking for women of good character and child-bearing age who could serve a utilitarian role in the new colony, which they promoted as being 'socially superior' and full of opportunity. Eliza seemed an ideal candidate. She later wrote: 'I seen in the paper that the Government was going to charter a vessel to Australia and they wanted young women to go as servants. It was an immigrant ship so I applied for a berth and was accepted. The name of the ship was the *Norman*, bound for Adelaide, South Australia.'[1]

In December 1854, Eliza and 224 other immigrants sailed from Southampton for a new life in Australia. She was one of fifty-five single women, most of whom were servants, who were regarded by the ship's surgeon, Thomas Alexander, as 'generally well behaved' although some did have cause to complain about the captain who was accused of 'gross familiarities towards some of the unprotected females'.[2] Whether Eliza was one of them history does not record. She claimed they had 'a very good voyage and enjoyed it very much'.

After a four-month voyage, the immigrants were both relieved and excited when they finally reached Port Adelaide in March 1855. As was the custom, crowds of Adelaide 'ladies' were waiting at the dock to come on board and choose servants who pleased them.

'Of course they did not engage all of us,' Eliza later recorded. 'Some of us had to go to the depot in Adelaide until they got places and I was one of them. We were at the depot for three days when three of us were engaged to go to St Peters College. Two laundry maids and one housemaid. Our wages were ten shillings a week. We thought it was great wages but it didn't last long. We all left and the next place I only got five shillings a week. There were so many immigrants coming out.' This last remark is substantiated by the records, which show that Eliza was one of 3481 female domestic servants who arrived in South Australia during 1855.

Eliza soon found a job at a coach builder's in Franklin Street and then at the flour mills in Hindmarsh, both jobs earning her seven shillings a week. About this period of her life Eliza later said: 'I was not married then and a very good job I was not, as I had no end of trouble.' It thus probably came as some relief to her when she met Ned Tuckwell who was then a foreman in the government workshops at the Bowden railway sheds. Soon the couple began courting and, as Ned's sweetheart, Eliza was invited to take a free ride on the first train that ran in Adelaide in 1856, an event she recalled with pride in later life.

In February 1857, just after Eliza turned twenty-one, she married twenty-seven-year-old Ned and settled down to respectable family life, giving birth to her first child, Mary Ann, in November of that year. Mary Ann was followed by Edward in 1860, George in 1863, Caroline in 1865, and Eliza Sarah in 1867. Caroline was the only one not to reach adulthood.

Eliza soon found that the main responsibility for raising the family was left to her while her husband pursued work, developing the links which would ensure the family's place in Territory history. In 1864, a year after South Australia had gained control of the Northern Territory, he left a heavily pregnant Eliza at home and joined the second expedition to Escape Cliffs, the site chosen by Boyle Travers Finniss to be the capital of the north. A carpenter and shipwright by trade, Ned's skills played a crucial role at the ill-fated temporary settlement.

He arrived there early in December and served under Finniss until the following December when Finniss was recalled to Adelaide to answer allegations

Eliza Tuckwell (seated third from right) was a stalwart of the Methodist church, living only a few doors from the manse. She is pictured here at a church picnic with a group of other Darwinites including her daughter Eliza Sarah (fourth from the right) and Charlotte Witherden (standing, third from right), who was a leading figure in Top End charity and Red Cross work, later receiving an OBE, the first to be awarded in the Territory.
Northern Territory State Reference Library.

about his mismanagement in choosing Escape Cliffs as the settlement site. Tuckwell then joined John McKinley, who had been sent to the Cliffs to assess the situation and explore the country overland. Ned accompanied him on an exploring expedition which, contrary to advice, he undertook in the middle of the rainy season. The party was well equipped, with about forty horses, but as they approached the Alligator River, floods forced them to stop. Having exhausted their stock of provisions, they were compelled to eat their horses. They escaped by constructing a boat with the horses' hides, in which they floated down the Alligator River and around to Escape Cliffs, a few miles from the mouth of the Adelaide River. Ned helped build the boat and navigated the frail craft on its perilous journey. It was later acknowledged that the escape of the party was due in a great measure to his seamanship.

Ned remained at Escape Cliffs until that settlement was abandoned, returning to Adelaide in February 1867. Eliza immediately became pregnant and in November gave birth to Eliza Sarah, who was destined to become part of another of the Northern

Territory's most well-known and enterprising families.

The lure of the north and the need for a steady job to support his expanding family soon found Ned heading for the Northern Territory once more, this time for good. In December 1868 he joined Surveyor General George Goyder's *Moonta* expedition to Port Darwin as ship's carpenter. For the next year he became part of the energetic group of men who surveyed the township of Palmerston and the surrounding area. When the job was finished, Goyder packed up the equipment and headed back to Adelaide. He left behind a core group, including Ned Tuckwell, to hold the fort until the first settlers began to arrive.

Eliza had made up her mind to be one of them. She organised passage for the family on the *Kohinoor*, which left Adelaide in December 1869 and arrived in Port Darwin in January 1870 at the height of the wet season. It was the first ship to bring civilian passengers to the northern capital. Also on board were Dr John Stokes Millner, the acting government resident; Paul Foelsche, the inspector of police; Escape Cliffs veterans Mary Packard and her family; James and Ann Devine and their child; Eliza Edwards, wife of one of Goyder's chainmen, and her three children; Emily Hayball, wife of a teamster, and her two children; Mrs Charles Fry, wife of another teamster, and her three children; and a Mr and Mrs Spencer, with one child.[3]

The voyage up was less than pleasant—Eliza later described the ship as 'very bad, only fit for cattle'—but when they rounded the heads and gazed on Fort Hill and the beautiful port of Darwin, the discomfort was forgotten and anticipation of the new life they were about to begin became paramount. Eliza later recalled that day:

The morning we arrived in Darwin was very nice and we dressed our children to meet their fathers in the afternoon but on coming into the harbour we ran into a sand bank so that delayed us for some hours to get her off and when she got off the sight was to see the *Gulnare* in the harbour, so you may be sure we were pleased. Crowds came aboard. No women were expected. There were several log huts built for the men, so they turned out and let the women have them. They had to put up tents for themselves. Next day our luggage had to be landed. There was no jetties, only the beach, so we had to settle down in the huts. We had very little room you may guess, there were five huts built on the piece of land opposite the doctor's house at the camp...We got on alright. We had to make our fires under the hill and all the women of the working class took in washing from the men who were going away and we made a good bit of money.

Isolation was part and parcel of living in the north. News and rations were dependent on the spasmodic arrival of ships sent from Adelaide. The small population was delighted when the *Bengal* arrived several weeks after the *Kohinoor's* departure. Eliza recalled that when the government resident Bloomfield Douglas and his family arrived with renewed rations 'the men were all tight that night'. With more residents and government officials arriving, the men of the camp began to build huts along the foreshore, known as Fort Hill Camp for many years. When Mr J. A. G. Little, who was in charge of the overland telegraph station, arrived with his staff, some of whom brought their families, Port Darwin began bustling with the activity of servicing the men who were sent to build the vital telegraph link.

Ned Tuckwell, who had been put in charge of boatbuilding and repairs, was one of those who found extra work for a while on the overland telegraph construction

Second-generation Territorian Eileen Styles (later Fitzer) prepares to travel 'down the track' on one of her many adventures in the Territory. Photograph courtesy of Eileen Fitzer, reproduction Gavin Perry.

Left:
Myrtle and Eileen Styles, second-generation Territorians of the pioneering Tuckwell family, dressed up at Brock's Creek in the early part of the twentieth century when their father was manager for the Zapopan mine near Pine Creek. Photograph courtesy of Eileen Fitzer, reproduction Gavin Perry.

'The camp' at Darwin's Fort Hill was home to Eliza Tuckwell and her family in their first few years in Darwin. Here Ned Tuckwell is pictured by the boatshed not far from the log hut that was the family home. The Tuckwells later moved to a more permanent site 'up the hill' in Mitchell Street.
Northern Territory State Reference Library.

parties. Along with his great mate Jerry Ryan, he kept early overlanders amused for hours telling tales of their days at Escape Cliffs. With his other great friend, stonemason Ned Ryan, he helped build the first government residency, a large log hut with a canvas roof. They earned two guineas a week for a six-day week. When the timber dwelling proved too small and too delicious for the white ants, they built a new one-roomed stone residency, around which the present government house is built. Eliza, now in her forties, was still expanding the family. First came a son, Charles Palmerston, born in September 1871, followed in April 1873 by Eleanor.

In August 1874, Ned and Eliza's first-born child, sixteen-year-old Mary Ann, married John Arnold, the son of a Scottish publican. He was a storekeeper at Southport, the nearby starting point for the Pine Creek goldfields, then in the middle of a rush. They were married in the Tuckwell's Palmerston home, and soon began raising their own family.

Ned, who by now was advertising his carpentry business in the newly launched *Northern Territory Times* , was joined in the business by his son Ted, and together they helped build many of Darwin's early establishments. When Ned occasionally indulged himself and drank away some of the family income, Eliza displayed a strength of character and stoic determination which helped her cope with many adversities throughout her life. In 1874 she took out a newspaper advertisement stating: 'I will not be responsible for my husband's debts.'

Whether Ned was influenced by this threat or whether he had come to respect Eliza's better business judgement is not known, but in 1875 when he took a job in Yam Creek, a mining community near Pine Creek, he gave her his power of attorney. He also built her a bigger house. Using those same innovative skills which had helped save the lives of the men at Escape Cliffs, Ned turned the remains of one of Darwin's first hotels, the Commercial, into a home that would serve the family for many years.[4]

In 1876 formal religion arrived at Port Darwin in the form of the Reverend Archibald Bogle and his wife, Hilda. Troubled about her soul, and that of her sometime errant husband, Eliza sought Reverend Bogle's help. He launched a campaign to get the community's drinkers, including Ned, to sign a no-drink pledge. But the signatories found their thirsty habits hard to overcome, as Eliza vividly described:

There were several boats arrived...with passengers and cattle and yes you may be sure that they brought plenty of bottled stuff. They got sale for this as this was a dreadful place at the time. The foolish men drank themselves blind. I have seen them have to walk on crutches. One also went blind and I am sorry to say some of the so-called ladies were as bad as the men. I could mention their names but it would not do.

Eliza also recorded that in Palmerston's early years there were 'several public houses...and plenty of sly grog shops round about.'

Bogle, Darwin's first Wesleyan minister, was a keen observer of the Territory's intemperate habits and his earnestly kept diary records that Ned Tuckwell was often in his prayers. He was particularly dismayed at the scenes he witnessed in March 1876 after he had given a sermon about the evils and perils of over-indulgence: 'At Bennetts' as usual noise and uproar for over three hours up to 11 o'clock. Ned Tuckwell and others were using profane and disgusting language plainly to be heard on our verandah.'[5]

Nine months later he wrote: 'Mrs Tuckwell sent over for me to come and see her. I went, found her ill with fever and in trouble about her soul. I read, prayed and spoke.'[6] His counselling was rewarded. Eliza became a stalwart of the Wesleyan church and for the rest of her life she was an active helper in many charity bazaars, picnics and other socials which raised money for needy causes and church equipment.

Eliza clearly worried about the effects of the Territory lifestyle on her daughters and in 1881, when a male resident used abusive language and repeatedly swore at them saying that their 'paternal parent might go to hell and he didn't care a damn', Eliza made sure the matter went before the courts, where the offender was fined and cautioned.[7]

Despite his problems with over-indulgence, it is clear that Ned was held in high regard. When he died suddenly in April 1882, the *Northern Territory Times* wrote:

Mr Edward Tuckwell, one of our oldest residents, has passed from amongst us very suddenly at the comparatively early age of fifty-two. Probably no man met with more vicissitudes, more ups and downs, than our deceased friend during his life in the Northern Territory. For some years he has been employed as overseer in the Government workshops and many are the buildings in and around Palmerston on which Mr Tuckwell was employed. Probably no European knew so well how to manage the Chinese workmen as he did, and as a proof he was no hard taskmaster, all the workmen asked for leave to attend his funeral...His remains were followed to the cemetery by nearly the whole of the residents of Port Darwin...By his death the Government have lost a good honest, and faithful servant and one whom they will find it difficult to replace.

Ned's death meant that Eliza had to find another income and she decided to open a boarding-house which she called Resolution Villa. An advertisement she placed in the *Northern Territory Times* in June 1883 stating she had 'sleeping accommodation for four steady respectable young men' left little doubt about the type of people she would accept. On Ned's death, the family property was transferred to Eliza and she became one of the first resident women ratepayers in Palmerston. Known as the 'Sarah Gamp' of Darwin, Eliza supplemented her boarding-house income by acting as midwife and nurse to the Palmerston community. She delivered many of the Territory's early babies, including most of her own grandchildren, some of whom had tragic fates.

Between 1879 and 1881 her eldest daughter Mary Ann lost all of her three children, as well as her husband, who died of consumption. Almost five years later to the day, she gave birth to a son, Claude Arnold, who survived. His father was Heydn Pelham, a Palmerston engineer whose family the Tuckwells had known in Adelaide. When Mary Ann, who had been sick for several years, finally died of consumption two years later, Eliza took charge of her young grandson, who would become the main beneficiary of her will. Three years later Eliza also lost her second son, George, who had set up a blacksmith shop at the rear of her boarding-house. He died in January 1891 after a long illness.

The only daughter to outlive Eliza was her namesake, Eliza Sarah, although she caused her some moments of anxiety, such as when, at the age of fifteen, she had a near-fatal accident while using kerosene to light the fire for her mother's stove. Some of the fuel had spilt on the sleeves and skirt of her dress and ignited with a spark from the fire, setting her clothes ablaze. One of her arms and her neck were badly burnt and it was some time before she was fully recovered. A short time after the accident, Eliza Sarah became housemaid to a prominent Darwin businessman, the recently widowed Victor Voules Brown. His first wife, Julia Solomon, had died giving birth to their sixth child, who also died. The five remaining children had been taken to relatives in Adelaide and Victor had returned to Darwin to carry on his auction-eering, mining and shipping agency, in the stone building still known as Brown's Mart.

Eliza, who was twenty-seven years younger than Victor, was only sixteen when she had their first child, Adelaide Victoria, in 1884. Between then and 1901 she had six more children. Although obviously devoted to each other, Victor and Eliza did not marry until 1901 when the Bishop of Carpentaria, Gilbert White, visited the Territory. Following the marriage, Eliza and Victor's earlier children were 'regis-tered' through the authority of the Legitimisation Act of 1898. This situation occurred in several Territory families, particularly between couples who lived in isolated situations and had no way of solemnising a marriage until they visited town or were visited by someone who had the authority to conduct such ceremonies.

Eliza's youngest and only Territory-born daughter, Eleanor, married a handsome railway ganger from Queensland in 1893. He was Tom Styles, whose gregarious nature and somewhat nomadic lifestyle did not always meet with Eliza's approval. Over the next ten years, Tom and Eleanor had nine children, only five of whom lived beyond infancy. Tom's work, which ranged from railway repairs to mines inspections, took the family to many of the more remote regions of the Top End, including Pine Creek and Brock's Creek, where they were living when the cyclone of 1897 devastated Darwin. The wild storm lashed the community throughout the night and by morning most homes and buildings had been destroyed, including Eliza's, which had been totally flattened. Although Eliza complained that 'the Chinese carpenters rose the wages to a pound a day', she was grateful to be one of the recipients of subscription money raised by people around Australia for the cyclone victims, particularly by the many ex-Territorians who had returned to South Australia.

Although Eliza did not have to endure any more serious cyclones, her suffering was far from over. Early in 1910 she lost her son-in-law, Victor, who died very suddenly. A few weeks later her daughter Eleanor died of cancer. This left Eliza with only three surviving children—her daughter, Eliza, who soon gave birth to her ninth child, Victor Voules, named after his late father; her youngest son, Charlie, who had spent much of the past twenty-five years in Western Australia; and her eldest son, Edward, who had moved to Sydney in the 1880s, the only one of her children to leave the Territory permanently.

In 1912 Eliza decided to take her first trip south since arriving in the Territory in 1870, to visit him. He had married Mary Jane Wright in Campsie in 1885 and they had several children, none of whom Eliza had seen. Her grandson Claude Arnold helped organise the trip, first trying to get the Territory's new administrator, John Gilruth, to pay her passage. But Gilruth believed a public subscription would be a better idea and offered to assist. The subscription was raised for a one-way fare to Sydney and she sailed on the *Eastern* in November 1912. But she still needed her passage back to the Territory and the *Northern Territory Times* pleaded her case the day she left, paying tribute to Eliza's pioneering spirit and revealing an interesting mixture of patriotic and parochial views:

Mrs Tuckwell's husband died in the NT many years ago, leaving her to face the world with a young family...During the whole of this long period (43 years) she has never once been away for a change of scene and yet at the present moment is perhaps as healthy and sturdy looking an old lady for her years as could be found in any part of the Commonwealth. This is something of a record and is calculated to raise doubts respecting the absolute correctness of the theory that white women cannot live continuously in this climate and retain normal health. Add to the above that Mrs Tuckwell has reared a fairly large family here and has quite a flock of sturdy Northern Territory-born grandchildren and it will be seen that she is a good example of the type of hardy pioneer that is essential to the settlement and progress of every new country. The old lady is now on her way to Sydney to spend a few months with her eldest son upon whom she has not set eyes for over thirty years. She does not propose to winter

All the daughters of Eleanor and Tom Styles were talented musicians and entertainers and always entered into the spirit of Territory social life. Here Eileen Styles (later Fitzer) poses as Fatty Carmichael, for which costume she won a May Day prize. The Styleses were great friends with the family of union leader Harold Nelson, and Eileen drove a sulky all over Darwin campaigning for him when he successfully stood for federal parliament in 1922.
Photograph courtesy of Eileen Fitzer, reproduction Gavin Perry.

south fearing she could not stand the cold after all these years in the tropic north. Mrs Tuckwell has been a toiler from the day she landed here, under all the disadvantages and discomforts so prevalent in the earlier days of settlement and has often been hard put to make both ends meet. The Territory requires many settlers of the type of Mrs Tuckwell if it is to progress.

In any case...Mrs Tuckwell is a woman who has successfully battled for existence in this Territory for forty-three years and we think it would have been a graceful and kindly action on the part of the authorities to at least pay the old colonists passage down and back again. The objection would probably be that old bugbear establishing a bad precedent. But such an objection can have no force in this instance for it is an exceptional case which cannot possibly recur.

But Eliza could speak for herself, and when she reached the southern states she made direct representation to the responsible federal minister, Sir Josiah Thomas: 'I told him that I was quite entitled to the return passage having been the oldest female resident in the Territory. I [had] been here over forty years and had great hardships to go through.' Clearly impressed, the minister granted her a second-class passage back to Darwin and in return asked Eliza to have her photograph taken to be shown in Adelaide and elsewhere as an example of a pioneer Territorian. This she did and was delighted to find that many South Australians recognised her and sent her their regards. She spent several more weeks in Sydney with her son and his family before returning to Darwin.[8]

Eliza also had to battle for the pension, after federal legislation granting it was introduced in 1909:

I read in the papers about the Old Age Pension, so I applied for it and got the order to get it signed by several people and I got that done but made a slight error in the valuation of my property so I had to go up to the then Government Resident and explain everything to him. He seemed to think I wasn't entitled to it on account of having a small house to live in so sometime after I got a notice stating that I was not entitled to the Pension. I kept the notice and thought no more but I feel sure that he didn't want me to get it.

Eventually, with the help of the local Methodist minister, Reverend Bennett, she managed to convince the authorities she was entitled to it.

But there were troubles and trials still ahead for Eliza. In April of 1914, one of her grand-daughters, Gertrude, died and in August her son Charlie died at Pine Creek, aged forty-three. A few weeks earlier Eliza had narrowly escaped tragedy herself: 'I had a narrow escape of being burned. I had gone to bed and a man and a woman were passing and saw the fires and they came to the window and where my bed was. Then some more came and managed to put the fire out. I shall never forget that night and I could not thank God and the people enough,' she said with the stoic Christian faith and acceptance which seems to have been a major source of her strength.

In 1915, her grandson, Walter Styles, became the first Territory victim of the Great War only days after he had written to his father and sister telling them he had been wounded but was recovering and how anxious he was to get back into the fighting. The letters were printed in the *Northern Territory Times* the same day as the telegram advising of his death. A few years later Eliza witnessed the unveiling of a monument to pay tribute to the Territory boys who had lost their lives in the war. The *Times* reported:

the tears in her eyes on that occasion betokened the solemn fact that one of her grandsons had written his name on the granite pages of the history of the Empire. In speaking of her bereavements in the Territory the grand old lady regretfully and yet gratefully had said 'I have had my share of trouble, thank God for giving me strength to bear the cross'.

Finally Eliza 'Granny' Tuckwell reached the end of her struggle-filled life and in August 1921, aged eighty-five, she died—the servant girl from London town who had become a pioneer social builder of the Territory and, as the *Northern Territory Times* put it, had been 'a Christian pioneer for over half a century'.

Of her small estate, Eliza left twenty-five pounds each to her daughter Eliza Sarah, and to her son, Edward. The remainder went to her grandson, Claude Arnold, whom she had raised from childhood. Four years after Eliza's death, her only remaining daughter was killed in a tragic buggy accident outside her home.

FOLLOWING ON FROM ELIZA

Despite the many tragedies and tribulations the family experienced, the Tuckwells drew strength and spirit from Eliza's indomitable attitude to life and by 1988 five generations of Territory-born Tuckwells were still pioneering the Territory. They were the descendants of Eliza's daughter Eleanor and her husband Tom Styles. One of their four daughters, Eileen Fitzer, was still going strong in 1988 and exhibited all the strong spirit of her locally famous grandparents—a spirit reflected in bright, blue-grey eyes, forever ready to see the lighter side of life. Her memories of her more stoic grandmother are sparse, but strong:

I remember very well this little lady always wearing a black bonnet and shawl and always sitting in her rocker on the verandah and singing hymns in the latter years of her life. There was a paddock between my grandmother's house and the Wesleyan church and I can remember her going off to church every Sunday. She helped deliver many of the babies in Darwin and most of her own grandchildren. She delivered my eldest sister Lil, who was born in grandma Tuckwell's house in 1893 with grandma as mid-wife.[9]

Eleanor, who had already had a son, Walter, had three more Territory-born daughters—Gertrude, Eileen and Myrtle. Eileen, who was born in 1902, spent most of her younger years at Brock's Creek, where her father was underground manager for the Zappopan mine, and recalled the happiness of her childhood:

Mother was so young and full of life. I can always remember her driving through Chinatown at Brock's Creek and across to Burnside station where we went on picnics with the Byrnes children, our nearest neighbours, a few kilometres away. My mother was a gay sort of person, played the concertina and danced—my father was very musical too; he had a wonderful voice. I remember my fifth birthday—they had a party and danced on the antbed and ash floors, and the next morning we swept up all the dust. All of us girls inherited the musical streak, especially my sister Myrtle who was a wonderful singer and dancer and entertainer when she got older.

When Eileen was seven she and Myrtle went south with their mother who was seeking medical help for cancer, but it was too advanced and they returned to Darwin where Eleanor died in 1910, at the age of thirty-six, leaving her husband with four daughters to look after. Eileen recalled:

For awhile my sister Lillian took Myrtle and they lived with grandma while Gertrude and I were put in the convent in Darwin where we went to school for three years. Our brother Walter went to Queensland because he felt he had to battle out on his own. We used to hear from him nearly every week. He was a wonderful brother, but we never saw him again—he enlisted and was killed at Gallipoli.

Eileen fondly recalled her school days in Darwin:

We used to play cowboys and Indians down at Fort Hill, where my grandparents first lived so many years before, and we would go exploring in Chinatown, down Cavenagh street. It was the most fabulous place in the world and the New Year celebration was the most exciting time in a European child's life. We would follow the processions with their beautiful costumes, hundreds of crackers and big Chinese dragons. The Chinese storekeepers used to give all their customers big Christmas boxes, loaded with ham, ginger plums and pumpkin seeds. Then there were the Chinese laundries where most men had their white suits cleaned; the old Chinese men would blow water on them and then iron them dry—probably not too sanitary, but effective.

Meanwhile Tom Styles had been sent to Port Essington to restore the graves of the pioneers there, including Emma Lambrick's, and when he returned in 1913 he gathered his girls and headed back to Brock's Creek, where Eileen and her two younger sisters walked two miles to school each day. From Brock's Creek the family moved to Pine Creek. Eileen recalled with affection her father's efforts at the time:

I think my father greased every bolt that went on the railway line between Pine Creek and Emungalun, the town that preceded Katherine. That was his job. My father was a very versatile man; he was a blacksmith and built buggies and all kinds of things. There was nothing my father couldn't do, even mend broken arms in the bush. I was always falling out of a buggy of some description because I was like a little boy.

Towards the end of the First World War, Tom Styles decided to try his luck at peanut farming in Katherine and Eileen and her sisters moved to Darwin and set up a 'bachelor pad' in Smith Street near Brown's Mart, their uncle's auctioneering agency, now a Darwin theatre. Eileen worked as a salesgirl for the big European store, Jollys, which was then managed by Jim Fawcett, whom her musically talented sister, Myrtle, had married. The four sisters were all talented and in popular demand, participating in most of Darwin's fancy dress dances and concerts. Later, during the Second World War, Myrtle was the only woman to travel with an entertainment troupe performing for the thousands of soldiers stationed in camps throughout the Territory.

The early 1920s were heady days in Darwin and Eileen shared some historic moments with her friend Mary MacDonald, who for years was matron of the Kahlin compound.

We used to bring Sunday lunches out to Fannie Bay jail when Harold Nelson and his colleagues had been sent to prison during the no taxation without representation fight in 1921. We cooked such delicious meals that most of the men gained weight during their voluntary jail terms! And then when Harold ran for parliament the next year, Mary and I drove a sulky all over Darwin campaigning for him. We sat up all night at the police station waiting for the votes to be phoned in from the different areas and I remember how excited we were when he won. They were good days— everyone knew everyone else and everyone seemed to get on.

'Then in 1928 my sister Gertrude decided I should train for something and financed me to do a nursing course in Melbourne,' Eileen said. She spent four happy years working to get her double certificate in nursing at the Queen Victoria Hospital, but she could not wait to get back to the Territory. As soon as she had sat for her exams Eileen headed straight for Alice Springs where she stayed for a while with her sister Lillian, who had married one of the Territory's most well-known policemen, John Lovegrove.

Soon she was appointed as a nursing sister at the Bungalow, where she administered health care to children of part-Aboriginal descent, and even helped teach the very young ones.

While I was there, I think we made medical history in Alice Springs because a very, very severe trachoma eye epidemic broke out in the Alice and I was in isolation with seventeen patients in the old Police Station through the Gap, while we treated them. With me were a couple of teenage girls, part-Aboriginals, who were helping me. We only saw the doctor, the baker and the butcher all the time we were there. The treatment was drastic and continuous and I think we were there for two months administering the treatment to at least a hundred patients.

In 1934 the Territory's chief medical officer, Dr Cecil Cook, transferred Eileen to Pine Creek as sister in charge of the hospital:

At that time the hospital was really a casualty station, catering mainly for the gold miners. Most of our cases were caused by mining accidents or pub fights and we were visited at least once a week by the famous flying doctor, Clyde Fenton, who was stationed in Katherine. He was an amazing and fantastic pilot. He was also one of the most mischievous people I've ever met, always ready with a practical joke.

She recalled her first meeting, and her first flight, with the good doctor. After a long and bumpy ride in a Model-T Ford on the then roadless trek from Alice Springs to Birdham (now Larrimah), she boarded the train for Katherine, on her way to take up nursing duties at Pine Creek.

'When we stopped in Katherine, Clyde was there to greet me and he looked so very different from what I expected...He wore a beard in those days and had great blue eyes, and if ever I saw anyone who looked like Our Saviour, it was him.' It did not take Sister Styles long to discover Fenton's more devilish side, however. As soon as she had settled in at Pine Creek, Fenton made weekly visits to the hospital, commuting in his Tiger Moth plane from Katherine:

I used to have to help him tie the plane down as there was no hangar in Pine Creek. I remember once some goats started to try eating the wings! The first time I ever flew with Clyde, he bet me six bottles of beer that he could make me sick. He said he would tap me on the shoulder and if everything was OK, I should smile. We flew around for about thirty minutes and he did everything that little plane could do, rocking it, shaking it, and finally turning the engine off and putting it into a spiral spin. I just turned around and grinned at him and I won the bet.

She also went up with Fenton for an illegal spin in the moonlight the night before he performed one of his most famous Darwin stunts by flying between the screen and the audience at the popular open-air Star Theatre in Darwin's main street. It is a feat still talked about by those still alive to remember, and one of several which landed him in trouble with the authorities. But his services were too valuable for him to be out of action for long. 'He was a fantastic pilot and a marvellous doctor and he would fly anywhere to see a patient. When he was on duty, nothing interfered with his work.'

Meanwhile, the sister who had helped Eileen through nursing, Gertrude, had married Bill Easton, a member of the North Australian commission, and moved to Perth, where she had several children. When news came in 1936 that she had died, Eileen was deeply distressed and decided she did not want to be on her own any longer, and so she married a long-time friend, Harry Gribbons, whom she affectionately called her 'wild Irishman'. 'He was a fascinating character, everybody loved Harry, he did everything and made a success of it—but then he used to drink a lot. He just lived from day to day—that type of person.'

Harry and Eileen moved to Darwin, where Harry worked as an auctioneer for a while before the couple tried their luck on the Wauchope mining fields, some sixty miles south of Tennant Creek, where wolfram had been discovered. It was 1939 and Eileen was the only white woman on the field for eighteen months.

It was an experience. I lived in what was called the mansion, a little tiny shed, the floor made of filings from the mine, and stones sticking out through the mats that I had down, there was a huge mosquito net to have our meals under because of flies— it's a country of sand and spinifex. I always wore a pith helmet with a fly veil on it.

Eileen did some more nursing at Wauchope, especially with people needing eye treatment. Then she was asked by the chief medical officer, Dr Cook, to be relieving sister at the leprosarium on Channel Island, several miles from Darwin. When she left Wauchope, the miners gave Eileen 'a big fat cheque' in appreciation of her nursing care. At the leprosarium she looked after about 120 lepers for three months, a time she describes as very happy and satisfying. She next worked for a while at the Bagot compound, where Aborigines and people of part-Aboriginal descent had been moved from the Kahlin compound.

A short time later Harry and Eileen bought the Adelaide River hotel and moved there—until Harry's illness and the Second World War. They were evacuated in December 1941, on the *President Grant* and went to Sydney, where Harry was put in special care. When he was safely settled, Eileen was given permission to return to Adelaide River and settle up their hotel business.

When I got to Port Pirie I heard that Darwin had been bombed and I arrived in Alice Springs in time to see all the evacuees arriving in convoys. It was a distressing scene. We were all terribly upset—we knew all those who were killed, although not many names had been released.

Eileen managed to catch a ride with a friend in a convoy of seventy-seven trucks heading north to Adelaide River. 'There were thousands of soldiers in Sidney Williams huts and tents for miles and miles,' Eileen recalled. When she arrived at Adelaide River she told her friend, Matron Edith McQuade White, who was in charge of the women's medical service there, to take all the furniture in the hotel and use it in whatever way she felt best. After a month's stay at nearby Mt Bundey Station, Eileen returned to Sydney, where her husband died in February 1943. She remained in Sydney for eight months until she got a telegram from a friend asking her to come to Tipperary Station in the Top End as a trained nurse. Eileen jumped at the chance, anxious to get back to the Territory. There were still soldiers everywhere, living at staging camps.

It was at Tipperary that Eileen renewed her acquaintance with one of the Territory's most famous policemen, Tas Fitzer, then policeman in charge of the Daly River Station. Tas had been breaking in a wild colt when it kicked him on the knee, causing severe pain and injury. He lay in agony on his verandah for seventeen days, attended to by his faithful Aboriginal trackers. It was in the middle of the wet season and he knew there was no chance for the flying doctor to land, so just before he became semi-delirious he scribbled a note and gave it to one of the trackers, who travelled on foot over thirty miles (48 km) to reach 'Sister Eileen' at Tipperary. The tracker returned in three days with a note from Eileen explaining how, with the help of fourteen Aborigines, she had penetrated bogs and swollen creeks to get within nine miles of the police station. She sent instructions for the trackers to improvise a stretcher and carry Tas back to her, a feat they accomplished after a gruelling five-hour trudge through the thick tropical scrub. Eileen gave Tas morphine and organised for him to receive further treatment at an army hospital. In April of 1945 Tas and Eileen were married in a 'beautiful ceremony' among about fifty friends at Tipperary, before moving to their home on the Daly River, about eighty miles (130 km) from the mouth.

It was while at the Daly in 1946 that Eileen had a close call with death herself. When she became desperately ill with abdominal pains which worsened over several days, Tas sent an urgent message to Adelaide River with his Aboriginal tracker, Nipper, who had to run more than ninety miles (145 km) through flooded country to get the message through, as Tas's radio transceiver was out of order, the airstrip was under water and the Stuart Highway was impassable. After two days and nights of running, Nipper reached his destination with the urgent message to bring medical help. The message was phoned through to Darwin where officials immediately sought help from all available sources and made the boom-defence vessel HMAS *Kangaroo* available to the rescue party. On deck they carried a crash launch with two powerful engines so that they could negotiate the narrower parts of the river, which a vessel the size of the *Kangaroo* would find impossible. They reached the mouth of the Daly in about half a day and then used the crash launch to negotiate their way through the treacherous tidal river. They travelled through the crocodile-infested river for the rest of the day and well into the next before finally reaching Eileen who was by now not only in great pain but also severely jaundiced. After injecting her with morphine, the party loaded her on board the small vessel and made the return journey, this time going with the tide and at frightening speed. They finally reached the *Kangaroo* and proceeded to Darwin, where they found that their venture and Eileen's plight had been spread across nearly every paper in the country, and thousands of readers were waiting to see if the dramatic rescue had succeeded. It had, and within a few weeks of treatment at Darwin Hospital Eileen was well again and was able to resume her life at the Daly.

After the Daly, the Fitzers spent several years at the Timber Creek police station and eventually retired to travel and live for a time in Sydney. But when Tas died in the 1960s, Eileen returned to her beloved Territory, where she was still living in 1988. Among her constant stream of visitors are the children and grandchildren of her sisters, Myrtle Fawcett and Lillian Lovegrove who are producing the fifth generation of Territory-born Territorians. The various family members are spread throughout the Territory. They cover a wide range of professions—from policemen to pastoralists to modern-day 'urban pioneers'—and they are all proud of their pioneering Tuckwell heritage.

GRANNY LUM LOY, SOWING SEEDS FOR THE FUTURE

It was not, of course, just Anglo-Saxon women who were Territory urban pioneers. Women of many races made their own particular, often unsung contribution to the cosmopolitan atmosphere which has characterised so much of Territory history. Among the most prominent cultures has been the Chinese.

Although there were very few Chinese women in comparison to Chinese men in the early days of the Territory (in the 1880s they were outnumbered by the men by as much as 400 to 1) some made a very firm mark on the place. One of the most notable was Lu Moo, also known as Lee Toy Kim, but more commonly known in Darwin as the ever-sprightly Granny Lum Loy.[10]

She was about ten years old when she arrived in Darwin on a ship from South China, around the time of the disastrous 1897 cyclone. Apart from a few years during the Second World War, she remained in the Territory until her death in 1980. She was one of two adopted daughters of a Chinese family who started a grocery and general store in the heart of Darwin's Chinatown. She later described it as a bustling place with more than fifty shops representing almost every type of trade and with many fringe businesses, such as fishing, gardening and gambling.

The Chinese of the time dressed in their traditional costumes—hers was trousers and a top, the garb of the working class—and most wore pigtails. During interviews at the end of her life, she delighted in the recollection of the policeman who arrested some Chinese men for running illegal gambling games and, because he had too few handcuffs, tied their pigtails together before marching them off to the police station. She also remembered how some Chinese immigrants outfoxed the authorities when the government was restricting Chinese immigration just after the turn of the century. As the ship sailed into Darwin harbour, the Chinese passengers would hide beneath a bunch of cabbages or other vegetables and be carried to safety with their clever camouflage.

For several years after her arrival, Lu Moo worked in her adopted family's shop and, although she spoke only her native language of See Yup, she came to know many of the locals, including countless Aboriginal people whom she liked and respected a great deal. About the time of Australia's federation in 1901 she married a Chinese mining engineer named Lum Loy. Together they travelled by train about 120 miles (193 km) south of Darwin to Wandi, a mining camp near Pine Creek, where a large deposit of wolfram had been discovered, later moving up the rail line to Brock's Creek. Now one of the Territory's many ghost towns, Brock's Creek was then a bustling mining town of about 2000 people, with a host of Chinese shops, a myriad of self-supporting farms, Fannie Haynes's famous Federation Hotel, and three joss houses. Lu Moo especially remembered the lions that once guarded the joss house in which she worshipped, which were later moved to the Chinese temple in Darwin, where she was a regular worshipper until her death.

In December 1906, at a railway siding near Brock's Creek, she gave birth to her one and only child, a daughter called Lizzie Yook Lin. For the next ten years the family lived in the Pine Creek-Brock's Creek area, where there were many Chinese mining the wolfram and gold fields. In 1908 Lu Moo had to appear in court to give evidence in an opium case against one of her countrymen, and, speaking virtually no English, she did so very reluctantly. It was perhaps then that she determined that her daughter would learn the language of their adopted land so that she could better deal with such situations. When her husband died in about 1918, Lu Moo and Lizzie returned to Darwin, where Lizzie entered school and not only learned to speak English but became a top student. In fact she was so proficient in English that she became one of the three Chinese residents who were used as interpreters in court cases involving Chinese, many of whom faced charges of possessing opium, to which they had been addicted long before it became illegal.

Lizzie eventually married a prominent Darwin businessman, Chin Loong Tang, and soon their nine children began arriving on the scene, with the well-known Chinese midwife, Sarah Lee Hang Gong, helping to deliver most of them. When the Tangs moved to Katherine for a while, Lu Moo, by then known to most as Granny Lum Loy, decided to find a business to support herself.

She rented ten acres (4 hectares) of land from Vesteys, near what later became the Darwin Bowling Club in Fannie Bay. She paid four pounds a year for the block which she single-handedly converted into a mango orchard. She planted and cared for the 200 trees, carrying water from the well and compost from the large compost pit, year in and year out, until she had a prolific fruit-growing enterprise. At harvest time she toiled with a long picking stick until all the fruit had been plucked from the trees and put in containers to be sent to Western Australia. 'You could not sell many locally because most people grew their own,' she explained.

Four years before the outbreak of the Second World War, she sold the mango plantation and moved back into Chinatown to help her daughter run a cafe business while Mr Tang was in Hong Kong on business. When he returned, the ever-enterprising Granny looked for yet another project.

This time she decided on chickens. She rented a block of land in Stuart Park, about a mile (2 km) from the city area, and set up a chicken farm, walking daily from town to the farm to tend the chickens and collect the eggs, which she sold to the Gee Fong Ming Cafe. Granny sometimes stopped to visit one of the three Chinese herbalists in town or to pray at the joss house, and she was at the latter when the Japanese bombed Darwin on 19 February 1942:

I was just coming out of the joss house when I saw smoke rising in the harbour and heard all this noise. I wondered why the harbour was alight and I started to run towards the police station. I met some of the Que Noy family and they put me in their vehicle and we drove to Adelaide River. When we got there everyone was in such a panic that when some hawks flew over the town everyone started screaming that the Japanese planes had come back and they scrambled everywhere.

Granny waited for the train to Katherine and there met up with her daughter and grandchildren. They moved into a house in the main street and were there the one and only time the Japanese bombed the Katherine aerodrome, killing an Aboriginal man. The family was told to evacuate and they made their way to Alice Springs and on to Adelaide, where they opened a fruit shop in Hanson Street. Later

Chinese matriarch Granny Lum Loy came to Darwin in the late 1890s and become one of the Territory's best-loved and most active pioneer women. When Darwin photographer Clive Hyde photographed her in 1979, the year before her death, artist Geoff La Gersche was so inspired by the character of her face that he painted a huge portrait of her for his entry in the Archibald Prize. When shown the portrait, Granny was overwhelmed, explaining to her family that in the China she knew as a young girl only emperors had their portraits painted. Photograph by Clive Hyde.

they moved to Sydney, where Granny's beloved Lizzie died on the day Hiroshima was bombed.

After the war, Granny returned to Darwin and discovered that it was fortunate she had sold her mango plantation—the trees she had so lovingly established had been destroyed by army troops who were worried that if the Japanese had landed they could have used it as a camouflage. Although still grieving for her daughter, Granny was determined to start a new life and again turned to gardening pursuits for her main source of income, and pleasure. Her son-in-law gave her half of some land he owned in Stuart Park to help compensate for the chicken farm she lost during the war. Her grandson, Ron, built her a house and immediately she set about establishing her beloved garden. Little did she know that nearly thirty years later she would have to do it all over again when Cyclone Tracy wreaked havoc in 1974.

Not that such foreknowledge would have stopped her. Granny Lum Loy's vitality was renowned. In her nineties she was still leading the life of someone half that age. Ron described her lifestyle:

She was up every day before any of the rest of the family and out in the garden all day. She had everything growing—mango, guava, five corner, custard apple, ginger, garlic, banana, chilli, yam, Chinese melon, bitter melon, everything. She was also a regular worshipper at the joss house and usually walked the distance — about a mile — because she was too impatient to wait for a lift from one of the family.

Her tiny figure, always garbed in her traditional black trousers and top and broad-brimmed black hat, was a familiar sight to Darwinites for many years. When Cyclone Tracy did devastate Darwin, and much of her garden, she simply picked up the pieces and started once again.

Although she had no formal education, she could read and write Chinese and could quote at length from Lo Puk Woon, a Chinese philosopher. This thoughtful side to her otherwise vibrant personality emerged in a description she once gave of Darwin: 'Darwin is like a crab. It looks like a crab from the air, and like a crab it can become very weak, almost empty at times—but it always comes back again, full and strong.'[10] As someone who experienced the Darwin way of life for more than eighty years, surviving three major cyclones and a war, she probably knew what she was talking about. When Granny Lum Loy, astute businesswoman and a matriarch of the Darwin Chinese community, died in 1980, her funeral was one of the largest seen in the community for many years. A housing block was later named in honour of her many pioneering ventures and spirit.

HILDA MUIR

Another large portion of Darwin's cosmopolitan population is made up of Aboriginal women and Aboriginal women of mixed descent. One of them is Hilda Muir, whose life reflects what many Territory Aboriginal women experienced.

Born Hilda Rogers in the tiny Gulf township of Borroloola in about 1920, she spent the first eight years of her life with her Aboriginal mother, who worked at the police station there. She never knew who her father was. Like many Aboriginal children of the time who were victims of the new government policy regarding Aboriginal protection, Hilda's life soon changed in a dramatic way.

In 1928 the local policeman, Sergeant John Bridgeland, had to escort some prisoners from Borroloola to Darwin and he received instructions to bring any part-Aboriginal children in as well. A young girl named Clare, who was also of part-Aboriginal descent, was rounded up at the McArthur River and brought into Borroloola, where Hilda lived. From there the party made the trip to Darwin. The first part of the long journey was on horseback to Larrimah, the end of the railway line. Hilda, Clare and an Aboriginal girl named Ada shared one saddle. The prisoner and the witnesses for the courtcase walked. When they reached Larrimah they took the train to Katherine and then boarded a freight truck for the rest of the way to Darwin and the Kahlin compound. Today many refer to this process as 'legalised abduction'.

During one of the first inspections of the compound after their arrival, Clara was declared 'too white' to stay there and was sent to the convent. Hilda remained in the compound for the next six years. Along with the other children, she had her hair shaved—the bureaucratic solution to having no combs available.

They used to just spread blankets on the floor and we slept there. If you did something wrong, the matron used to get her husband, an ex-soldier, to flog the person. I don't know what a wrong person used to do, but I know when we did get punished, we got really punished. They had a great big cane, and used that on your hand, if not on your legs...I know that it was very sore.[11]

All the children were dressed alike in one-piece rompers, usually of khaki and jute. Food was meagre, consisting of a ladle of porridge or a piece of bread in the morning, boiled stew at lunchtime and bread and jam in the evening. 'One time there it was really bad. We children got so desperate with hunger that some kids got the bright idea to ringbark poinciana trees and get the stringy part out of it to chew and get the juice out of it,' Hilda recalled. The matron, however, made the children promise to tell the Chief Protector of Aborigines, Dr Cecil Cook, that they were getting enough food, threatening punishment if they did not.

Their lives were strictly supervised all day. Before sundown the children were lined up to be counted and at six o'clock they were locked up for the night. The children were not allowed in the town area, unless they had permission to do work for someone.

One of Hilda's happier memories of life in the compound was of a time when a whooping cough epidemic broke out and, to ensure that it didn't spread to the larger community, the children were taken across the harbour to Channel Island, later the site of the leprosarium. They were there for about eight weeks. 'We had a very good time. We could bird hunt and fish all day. It would have been a lovely place to stay because we could get food off the land, like honey from the trees.'

A visiting teacher gave lessons to the children at the compound. Hilda loved her teacher, Mrs Carruth, who had taught for years at Pine Creek:

She used to feel sorry for us. She could see what our lifestyle was like. She wanted to adopt me and went to ask Doctor Cook if she could. But the matron didn't want her to and told me I was to say no when Doctor Cook asked me. I was very timid so I had to carry out the matron's word because I was too frightened that if I didn't she would give me a hiding and I was frightened of big hidings.

One of the most controversial policies developed when the commonwealth took
responsibility for the Territory was that of taking young children from their
Aboriginal mothers and putting them in a compound. Most of the girls were
trained to become domestic help for European families. Pictured here are (from
left) Maggie Smith, Daisy Ruddick, Cathy Choung, and Phyllis Wilson. Daisy's
story is typical of many. She was born on a cattle station near Wave Hill in
1916. Her mother was a Gurinji Aboriginal woman and her father Jack
Cussack, the white station manager. At the age of eight, Daisy was taken away
by the police to Darwin, where she was placed in the Kahlin Compound with
other part-Aboriginal children who had been rounded up and removed from
their parents. Daisy remained at the compound for four years, until the Crown
Law Officer, Eric Asche, and his wife Beryl, asked Daisy to come and work as
nursemaid to their children. Although she objected at first—she didn't want to
be 'taken away' again—she soon came to love the family, and when they
returned to Melbourne in the 1930s, she went with them. She later returned to
Darwin and worked for four years as a nursing aide before marrying an
Englishman, Joe Ruddick, by whom she had three daughters. When the
marriage ended, Joe put the girls in boarding school and it took Daisy, as an
Aboriginal woman without many rights under European law, many months to
convince the courts to put the girls in her care. She raised the girls to be proud
of their Aboriginal heritage and by the 1980s all of them were active in
movements attempting to improve the lot of Aboriginal people.
Photograph courtesy of Chief Justice Austin Asche and Dr Val Asche.

'I was weak,' Hilda said, laughing at her timidity.

Eventually, when Hilda was fourteen, she was one of a few girls who were chosen to train as nurses at the hospital. They worked six days a week and were paid thirteen shillings, but not in cash. Their money went into a trust fund and every once in a while they were issued with a money order and allowed to buy a few necessities from selected stores.

During this time Hilda met her future husband, Bill Muir, who was then a deckhand on a ship. When he was caught inside the girl's dormitory visiting Hilda, he was sent to gaol and Hilda was sent to Katherine. After several depressing months, Hilda was allowed to return to Darwin to give birth to Bill's child. His parents did not approve of the match because Hilda was a 'compound girl', but they stuck together and were finally married in 1940. Two years later Hilda and her children were evacuated to Brisbane, where they stayed for the rest of the war.[12]

For Hilda the evacuation offered her an opportunity to see a whole new world. For a while they lived with her husband's foster mother in Brisbane, but eventually Hilda and her children moved into a home on their own.

I wanted to live on my own and go my own way. I had enough of being, you know, watched over when I was a kid and I wanted freedom. Be my own boss and have my own way of life to live with my children...you were sort of sorting things out in yourself and as I was going along I was sort of learning, educating myself how to live and survive. We had to survive in the Home you know but this was different...it was a big thing to go to Brisbane.

Hilda stayed in Brisbane until 1946, when she returned to Darwin with Bill who had been sent in the meantime to New Guinea and fought at Milne Bay.

Hilda returned to Darwin with a new strength and confidence. This, combined with a delightful optimistic nature, helped her cope with many moves and many different living conditions over the next thirty years. She needed all her inner strength when Cyclone Tracy struck Darwin in 1974, killing Bill and injuring Hilda and some of her family. Again they were evacuated to Brisbane, where Hilda remained until 1976, when she returned to Darwin for good.

Despite a childhood that many would regard as horrific, Hilda looks upon the experience in a philosophical way, appreciating that it gave her an education and thus opportunities which she would never have had had she remained with her mother at Borroloola. She has returned to her Borroloola home several times and has re-established contact with members of her Aboriginal family. Her own children have excelled in various areas of Darwin life, especially sport and education. Hilda, using her pension and money left to her by Bill, has travelled overseas several times. She has thoroughly enjoyed her travels and is pleased with herself for venturing overseas. She is proud of her Aboriginal heritage and the community of which she has been so integral a part can be justly proud of the contribution that she, and many other 'compound girls' have made to the Darwin way of life.

Eliza Tuckwell, Granny Lum Loy and Hilda Muir are only three of the Territory's urban pioneers who, by their choice to remain in the Territory through various types of adversity, have discovered the freedom and opportunity the Territory way of life offers. And by choosing to make the Territory their home, they, like many other women of many other cultures, have provided enviable role models for generations of women to follow.

Chapter 9

Ellen Ryan

AND WOMEN OF THE TOP END'S PUBS:
MORE PLUCK THAN WISDOM?

'In [1874] there were only three or four white women, including the late Mrs Ellen Ryan, on the fields and they naturally drifted into the hotel business, a profitable pastime when men not engaged in digging for alluvial were earning five to six pounds a week and as much keep as they required.'
Northern Territory Times. 7 March 1924

When London-born Ellen Ryan spent more than 4000 pounds in 1890 to erect Darwin's first two-storey hotel, the *Northern Territory Times* admired her pluck but questioned her wisdom. History has shown she had both. Not only has the Hotel Victoria proved to be one of the Territory's most famous and profitable watering holes, it has also survived three major cyclones and a world war to become one of the few buildings left to remind Top End Territorians of their colourful pub-filled past. Ellen Ryan and her many hotels featured in that past for more than forty years when pluck and wisdom, not to mention good humour, were part and parcel of her character. A look at her life is a look at a vital slice of Territory history, in which women in particular played an essential and enterprising role.

Ellen was born in London in 1851 and in 1853 travelled to Western Australia with her parents John and Bridget Freeman and their two other children. John, an ex-soldier, was a guard on the convict ship *Dudbrook*, which brought 208 convicts, thirty pensioner guards, twenty-four women and forty-five children to Western Australia. In 1856 John and Bridget, who by now had another child, decided to sail to Adelaide and begin a new life in a 'free' colony. When John died, Bridget married a shepherd, John Heaphy, by whom she had several more children. When Heaphy died she married John Boyd. In 1867, at the tender age of sixteen, her eldest daughter, Ellen, decided to leave the family nest and marry a thirty-three-year-old Irish immigrant labourer, William Ryan.

Six years later the couple, seduced by news of gold discoveries, decided to venture to the Northern Territory. The cry of gold had gone out months before and diggers from all over the country swarmed north. Along with 120 others, including Ellen's future brother-in-law, Dudley Kelsey, they set sail on 12 June 1873 in the 880-ton barque *Birchgrove*. They arrived in Palmerston on 12 July 1873, a beautiful dry-season day which paid full tribute to Port Darwin's magnificent harbour. After spending the first night on board, William and Ellen disembarked near Goyder's old jetty by Fort Hill and wound their way up the narrow footpath to the main streets laid out by Goyder's survey crew. Though it was three years since Eliza Tuckwell and other early pioneers had arrived, the town was still in the main a motley collection of roughly built log and bark buildings, a few galvanised-iron stores and numerous canvas encampments. Apart from the government residence, the only substantial buildings in town were the impressive stone submarine cable quarters and the overland telegraph offices on the Esplanade, where the elite of early Palmerston were housed.[1]

Ellen and William spent only a few days in Palmerston before heading for one of the most promising runs at Yam Creek, a few miles northwest of Pine Creek. At the time there were about 1500 people in the area, a lucrative market to an enterprising eye. Ellen's eye was particularly enterprising and it did not take her long to realise where the Territory's real wealth was to be found. Within a few weeks, she had leased the Miners' Arms Hotel, the first hotel in the area, and as she had little or no opposition she did a good trade. She quickly developed a reputation for hospitality and quality that was to remain with her throughout her Territory life.

Her style was a welcome change. Harriet Daly described the period previous to Ellen's reign: 'Drinking saloons were very soon opened. Did ever a settlement start without one?...The grog shanties were always full [and] they drove a stirring and paying trade...a sample of what was sold to the poor fellows so lately recovering from fever [was] gin and kerosene mixed with Worcester sauce, and flavoured with ginger and sugar...'[2] In this rough and ready atmosphere Ellen's reputation spread quickly and it was soon acknowledged that she 'kept the best table out of Darwin...equal to anything one could get even in Darwin'.[3]

It was not just Ellen's better quality product that interested the diggers, it was also the fact that she was a woman, a rare sight on the frontier. In February 1874 a *South Australian Advertiser* mining correspondent, who had just arrived on the Territory mining fields and discovered that Ellen was one of the very few women in the region, described the atmosphere this way: 'That portion of humanity that "when pain and anguish wring the brow" act as ministering angels is scarce; and as the sterner sex are left to enjoy themselves as best they can in the wild bush of Australia, society is in rather a rude state.'

Ellen, as far as is known, concentrated on providing the more respectable range of services, capitalising on promoting the 'home away from home' image. She was soon joined in the hotel competition stakes by another enterprising woman, Amelia Traversi, who had been running a temperance bar, featuring 'cordials of every description', in Palmerston. Realising that the profits were to be made from intemperate miners she went to the fields and built the British and Foreign Hotel. By February 1875 she was advertising an intriguing combination of services, promising that travellers would meet with 'all the comfort that can be expected in the Northern Territory. Good stock of all kinds, spirits and provisions... A professional French cook ...Good Billiard Table. Good bedrooms... Horse Feed [and] As the doctor [was] residing at the Shackle a private room [would] be restored for invalids.' She also promised that a garden to supply fresh vegetables would be planted at once.

But competition didn't bother Ellen. In fact it may have been at least partially responsible for saving her life. At the end of 1874 Ellen booked a passage on the *Gothenburg* to have a holiday in Adelaide. Off she went to Palmerston to wait for the popular steamer, but while there she was induced, quite possibly by news of the prospective competition from Amelia Traversi's new hotel, to return to the Shackle

Ellen Ryan added more than a touch of class to Darwin's social scene when she built the Vic Hotel, Darwin's first two-storey building, in 1890. It was one of a number of hotels she built and/or managed from the time she arrived in 1873 to the time she left in 1915. Kelsey collection, Mortlock Library.

and look after her own investment. She cancelled her ticket and returned to the Miners' Arms.

This snap decision meant she did not share the tragic fate of all the women and most of the men who sailed on that vessel and lost their lives when it sank off the Queensland coast during a cyclonic storm in February 1875. As the shock of the news subsided, Territory residents did what they seem to have done in remarkably consistent fashion for so small a population — they 'passed the hat'. Acutely mindful of her own narrow escape, Ellen Ryan was a generous donor, as she was for many other charitable causes over the years.

Ellen finally took her first holiday back to Adelaide in 1876, returning to Palmerston with her younger sister, Mary. After a short stint at a hotel in Palmerston, Ellen moved to the nearby mining depot town of Southport where she took a short lease on the Royal Hotel.

Meanwhile, early in 1877, her husband William applied for another licence for the Miners' Arms Hotel at the Shackle but was refused. The versatile John George Knight, the chief mining warden at the time, recommended to the government resident, Edward Price, that it be used as a much-needed hospital, and after considerable lobbying, the minister for the Territory agreed. The government purchased the hotel and handed it over to Knight who used his architectural skills to make the necessary alterations.

Ellen may well have been one of the first people in need of attention as it is clear that by this time William had become violent and threatening to her. Finally in 1877 she left him and branched out on her own. Perhaps she was encouraged by the actions of another Territory publican, Eliza Blankley, who the year before had used South Australian legislation to take out a protection order against her husband and had successfully applied to the courts to have their Exchange Hotel in Palmerston transferred to her name. Eliza had taken out large advertisements in the *Northern Territory Times* in March 1876 to let the public know she had 'now taken entire management and control of...the hotel...Mr Blankley not being in any way connected with the business'.

In May 1881, Ellen took similar decisive action against her estranged forty-five-year-old Irish husband. Under South Australian law, married women could take out protection orders against their earnings if they could show they had supported themselves from the time they had separated from their husbands. The court transcript printed in the *Northern Territory Times* of 7 May clearly shows that Ellen had no trouble providing such proof:

Ellen Ryan, sworn said: her husband's name was William Ryan and for some time past had supported himself; they had agreed to separate; they were not living together; she left her husband in May 1877, owing to his threats, cruelty and drunkenness; she had not lived with him since; he had never sent her any money and she had no children living; she desired a protection order for her earnings; she had authorised her husband to receive 50 pounds to clear him away; when she left him she had about 700 pounds, the money had been made by her in the hotel.

The Bench being satisfied, granted the usual order.

The *Northern Territory Times* added: 'The poor old man, we hear, gladly pocketed the fifty pounds and sailed by the steamer *Meath*, he having had quite enough of the Territory and the people in it.'

Freed of her domestic burden, Ellen concentrated totally on her business ventures, always careful to specify in any transactions that the land concerned was 'for her own and separate use'. At times she was diverted by personal concerns, such as looking after the welfare of her fourteen-year-old sister Mary, who had come to stay with her at the Shackle. When she discovered that the twenty-two-year-old gold warden, Charles Nash, was visiting her sister in the small hours of the morning, she complained first to the police chief, Paul Foelsche, and then directly to Government Resident Price. She wrote that she had at times had to beat him away with a stick but he still kept returning. She claimed that:

Since this time...he has taken every opportunity of showing his spite and on one occasion when I had permission to place my horse in the police paddock he threatened to turn the horse out and also used very insulting language. There are also several men who owe me money...but I feel sure it would be of no use [to charge them] as Mr Nash would decide against me.

Pointing out her sister's young age, she appealed to Price to use his influence to put a halt to the situation:

The affair has caused great scandal, for many people have seen him waiting for my sister to come out in the morning and know that she has...been meeting him without my consent or knowledge...I feel sure his intentions to her are not good and if he was an honourable man he could never bring a child like her to the scandal he has done...I beg you will pardon me for troubling you with this long letter but I can see no other way of stopping Mr Nash's visits to my house and saving my sister from scandal or possibly much worse.[4]

It is not clear what the result of this plea was, but Nash remained warden for many years and Mary eventually married someone else.

There were, of course, many light-hearted moments in Ellen's life. Some of the most entertaining stories were the result of the keen but good-natured competition that existed between the enterprising Ellen and her Southport publican neighbour, Sam Brown. Their patrons entered into the spirit by donning 'uniforms', which, while not designed for tropical living, certainly added to the atmosphere of the two hotels. Boarders at Brown's Hotel dressed in white for dinner and became known as 'white coaters' while Ellen's customers donned navy blue flannel and were known as 'blue coaters'. On many a Christmas Eve, blue coaters could be spotted stealing pigs, eggs, hens, sandwiches, cakes or other festive fare from the Brown Hotel while light-fingered white coaters were similarly occupied at the Globe. Tricks to obtain free grog also abounded, but the larrikins responsible were treated with good humour and usually continued to receive excellent service.

The lucrative pub trade boomed to such an extent that at one point even the Southport post office was used as a boarding-cum-liquor house, much to the annoyance of some more temperate residents. In fact in 1880, with the Top End's Margaret River gold rush in full swing, Ellen and Sam were so busy with their respective pubs that they hired Vaiben Solomon, one of the town's prominent businessmen, to plead for their licence renewals in their absence. Solomon stressed the hardships which the teamsters and others would undergo by the house being closed. While the judge remarked that 'three months sobriety would do them good,' he did grant the renewals, as well as new licences to cater for the Margaret River rush. It was another woman, Mrs Ralph Moss, who was first to open a hotel on those digging fields and, as the *Northern Territory Times* noted, 'not before it was wanted'.

Some saw it as 'a woman's job' to run boarding-houses and pubs on the goldfields. The reason given by one Territory scribe was a very practical one: a woman could better protect the alcohol supply as 'she could have the liquor stowed away in her bedroom and no policeman was game to go there in search for evidence. A woman's bedroom was sacred and God help the policeman or any other person who entered there against her will.'[5]

Whether some provided bedroom services as well as liquor supplies is difficult to discover. While there are no really direct references to brothels, which were part of life on almost every other goldfield in the world, there are mentions in the early newspapers of 'little businesses' and the 'notorious Kitty Chown at Tumbling Waters', but further details are left to the imagination. Many years later Territory author and resident Bill Harney made reference to two travelling prostitutes with the intriguing names of Tiger Lil and Olga the Brolga, and it is difficult to believe that such women were not part of the Territory's earlier history too. It has been suggested by some that the presence of Aboriginal women meant that many men turned to them for companionship and to fulfil their sexual desires, lessening the 'need' for the traditional brothel.

There was, however, some unruly behaviour associated with hotels belonging to a number of Ellen Ryan's contemporaries. The March 1883 licensing report on the Territory's public houses described the landlord and landlady of the Margaret Crossing Hotel to be unfit to hold a licence, noting that:

on more than one occasion the landlord or his wife [had] smashed everything in the bar [and] several persons have been assaulted—one of them very seriously by the landlady...on being spoken to about it she exhibited an utter disregard for the consequences. There is no doubt that half-drunken men say things at times that they should not do, but there is no reason why either a landlord or his wife should take the law into their own hands.

The report also slated Elizabeth Turner of the QCE (Quiet, Comfort and Ease) Hotel at Adelaide River for running a house that was 'dirty and in bad order, being very much out of repair...four of the bedrooms [having] no proper windows [and] the partitions between the bedrooms composed of dirty calico'. The licensing inspector added that she did not appear to have 'much idea of the requirements of the business'.

Not so Ellen Ryan. She knew her business well and in 1884, with the promise of a railway between Palmerston and Pine Creek becoming a reality, Ellen dismantled her Shackle hotel and moved it to Port Darwin Camp, about four miles (6.4 km) to the east and several miles north of Pine Creek, closer to the railway line. By the following year she had made enough money to expand her business ventures even more. She bought more land on the goldfields, became involved in some mining leases in the Pine Creek region, and invested in land in Palmerston, much of which she still owned at the time of her death. By 1885 Ellen and Eliza Tuckwell were the only two Territory women listed on land tax statistics as earning more than 300

Ellen Ryan's Vic Hotel was the most prominent building in Darwin's Smith Street for many years and is now a major feature of the Smith Street Mall.
Mitchell Library.

pounds a year. Ellen shared her wealth with others and was a generous donor to worthy causes such as the Irish Famine Relief fund and the subscription guaranteeing a medical man on the goldfields.

Ellen was also still dealing with business competition, this time in the form of the newly built nearby Grove Hill Hotel, run by Sydney Budgen and his new bride Florence. Florence had married Budgen in Sydney in 1885 and immediately afterwards had travelled with him to the Territory, where he had been since the Margaret River rush of 1880. Florence was also destined to become a major business force in the Top End, although not as famous or flamboyant as her younger sister, May Brown, whose story is told in the next chapter.

It was Ellen who was first to move into the relative 'big time' of the Top End hotel trade. In 1888 Ellen accompanied her sister Mary back to Adelaide so the latter could spend a few weeks recuperating from a tropical illness. While there, Ellen took the opportunity to consult some architects, and a short time later she returned to the Territory with plans for a major business expansion. She began building a new hotel at Union Reef, on the Palmerston to Pine Creek railway line, and had plans for a grandiose hotel for Palmerston. When the Union Hotel was opened in October 1889 the *Northern Territory Times* described it as the 'best and most commodious north of Townsville,' adding the view that now that there was a licensed house in the region the authorities should try harder to curtail the sly grog merchants.

Ellen did not hesitate to point out to the government business practices that she regarded as unfair. In December 1889 she wrote a letter of protest to the government resident, John Langdon Parsons:

I beg respectfully to call your attention to the following facts—I bought from the government an allotment at a cost of 25 pounds—and am now building on that allotment a house at a cost of 500 pounds. I now find storekeepers and others carrying on business outside of the surveyed town at no cost other than a business licence and thereby injuring the users of allotments in the government town. I point out to you it is hardly fair of the government to allow an opposition township on the outskirts of the surveyed one.[6]

She was supported in her protest by the chief mining warden and other business people in the area and the government ceased issuing licences to people outside town boundaries. Ellen did not stay much longer at Union Reef, however. She sold her new hotel so she could concentrate on the 'great lady' of pubs she was building in Darwin. Before leaving Union Reef, however, she was hostess at the wedding of her sister, Mary, to Dudley Kelsey, a telegraph operator who had been an eight-year-old passenger on the *Birchgrove* with Ellen and William seventeen years earlier. The wedding was the first to be registered in the township.

By June 1890 Ellen was ready for the grand opening of her new stone hotel in Palmerston, even though she had to fight, unsuccessfully, a court battle over fees for the architect and builder, fees which turned out to be almost double what she had originally been quoted. At first Ellen was going to call her new project the Royal Hotel, but she changed her mind and chose a more parochial name, the North Australian. Descriptions of its structure demonstrate that Ellen tried hard to ensure that it could withstand the ravages of the ever-hungry white ants. However, the 11 July issue of *Northern Territory Times*, while acknowledging the hotel was 'the first building of its kind erected in the northern portion of the Territory', doubted that it would stand up to other rigours of the climate:

The walls are of stone, the timber used is exclusively cypress pine, the ground floors are of cement, and the roof galvanised iron. Lath and plaster partitions divide the rooms and the same material forms the ceiling, but this, we think, will in time prove a very troublesome and expensive mistake for we hardly expect that such material will stand the wear and tear of time in this country where thunderstorms are so severe and the wet and dry seasons are so regular.[7]

Despite such fears, the paper readily acknowledged the building's other assets and the contribution it could make to the Palmerston lifestyle:

A staircase leads to the second storey, where there are nine rooms — an assembly room 28 x 17 and eight bedrooms — besides a ladies' bathroom. A 10-ft balcony runs along the back of the building, both sides, and portion of the front and this should be a most charming retreat at all times from the dust and worry of the lower world. It is the first two storey hotel that has been built here and its erection reflects the greatest credit upon the ability of the contractor, Mr H.M. Debross, whose work throughout appears to have a first class stamp about it...We take it for granted that with a house like this Mrs Ryan will secure a fair proportion of the hotel business of the town.

And when Ellen's 4000-pound hotel finally opened its doors for business in September 1890, the *Times* paid tribute to her courage and enterprise:

It has been commonly asserted that Mrs Ryan exhibited more pluck than wisdom in entering upon such an expensive undertaking. Be that as it may, the fact remains that she has departed from the old weatherworn system of wood and iron houses and has now placed at the convenience of the public an hotel which is a credit to her enterprise and an estimable token of city improvement and the least we can do is to wish that she may find as time goes on that her confidence in the resources of Palmerston was not misplaced.

Acknowledging the post-gold-rush depression the Territory was now entering, the *Times* added: 'The outlook at present is not particularly cheering for any branch of business, but the North Australian Hotel is bound to secure its share of what trade is going in its peculiar line.' This it certainly did, even though because of the heavy mortgage Ellen had to take out on the hotel, she ended up holding the hotel licence and managing the hotel, while the large European firm of A. E. Jolly's actually owned the hotel.

As the proprietor of the town's most prestigious hotel, Ellen Ryan quickly had her hands full with many events, including, in 1892, providing accommodation for the South Australian premier, Thomas Playford, staging the wind-up party for Palmerston's annual Athletic and Sports Day, and attending the fancy-dress ball given by the very active Palmerston Dramatic and Musical Society. Ellen, who had worn an evening dress to this last event the year before, donned a costume and went as a Red Cross nurse, in which attire she consolidated her reputation as hostess. The *Northern Territory Times* gave credit where it was due:

About midnight there was an adjournment to the stage to refresh and rejuvenate on the profusion of delicacies tastefully laid out by Mrs Ryan of the North Australian Hotel whose success as a caterer was accorded very great praise and every bit of it well deserved.[8]

Like many Territorians, Ellen also took a keen interest in racing. She owned and raised horses in her own stables, although at times she ran foul of the district Council for allowing the animals to stray onto the roads and footpaths. However, Ellen's horses competed in most Top End racing meets for many years. In 1893 and for several succeeding years she also won the tender for the Northern Territory Racing Club tattersalls, and course privileges, with the settling up usually taking place at her hotel. Ellen also interested herself in local cricket and one year donated a cricket bat to the Palmerston District Cricket Club as a prize for club competitions. Whether this was motivated by an actual interest in cricket or simply by the rules of good business it is difficult to say, but in the sports-obsessed Territory it certainly helped to enhance her already solid reputation.

Always looking for a new challenge, Ellen decided in 1896 to relinquish her lease on the North Australian and try her hand at running the Palmerston Club

Hotel, which had been built in 1883 by Edward and Margaret Hopewell. At the time they were commended by the local press for finally providing a Territory hotel 'where a lady could be accommodated with lodging fit for one of the gentler sex'. They even had the hotel fitted with electric bells so patrons did not have to run after the barman, and they introduced Darwin to its first ice machine, a welcome innovation indeed in the hot and humid tropics. Ellen held a private sale of the furniture and effects she had accumulated for the North Australian and in May 1896 took over the running of the Club. In turn, Mr and Mrs G.H. James took up the lease on the North Australian, which they promptly renamed the Hotel Victoria, today known fondly amongst the locals as 'the Vic'.

During negotiations for the exchange of the leases, the three of them were involved in a court case in which a local male was charged with 'violently and feloniously assaulting Mrs James with intent to ravish her'. As part of his evidence, the accused admitted he had had about five glasses of wine at Ellen Ryan's hotel. He stated that 'the champagne wine at Ryan's [was] a sparkling wine and if you [drank] half a glass you felt it all through you'. [9]

Whether she took her special stocks of liquor with her to the Club Hotel is not known, but Ellen did make improvements. She installed one of Palmerston's first telephones in the hotel and advertised that she hoped 'by a close personal attention to the wants of her patrons to merit a fair share of public patronage'. She offered to give quotes on special terms for board and residence and to provide estimates for catering for picnics, tiffins and other parties. She promoted the Club as having 'excellent cuisine, large and well ventilated bedrooms, four sitting rooms, piano and billiard room, shower, baths, and horses and a wagonette for hire'.

Although Ellen's reputation as a genial hostess was widespread, she did have her conflicts with authority. One of her most persistent antagonists seems to have been Mounted Constable Thompson, with whom she first crossed swords in September 1896 when Miss Scott, one of her barmaids, was fined two pounds and costs for supplying an Aboriginal woman in Ellen's employ with a glass of liquor after she had done her day's work. This was against the law and Constable Thompson had waited about the hotel in plain clothes in order to catch the offender. When Miss Scott was convicted, Ellen, as proprietor of the hotel, had to pay the fine. Unhappy with what he thought was too lenient a punishment, Constable Thompson began spreading the word about town that 'Mrs Ryan had now trodden on his corns and he would be on to her like a scorpion'. When one of Ellen's gentlemen friends, waterman George Riddell, remonstrated with him for 'running a woman down', Constable Thompson challenged him to a fight. Riddell wrote a letter to the *Northern Territory Times* outlining the whole story and said he hoped that its publication would result in Constable Thompson 'treating respectable citizens with more respect'.

Although this was not the end of conflict between Ellen Ryan and Constable Thompson, all social squabbles soon paled into insignificance for a while when Palmerston was hit with its most devastating disaster to date—the cyclone of 1897. The storm struck late at night on 7 January, battering the township until daylight. Ellen's sister, Mary Kelsey, was one of the many residents who had a narrow escape when, at the height of the storm, she decided that her own home was too vulnerable and that she would try to reach Ellen's hotel and take shelter there. Grabbing her young son by the hand Mary fled with neighbours towards the hotel, but the force of the wind separated them from the others and hurled them into the open. She clutched her son to her and sought safety under the nearest tree, pulling loose branches around them for protection. Through the branches she could see a 'strange light, like a searchlight, hit the town' during the height of the cyclonic blast. She remained under the tree, cradling her son in her arms, until the storm subsided and Ellen and others found her.

Both the Club Hotel and the Hotel Victoria were damaged in the storm, but Ellen, after a short trip back to Adelaide, picked up the pieces and, along with the rest of the community, began the arduous task of reconstruction, a task which would be repeated several times in the history of the tropical north. By May both hotels had been repaired, although it was some time before the town itself was back to normal.

In August of the next year Ellen had another misfortune occur in her hotel when one of her guests, a man named Harry Harvey, contracted fever and died, despite Ellen's use of the telephone to get the doctor to attend to him as quickly as possible. In December she had more trouble when she was told by her Chinese messenger boy that the customs officer, Mr Finniss, was touting for business for the Hotel Victoria against the Club Hotel. When she complained to government resident Charles Dashwood, Finniss denied the allegation, saying he had not compared the Club with the Victoria but had simply been asked to recommend a hotel and he had recommended the Victoria. Ellen claimed that his behaviour was doing a serious injury to her business.

Whether it was due to these stresses and that of having to start again after the cyclone, or whether it was the result of more than quarter of a century living in the Top End is hard to say, but Ellen became very ill and was confined to her room for several weeks. When she had to travel south for medical help in September 1899, comments in the paper of the day illustrate the esteem in which she was held: 'We hope, and we are certain we are backed by all those who know the lady, that Mrs Ryan may soon be back amongst us, having completely recovered her health and strength.'

Sure enough, by February 1900 she was back, and by June she was embroiled in another confrontation with Mounted Constable Thompson. Thompson was in charge of a jury which was hearing a particularly sensational murder trial involving a Chinese riot at Wandi goldfields. The jury was staying at Ellen's Club Hotel, where Constable Thompson had to stand guard. When he suggested that he had seen a man coming out of a woman's hotel room in the small hours of the morning, Ellen complained to police chief Foelsche that Thompson was harming the reputation of her hotel and demanded that Foelsche seek an explanation. Thompson claimed: 'The whole affair has arisen out of my refusing to sleep in a bed Mrs Ryan offered me on Saturday evening and from beginning to end, it is one of personal spite against me.' Ellen in turn accused Thompson of 'unwarrantable slander and impertinence' and asked that the matter be brought to the attention of the government resident for review. Although Foelsche's report stated that two of the jurymen concurred with Thompson's story and that Mrs Ryan appeared to be at fault, the case does not seem to have damaged her reputation or her business. By 1901, the year of Federation, Ellen was in full swing again, racing her horses, running the tattersalls, catering for fancy-dress balls, and organising picnics and shooting parties for hotel patrons.

In October she decided to return to the Hotel Victoria and negotiated a transfer of leases with the then proprietors, who in turn took over her lease of the Club Hotel. Ellen continued offering fine service and occasionally organised special events. One of the most popular was when she secured the use of the good ship *M.L. Bolworra* in

November 1904 and took a large party for a few hour's excursion in the harbour. The *Times* reported that 'Mrs Ryan with her usual tact, had secured among her guests considerable vocal, musical and otherwise entertaining talent, with the result that moments and hours were not allowed to drag'. When part of the motor mechanism broke on the return journey, the trip had to be completed under sail, much to the delight of most guests, who thought the time had gone all too quickly.

By now Ellen had added yet another enterprise to her list of business ventures and established a dressmaking emporium in Smith Street, promising 'civility, attention and reasonable charges'. She also continued her interest in racing, owning and looking after several horses in her Darwin stables.

Her life was not completely trouble free, however. On a dark March night in 1909 she was farewelling friends who were leaving on a steamer when she fell off the Darwin jetty into the harbour, where both a large shark and a crocodile had been sighted that day. Fortunately two quick-minded local residents were nearby and able to rescue her. The *Times* commended her for having 'acted with rare presence of mind considering the sudden and surprising character of her adventure' saying she had the 'good sense to keep her mouth tightly closed and refrain from struggling'. It went on to use the incident to plead the case for better lighting in the vicinity of the jetty.

When the First World War broke out, Ellen was among the many women of the Territory who came to Australia's aid. Through the Territory branch of the Red Cross, which Jeannie Gilruth had founded, Ellen worked tirelessly to help raise money and supply equipment for the front. She was proud of the fact that the Territory Red Cross raised more money per capita than anywhere in Australia.

But while she was busy helping Territory boys who were fighting a war overseas, Ellen was embroiled in her own war at home. In 1915 she became one of the unfortunate victims of the decision of the ill-fated Gilruth administration to take over the wholesale and retail sales of liquor in the northern part of the Territory. The hotel acquisition led to direct conflict between the government and the growing union movement, the forced resignations of hotel managers, increased prices of grog, the emergence of sly grog shops and two separate six-week boycotts of the government-run pubs.

It had a telling effect on the men and women who owned or held the licences for them, including Ellen Ryan. When the takeover occurred A. E. Jollys actually owned the hotel, but Ellen, as licensee, managed it. She said the government had promised her several weeks of free accommodation in the hotel until she could make alternative arrangements. But later when she sought compensation of 2500 pounds as licensee at the time of the acquisition, the government said she owed eight guineas for board and lodging and Callan, the hotel supervisor, claimed he had not promised her free lodging. When Ellen protested, Callan did not pursue collection of the bill. However, the government did argue over her compensation figure and the final settlement was 1000 pounds less than the amount Ellen had requested.

Shortly after the government seized control of the hotels, Ellen, who was by now in her sixties and beginning to suffer from a crippling disease, packed her bags and reluctantly left the place that had been her home for more than forty years. For her farewell the women of the town held a progressive euchre party, at which they presented her with a thread bedspread and pillow shams as a token of their 'friendship and goodwill'.

Ellen moved to Adelaide, where she spent most of her remaining years in a home she fondly called The Shackle, a nostalgic reference to her enterprising youth. Sadly, the woman who had generously given so much of her spirit to the Territory had to spend much of her remaining time locked in a long and worrisome battle with government officials over the amount of compensation she was to be paid for the lease on her beloved Vic Hotel. It was a less-than-just way for the bureaucracy to treat a woman who had contributed so much to the Territory.

When Ellen Ryan died in Adelaide in May 1920, she received many tributes from her friends in the Territory, but perhaps her brother-in-law, Dudley Kelsey, said it best and most succinctly: 'Mrs Ryan was one of the very early pioneers of the North and was widely known for her kind and charitable nature and was the most popular and well known person in the Territory.'[10]

Ellen Ryan had no children, so her estate, which included several blocks of land in Darwin and the Pine Creek area, was divided amongst her nieces and nephews. While she left no legacy of children to carry on her pioneering spirit, she did leave a legacy in the form of the Hotel Victoria. It stands today in Darwin's central business district, concrete proof that women not only played a part in the social life of the Top End but also in its economic development.

As this book was being published, another colourful chapter in Ellen Ryan's life emerged in mysterious circumstances. When, in 1988, the lessee of the Hotel Victoria was knocking down a stone wall to enlarge one of the bar areas, workmen claimed they had discovered two stones which had apparently been hidden inside the wall's hollow cavity for decades. On one side of one of the stones was a sketch of Ellen Ryan. On the other side, and on a second stone, was a poem, printed in pencil, supposedly by a former lover who, after returning to Darwin and finding Ellen had died in Adelaide, was inspired to hide inside the Vic one night and etch her face and his love for her in stone and then seal the stones inside the wall, to be read 'at some far distant time'. While the authenticity of the find was doubted by many, others acknowledged that it had a ring of truth about it. The stones, now encased in glass in a new bar named after Ellen Ryan, certainly revived interest in the woman who gave Darwin one of its most famous landmarks. Drinkers are left to ponder the thoughts of her supposed lover, who wrote, in part:

She promised she would seek me here
If death was as she thought
Sometimes, less drunk, I think I see
Her lovely ghost form beckon me
Or could it be the liquor has me caught.

At the Vic Hotel in Darwin Town
They'll all be drinking still
Not knowing that her face lies hid
May it haunt them as for me it did
Oh God! This life's a bitter pill![11]

Whatever the truth of the story in stone, it is undoubtedly true that Ellen's pioneering spirit inspired other women to grasp the opportunities the Territory's hotel trade had to offer. Her own famous Hotel Victoria was destined to be managed by two of the Territory's most colourful and memorable women, May Brown and Christina Gordon, while 'down the track' women like Fannie Haynes, Tryphena Benstead, Kitty Bernard, Eileen Kilgariff, Myrtle Fawcett, Catherine O'Shea and her six daughters, and many others became legends in their time. Although they all deserve to have their stories told, no history of Territory women in pubs would be complete without reference to May 'Wolfram' Brown (whose story is told in the next chapter), Fannie 'Brock's Creek' Haynes and Christina 'Tanami' Gordon.

Fannie, who was born in London in 1869 to Albert and Eileen Dominey, began working as a domestic servant when she was a young girl. In September 1891 Fannie, aged twenty-two, and her younger sister Emily sailed for Queensland, where they hoped to find work and a new life. Within three months of arriving Fannie had found both.

In December Fannie married a forty-five-year-old widowed Irish miner, Michael Ryan Cody, at the Primitive Methodist Church in Croydon and together they headed almost at once for Charters Towers and then on to Wandi, east of Pine Creek in the heart of the Northern Territory's goldfields. There they opened a little hessian store, and ran it until Michael's death from dysentery in December 1897.

Fannie's lively Cockney personality and curly-headed good looks — not to mention the shortage of women on the fields — ensured that she could have her pick of new husbands if she so desired. She did, and within nine months, on 3 August 1898, she married English-born Thomas George Crush in the registry office at Wandi.

A short time later the newlyweds moved up the railway line to another mining community, Brock's Creek. There they built what would become Fannie's life, the Federation Hotel, a name which reflected the major political issue of the time. They opened the hotel in 1899 and together established a reputation for generosity and hospitality, both to travellers and to the people of the surrounding district. They presided over the popular race meetings that drew crowds of people from the surrounding area, including Ellen Ryan, who usually sponsored a horse in the regular 'Lady's Bracelet' race, among others.

Eventually profits from the hotel allowed Fannie and Tom to make an extended trip to London, where they visited Fannie's family in 1907. The following year Territorians elected Tom as their Labor member in the South Australian parliament. His parliamentary career was short-lived, however. When the commonwealth formally took control of Territory affairs from South Australia in 1911, for reasons still not totally explained, it did not allow for Territory representation in federal parliament. A decade of struggle would follow before this representation was achieved, but Tom would not be there to stand again. He died suddenly in 1913, leaving Fannie a widow for the second time. She carried on by herself for two years until early in 1916 when she married her third husband, one-legged grazier Harry Haynes.

At the time of their marriage Fannie was embroiled in her own fight with the government over its decision to acquire all Top End hotel licences. In the case of Fannie's Federation Hotel, the government announced that it was taking over both her hotel and store licence. If he did not already know about Fannie's strong will and determination, Harry was to learn. In numerous blunt and emotive letters to the officials of the day, Fannie put her case to the government, listing her stock, which she claimed was worth 1500 pounds. When she had still received no compensation by the following January she wrote to both the responsible minister, Atlee Hunt, and

Fannie Haynes (centre), one of the Territory's most colourful hotel owners for forty years, had to be forcibly evacuated from her beloved Federation Hotel at Brock's Creek when Darwin was threatened during the Second World War.
Northern Territory State Reference Library.

the supervisor of the state hotels, J.W. Callan, asking that the matter be settled quickly as she was getting married and wanted to join her husband on a holiday down south. Callan went at once to visit her, returning with the message for the administrator Gilruth that she now wanted 5000 pounds compensation and would take nothing less. Gilruth wrote to Hunt saying the government could not afford to take over the store contents. After further pressure from Fannie to get the matter settled, Gilruth finally advised Hunt that the government could not really utilise Fannie's premises and had failed to find a tenant for it. He thus recommended that the government pay Fannie 444 pounds compensation and let her again have and run the property. Hunt queried the justice of this from the government's point of view and the correspondence continued for another year. Eventually the liquor ordinance appears to have been amended to exclude Brock's Creek and Fannie was able to return to her normal business practices.

Throughout her battle with the authorities, Fannie got strong support from friends and neighbours, in particular the Byrnes family of nearby Burnside station, who wrote to the government demanding that the hotel should be allowed to remain open 'for the benefit of the general public'. Long-term Brock's Creek resident Tom Byrnes argued to the federal authorities that 'many cases of sickness' and people involved in 'important cases such as murder, suicide, etc.' had to wait at Brock's Creek for the train to Darwin and needed proper accommodation and service. 'Why should country people be ignored?' he asked.[12]

It is not clear whether Fannie obeyed the instruction to close her premises during the many months of squabble with the government but it is doubtful that she would have refused her customers service if she could provide it. Although stories abound about Fannie's rough and ready nature, her love of horse racing and gambling, her court battles to protect what was hers, her eavesdropping on all telephone conversations between Adelaide River and Darwin, and her colourful use of language, Fannie had a soft and generous side as well. Many were the ever-hopeful but seldom successful prospectors she had grubstaked while they sought to strike it rich. And many a weary traveller found refuge and hospitality in her pub, listening for hours to the yarns of the visiting bushies and of Fannie herself, who could spin tales and instigate practical jokes with the best of them.

There were plenty of stories around about the near-twenty-stone Fannie of course. She was renowned for ridding herself quickly of unwanted or unruly customers, earning herself the title of 'Fighting Fannie'. One famous Fannie story that illustrates her practical nature is recounted by Ernestine Hill in her book *The Territory*. According to Hill, a travelling man of religion happened by the hotel one day when a fierce tropical storm was ripping through the bush. Concerned for his and everyone else's safety, he cried, 'We'll pray'. 'No we won't,' growled Fannie. 'We'll cover up the bloody flour.'[13]

Her strong will was never more apparent than when the Second World War loomed close to Australia's shores and officials decided to evacuate all women and children from the Top End 'war zone'. Seventy-two-year-old Fannie stood her ground with a gun and a bottle of lysol, threatening army provosts who tried to evict her that she would shoot them with one and drink the other. But in the end the strength of military regulations and the army officers won out. Fannie and Harry were lifted bodily from their Federation Hotel and evacuated to Adelaide. There Fannie spent several months very ill in bed but eventually she recovered and went to Sydney to join her sister Emily, whom she had not seen since they had parted nearly fifty years earlier when Fannie went north.

Fannie's niece later remembered her aunt's arrival well: 'She was a broad lady with long silver grey hair, toothless and a florid complexion. With dresses of floor length brocaded silk she was like someone out of another era.' Always ready with a practical joke, Fannie delighted in scaring the refined Sydneysiders with her 'mad woman from the north' routine. She also told bitterly of her evacuation and claimed the soldiers had pillaged and looted her beloved home. But the humane side of her nature remained intact too, and she gladly gave her clothing coupons to her niece to buy her wedding gown.

Sadly and suddenly Fannie died, just before the war's end, nearly 3000 miles (5000 kilometres) from the only home she knew. She was cremated in Sydney and her grieving husband Harry, who arrived too late for her funeral, flew her ashes back to be buried at her beloved Brock's Creek. She would have liked the tribute author Ernestine Hill paid her when, years later, she wrote, 'Fannie Haynes *was* Brock's Creek'.

More refined than Fannie, but no less endowed with fortitude and courage, was Christina Gordon, who, during her long life, earned herself an Australia-wide reputation as one of the Territory's most prominent publicans and citizens. Born on Christmas Day in 1863, Christina first came to the Territory just after the turn of the century with her husband, Duncan Gordon, whom she had met and married in Queensland. They had first gone to Western Australia where they worked on the goldfields, Christina proving herself 'as good a miner as any man, handling pick and cradle with the best of them'. [14] From there they went on to build thirty-six miles (58 kilometres) of the Western Australian dingo-proof fence, with Christina again sharing in the physical labour. It was in Western Australia that their two sons were born. When they heard news of a Territory mining rush at the Tanami in about 1908, the Gordon family packed their meagre belongings and headed for the fields.

Accompanied by Duncan's twin brother John, who remained with them all his life, they staked a claim and for two years worked solidly, reaping a small fortune. Existence was isolated and supplies were scarce. At one stage, when they ran out of food, Christina fed the family on milk taken from their camels each day.[15] As there was seldom any other white woman on the fields, and no resident doctor or nurse, Christina nursed hundreds of miners, ill with fever or injured in the course of seeking their fortune from the elusive gold. She earned the title of 'Mother of the Tanami' and years later was frequently referred to as Mrs Tanami Gordon.

Perhaps it was from this experience that she came to appreciate the important role the Territory pubs played in the lives of people so isolated from the rest of the world, for it was as a publican that she was destined to become best known and loved. When want of water compelled the family's evacuation from the goldfields, they moved to the Pine Creek area, where Christina continued her charitable work by becoming a foundation member of the Red Cross and eventually, in 1921, took up the lease of the Playford Club Hotel, strategically located on the railway line. There she established the reputation which would stand her in good stead for the next thirty years.

When Lord and Lady Apsley met her in 1925 in Pine Creek during their trip through parts of the Territory and Western Australia, Lady Apsley praised Christina's pioneering efforts, pointing out she was one of the first white women to come to the Northern Territory from Western Australia after the Kimberley gold rush. In tribute, Lady Apsley wrote:

Some day, when there is a history of the Northern Territory to be written, her name and others like her ought to go down the Ages among the great women of Australia — the pioneer women who have shown it possible to carry the ideal of homelife out into the untamed Bush, and whose names should mean to future generations of Australians what Boadicea, Queen Elizabeth, Florence Nightingale and Queen Victoria mean to us in the Old Country. In comparison with hers, our little trip over her route was like playing with a toy cart-and-horses compared to riding the winner of the Melbourne Cup, but, as is usual with prophetesses and heroines, Mrs Gordon lived an ordinary life and gave us a most extraordinarily good tea and breakfast.[16]

In 1926 the family moved to Darwin where Christina took over the lease of the famed Hotel Victoria from May Brown who in turn took up ownership of Christina's Playford Pine Creek Hotel. Christina offered her own distinctive kind of hospitality, assuring her patrons of 'a home away from home'. During the twenties and thirties when some of the world's pioneer aviators were passing through Darwin on record-

When the railway was extended to Katherine and beyond, Nellie Fisher, newly widowed at the time, established a bush timber and galvanised iron boarding house and hotel at Mataranka, near the Elsey Station homestead of 'Never Never' fame. She is pictured here with her grand-daughter Jaci Seale, who occasionally was sent to stay with her from Darwin, where her other famous Territory grandmother, May Brown, was managing the Vic Hotel. Photograph courtesy of Jaci O'Brien (née Seale).

breaking flights, Christina played hostess to them at her hotel and had them sign their names to one of the stone walls that Ellen Ryan had had built some forty years earlier. She soon became known as 'The Aviator's Mother' and decades later one of her grandson's prized possessions was a hat given to her by Kingsford Smith on one of his trips to Darwin. Christina also involved herself in other aspects of Darwin's social and sporting life. As well as donating prizes to various sporting events, she held the distinction of being elected vice-president of the Rover's Football Club and as such, she hosted many sporting functions at her hotel.

Christina's first few years of managing the Hotel Victoria had their times of sorrow. In 1928 her husband's twin brother, John, died of pleurisy and a year later Duncan died, a devastating blow to the family. Following his death Christina went into business with her two sons. Realising the importance of good entertainment to an isolated community like Darwin, Christina soon branched out into the picture theatre business and became part of a syndicate that built the Star Theatre in Smith Street. Christina bought the syndicate out in 1930 and gave the talented Tom Harris free hand as manager. When he began putting on special shows for the unemployed, the Star soon secured itself a reputation as one of Darwin's most popular entertainment venues.

The family also maintained the Hotel Victoria and built Gordon's Don Hotel as well as a popular city cafe. When Qantas first began its flights south from Darwin, Christina and her son Duncan were chosen to be the first civilian passengers. They received a hearty ovation when they returned a few weeks later.

Eventually Christina retired from the hotel business and settled down to a private life in her Daly Street home. In 1937 she received an OBE for her charitable work in the Territory. However, her retirement was soon interrupted. Like most other Darwin women, Christina was evacuated during the Second World War, an evacuation to which she strongly objected, in common with other Territorians. As soon as civilians were permitted to return, Christina and her son came back to Darwin and again took over the Hotel Victoria. Various factors, including shortage of staff and materials, coupled with Christina's increasing ill health, forced her to dispose of the business and retire to Queensland, where she spent her few remaining years, suffering from a severe illness.

There she died in 1952 and, although she had been gone from the Territory for several years, news of her death was greeted with sorrow there. The paper of the day wrote an extensive obituary, referring to her as 'one of the most colourful characters which the Territory has known'.

But the most colourful character of all was arguably the woman with whom Christina, Fannie and Ellen had all shared many an entertaining time — the thrice-married May 'Wolfram' Brown, whose story is told next, and who, like Christina Gordon, helped mine both the Territory's mineral and its liquid wealth.

May Brown takes her only grandchild, Jaci Seale for a ride in her latest car in the 1920s in Darwin. Jaci has mixed memories of being babysat by her grandmother. 'She was very generous and had magnificent jewellery and furniture and fashions, but when she lost her temper she was absolutely terrifying'

Chapter 10

May Brown

THE RISE AND FALL OF AUSTRALIA'S WOLFRAM QUEEN AND OTHER WOMEN WHO MINED THE TERRITORY'S WEALTH

'May Brown was always interested in the miners; she herself, the most colourful figure in the mining world. As proprietress of the Hotel Victoria, she was noted for her generosity to genuine friends; but should anyone play her false, she would wind him with a straight right to the solar plexus. Married three times, a previous husband had been a professional boxer; he taught her the art; she knew it well, and made use of it.'

Vanda Marshall, We Helped to Blaze the Track

May Brown may have been the most flamboyant of the women engaged in mining the Territory's rich mineral deposits, but she was certainly not the only one, or the first. Although seldom mentioned in official reports, women were there, pioneering mining ventures along with the men in both the Top End and Central Australia. As gold, copper, tin, wolfram, mica, iron ore and other minerals were discovered at various times throughout the Territory, the cry went out and periodic 'rushes' became an integral part of the Territory's boom-and-bust history. Unfortunately very few women seem to have left records of their lives on the fields, although some details of their movements and lifestyle can be gleaned from other sources such as from descriptions found in official and unofficial records, newspaper reports and oral histories. One woman who did record her observations was the talented daughter of the first government resident, Harriet Daly who, along with her husband and child, joined in the Territory's first real rush in 1872. Harriet later recalled the excitement that seized the population when gold was discovered:

Of course, the one and only topic of conversation was gold mining. Each day brought news of a fresh discovery. Regulations were drawn up, and officials were appointed to supervise the goldfields. I was soon the proud possessor of a miners right and my claim was pegged out for me away on the reefs. The excitement of those months has, I believe, never been equaled, nor do I think it improved the morale of the Territory. Men left the steady employment and good pay given them by Government, and rushed to the diggings. No roads were made, nor was any attempt to make any begun and the wet season was rapidly approaching.

Each day saw a new company floated, regardless of any certain information, even as to the whereabouts of the newly discovered mine; and the feverish excitement that ensues whenever a gold rush is on, ran to a most dangerous height. By degrees the precious metal began to come into camp. Rough men brought pickle bottles full of nuggets...The mania spread everywhere; even the children were seen groping about amongst the rocks on Fort Point, picking up quartz and smashing it up with their hammers. Every week fresh arrivals took place, and fully equipped prospecting parties sent up by the newly formed companies from Adelaide, Melbourne and Sydney by degrees reached the scene of operations; indeed, for a time it seemed as if the early days of the Victorian goldfields were on the point of being lived over again.

Like the Victorian rush, the first Territory rush also ended, although the Top End region in which the gold was discovered has been the scene of many similar rushes.

The first real rush to Central Australia followed the discovery of gold in 1887 at Arltunga, some seventy-five miles (120 kilometres) east of Alice Springs. It brought the greatest influx of people to the area since the construction of the overland telegraph, an influx which continued, at a varying pace, for the next twenty years. There were goldfields at Arltunga, White Range and Winnecke, all of which are in the same general area.

Although there is virtually no mention of European women in the area for the first decade, some were almost certainly there, as is indicated by a photograph, held by the Northern Territory Conservation Commission and dated 1896, showing an unnamed, rather unhappy-looking woman standing outside a tent home on the Arltunga fields. Aboriginal women were certainly present and, apart from being engaged as laundry maids, goat shepherds, cooks and water and ore carriers on the fields, some lived with white miners.

There is evidence that by 1903, when the second rush was under way, European women were in the area. With more than 500 people flocking to the fields, this is hardly surprising. An Adelaide *Advertiser* report of 13 May 1903 referred to the arrival of one of the largest mixed trains ever seen arriving from the south and carrying a large number of passengers, about half of them heading for Arltunga. Among them were two women from Victoria who were going to join their husbands on the fields. One was married to George Lines, manager of the crushing battery at Winnecke. Doris Bradshaw, daughter of the Overland Telegraph Master at Alice Springs at the time, visited the Lineses and later described their lifestyle at the isolated settlement: 'I found Winnecke a calico village, a straggling land of tents and bough shelters. George Lines and his wife lived in two big square tents connected by a breezeway and insulated from the sun by brush walls and a rubberoid roof. This material was also used for the floor. There were deck chairs and improvised furniture, all of it quite comfortable. They even had a small portable organ used for sing-songs in the evening. My diary complains that it was pitched a little too high for the songs I sang and for "Juanita," which I sang as a duet with Mr Lines. No television, no radio, no theatre, no cinema...and yet we had simple fun that kept us very happy.'[1] The Lines remained on the fields for several years.

Following the typhoid epidemic of 1903, in which at least one woman died, there was a request for another doctor on the fields. In support of the request, it was pointed out that there were six white women with their husbands and children at White Range, and three others were leaving for Winnecke. One of the women at White Range was Betty O'Neil, who had arrived in about May 1903 to join her husband Patrick, who had managed to obtain a much coveted billiards licence. A

Life on the Arltunga goldfields was harsh and only a handful of European women accompanied the men who ventured forth to reap a fortune. One of the few was this woman, pictured outside her tent in the late 1890s. There was a scarcity of European women, and Aboriginal women were crucial to the development of the fields, often carrying the precious mineral many miles over barren rock in the scorching sun, to the nearest battery where it could be processed.
Northern Territory Conservation Commission.

man who was passing through the area observed them putting up their home and wrote in his diary: 'White Range seems to be going ahead. The man with the billiard table is putting up a mulga shanty there. He started with us and the table has only just arrived, his wife is up also and she was holding the posts whilst he was ramming them.' Betty was still on the field in 1908 when she was listed as owning a quarter share in the Excelsior mining company.

In 1909 another woman, Jane Webb, accompanied her husband, teamster Ben Webb, to Arltunga, where they lived for many years in a primitive dwelling they built themselves. There Jane gave birth to their children, reading instructions from the

Mrs George Lines, pictured with her husband and child outside their home at the Winnecke goldfield, where George was manager, was one of the few European women to venture to the Arltunga goldfields in central Australia. She arrived in 1903 and stayed for several years. Bradshaw collection, Northern Territory Conservation Commission.

family medical book to a young Aboriginal girl, Stella, who lived with them and acted as midwife. Eventually, however, isolation took its toll and Jane contracted a fatal illness, leaving Stella to look after the children she had helped deliver.

For the most part, European women did not go to the mining fields because living conditions were not considered suitable for them. Men on the fields often turned to Aboriginal women for companionship and together they raised families, some of whom are still part of Centralian society. One of the best known was the family of Walter Smith, whose life has been outlined in Dick Kimber's book *Man From Arltunga*. One of the Smith children born at Arltunga was Ada, who later went on to become a prominent citizen of Alice Springs.

Some women played a part in the development of the Arltunga goldfields without living on them. One of these was a Mrs Bagot of Oodnadatta, who organised camel teams to leave weekly with stores and supplies for the miners.[2] Others ran stores or hotels in the little centres that were dotted along the long and rough track to the fields.

Although the gold eventually petered out, many of those who came to central Australia during the rush took up land and stayed. One of the best known of those families was that of Sam and Lizzie Nicker, who named among their close friends Breaker Morant. After many years travelling by horse and buggy on outback tracks in Queensland and the Territory, the Nickers eventually found their way to Arltunga, arriving in December 1905. With them was their ten-year old daughter, Anne Jane, and their young son, Claude, who had been born during the journey. They built a stone hut between the police station and the store and for some time made their living selling sly grog. Lizzie, who had two more children while at Arltunga, became a midwife and nurse for the region. From Arltunga the Nicker family moved on to Ryan's Well where Lizzie again worked as a nurse and midwife while Sam ran the post office. When Sam died, she stayed on, refusing to be evacuated during the Second World War. Their daughters, Anne Jane and Margaret, eventually married Centralians and became pioneers in their own right.

At the time the Arltunga gold rush was in full swing, mining in the Top End was also having a resurgence. One of the centres for mining activity was Brock's Creek. Apart from the irascible publican Fannie Haynes, one of the most prominent women in that area was Susannah Mansfield, a woman who came to the Territory with a vast amount of experience of Australia's goldfields.

Susannah was the daughter of John Marritt, a soldier who had fought at the battle of Waterloo under the Duke of Wellington, and his wife Sarah.[3] She was born in 1843 in Oaklands, Tasmania, and travelled with her family to the Victorian goldfields in the 1850s where, as a child of eleven, she observed the Eureka uprising. She later recalled how the miners armed with pikes stood up to the rifle fire of the government troops when they launched their surprise attack on the stockade, and remembered seeing those who fell mortally wounded. Susannah was also among those who welcomed the Victorian governor Sir Charles Hotham to the goldfields, and saw the colourful entertainer Lola Montez perform her controversial 'spider dance' for the miners.

It was in Victoria in December 1864 that Susannah met and married a miner, William Mansfield, the son of an English surgeon. They appear to have followed various gold rushes in Victoria and New South Wales for many years. In 1868 they had a daughter, Susannah Elizabeth, who died in Ballarat two years later. Their son William Henry was born at the nearby Canadian goldfield in 1874 and their daughter Lily Warren was born at Home Rule in 1877. They moved to the Territory in 1898 when William was appointed manager of the Zapopan Mine at Brock's Creek where Fannie and Tom Crush were preparing to build their Federation Hotel. Although William was replaced as manager in September of 1905, he and Susannah continued living in the mining community. By 1914, both their children had married, though their son's marriage did not last. William Junior then enlisted in the First World War and went to England, where he remained for the rest of his life. When William Senior died at Brock's Creek in September 1914 Susannah elected to remain in the tiny township. In 1920, however, she was badly injured during a severe storm, and was trapped for several hours under debris. After spending several months recuperating in the Darwin Hospital she moved into a Darwin house.

There was more adversity in store for her. In 1921 her son-in law, Dave Byers, disappeared forever in strange circumstances while he was managing one of Joe Bradshaw's stations, and four years later she witnessed her only daughter's tragic death in a buggy accident with her good friend Eliza Tuckwell Brown. Susannah, by now widely known as 'Granny', took over the raising of her grandchildren. Lively and always full of humour, she was greatly loved and respected by the Top End community. When she died in 1937 at the age of ninety-three, she was Darwin's oldest woman resident, and her funeral was attended by most of the townsfolk.

Another woman associated with Top End mining was Lucy McGinness, or Alyandabu as she was known in her Aboriginal community. A tall and dignified woman, she met and married Irish-born Stephen McGinness when he was a ganger on the railway line. For years they lived in fettlers' camps up and down the line until Stephen lost his job and he and Lucy and their growing family went on a prospecting trip to the Bynoe Harbour area, about sixty kilometres from Darwin. One of their sons, Valentine, recalled how his mother made a discovery which made her locally famous:

They had a dray, three horses, a herd of goats and a mob of chooks. Mum and the kids were bringing the goats. They camped near a big long billabong about eight miles [13 km] from Bynoe, when Mum realised she had lost two of her best milkers. She went back to find them and where she did was a big upturned tree with some specimens hanging on it. She brought them back to the camp and her brother, Frank, told her it was tin. So they went back to the site and found the mine and mined it from then until Dad died.[4]

Stephen named the mine Lucy, in honour of his wife.

Val remembered sending the tin by dray to the pumping station near the present Darwin dam where it would be put on the train and sent to Jollys, Darwin's main European store, or to one of the Chinese merchants in Darwin. 'Everything was done by hand; we had no compressors. We did have a government steam tractor for a few years which we used to drive a machine to crush the stone. We used to call it a dingledarcedingledun because that's the sound we thought it made.'[5]

When Stephen McGinness died in 1918 after years of working down the extremely hot mine-shafts, hard times struck the family. Although Lucy had been a legal partner in the mine, because she was Aboriginal she was not allowed to own property and the mine was forfeited. Her Aboriginality did entitle her, however, to live at Darwin's newly built Kahlin Compound for Aborigines, where she moved her family. Valentine remembered the time with sadness:

We were virtually starving. We were given one slice of bread for each meal and we could get a drink of tea. Sometimes we got jam for breakfast and sometimes for lunch and dinner we were allowed to put our slice of bread on top of water which had been used to boil meat for working natives and soak up the juice. For a while mother cooked and worked for Judge Hogan at Myilly Point and she would sometimes sneak us a little food.[6]

Although the family went through hard times, Lucy lived to see her children become part of the movement which fought for the emancipation of their people and improvements to their lives. Her eldest son Jack became the first person of Aboriginal descent to be president of the North Australian Workers Union and he was the first president of the Half-caste Progress Association, formed in the 1950s to fight for citizenship and better conditions for his people. When Lucy died in September 1961 the *Northern Territory News* paid her tribute:

Mrs McGinness undertook her giant task with tremendous energy and complete devotion to her family. Although her daughter was in her home and her sons in a compound she still tried throughout to give them something of herself and keep the family ties strong. This became the centre of her existence and later extended towards her numerous grand and great grand children. Although all her life she had little material wealth, many have benefited through her generosity. Those who knew her will remember always the fierce spirit of independence that lasted until the end of her days.

Eighteen months later Lucy's own Aboriginal people performed a huge ceremony in her honour at the Darwin River property of her grand-daughter, Vai Stanton, a latter-day pioneer in her own right, whose story is told elsewhere. In 1988 Territory singer Ted Egan honoured Lucy with a song in his 'Faces of Australia' series and paid her further tribute by successfully entering her story in the bicentennial publication *Unsung Heroes and Heroines*.

The Tennant Creek and Tanami rushes in the 1930s brought more women to the outback centres of the Territory, and although they were far outnumbered by men they made their own contributions, not the least of which was to help establish the town of Tennant Creek itself. Some of their stories are incorporated in other parts of this book.[7]

In Tennant, as in other parts of the Territory, Aboriginal women were often the unsung heroines and the real toilers in the mines, reaping wealth for others. An incident reported in the *Northern Standard* in 1935 serves to illustrate the dangers they faced:

More than a local police inquiry is needed into the tragedy of the [Aboriginal woman] crushed to death by a falling mass of rock while working in an ochre tunnel near Alice Springs. Both outback missionaries and union officials have opposed the employment of any Aborigines in such out of the way mines and it will be a shock to many people that native women have to face such underground risks. We pride ourselves on having made great humane advances since the early 19th century in the United Kingdom when women, stripped to the waist, hauled coal trucks by chains fastened round their bodies. The conditions under which [Aboriginal women] now toil underground in Central Australia may not be nearly so severe, but more than one of them has lately suffered a mishap that clearly calls for full investigation.[8]

This tragic story serves to remind us that women of all races were very much part of the Territory's many boom-and-bust mining ventures.

THE MAY BROWN STORY

But the woman whose story perhaps best illustrates the substantial role women have played in the Northern Territory mining industry, and in the Territory's social and economic development in general, is the flamboyant thrice-married May Victoria

Brown, Australia's 'Wolfram Queen', one of the Territory's truly larger than life characters.

During her near-fifty-year association with the place (1890-1939) May became actively involved in nearly every facet of Territory life. Although mining and pubs were her major preoccupation, and the means by which she made and lost her fortune, she also took an active interest in gambling, giving, racing, politicking, drinking and marrying, thus ensuring that her name was indelibly etched in the memories of all who met her, and many who did not, but heard of her exploits.

She may have inherited her flamboyance from her mysterious paternal grandmother, actress Eliza Pailing, and her grandfather, prominent Tasmanian politician-auctioneer, Charles James Weedon. May's father, also named Charles James, was their son, the product of their liaison in the early 1830s in Launceston, several years before Charles Senior met and married Charlotte Hardwicke and settled down to become 'the principal man in Launceston amongst the genteel people'.[9]

Although May's father appears to have stayed in Launceston until he was a young man, her grandmother very quickly disappeared from the scene. Charles Junior went to Sydney when he was in his late teens, became a labourer, and met and married May's mother, Mary Chiodette, the daughter of a wealthy bandmaster. May was born on 24 May 1875, the sixth of seven Weedon children.

May's first contact with the Northern Territory came ten years later in 1885 when her elder sister, Florence, met and married a Darwin saddler and would-be miner, Sydney Budgen, who had arrived in the Territory in 1880 in search of gold on the Margaret River. They were married in Sydney but headed straight for the Territory, where they began trading in liquid gold, which in Territory terms was usually more profitable than the elusive and coveted mineral itself. They opened pubs at Grove Hill, then Burrundie, near Pine Creek, where they were soon joined by May and Florence's brothers, Sydney and Percy, who both established reputations for their skill in local cricket and racing circles.

May made her first visit to the Territory in June 1890, just after her fifteenth birthday, to help her sister and brother-in-law manage the relatively new Terminus Hotel at the end of Darwin's Chinatown. While this experience probably affected the direction her life took, May would almost certainly have been influenced and inspired by Ellen Ryan, who was about to open her famed Hotel Victoria, which May was destined to manage thirty years later. Ellen's strength and business acumen in a male-dominated environment were traits which May also developed, albeit in a more flamboyant style than Ellen. The feisty and independent spirit that was to make May a legend in her own time was probably also shaped by national trends of the time, to encourage women to learn more than just a domestic trade, to throw away their corsets, and not to be ashamed of the 'bachelor girl' image.

May made several visits to the Territory over the next decade but in 1901, when she was twenty-six and living in Sydney, she decided to marry a dashing former Australian amateur boxing champion, George Seale. George, who was fifteen years older than May, was the son of a wealthy Irish agriculturalist and hotel owner in Sydney and had been a prominent Sydney cricketer and rower. Legend has it that his family did not approve of the working-class girl he chose to marry and this may help account for some of May's outlandish behaviour when later she became wealthy. At the time May and George were married their income was moderate, but their life was fascinating. George was managing Sydney's Amateur Gymnastics Club in Castlereagh Street and they lived on the premises, running both the club and an accompanying bar, May's second close encounter with the hospitality trade. Here May met many of Sydney's most prominent sportsmen and here, too, she learned her husband's pugilistic skill, a skill which would come in handy many times during her Territory life.

In 1902 when May had her first and only child, George, the Sydney papers speculated on whether the boy would follow in his famous father's sporting footsteps. But he was not to have the chance. In March 1906, after battling pleuropneumonia for seven weeks, George Seale died, leaving May and young George with an estate worth 266 pounds. The Sydney papers sang George Seale's praise, the *Sydney Mail* claiming that 'in his day he was about the best all round amateur athlete in Australia [and] for his weight...probably the best amateur boxer in the world'. The esteem in which he was held by his colleagues was made clear when they organised a huge benefit for May at the National Sporting Club's Athletic Hall. About 700 people attended the event, which included several boxing bouts as well as entertainment by performers from the Tivoli and music by the Purnells Band. A 'goodly sum' was raised by the benefit along with 80 pounds in subscriptions.

Grieved though she no doubt was, May was not one to wait around for something to happen. A little more than six months after George died, May married James Burns, one of the partners in the rich Wolfram Camp mine near the Territory mining community of Pine Creek. It is likely that James, who came from a Newcastle mining family, had met May through her brothers, both of whom lived in Pine Creek. May and James were married in Sydney but headed for Darwin a few weeks later.

When May, James and young George arrived in the Territory in January 1907, the *Northern Territory Times* accurately noted that 'with wolfram quoted at over 100 pounds a ton, they appear to be coming back to one of the best things in the NT'. In August 1907 James and one of the other partners, Goggins, bought out the third partner, Brock, for 1710 pounds. This was a surprisingly low price given the reputation of the mine that only four months before had prompted the well-known auctioneer, V. V. Brown to advertise: 'I have no hesitation in saying that with machinery and brains this will prove one of the most remunerative things ever found in the Northern Territory. It is a rare chance for investment.' Indeed it was, and although May suffered many hardships and trials in years to come, the wealth from this mine, and their nearby Crest of the Wave mine, supported her extravagant, flamboyant and generous lifestyle for most of her life.

That wealth enabled her to travel frequently and extensively. In December of 1907 she took young George on the first of many trips south to visit his grandmother and other relatives. They sailed on the *Eastern*, along with the largest exodus of Europeans from Port Darwin for many years. Within a week of their departure, James suffered a serious accident which illustrated the hazards of their isolated life. He had been riding about seven miles [11 km] from the Wolfram Camp mine when he was thrown from his horse and injured to such an extent that he was unable to move afterwards. An Aboriginal boy found him and went to the mine site to get help. A buggy was sent to get him, and when it was discovered how badly he was injured, his rescuers decided to try and get him onto the train at Pine Creek on Saturday morning. It was raining and the roads were heavy, so the journey took the whole night, but by

The Wolfram Camp was home for many years to May Brown, who made her fortune mining and selling wolfram during the First World War, earning herself the title of the Territory's Wolfram Queen. Her square, thatched residence (bottom right) was a far cry from the glamorous accommodation of the Scotts Hotel in Melbourne and the Hotel Australia in Sydney where she often had suites booked permanently when the Melbourne Cup was on. The Wolfram Camp mine also accommodated the largest Chinese community on the Top End mining fields.
Kirkbride Album, Latrobe Collection, State Library of Victoria.

daylight they reached the Pine Creek terminus and by Saturday night James was finally in Darwin receiving medical treatment.

Shortly after May returned to the Territory a tin rush was under way, which the *Northern Territory Times* described in hopeful terms:

During the past week further contingents have left Pine Creek in quest of Dame Fortune's silvery secrets between Pine Creek and the Gulf and there must be some fifty men engaged at the present moment in this last attempt to find something big that will lift up the NT with a jump. Whether a big find eventuates or not, it is certain that the boom has come in the nick of time to provide occupation for the idle miner and to keep adventurous spirits within our borders.

But mining in the tropics had distinct drawbacks, which at times brought out the best in May. When a fever epidemic broke out at the Umbrawarra field, where tin and wolfram had been discovered in February 1909, she became Florence Nightingale to the sick miners. Author Ernestine Hill paid her this tribute: 'Forgetting her own interests, riding with food and water for the dying, [May was] a nurse of unexpected gentleness in many a man's last hours, and then, with a black boy, burying the dead.'[10] The *Northern Territory Times* also praised her for playing 'a truly womanly and kindly part in nursing the poor men brought in from the tinfield and suffering'.

The manager of the Pine Creek Hotel at the time was Fannie Bell, who often went out on horseback to prospect herself. She later recalled the fever outbreak and the difficulties caused by living in isolation without medical help:

Several men were brought into our hotel suffering from malaria fever. They were miners from outback and there were no doctors or nurses about to attend to them. Next thing [Mrs Burns] arrived and took charge of them. More sick men came in from the far flung mining areas—they were attended to at the hotel until the train arrived. [Mrs Burns] made all the men as comfortable as possible for their trip to hospital in Darwin [where they] were treated by good nurses and a wonderful man Doctor Strangman...All we had in those days in Pine Creek to give to anyone who was ailing was Strangman's Fever Mixture! What a dreadful thing to live so far away from a Doctor.[11]

The fever was no discriminator, and eventually reports arrived that May had been brought in very ill, along with two other well-known Pine Creek women, Mrs Schunke and Mrs Frith. They recovered, however, and May was soon playing the Good Samaritan again, this time to Fannie Bell's infant daughter, Heather. Once more Fannie remembered May's help in her time of trouble:

I was nursing my infant daughter when I noticed she was in a convulsion. I had no one to advise me so I quickly took all her clothes off and put her in a large washing up dish—still with cutlery in the bottom! [Our Chinese cook] looked at me in amazement and said the water [was] hot. And so it was. I was in despair. Suddenly a voice said "give the baby to me." Who should it be but [Mrs Burns]. She took Heather from me and told me to go and rest. I went to my bedroom crying and thinking that I shouldn't be so far away from medical assistance. When I had composed myself, I went out to [Mrs Burns] and there was my beautiful girlie all wrapped up in a blanket. I was not able to hold her, only to massage her gently with brandy and water. After working on her all day, she started to tremble and her eyes moved at last. Oh! I will never forget that dear soul coming to me in my trouble.[12]

Fear of the fever eventually caused Fannie and her husband Jim to pack up their family and leave Pine Creek for Darwin where they were nearer medical help. But May stayed and continued to work the mine with James and their Chinese tributors who helped with the operation for a share of the profits. May usually worked down the mine-shafts attending to the cleaning and dressing of ores and helping to mend the pumps when they broke down. Life on the isolated mine site was far from easy. The heat from the tropical sun was intense, the flies numerous, the equipment primitive and working conditions less than luxurious. In 1910 a huge flood wiped out the crushing battery and plant at Wolfram Hill along with 1000 pounds worth of wolfram. By then, however, May and James were able to sustain such disasters; they had bought out their partner and their mine was extracting record amounts of ore. The year's government report stated that 'a splendid shoot of wolfram ore has come from the Wolfram Camp, the richest and best wolfram mine in Australia, the holders having made thousands of pounds'.

Despite, or perhaps partly because of, her increasing success and wealth, May was beginning to succumb to one of the hazards of Territory life and was already no stranger to drink. After her arduous buggy rides into Pine Creek to cart the wolfram ore to the train for storage in Darwin until the price was right, May usually headed for her brother Sydney's Playford Hotel. According to one who knew her at the time, May, a brandy drinker, tended to 'tear things apart'. On several occasions, she had to be nursed out of the DTs after a binge with her friends.

When the Bell family left Pine Creek, May's brother Sydney took over the Pine Creek Hotel and at times May helped him run it. She probably also gave financial help at times to Sydney and to her other brother Percy who had taken over the management of the local butchery. Sydney was praised in the *Northern Territory Times* for changes he made to the hotel including the supply of 'aerated waters of various kinds made on the premises' and, in keeping with the 'White Australia' policy, 'the introduction of a white cook and white laundress from the south'. May and James, on the other hand, were the target of some criticism for disregarding the policy and employing Chinese labour at their Wolfram Camp mine. They were certainly not alone in this practice, however. The Chinese usually worked longer hours for less pay than did European workers and were thus more appealing employees for many mine owners. The Wolfram Camp region was known for having the most substantial Chinese quarters and population of any Territory mine of the day, however, and as such was sometimes singled out.

In fact May and James sometimes left one of their tributors, a long-time Chinese businessman and miner, Mee Wah, in charge of the mine while they travelled south. They made one such trip at the end of 1911 when, as usual, they stayed at May's mother's residence in Annandale. They stayed in Sydney nearly four months, returning to the Territory in March 1912 with their friend Ellen Ryan, who had gone south to recover from an illness. This appears to be when they left young George behind with May's mother, so he could attend school in Sydney, first at North Annandale and later at the illustrious King's School. May, who was concerned that George had begun speaking mainly in Mandarin because of his constant contact with the Chinese on the mine, had decided that he needed a more normal environment. It was a decision for which George, who did not want to leave the Territory, never forgave his mother.

May and James returned to good news. In August, Sydney Weedon sent a telegram to the *Northern Territory Times* saying that they had struck a lode of copper ore five feet wide with 50 per cent grey ore and wolfram, which was better than all past showings. Authorities were now referring to the Burns Wolfram Creek Mine as the biggest wolfram show in Australia. But James did not have the chance to see just how big his wolfram shows would become. In November, after a long bout with the quite common Territory malaise — alcoholism — James died. According to the will he had made out a few months earlier in Sydney, May inherited everything.

May did not waste time being a grieving widow. Within seven months she married Charles Albert 'Bert' Brown, a tall, good-looking drover-cum-pastoralist-cum-prospector then on Campbell Downs Station. It is not known exactly when or how May met Bert, but he had been in the Territory at least since 1910, when he shared a goldmining lease on the Tanami. May is reputed to have visited the fields at that time, the only white woman, apart from Christina Gordon, alleged to have done so. Witnesses to May's wedding, which took place quietly in the Methodist parsonage in Darwin, were two friends, Ellen Ryan and the manager of the English, Scottish and Australian Bank in Darwin, John Beale.

The Wolfram Creek Mine ceased production while the probate of James

Burns's estate was finalised. The main cause for the delay seems to have been May's lack of cooperation in allowing a full assessment of the mine's worth to be made. She refused to pump out the underground shaft so that a valuation could take place.[13] Eventually the probate was settled and the mines that had not already been registered in May's name were now transferred to her. She later transferred a portion of the land to Bert in his own name. This, presumably, was to allow him to develop his pastoral and cattle interests while May concentrated on the mines.

There was no doubt in the public's mind who was the power behind the wolfram throne. In April 1914 the *Northern Territory Times* reported:

Many and varied have been the owners of the Crest of the Wave...However, there is one of the partners who has shown unbounded faith in the mine since first becoming interested in it and that one is Mrs Brown of Wolfram fame, who is now sole owner of the Crest of the Wave mine. Mrs Brown owns, also, that well known wolfram mine at Wolfram Camp...[she] is to be congratulated on being the proud possessor of two such brilliant properties.[14]

May's perseverance and faith paid off, especially when the outbreak of the First World War increased the demand for wolfram, which was used as a steel hardener in the making of weapons. The price of wolfram skyrocketed, and by 1916 wolfram from May's mine, acknowledged as the richest mine of its kind in Australia, was valued at 20 000 pounds.

May helped the war effort in many ways. She joined the very active Red Cross movement led in the Territory by the administrator's wife, Jeannie Gilruth, and helped raise hundreds of pounds through subscriptions and raffles in the Pine Creek area. She donated an expensive saddle, which was raffled to raise money, and she and Bert also gave generously to such drives as the Territory 'battleplane' fund initiated by patriotic *Times* editor Charles Kirkland. Meanwhile, May's sister Florence, who owned Darwin's only silent picture theatre, the Don, was praised for providing movies free of charge to help raise war funds. Sadly, in 1917 Florence's son Willie Budgen was amongst the many Australians killed on the battlefields of France.

During the war years May adopted the son of Harold Seale, one of her first husband's relatives who had managed Wave Hill Station until his sudden death in 1915. The boy, James Seale, was the product of Harold's relationship with a woman of mixed Aboriginal descent who lived on the station. After Harold died, May decided to adopt James and send him to Sydney to be raised by members of her family.

Not long before she sent him, May nearly lost her own son, George, who was resentful towards his mother for making him leave the Territory to attend The King's School in Sydney. In 1917 George had an accident on the new motorbike he had convinced his indulgent mother to buy him, and sustained serious head injuries. The doctors told May he probably would not live, and that if he did, he would have massive brain damage. With her determination and her wealth, May defied the odds. She sent for one of America's top neurosurgeons who successfully implanted a steel plate in her son's head. George went on to live a normal life, although many who knew him later claim the implant caused him to have a vile temper and unusual behaviour at times.

Back in the Territory, another stressful situation occurred for May and Bert, although the exact details of what happened are not clear. In March of 1917 Bert was charged in Pine Creek for the murder of a Chinese man named Ah Quee at Wolfram Camp. He was committed for trial at the Supreme Court in Darwin where the case drew a great deal of attention. Several elderly Chinese men were brought in as witnesses for the prosecution but more attention was given by the press to the fact that they had to use a Chinese interpreter to present their evidence than to the evidence itself, so the circumstances of the case are not clear. According to the report, Bert made a long statement from the dock, during which he calmly and coolly denied the charge. His lawyer suggested that vengeful motives lay at the bottom of the prosecution. The prosecutor countered with the claim that the case had been proven and then launched into passionate address about people of all races and colours being entitled to equal protection under British law. This appears to have been an attempt to squash any prejudice the jury might have had resulting from the strong emphasis at the time on the 'White Australia' policy. The jury does not appear to have been able to come to a decision and the matter was held over to the next sittings, the charge was reduced to one of assault and eventually was dropped. Unfortunately, the actual court records are not available and the newspaper reports are unusually vague, given the seriousness of the accusation, so the real story may never be known. However, according to Alex Gorey, who was living in Pine Creek at the time, May was not impressed with Bert's behaviour in the incident and is alleged to have 'bushed' him for a time. This may be when he took up his droving and pastoral interests again and began to live a life more independent from May, although within a year they were reported as attending several events together.

One of them, in July 1918, brought tragedy and involved their good friends, the well-known Frith family of Pine Creek. It was race day at Pine Creek and May and Bert were among the many country folk who had come to town for the event. As usual, May was decked out in one of her flamboyant outfits for the occasion. Young Frank Frith, who was newly married, approached her and said: 'Boy, Ma, I love those strawberries in your hat.'

May turned to him, eyed him squarely and said, 'Win the next race and it's yours.'

'You're on,' Frank replied and headed off for his horse.

He didn't win the race, or the hat. What began as a playful bet ended in tragedy. Midway through the race he fell from his horse, Cropier, and was knocked unconscious. May, along with the Territory administrator, Dr John Gilruth, rushed to his side and got him to Pine Creek hospital where they stayed by his bedside until he died. The family placed a special notice in the paper thanking May for her help and compassion.

In 1918 May refused an offer of 14 000 pounds for her Crest of the Wave show, which, according to the July issue of the *Northern Territory Times*, was still the richest tin mine in the Northern Territory. Her decision not to sell was perhaps unfortunate. The tide of the war had turned, and when the armistice was signed the market for wolfram plummeted. Mining from Wolfram Hill had virtually ceased by July 1919, though the Crest of the Wave mine continued to give profitable yields of ore and earned May revenue through much of the 1920s.

It became clear that May would have to diversify her financial activities if her level of income was to be maintained. Like others who had made their start on the mining fields, May turned to the hotel trade. She was the first to win the lease for Darwin's Hotel Victoria when the controversial six-year period of the Gilruth-

May Brown (left), pictured here with her niece Florrie McKinnon and some Vic Hotel customers. Most photographs of May were lost in Cyclone Tracy and this photo was found on an Australian Joint Copying Project microfilm in a diary kept by a visiting English pianist, T. P. Fielden, who stayed at May's Hotel in 1925. He wrote beside her photo: 'You will see by the photo what manner of woman she is and no doubt needs to be as she probably has to cope with some hard cases.' The original photograph was eventually tracked down in London, where a relative of Fielden's kindly provided a negative to be used for this book.

initiated state control of the Darwin, Pine Creek and Brock's Creek hotels ended in 1921.

Ever mindful of the special needs of miners, drovers, pastoralists and country folk who spent so much of their lives in isolation enduring physical hardships, May turned her attention to providing special comforts for them. She completely renovated the hotel, and advertised that it catered for country visitors, especially families, who were able to stay in the separate cottages adjacent to the hotel. She also advertised that country customers no longer had to purchase liquor supplies through the government stores, as they had been forced to do during the Gilruth regime, but could buy directly from her.

May's business acumen was acute and she knew how to draw the crowds to her hotel. In March 1922 she reduced the price of draught beer, whisky by the nip and bulk whisky, forcing her competition, the Club and Terminus Hotels, to follow suit. It may be that she had one too many nips herself on occasion — such as the time she strained her leg when she fell to the bottom of her cellar, claiming she had not seen that the hatch to it was open.

May in fact spent a fair proportion of time in the hospital, and perhaps because of this she gave generously to other patients, particularly at Christmas, as the *Northern Territory Times* recorded in December of 1920:

Always mindful of suffering humanity, Mrs Wolfram Brown, of the Victoria Hotel, has collected the sum of forty-two pounds to provide a Christmas treat for the patients at the Hospital. There is a thoughtful generosity about this annual effort which is highly commendable. Last Christmas a similar amount was collected by Mrs Brown, which proved a godsend to the sufferers at the Hospital.

In 1921 she joined with the Victoria River Racing Club to help buy cane lounges from Singapore for the patients.

While May was known for her compassion, if anyone crossed her, as several tried to do to their peril, she had no hesitation in using the pugilistic skills learned from her first husband to teach them a lesson they would not easily forget. She used the same skills to box unruly patrons out on their ears. There was no need for May Brown to hire bouncers. She is reputed to have worn a stockwhip around her neck just to intimidate any would-be trouble-makers. Alex Gorey, a Russian-born Pine Creek miner and peanut farmer who arrived in the Territory as a young man in 1915 and was still around in 1988, confirmed May's dual nature, describing her as 'a real fighter, but a good woman'. He said she grubstaked many people, including himself, and was well-known for her humanitarian deeds. She enjoyed spreading her wealth around to those in need, particularly the 'bushies'. As hotel proprietor, she would grubstake them in the bush and 'shout' them in town. As one of her contemporaries, Vanda Marshall, told it:

She spent her money recklessly and gave it away liberally. As a weekend special she sometimes tossed a handful of sovereigns in the air, and scattered bank notes on the wind. Let catch as catch can, as men scruffed and scrambled in the dirt for the gold, and chased bank notes down the windy street.[15]

When she wasn't giving money away, May was quite frequently gambling it away. Her favourite Australian money-spending event was the Melbourne Cup, which she attended as often as possible. She often spent several weeks living it up during the trips. She is reputed to have had a permanent suite booked at the Hotel Australia in Sydney and the Scotts Hotel in Melbourne, where, according to her grand-daughter, she sometimes also stayed in the home of a leading clairvoyant. She tipped generously and expected the best. According to Vanda Marshall, 'The wealth of the Wolfram Queen was widespread and her good name, honesty and generosity would have taken her round Australia on an IOU.'[16] Her favourite overseas destination was Monte Carlo and its gambling tables, which she is believed to have visited on several occasions.

She usually returned from these trips with the latest French fashions, which she delighted in showing off to acquaintances who imagined that any woman from the Territory would be totally out of touch with anything remotely in vogue. Her costumes included diamond-studded shoes, ostrich feather boas and matching hats, gowns of brocaded crepe de Chine and ermine. According to those who knew her, she had an umbrella to match every purse and outfit. Her jewellery collection was also renowned, and included a selection of diamond 'kitchen' rings worn only for everyday, while the really expensive items were saved for special occasions.

May was also amongst the first people in the Territory to own motor cars, purchasing several over the years, and her home, opposite Brown's Mart in Smith Street, was called, appropriately, 'The Mansion'. She bought the house in 1920, and fitted it out in the lavish style to which she had become accustomed. Stories abound of her magnificent silver, in particular an eight-foot [2.4 metre] silver carriage vegetable dish, which her Aboriginal houseboy and housemaid had the dubious privilege of polishing.

May was also well known as an extravagant and imaginative hotel hostess. The *Northern Territory Times*' description of a dinner she gave in March 1922 for about forty guests, to honour the Vesteys football team, proves the point:

Mrs Brown had spared no effort in placing before Mr Wedd's guests a most sumptuous spread and the large dining room was tastefully decorated with Vesteys colors (blue and white) and each diner had a very pretty true lovers' knot souvenir badge of the club's colours placed before the seat allotted to him at the table. The fair lady waitresses did their utmost to keep all supplied...the dinner was a huge success.

May's lifestyle did not always meet with the approval of the union-run *Northern Standard* newspaper, which sometimes criticised the conservative nature of her political leanings, and those of some of her colleagues. When in 1921 she was listed in the social columns as one of the ladies 'in evening dress' who attended a government house function, the paper claimed those who attended were traitors to the cause of enfranchisement for Territorians, pointing out that while they were partying, many of the town's residents were in gaol over the 'no taxation without representation' issue. The next year May was again in the papers when she became the central figure in a controversy over the municipal elections and her right to vote as a landholder. She won the battle and the right to vote in the election that saw her business partner George Wedd, along with others, defeat the union-backed candidates who had been in control of the council for several years.

May made sure she had her say in most decision-making processes of government. Her wealth put her in a strong lobbying position. She knew it and she used it to fight for what she believed was best for the Territory. Reputed to be particularly good friends with Country Party parliamentarians George Pearce and Earl Page, she never lost an opportunity to have a word in their ears. When she sent letters or telegrams about issues, and really meant business, she usually signed her name 'Mrs Wolfram Brown', a not-so-subtle reminder of her wealth and influence.

May was proud of her straightforwardness, as was evidenced during a court case in which she testified about the state of sobriety of one of her patrons accused of negligent driving while under the influence of alcohol. May gave evidence in his defence and when challenged about its accuracy, she indignantly stated that she 'would have no compunction in telling the truth about any of her customers if they deserved it. She was not like other hotel keepers and never hesitated to say what she thought.'[17]

In 1924 May's son, who had returned to the Territory, married a young Darwin woman, Mary Fisher. Although at first May objected to him marrying anyone and in fact had to be locked in her room during the wedding so that she would not disrupt the ceremony, she came to like her daughter-in-law a great deal. The fact that Mary was from a long-standing Territory family was certainly in her favour, as by now May had strong views about Territorians marrying anyone but other Territorians. Her opinion emerged during what was one of Darwin's most famous cases, a breach of promise case brought against well known pastoralist Matt Wilson who decided not to marry his fiancée. In his defence he reported to the court that 'Mrs Brown warned [me] against marrying anyone from the southern states'.[18]

May appears to have had her own formula for a successful marriage; as well as marrying a Territorian, each partner should retain a certain amount of independence. It appears that Bert and May lived such a life and, although they had their share of fights, a friend who knew them at the time said May was 'very cut up' when in 1926 she received a telegram saying that Bert had died of malaria in Queensland. He had been on a drove along the Birdsville Track, one of the loneliest and longest stock-routes in Australia, moving a mob of cattle from Wave Hill to Longreach for Sidney Kidman, when he contracted the fever and died, leaving May widowed for the third time. The *Northern Territory Times* said he was:

well and very favourably known by a large number of NT people. He was a cultured, thoughtful man, and when one secured his friendship, it was invariably found to be lasting. The delayed news of his untimely end came as a shock to his many friends. To his widow, Mrs May Brown, sincere sympathy is extended.

Bert, who had made his will a year after he and May were married, left his estate of 414 pounds to her.

Although deeply upset by Bert's death, May found some consolation in the birth of her only grandchild, a girl named Jaci. On her next trip to Monte Carlo May returned with gold spun shoes and a hand-made china doll for her new grand-daughter, who soon learned to treat her grandmother with a combination of fear, respect and love.[19]

In 1926, when May's first five-year lease was up for the Vic Hotel, she attempted to renegotiate it, claiming that she would paint it but that she wanted the government to erect a billiard room and pay her compensation for the cottage which was pulled down. In reply the government, by now familiar with May's forthright nature, pointed out that she was already obliged to paint the premises under the lease conditions and suggested that another lessee would agree to more appropriate conditions and make less demands than would May. It was decided to offer both the Pine Creek and Vic Hotel leases to Christina Gordon. Christina, however, took up the Vic lease but transferred her lease on the Playford Hotel in Pine Creek to May, who kept it for the next five years. She no doubt enjoyed being able to spend more time with her niece, Jess Chardon, the daughter of her eldest sister. Jess had married a Territory mail carrier and settled with him on Florina Station. She and May were great friends and while she shared many of May's outspoken characteristics, Jess became a Territory identity in her own right.

In 1931, with the depression setting in throughout Australia, May transferred her Pine Creek lease to another well-known woman, Maude Dowling, and moved to Darwin, where she established a cafe boarding-house in the heart of Chinatown only one block from her home. She turned half of the building into a soda fountain and ice cream bar, where she served home-made ice cream, and the other half into a dining room where the men who had paid a week's board could eat breakfast, lunch and dinner — as long as May wasn't on one of her regular drinking bouts. Former guests recalled that sometimes when they showed up for a meal, they would be greeted by one of her two faithful Aboriginal helpers, Elsie and George, who would announce, 'No dinner today. Missus got fever.'

But if May was physically beginning a downhill run, mentally she was as alert and assertive as ever, never hesitating to have her say. For instance, in 1930 when she had a dispute with Matron Ashburner over Darwin's hospital services, she sent this verbose but colourful telegram to the Minister for Home Affairs, Arthur Blakely:

Multiplicity excellently qualified nurses throughout Australia should make choice matron capable administering Darwin hospital easily accomplished with object securing distinct improvement existing most scandalous conditions. Administrative staff being permitted for years past usurp autocratic powers tyranny against subordinates flout established rights. Taxpayers demand best rather than worst service without personal responsibility or accountability for their actions Kindly acknowledge. Mrs Wolfram Brown.[20]

Although she appears to have lost this particular battle, it was alleged that May had influence with people in high places and it was even rumoured that she had a romantic liaison with one of Australia's most senior political leaders of the time.

While she enjoyed certain political power and privilege, May also had her share of problems and trouble, particularly in 1932, a year full of tragedy and challenge. It began when her mother died in Sydney in March, after long and faithful service to her flamboyant daughter. Soon after, May's adopted son James Seale returned to Darwin, having spent most of his eighteen years with her family in Sydney. He contracted pneumonia, and in June he too died. Before his death, May tried to get him work on the Vesteys-owned Wave Hill Station where he had been born. His story illustrates some of the prejudices and problems which confronted some Aboriginal people at the time.

When May asked Cecil Cook, protector of the Aborigines, to help get James work on Wave Hill Station, Cook lobbied on her behalf by explaining the circumstances in a letter to officials. He said that James's parents were both employees of Wave Hill Station when he was born there in 1915 and that May had taken him to Sydney when he was about four years of age where he had been ever since. Cook argued that while it was possible to apprentice him elsewhere, there was no disputing that, under the principles of the apprentices half-caste regulations, Wave Hill Station had a moral obligation to provide him with employment. Cook said it would be 'undesirable' that a firm of the magnitude and standing of The Northern Agency Ltd, a Vesteys company, should be able to evade its responsibilities under the regulations, as this was liable to be misinterpreted by less powerful organisations who had been forced to abide by the rules. Cook told the company officials that he had been assured by May Brown that Mr Alec Moray, pastoral inspector of the Northern Agency, had promised her before the regulations were gazetted that he would find James a job on the station. Cook asked the company to honour that promise.

Vesteys refused, claiming that James Seale was now a 'southern' boy and that it was too late to begin his training. They claimed that the accommodation and training of a youth 'of this description' would present difficulties. Cook countered by saying that James was 'quite white' in appearance and upbringing and for this reason his accommodation should offer no difficulty whatever, particularly as station had recently accommodated a 'definitely coloured' youth. Vesteys said the

the station was losing money and could not afford to hire James as an apprentice. Cook again reminded them that apprenticing of half-castes was an obligation of their licence. Unfortunately James died before the dispute was resolved.

Just three months later May's brother Percy, who had helped his sister Florence pioneer silent pictures in Darwin, died in Bowral where he had been proprietor of the Bowral Pictures. Despite three family deaths in a matter of months, May was not one to let life get her down for long and she soon involved herself in a new venture — the Tanami gold rush. There had been glowing accounts printed in the press about the richness of the field, but May was sceptical. Early in October of 1932 May and four others left Darwin in a Paige motor car to have a look for themselves. When she returned, May spoke her piece in a blunt article in the *Northern Standard*, in which she was highly critical of the optimistic publicity being given to the field, which she said had yet to be proved. She complained about the type of equipment being used and about the route being taken to reach the fields, claiming that by using the way chosen in 1910, she cut 400 miles (644 km) from the distance and had good supplies of water all the way. May said she was highly amused to find many travellers to the fields carrying guns and revolvers for protection. She reported that her party of five, including two women, slept out in the open each night, and carried neither gun or revolver, although a gun would have come in handy to secure a turkey or two for dinner. Given her reputation, May probably would not have needed a gun to ward off trouble-makers. She warned people not to make heavy investments until there was more proof of the richness of the field. Her warnings proved legitimate, as the rush soon petered out.

By 1934 May was in financial trouble herself. Her extravagant lifestyle, combined with the Great Depression, were taking their toll, and in February she was forced to forfeit both her Wolfram Hill and Crest of the Wave Mines for 'non-payment of rent and non-compliance of labour conditions'.

A court incident in 1935, however, clearly shows that her feisty spirit was still very much in evidence. The newspaper headline read 'Tussle at Star Theatre—Well Known Ladies in Court'. May Brown pleaded not guilty to a charge of assaulting a Mrs Walsh at the Star Picture Theatre, Tom Harris's popular open-air theatre in Darwin's main street. Mrs Walsh's story was that she had gone to the theatre, sat in her usual seat, and was then asked by the proprietor Tom Harris to vacate it as it was reserved for May. She refused, claiming she had occupied the seat for two years. According to Mrs Walsh, May Brown then 'stooped down and caught hold of [her] dress at the shoulder and waist and tried to lift her out of the seat but the dress gave way and she was frustrated in her attempt'.

Mrs Walsh claimed May caught hold of the chair and dragged it and Mrs Walsh towards the aisle in the theatre, tipped up the chair with Mrs Walsh in it and then threw the chair on top of her. Mrs Walsh, who had hurt her shoulder when she fell, claimed that May had been hostile to her ever since she had married Billy Walsh, a railway man with whom May had had a close association for several years.

May Brown had a different version. She said Mrs Walsh had only occupied the seat as May's guest and on the night in question May had specifically asked that her two regular seats to be reserved. When Mrs Walsh refused to vacate the seat, May said she had grabbed her by the arm and 'lifted her politely from the chair'.

'If [I] had hit her or used violence she would have been in hospital and would have had a port-hole in her,' May told the court.

After hearing somewhat confusing evidence from several other witnesses, the magistrate convicted May and fined her ten shillings, adding four pounds and thirty-five shillings for court, witness and professional fees, and six pounds seven shillings for 'damage to the dress'.

History does not record whether either woman tried to take the other's seat again, but May did not need hers for much longer. By 1936 she had sold off or transferred to her daughter-in-law most of her land in the Top End. By this time George and Mary Seale were running a successful pub and boarding house in Parap, where May had first set them up managing a club she had purchased from a local lawyer in 1931.

No one seems to know exactly when May left the Territory or exactly why, although it is presumed that she was in need of specialised hospital care for the cancer she had by then contracted. As one local resident of the 1930s said, 'all of a sudden Mrs Brown wasn't there anymore'. May moved to Sydney, where she lived out the rest of her life in a terraced house in Phillip Street not far from where she and George Seale had spent their short married life. Her grand-daughter Jaci, then going to school in Sydney, used to visit her there. Ever enterprising, even in illness, May converted part of her home into a boarding-house. And in Sydney on 23 July 1939 May Brown, the once wildly wealthy Wolfram Queen, died virtually penniless. She is buried in Rookwood cemetery with her first husband, thousands of kilometres from the Territory where she had won and lost her fortune.

Whatever rather mysterious force motivated and drove her in life, there can be little doubt that May Brown made a significant impact on the financial, social and political life of the Territory. Not only does a look at her life provide a deeper understanding of one particular phase of the Territory's history and of the type of people who helped shape its destiny, but her life itself, with its rise to enormous wealth and subsequent financial demise, reflects the many boom-and-bust periods that have characterised the Territory's history.

Chapter 11

Petticoat Drovers and Women of the Wayback

'Women, as the bushmen said, look a lifetime ahead. The roots of their faith and hope ran deep, binding that fickle earth. Though they themselves were deprived and forgotten, they knew it was not in vain.'
Ernestine Hill, The Territory, 1952

It was Jeannie Gunn who gave Australia its first and perhaps most indelible image of outback life for European women in the Northern Territory when she wrote of her experiences as the only white woman at Elsey Station on the remote Roper River in 1902. In her classic 1908 book, *We of the Never Never* , she depicted the 'Land of Plenty of Time' with the romanticised eyes of a new bride, who, though plucky and adventuresome, was almost certainly sheltered from much of the harshness and reality of life in the back of beyond. It was a life where men were kings (or 'malukas' as Jeannie's husband was called by the Aborigines) and a woman like Jeannie was the noble 'little missus'. Men ran the stations, drove the cattle, and protected the home and hearth while the woman took charge of the household and trained Aboriginal women to help with the domestic chores. Jeannie presented the 'never-never' as essentially a man's frontier where the crucial role of the Aboriginal women as 'drover's boys' was not mentioned, and only the 'right sort' of European woman gave up the comforts of civilised life in order to venture there.

In reality station life was mostly a partnership between men and women and between Aborigines and Europeans. Although there were times of conflict, the practicalities of living meant that typical role models for the sexes were less adhered to. Although greatly outnumbered by men, both Aboriginal and European women were very much a part of the daily attempts to reap a living from the harsh land. In some ways, perhaps, they learned better than men that one doesn't 'conquer' the land, but rather learns to live with it, including its challenges, its joys and its tragedies.

Aboriginal women, of course, were born to the bush and knew its lessons best of all. Whatever the rights and wrongs of the European intrusion on Aboriginal land, it is indisputable that Aboriginal women were invaluable to white outback pioneers. Even in the nineteenth century the fact was acknowledged by some, such as Territory customs officer Alfred Searcy who reported that 'besides the companionship, [Aboriginal women] become splendid horsewomen and good with cattle. They are more reliable [than men]...They...find water, settle the camp, boil the billy and track and bring in the horses in the mornings.'[1] They were also employed as house servants and station hands and often provided the only other female companionship for the wives and daughters of the station managers. The fact that they were sometimes abducted from their people to join the white camps, and thus became catalysts for racial conflict, does not negate the important role they played.[2] It is now also being acknowledged that many of them found a satisfying freedom from their own cultural restrictions through their liaisons with men other than those Aboriginal men to whom they had been promised.

The role of the few European women who were part of the Territory's development was equally important, and theirs was also often a freeing experience from the restrictions placed upon women in more settled parts of the country. Theirs was usually an isolated life, which demanded resourcefulness, courage and good humour. Not only did they have to make most of their own clothing and furniture and live in makeshift bough sheds for much of the time, but they also had to know how to ride, brand cattle, muster, administer medical aid, defend themselves against intruders, help manage the property, educate their children, and keep themselves and their families entertained. They had to learn to deal with a life which seldom brought them the company of another woman and which saw them get new supplies once or twice a year. Above all, they had to maintain an optimistic spirit and a hope in the future through all kinds of adversity — floods, droughts, sickness and death. The women of the Wayback in many ways embody the silent spirit of Australia, a spirit which even those who have never ventured beyond the city outskirts in some strange way rely on for a sense of national identity. By looking at the lives of just a few of those women who were part of the Territory's history, perhaps we can gain a better understanding of that spirit.

The first white woman known to settle for any length of time on a Territory pastoral property was Mary Augusta Sprigg, who married English-born pioneer Territory pastoralist Alfred Giles in Adelaide in early 1880. After a large wedding and a lengthy honeymoon in Mount Gambier, the newly-weds sailed to Darwin where Mary and her maid Lydia stayed with the family of the postmaster, John Archibald Little, while Alfred checked out the station home he had built for them the previous year several miles west of Katherine. Mary had already had to wait three years to be carried across the threshhold so a few more days would not matter.

In 1877 Giles had been hired by well-known and well-liked South Australian pastoralist and livestock speculator Dr William James Browne, to take stock to an area he had claimed on the Katherine River and select a homestead site. Attracted both by the proposal and its liberal salary, Giles agreed to the venture, and postponed his marriage to his fiancée Mary, until the expedition was complete, and a homestead established.[3] Once the epic pastoral journey was completed and the destination reached Giles built a home for his patient fiancée, and returned to Adelaide in late 1879 to marry her and bring her back to her northern home.

When all was ready, Mary and Lydia took a launch from Darwin to Southport where Alfred met them for the journey to Katherine. They loaded their furniture, including a Ronisch piano which Alfred had given Mary as a wedding present, onto the waiting buggies and proceeded to their new home. Alfred and Mary travelled in one, while Lydia and a driver travelled in the other, with two Chinese cooks behind. They camped by the wayside each night, where the Chinese cooked delicious outback meals. They arrived at Springvale on 20 June 1880.[4]

Mary and Alfred soon became well known for their hospitality to travellers and for their well-stocked and watered garden, which, Giles claimed, neighbours and travellers regarded as a 'sort of sanatorium', saving many from the common tropical ailments of scurvy and beri-beri. They lived in the Territory for forty years, first at Springvale and then at Darwin, returning to Adelaide only twice in that time. Mary's first visit home was in August 1883, when she travelled with pioneer female explorer Emily Creaghe and her husband Harry to Darwin and by ship to Adelaide.

The Gileses had four children at Springvale, and when Mary Giles died in Adelaide in 1940 at the age of ninety, two of her sons were still an integral part of the Territory. Leslie was Government Secretary in Darwin at the time of her death and Harold and his wife were still conquering the 'never-never' at their home on Elsey Station

Her youngest child, Maude, had a more unforunate fate but one which was not uncommon in the outback in the days before flying doctor services and improved communication. Maude had married Sir Alexander Cockburn Campbell and lived an isolated life at Waterloo station, a few hundred miles from Halls Creek. There, after giving birth to four children of her own, Maude died in February 1926, the tragic victim of isolation. When Maude had become desperately ill, it had taken a messenger five days to reach the nearest medical man, who then took the same amount of time to reach Waterloo, slowed by the flooded state of the country in the height of the wet. The doctor was too late, and Lady Campbell died, her death highlighting the need for outback aeroplanes and a wireless sending set, which would have reduced the time to two or three hours instead of ten days.

It was not long after Mary Giles's arrival as a young bride at Springvale that other pioneering women began arriving at other Territory pastoral properties. Among the first was Mary Costello, a daughter of the famous Durack family, who arrived in the Territory in the early 1880s with her husband John to establish a homestead at Lake Nash Station on the Territory-Queensland border. She battled dengue fever, malaria, isolation and, like other women of the outback, spent long periods on her own while her husband was tending to the stock, doing all he could to ensure that they survived the severe droughts that plagued the region. When Michael Costello wrote *The Life of John Costello* in 1930, he saved the last chapter as a tribute to Mary, 'A Brave Woman Pioneer':

She was one of the women who made the nation—the silent heroines of our race. Fearless, self denying, facing the relentless dangers of the unexplored wilds, these women of the West not only did and dared but kept a cheerful optimism through it all. Hearts of gold, great and heroic, such they had to be. They dared to live where few would go...There are many who can be heroines before a sympathetic and admiring audience, but the wives of the pioneers were the greatest heroines of them all. Patient endurance and hopefulness marked their characters, knowing no dangers, fearless, self sacrificing, magnificent exemplars of their sex, the women who rear the invincibles of our race.

The Costellos were responsible for bringing another family of pioneer station women into the Territory. In the early 1880s Jack and Mary Ann Farrar went to the remote Limmen River area to manage the Valley of the Springs station for John Costello. Jack, who had earlier travelled with the ill-fated Burke and Wills exploration as far as Cooper Creek, had been a faithful stockman for Costello for many years, and Costello had named Farrar's Creek after him. With Jack and Mary Ann was their son Bob, and a teenage girl from Albury, Phoebe Wright.

They left Sydney by steamer for Thursday Island and then went on to Normanton where Jack bought a buggy, harness and horses and set out for the Rankine River where they picked up 1200 head of mixed cattle and two wagons loaded with supplies necessary to build a house. On the long, hot and dusty journey into the Territory, Jack drove one buggy and Phoebe the other, with Mary Ann Farrar as her passenger. Phoebe also did the cooking for the camp, a job she continued when they reached their destination. They remained there for five years, during which time Mary Ann gave birth to two more sons.

Hostility from the Aborigines, who speared much of their stock, eventually forced the family to shift their home and cattle to the Hodgson River area, where they began Nutwood Downs Station.

Bob and Phoebe married and began raising their own family, with Mary Ann helping her daughter-in-law with the births. Mary Ann and Phoebe were often left in charge of the station on their own while the men went out mustering cattle, although Phoebe also often participated in this side of station life as well. In 1902, after they had sold 200 bullocks for 1000 pounds, the family decided to have a holiday in Darwin. They headed on horseback for the 'big smoke', with Phoebe's youngster riding on the saddle in front of her. On their way they stopped at Elsey Station, where Phoebe, tall and shy in her homemade dress and hat, and Mary Ann met Jeannie Gunn, the first white woman apart from each other, they had seen in almost twelve years. After this chance meeting Jeannie immortalised Phoebe as the 'Bush Mother' in her classic *We of the Never Never*.

In late 1917, after spending nearly forty years grazing cattle and running properties in the Territory, Mary and Jack decided to retire to a property near Maryborough. But as writer Billy Linklater later observed 'fate is always against the pioneer ending their days peaceful'. There they both died within a year, Mary after a tragic accident when a petrol lamp exploded, setting fire to her dress, and Jack a year later of pneumonia. On learning of Mary's death the *Northern Territory Times* wrote that she was 'one of the oldest residents of the Territory and ranked absolutely first among the women who nobly pioneered the Northern Territory bush'.

Bob and Phoebe continued to run the family properties, and Phoebe continued to draw admiration, such as this 1924 tribute by the *Northern Territory Times*, describing her as:

one of that admirable type of women who take a real and practical part in the Territory's development—one of the real trackblazers who with extraordinary courage and endurance shoulder a man's task in station operation and in following the mustering camps and attending to the ordinary requirements of her menfolk. In spite of work she does Mrs Farrar looks young and comely and our hope is that the Territory may long be blessed with such ladies.

Phoebe was regarded as the best rider on any property the family owned, and as her husband was often ill in later years, it was Phoebe who did most of the work, mustering, living for weeks at a time in stock camps with only Aboriginal companions and doing all her own branding. Her daughter once recalled the time Phoebe drove a mob of 300 cattle 400 miles (640 km) to the family's new station at Ban Ban

Springs. She was accompanied by one stockman and a dog. The two of them shared all the night watches. In the mid-1930s Phoebe suffered a broken hip when she was crushed by a bull during a branding operation and was told by the doctor who operated on her in Darwin that she would never walk again. A year later she walked into his office nearly as good as new, claiming she had overcome the odds through 'sheer hard work and plenty of guts'.[5]

The Farrars remained in the Territory for the rest of their lives, except for a short period when they tried to retire to Queensland. They became so homesick for the Territory that they moved back and ran Glencoe station, still pioneering after their children had married and were living their own lives elsewhere. A horse remained Phoebe's only means of transport for the greater part of her life. When her husband bought an old Model-T Ford, she used to pull back on imaginary reins and call 'whoa' when she wanted to stop. At seventy-five she was still riding horses despite her encounter with a bull fifteen years earlier. For a woman of such activity and spirit, her last few years were sadly restricted. In 1955 she entered the Darwin hospital, where she spent the last five years of her life, as the Territory at that time had no accommodation for pensioners. When Phoebe died in August 1960 at the age of ninety-two, the *Northern Territory News* was more than justified in saying that her death marked 'the passing of one of the few really Grand Old Ladies of the Territory'. In 1988 her daughter, Phyllis Uren, successfully nominated Phoebe for inclusion in the bicentennial book *Unsung Heroes and Heroines*, which honoured 200 such Australians out of thousands of nominations.

About the time the Farrars and Costellos were pioneering Top End stations, a few families were also moving into central Australia. Among the first women to pioneer this area was Mary Hayes, who arrived with her husband William and their family in 1884. Liverpool-born William, who had emigrated to South Australia at the age of twenty-one in the early 1850s, had married Mary Stratford of Goodwood, and together they began a lifetime of pioneering pastoral properties in northern South Australia and central Australia. Their venture into the Territory came when William signed a contract with Sir Thomas Elder to do all the fencing and dam sinking at Mount Burrell, about 100 miles (160 kilometres) south of Alice Springs. They loaded three teams of horses with rations and goods for the family and another two teams with the fencing material and set out on the arduous trip, which took several months.

At the head of the railway, they loaded up more teams with steel telegraph poles for Alice Springs — to replace the rotting wooden ones. The family carried on for a while, dam sinking and working on various stations until Mary, by then mother of six children, finally insisted on a permanent home. Eventually the nomadic William agreed, and they took up country at Deep Well in central Australia, part of the first pastoral lease issued in the Territory. Despite setbacks and hardships, within a few years the family had expanded its holdings to include Mount Burrell, Undoolya, and a new station they called Maryvale, after the stalwart matriarch of the family.

Like most of the women who went with their families to the isolation of Territory pastoral life, Mary Hayes and her daughters undertook their full share of the station work. They could muster, brand, drove, slaughter and dress cattle and build fences as well as any man. On one occasion, when the men of the family were engaged in another task, Mary Hayes and her daughters drove a flock of 1000 sheep

For many years in the early part of the twentieth century, Love's Creek station was home for (right to left) Lillian Bloomfield (née Kunoth), her two daughters Peg and Jean, her sister Maggie, and the children's governess, Annie Fox Denton.
Because there was no doctor servicing the region, Lillian drove a horse and buggy to Oodnadatta to have her children. Peg and Jean both went on to marry into Territory families. Photograph courtesy of Peg Nelson (née Bloomfield).

more than 350 miles (560 kilometres) to Mount Burrell, managing to nurse and save most of the lambs born during the arduous journey. Mary Hayes walked nearly every foot of the way.

William died during a rare visit to Adelaide in November 1913 at the age of eighty-six, not long after the tragic death of his eldest son. His last words were about his family and the help he had had from them. Eventually most of the family returned to Adelaide, except for one son, Ted, who stayed and maintained the family property. His son, Ted, later married Jean Bloomfield, daughter of prominent central Australians Lewis and Lillian Bloomfield, who owned Love's Creek Station. Ted and Jean lived on the Hayes family property and eventually took out a lease in their own names. By 1988 there had been five generations of the Hayes family who had worked the property and remained in the Territory to carry on the family's pioneering pastoral spirit.

Ted Hayes, who died in 1988, reflected on the pioneering contribution the women in his family had made and the significance of living in isolation when he delivered the 1986 Doreen Braitling Memorial lecture in Alice Springs:

My own ancestors were typical of the battlers who were successful after the failure of the big pastoral firms, who were unable to cope with the vast distances from the markets...Being born and bred in the bush I have often been asked about the isolation, but it never occurred to me that we were isolated, and looking back over those years, I now realise the great responsibility and worry our mothers had to bear as there was no medical facilities available for perhaps hundreds of miles and then as now accidents did occur...Station women were great at improvising. Furniture would be created from packing cases. The twice a year arrival of station supplies were always a welcome sight, as much for the material to build furniture from, as the goods they contained.

In 1891 there was another surge of interest in Top End stations, bringing a few more women to the isolated north. One was Euphemia Lydia Oakes (née Gregory), wife of the manager of Elsey Station. She is believed to have been the first white woman to reside at that station, along with her two daughters—although there is an anonymous reference in the *Northern Territory Times* to a woman at least passing through the area several years earlier. An article in the 19 September 1933 issue of the *Women's Mirror* also quotes Euphemia as saying that the previous occupant had been a white woman too, information she had gleaned from the Aborigines living on the station. Aboriginal people certainly remembered Euphemia, and her arrival at the property. Harold Thonemann, who wrote an intriguing book called *Tell the White Man: the Life Story of an Aboriginal Lubra*, describes the meeting:

Kimberley's lubra, Mary, who was the house girl, was very excited. Kimberley speared fish, which Mary prepared as a feast for the new arrivals. She rolled it in mud and cooked it in ashes until it looked like lumps of clay. Mrs Oakes, who was the new Boss's lubra, arrived at 'sun-sit-down.' When Mary saw her, so tired and dusty, she was pleased that she had gone to so much trouble with the meal. But she was distressed to see that Mrs Oakes did not know how to serve fish cooked in this manner. Although Mrs Oakes seemed a very kind woman, the house and food had not pleased her. So the next day she called the lubras together and showed them how a white lubra cleans her house and prepares her food.

Euphemia had one child when she arrived at the Elsey, and she travelled to Darwin to have her second one. Living in the isolation of Elsey Station, where many poisonous snakes abounded, Euphemia feared they might hurt the infants, whom she kept in fenced cages that she had built off the ground, causing much bemusement among the Aboriginal people.

Euphemia and her family stayed at the Elsey a little more than a year. It was another decade before Jeannie Gunn would arrive and immortalise her experiences and impressions there to such an extent that many people do not realise that there were pioneer women who preceded her into the vast outback regions of the Top End.

In fact, as early as 1891, Jeannie's future husband, Aeneas Gunn was included in a party that had brought another potential woman pastoral pioneer to the Top End. She was the cultured, musical Mary Jane Bradshaw (née Guy), new bride of the wealthy entrepreneur and Territory pastoralist, Joseph Bradshaw. Joseph and Mary had married in Melbourne in August and headed at once for Darwin, where they were to continue on to a promising pastoral settlement at the remote Prince Regent River in Western Australia. The idea of white women going into unpioneered land was still most unusual and when they arrived in Darwin in October, the *Northern Territory Times* noted that Mary Jane was 'displaying commendable spirit in resigning the pleasure of southern society for life in the far Northwest where no white woman ever set foot before and hundreds of miles from the nearest neighbours'. In fact, she had with her her maid, a Mrs De Bois and her two children, about whom little is known.

Before they travelled to their isolated home, Mary Jane was able to attend a fancy dress ball in Darwin where she drew admiration for her costume, put together at short notice. It was the last bit of civilisation she would see for some months. Aeneas Gunn wrote an account of their trip to the remote river region in a series of articles later published in the Melbourne *Leader* called 'Pioneering in Northern Australia'. He describes the arrival of the 'twelve roasting human beings' who would form the first white settlement in the area, and relates some of the more unnerving events, such as the time Joe and Mary Jane awoke to find a large snake wound around part of the legs and bellows of the treasured organette that the talented bride had brought to bring music to the wilderness.[6]

But it was Mary Jane's birthday celebration that brought the most descriptive phrases from Gunn's pen and which perhaps best captures the isolation and strangeness of the place, particularly for a white woman so used to the culture and class of Melbourne:

The bizarre nature of our life at Marigui was never more characteristically expressed, or more forcibly impressed upon the participators than it was when Mrs Bradshaw gave a party in celebration of her birthday...the canorous notes of Mrs Bradshaws organette and Hugh Youngs flute made unfamiliar melody in his ears...there was an element of unreality about the whole scene...Our appearance would have suggested that we were either a castaway theatrical company, entertaining ourselves, an out west Pison Creek tea party or an assemblage of very material ghosts...Mr Bradshaw and I had military sabres dangling at our heels much to our inconvenience, although they were reminiscent of old volunteering days and rifles ere stocked by the table or leaned against the tent ropes...We all wore broad brimmed felt hats, jauntily tipped to one side and generally comported ourselves with the easy swaggering rolling air of typical swashbucklers. Mrs Bradshaw entered freely and fully into the spirit of that I am sure most memorable of her birthday parties and kept the fun going with many a witty, silly and humorous rejoinder. We one and all yielded her the homage the woman of culture and innate refinement will command anywhere, except in a Parisian enroute and with a charming graciousness and courtly gracefulness she plied us with music and song and won from us tributes of praise and applause...all people came to the party fully equipped with arms and ammunition.

Although she no doubt appreciated the efforts made on her behalf, Mary Jane decided she preferred Melbourne to this remote place, and shortly after the new year decided to return on the first available vessel. Gunn lamented but understood her decision to depart and commended her contribution to the lonely lifestyle:

Mrs Bradshaw leaves for Derby...she [has] shown no little heroism in going to such an out of the way corner of the funny old round world at all, had, after a fair trial of it, decided that she and life at Marigui could not agree. Tent life in the Australian tropics even during an ordinary summer season and in the most favourable circumstances has not a great many features to recommend it to a lady who has been brought up in the lap of luxury and refinement and when, as was the case during our first season at the Prince Regent, the more austere features of the life were exaggerated by an exceptionally hot season...Mrs Bradshaw must have found the absence of congenial feminine society a sore trial and a sufficient reason for shaking the dust of Marigui off her feet.

Her departure from the far north, it would appear, was permanent, even though her husband became a well known pastoralist and entrepreneur in the Territory and experimented with many ideas for development. She and Joe remained married, however, with Joe dividing his time between Melbourne, England and the Territory. They had one son, Joseph Guy, who was born in 1893 and died in Melbourne in 1922, six years after his famous father, who died in Darwin Hospital in July 1916 of diabetes and gangrene of the foot, after an accident on his property at Victoria River Downs. He left his quite substantial estate of 2540 pounds to Mary Jane, who died in Kew, Victoria, in February 1942, only a few days before the bombing of Darwin. Her death notice recorded that she was aged eighty-one and 'the widow of the late Captain Joseph Bradshaw', and made no mention of the months she spent as the only white woman of that far north region.

It is not known what influence Mary Jane had on her husband's life in the Territory, but it is a matter of record that he had some considerable influence in ensuring that several other pioneering women ventured north with their families, not the least of whom was a spirited woman who wrote her own valuable account of life in the Territory at the turn of the century.

She was Mary Niemann, who, as the wife of leading Melbourne chemist John Henry Niemann, found herself bound for the Victoria River district of the Northern Territory in 1899. In 1896, as Mary Nicholson, she had married the widowed Niemann, who had a young daughter by his first marriage. In 1898 Mary gave birth to a daughter, Catherine. Niemann had been working on a meat extract wanted by the British Navy and, when Catherine was still a babe, Joe Bradshaw persuaded him to come to the Territory and work on a similar project at Victoria River Downs. Bradshaw hoped to use his supply of cattle to produce the extract and market it to the British.

John and Mary eagerly accepted the offer as doctors had told the sickly John that he needed a change of climate. Their friends thought they were slightly mad — if John was so sick he could not live in Melbourne, the Territory would surely kill him, they proclaimed. They were wrong, although the adventures that lay immediately before them would have convinced fainter hearts that the Territory was certainly going to try. Fortunately for posterity, Mary, a strong and spirited woman of many talents, recorded the events of their first years in the North and later published them as a series of articles in the Melbourne *Leader*, under the somewhat deceptive title, 'Land of the Lotus Eaters'.

Her picturesque description of their arrival in Darwin emphasised the Asian and cosmopolitan flavour of the time:

Boats were everywhere. Pearling luggers with furled sails rocked lazily at anchor while close about us jostled a host of smaller craft, manned by vociferous gesticulating crews, infinitely varied as to race and colour, but alike in their amazing volubility and their insistence that we should buy their wares. Malay traders offered us everything from pearl to turtle shells; Chinese hawkers pressed upon us luscious tropic fruits, while other Chinese proclaimed the rival merits of Darwin's three hotels, each one urging us to trust ourselves and our luggage to his particular care.

They soon discovered that the steamer in which Bradshaw had intended to take the family to the Victoria River had been bought by Americans, and after some discussion it was decided to hire a pearling lugger named the *Midge*. Mary was warned about travelling aboard the vessel with two small children and was advised to go overland instead. Characteristically, she refused. The decision resulted in Mary and her children experiencing one of the most dramatic life-threatening events to occur at the mouth of the mighty Victoria River.

The Victoria is notoriously difficult to navigate by sail due to the enormous rise and fall of the tides in the area. The day after the *Midge* left Darwin it ran into an unseasonal dry-season storm, which blew it off course. During the ensuing days, while they were searching for the right estuary of the Victoria, at one spot they observed the tide eat away ten feet of the mainland in three days and create a six-foot-by-forty-foot (2metre x 12metre) hole by the boat. After dodging banks and negotiating various inlets for ten days their luck finally ran out, and on 26 June, 1899, with the fearsome tide at its highest, the little boat and its passengers were carried nearly fifteen miles up an inlet and left stranded on a small sandy flat, the boat leaning at a precarious and most awkward angle.

There they remained for a fortnight, helpless until the next high tides arrived to sweep them back into the water. It was a fortnight of fear and increasing hunger, particularly after all the ammunition had been used in the first week and all that was left was two packets of starch, two pounds of self-raising flour, the odd fish or crab, and the nutrients in a few nearby plants. Niemann's knowledge of botany helped the party in this regard, but fear of an attack by understandably wary Aboriginals in the area restricted their gathering expeditions. Fortunately, they were able to get fresh water from a condenser that Mary's brother made for them. Finally, the sea that had landed them in their predicament arrived again, with just enough breeze to float them back into the water and head for the open sea and Darwin.

When they arrived, forty-four days after they had left, they found that Darwin had given them up for dead and that Bradshaw had been out searching for them by land. To add insult to injury, Niemann's Melbourne partner had also given them up for dead and had left with all the money from the business.

The experience caused them to re-think their plans and in the end they decided to abandon the Victoria River Downs project and head instead for a place on the newly vacated Daly River Mission, which one of the Niemanns' friends had recently purchased. There they would recuperate and continue with the meatworks and meat extract idea, with the cattle supplied from the Daly River instead of from Bradshaw's run.

This time they went overland. In her later writings, Mary described the journey by train 'with its elastic time table' to Brock's Creek and the three-day drive in horse and buggy to the mission.

They were all enthralled with the beauty and relative luxury of their new home, which had been well built and maintained by the missionaries, who had spent sixteen years turning it into a veritable tropical paradise. Lush gardens, attractive and comfortable buildings, goatherds and a fenced swimming area greeted them, along with sawmills, a pumping plant, a fish curing room, a tobacco curing room, goat sheds and friendly nearby Aboriginal people.

Both Mary and John at once began working with and adding improvements to the environment, planting many species of trees and sending plant, bird and insect specimens back to Melbourne for study. Mary made a particular effort to understand the Aboriginal people, and, in particular, the women. She was determined not to adopt the usual European way of communicating with them, by Pidgin English, and instead learned to speak several dialects of their own language. A teacher and people enthusiast by nature, Mary would sit with Aboriginal women on lotus leaves spread out on the ant-bed floor and teach them what she knew. In turn they taught her their language and their customs. Some fifteen years later, when the government was proposing to bring two women from Oxford out to study the Aborigines of the area, the locals decried the scheme, claiming that the money would be better spent on food and clothing. The *Northern Territory Times* argued that 'Mrs Niemann, who speaks at least three dialects fluently, has lived amongst them for many years, and has made a study of Aboriginal women and their folklore', was much better suited to the job and could do the work at a tithe of the cost of importing two women.[7]

While at the Daly, the Niemanns experienced a cyclone and an earthquake and Mary once warded off an attack by Aborigines when she was on her own at the homestead. But Mary held no grudges, wisely observing that the 'blacks are lovable people and against tales of savagery and treachery must be set the fact that in their eyes we are intruders who have driven them from their hunting grounds and are gradually exterminating their race.'

Although the Niemanns were isolated by distance from other Europeans, particularly women, they received many male visitors, causing Mary to remark, rightly or wrongly:

The Territory is nothing if not democratic and men of all sorts and conditions gathered...during our too brief stay. [They were] touchingly grateful always for the little one could do for them and unfeignedly thankful to be once more in touch with a woman of their own race.

But Mary and John Niemann's stay at the Daly did not last terribly long. As well as suffering frequent losses of cattle through spearing attacks by the Aborigines of the area, they found their project set back when tick restrictions were eventually removed and the Queensland markets were thrown open to Territory cattle. This sent the price up too high to make meat extracting profitable and the project had to be abandoned. For a short time they turned to mining silver-lead deposits, but after collecting their first load they had the misfortune to have the cargo of ore sink while being transferred from the barge to the steamer.

Despite the problems, the magic of the Territory had captured them and they decided to stay, moving first to Darwin, where John ran a chemist business and for a short time managed the newspaper office, and then to Pine Creek where John became government chemist and Mary the town teacher. There they continued to serve the Territory and its many sojourners, causing one Queensland prospector who survived the Umbrawarra fever plague of 1909 through the Niemanns' help, to say:

'Mr Niemann and his splendid wife are worth their weight in diamonds to the people up there.'[8] They remained in Pine Creek until the middle of the First World War, when financial circumstances forced them to move to Adelaide, where they lived until their deaths during the Second World War.

When Mary wrote later of their decision to stay in the Territory despite their experience of business failure at the Daly, she captured some of the subtle seduction of the Territory:

But the Daly was not the Territory and though our dual failure compelled us to leave the Daly we determined still to stay in the country we had come to love so well. It had granted us my husband's restored health...and more than that; friends whose affection and loyalty have never failed us, new knowledge and new experiences and the memory of years of unclouded happiness. He would be ungrateful indeed who counted such gifts as nothing or who turned his back on the land that offered them at the first reverse.

Many years later Mary's daughter, Kit, remarked upon the attributes that undoubtedly made her mother more than a match for the Territory's various degrees of adversity — attributes she shared with many women of the wayback: 'She was a very versatile person. She'd take up anything, she'd try anything. She was always pushing, "come on, let's get ahead." And she never would admit adversity at all. She wouldn't say "Oh well, we're done for." Never. It was always "What's on the other side?"'[9]

Optimism was a hallmark of many of the outback women, exemplified by another pair of women pioneers, Margaret May (Mabel) Cole and her mother, Deborah Bridge, née O'Shea. Deborah had come out to Australia from Ireland in 1882 and after working for a short time at Healey's Hotel in Normanton she married a young teamster, Joe Bridge, a descendant of Matthew Everingham of the First Fleet. By 1895 they had three children, Mabel being the oldest. They decided to head for the Western Australia/Northern Territory border to establish their own station property. Joe, who had been working as a carrier ever since their marriage, sold a load of goods in Cloncurry, and converted his cart into a covered wagon by building a frame from saplings and attaching a tarpaulin over it. Deborah and the two younger children rode in the wagon while Mabel, then only ten years old, drove it.

It is difficult today to conceive what conditions were like for the hearty Queensland pioneers. Australia's inland was vast, mostly unpopulated and waterless for long stretches. They travelled across the Barkly Tableland, passing through several isolated station properties until they reached Eva Downs, where the then owner, Harry Bates, gave them two milking cows as a fresh milk supply. Taking charge of the cows was added to young Mabel's responsibilities. Garbed in her self-made outfit of blue dungarees, with cossack-type boots on her feet, Mabel made a quaint figure on the long journey. The family finally reached the 220-mile (352-kilometre) rugged, lonely Murrangi track. Each morning Joe would muster the horses while his family stayed in the wagon, with Mabel holding the shotgun, ready to defend her mother and brother and sister should the need arrive.

Mabel later recalled the reaction of the Aborigines they met on the track: 'They were so taken up with seeing white children—one was a baby and another just walking—that they followed us for days. They camped near us at night and came over just to look at the white baby.'[10] The family was relieved when they finally completed the crossing, which had, allegedly, only been made by wagon twice before. Deborah, Mabel and Kate Bridge had made history by becoming the first white women to have crossed the Murrangi Track. They were also almost certainly the first white women to be seen by most of the Aboriginal people in the region. When they reached Flora Valley Station, they met Katherine and Nat Buchanan, two of the north's greatest pioneers.

When the Bridges finally reached their destination near Hall's Creek in Western Australia, after travelling for more than a year, the family took up an area of pastoral land which they named Mabel Downs. Joe and Deborah lived there until 1913, when they sold the property and purchased Springvale Station. Three years later Deborah, who had spent the last thirty-six years in the outback regions of Western Australia and the Northern Territory, died of a heart attack.[11]

Her daughter, Mabel, who had met and married stockman Tom Cole in 1909, continued her mother's pioneering efforts for many years. Tom was the first man to successfully take a mob of 500 head of cattle down the lonely 700-mile (1120 km) Canning Stock Route between Hall's Creek and Wiluna, north of Perth, while Mabel minded the station and looked after the children. Her determined spirit never let her down. At the time of the Second World War, Tom and Mabel were living in Wyndham and when the army began evacuating the town, Mabel refused to go, eluding army officers by riding a horse fifty miles (80 km) to Ivanhoe Station. After Tom died in 1943 while on active war service, Mabel spent many years travelling around Australia visiting relatives before settling in Alice Springs, where she died in 1985. The *Centralian Advocate* paid her tribute:

With the death of 'mum' Cole died the strains of 'The Skaters' Waltz' and 'Over the Waves', often coaxed so lovingly with aged yet nimble fingers from her old accordion. The quick Irish wit inherited from her mother, the ready humour and the twinkling eyes will long be remembered by those who knew her so well. The story of Margaret May Cole has not yet been written—but when it is told, hers will be a saga of indomitable courage and fortitude in the face of hardship in the loneliness of Australia's North.

Mabel is another whose story has been included in the bicentennial publication, *Unsung Heroes and Heroines.*

Katherine 'Kitty' Buchanan was one more pioneer woman of the Territory's outback. The daughter of a New England pioneer, John Gordon, Katherine married legendary explorer and pastoralist Nat Buchanan in 1863. It is usually Nat who is the focus of historians' attention, but Katherine spent many years travelling with him through north Queensland, often sitting up alone on the 'night watch' during their long and lonely journeys. When an acquaintance once described Nat as a madman because of the furious pace he insisted on, she simply replied 'Then God give this country more of his kind.'[12] Eventually they ended up on Flora Valley, in the Kimberley district, where Kitty was living when the Bridges passed through the country. When Nat died in 1901 near Tamworth, Kitty, along with her two brothers and her widowed sister, moved to Chatswood in Sydney and lived her remaining years in a comfortable home she named Flora Valley, a reminder of the years she spent in Australia's outback. During the First World War she became well known for her work in charities and for her hearty welcome to hosts of friends who visited her until her death in the spring of 1924.

One of the most remarkable of the pioneering women of the wayback was Kate Warrington Rogers, another whose first contacts with the Territory were influenced by Joe Bradshaw. For years Kate's husband John was Bradshaw's manager on an Arafura property planned to be the headquarters of a grandiose scheme to fill Arnhem Land with grazing and agricultural operations. Kate, who had been born to James and Mary McCaw in Victoria in 1876, spent much of her early life with her family in Queensland, first at Urangandie and then at Camooweal. A talented seamstress, she served as dressmaker to the district from 1896 to 1901 when she married John Warrington Rogers, member of a well-established legal family in Victoria. When, in 1903, John was offered the job of manager for Bradshaw's Arafura property, established with English finance and under the Eastern and African Cold Storage Company, Kate would have had little hesitation in encouraging him to accept the job. She had grown up accustomed to station life and was a first-class horsewoman.

In December of 1903 Kate and John and their newborn son arrived in Darwin to board Bradshaw's yacht, *White Star*, bound for the wild and remote areas of Arnhem Land. For a while Kate would have the female companionship of another woman, Mrs Muridge, wife of the chief engineer on the project. *The Northern Territory Times* acknowledged the pluck of the women who were:

...braving the discomforts not to say dangers of a coastal voyage in practically uncharted waters at this precarious season of the year [as well as] the further inconveniences likely to be met with before settled homes can be formed in the wild and barbarous Arafura country whither they are bound.

The party took along tents, which were erected as temporary accommodation. They lived in these uncomfortable dwellings for some time awaiting more permanent plans for the attempted scheme. In late March 1905, Kate and John visited Darwin, where they were entertained at Government House by the retiring government resident, Charles Dashwood, before returning to the isolated Arnhem area. Here they remained for the next two years until Bradshaw's grandiose scheme failed and they moved to the Roper River region. Here they took up land at Urapunga, also known as 'Paddy's Lagoon' and Kate's reputation grew as one of the Territory's most accomplished women.

A mere slip of a woman, Kate soon became known throughout the Top End as an exceptional horsewoman, a crack shot, and a first-class cattle manager. Outback life was in her blood. She was described by her male peers as a born stockman. Kate's brother, William McCaw, owned a property at Daly Waters and her sister was married to Blake Miller who brought the first mob of one thousand cattle from Victoria River Downs to Lake Nash in 1904. But Kate made and earned a name for herself among the pioneers of the Territory outback. She and John shared the droving and the station management of several properties, with Kate often on her own for many months.

Kate played a major part not just in the physical operation of the stations, but also at the managerial level. When her husband applied in 1911 for land at Paddy's Lagoon, where they had been since 1909, he was refused on the grounds that the government police stationed in the area needed the waterhole. When Rogers'

Darwin agent, Walter Bell, suggested they amend their application to exclude the lagoon, Kate wrote telling him not to do it, as they had made many improvements to the property and wanted to settle there: 'If our present home has to be broken up there is no further inducement for us to remain in the Territory.' She added that at the end of the month she was taking delivery of a mob of heifers and 'had quite depended upon having [that] country to put them on'. She told Bell that the government's argument did not hold up and that the police in the area had a better waterhole accessible to them elsewhere in the area, a claim supported by the police. Eventually, after a couple of years of further persuasive and persistent letters to various government officials, Kate and John won out and their annual lease over the area was granted.[13]

A Brisbane *Daily Mail* reporter once visited Kate at Paddy's Lagoon and described her life:

Mrs Warrington Rogers...was managing her husband's station...with the greatest success while he was away droving his cattle to a distant market in North Queensland. This droving takes from ten to eleven months every year and during the whole of this time Mrs Warrington Rogers, with her staff of lubras is in sole charge of the station. This means that for months at a time the lady is out mustering and branding her beasts, building cattle yards, rounding up 'fats' for the markets and attending to the hundred and one other jobs of a big station. All this she does in one of the wildest parts of the Never Never country.[14]

Like many men, the reporter still needed to be reassured of Kate's feminine side, however, and made a point of noting:

For all her manliness and pluck Mrs Rogers is a most womanly woman, a delightful conversationalist and very well read. In spite of being always in the saddle, she was neatly costumed in an up to date tailor made riding dress. To meet this lady and her [Aboriginal women helpers], the latter clothed in brown holland Kate Greenaway dresses faced and braided with wide red ribbon, coming through the lonely bush of this far off land, is an experience indeed.[15]

According to those who knew her, the only thing that seemed to frighten Kate Warrington Rogers was the health and safety of her family. Isolation was the main problem, especially when sickness occurred, as it was 600 miles (960 kilometres) to the nearest doctor; and Kate is said to have buried one child at Urapunga, unable to get medical help in time.

In 1921 Kate contracted influenza and bronchitic pneumonia and was warned that she needed treatment down south, but she left it too late, claiming she was needed at the station, and when she finally reached Melbourne in August she died. When the *Northern Territory Times* got word of her death, it paid tribute to her as:

a woman of exceptional ability [who will] be remembered in the outback parts of the Territory for her skill and courage in everything pertaining to the management of the station and for her generosity and great kindness of heart. She was noted for her successful management of aborigines coupled on the station her motto being kindness contained with firmness. Despite the rough pioneering experiences she remained a kind and dainty lady to the last.[16]

Perhaps it was best that she did not live to see the fate of her beloved husband and son. Her husband, deeply saddened by Kate's death and disillusioned by the lack of success in his pastoral properties, finally shot himself at Mataranka in February 1935. The *Times* described him as 'one of nature's gentlemen with a history of fine achievements in the development of the Northern Territory'. It went on to pay another tribute to Kate's managerial capacity: 'She was a most capable horsewoman and knew nearly all that was to be known about cattle. During the frequent long periods of absence of her husband upon droving trips she managed his station property just as efficiently as he could have done himself.'[17]

Tragically, eight years later, on 16 May 1943, their only remaining son, John, died during a muster near Katherine when his horse slipped and fell on him. He was unmarried and left no children to carry on the name or tradition of his talented parents.

About the time that Kate and John were establishing themselves as Territory outback pioneers, so was another family, whose female members were also destined to become renowned for their strong spirit and ability. They were the Bohnings, and the female members of the family soon became known as the 'Petticoat Drovers'.

It all began when Esther Bennett, daughter of Thomas and Eliza Jenkins of Camooweal, met and married her second husband, German-born John Bohning of Rockland Station in 1902. They were both twenty-three years old. Along with Esther's two sons from her first marriage, the Bohnings began moving through parts of the Northern Territory and Queensland looking for a place to settle. Esther had already had a taste of Territory life when, as a child of eleven, she and her family had lived at Lake Nash Station for a time, her father serving as stockman and her mother as cook and district midwife. In 1907 they applied for a pastoral lease near Pine Creek. They built cattle yards near Katherine and by 1915 had taken possession of Helen Springs, a 1200-square-mile (3108-square-kilometre) property one hundred miles (160 kilometres) north of Tennant Creek. This would be their home for the next thirty years.

Esther, a small but well-built woman who as a young girl had achieved local fame as an excellent runner, soon learned to ride, muster stock, brand cattle, make all the family's clothes and water bags, and mend all the station boots. Like other women on isolated stations before the days of School of the Air, Esther also educated her children, both with books and with life experience. Her daughters, Edith and Elsie, as well as her sons, were an integral part of the station life and accompanied most of the cattle droves. Their nearest neighbour was one hundred miles (160 kilometres) away and it was seldom that they saw other white women. Once a year they travelled to Newcastle Waters to collect their stores. Esther often managed the property on her own for months at a time, particularly during the early 1930s when John and two of their sons were prospecting in the Tennant Creek goldfields. Once she went down the station well and the chain broke. Her children were too young to understand how to get her out so she calmly directed them to lower food to her while she waited for someone to get her out. Help finally arrived three days later.

Elsie was born with a desire to write and, educated by her father (as her mother had had no formal schooling), she put pen to paper very early in her life. By the time she was eleven, in 1921, she had begun writing for the *Northern Territory Times* and

Elsie Bohning, the 'Little Bush Maid' whose newspaper articles in the 1920s painted a vivid picture of life in the Territory's outback, with her pony on Helen Springs station. Photograph by Reg Harris. Hilda Tuxworth collection, Northern Territory State Reference Library.

some interstate papers under the deceptive pseudonym of 'Little Bush Maid'. She continued writing for at least a decade and her published articles provide a rare and passionate glimpse of station and droving life as seen through the eyes of a young girl growing into a young woman.

When her first article was printed on the Cinderella Page of the Sydney *Mail* in 1921, the *Northern Territory Times* heralded it with a small tribute:

Judging by the little letter appended there is more in the centre of Australia than meets the eye in the press controversy over the construction of the overland railway. The writer is a wee lassie of eleven, who with her parents, visited Darwin for the first time some six months ago. Her education and that of the family has been left entirely to a particularly busy mother and the result speaks volumes for the real bush people of the far inland.[18]

For the next several years she sent in regular reports of their station life, their droves, their droughts and their rains, and showed even then that she had a mind of her own about governments and bureaucracies. In 1924 she wrote:

The old mud spring, misnamed Renner Springs is just about dry. It needs fencing in and a few lengths of troughing would enable the mailman and travellers with small plants to water their horses. This is urgently needed and the cost would be very small. A five pound note would fence it in. I don't know why the Government have not taken this in hand. Perhaps they go about with their eyes in their pockets when out joy riding in the interior, or maybe we are too far away from the seat of govt. It is a well known saying that the further you go out back the worse the Government.

Just before closing she added 'Today is a day of jubilation for the rain god has opened his sprinkler for the first time...'[19]

A few weeks later she graphically described a drove on which their cattle ate poisoned plants:

The smash began just before sundown, cows calves, weaners and steers started tumbling over like so many fallen soldiers on a battlefield. Some of them died peacefully, some groaning with pain, some racing round and staggering like drunken men, others bellowing as if a pack of dogs had hold of them. The bullocks went mad; they raced around their fallen comrades seeking the invisible foe. It took all hands to hold them, the sturdy night horses sticking manfully to their tasks until daylight before the infuriated mob settled down. We had seventy dead out of four hundred. It's a sickening sight to see your cattle dying all around you and unable to do anything for them. We lost no fat bullocks that night, but the whole mob was affected. We had to travel six miles to water and it took all day to push the poor sick beggars along, a good many dropping by the wayside never to rise again.[20]

A few months later when she joined her family in another drove 700 miles (1120 km) to Alice Springs, she described the experience in poetic terms:

I am traveling down the O.T. Line and I'm a drover's hand
I am handy at making Johnny cakes, I am handy with the pan.
And I can bend a mob of steers.
Did you hear my stockwhip crack?
No; stockwhips are forbidden with fat cattle on the track.
Now, with all you jolly drovers from hut and camp and town!
Come, drink the health of the drover, the king of the overland![21]

At the tender age of fourteen she was already articulating strong views in the *Northern Territory Times*:

Now I just want to raise my voice in protest of leasing wells on the stock routes and not making proper provision for traveling stock. There is no justification for giving a few lessees the privilege of exploiting the traveling public. Every bore and well should have a small reserve where drovers could spell their cattle for a few days in case of sickness without having to pay heavy agistment fees...

The crushed cattlemen in our district have no less than four robbers. The king robber is drought. This is drought year and cattle are frightfully low in condition and some of the breeders are going out. Further inland it is worse.

The second robber is the poison bush. He takes a heavy toll when bullocks are padding the hoof to market

The third is the agistment fine on the government wells.

The fourth is the railway from Oodnadatta to Adelaide. It costs about three pounds per head to truck bullocks from Oodnadatta to Adelaide a distance of 700 miles [1127 km]. From Najara to Brisbane, a distance 1400 miles [2253 km], it costs only 35/- per head for trucking. Then there is rent, income tax, dog tax, wear and tear, carriage four hundred miles [674 km] inland and by the time they all get a cut out of it there is nothing left for the poor struggling cattlemen on the land.

Federal politicians attend public meetings deploring the desertion of the country side for the cities and with their hands and eyes raised towards heaven in search for the mystery of city invasion, then they appoint a fresh batch of high officials who don't know a tuft of mitchell grass from a bunch of barley grass. The powers that be seem to think the cure of all ills lies in appointing officials. Meantime population is decreasing. The small men are gradually being pushed off the land. We of the waybacks know they can rob us of our trade by not opening up the stock route to our natural market. But they cannot fool us, all the while, so far as the inland is concerned the settlers have cursed the day which placed them under Federal direction.[22]

By December 1925 she was taking a political stand, backing Labor man Harold Nelson against the conservative candidate Colonel Story. She explained her reasoning in a letter to the paper:

The elections will just about be over by the time this reaches you. I am tipping an easy win for Nelson. Owing to Story's drastic (and some say illegal) action over the dingo tax no self respecting wayback cattleman will vote for him. It seems rather over the odds that blunders committed in the administration office should put a penalty on the wayback settlers.

In the last election they blamed pastoralists for not getting their candidate elected. This was not so as the vote on the Downs was almost a block vote for Love. Why don't they face the issue like men and admit their own weakness? Personally I have small hope that political activity will ever strew our path with roses.[23]

Then, as if to apologise for her outburst she added, 'I do so hate to write about this sort of thing as it will be a nasty pill for some of the Darwinites but born and bred in the freedom of the bush has converted me into a bold and I hope a fair and just critic.'

In August 1929 Esther and Elsie made history by taking the first mob of cattle, most of whom they had given pet names along the long route, on the newly opened railway between Alice Springs and Adelaide. When a local official questioned whether the two women could handle the job, John Bohning confidently replied: 'If those two ladies can't handle the situation then it will be no use getting your men to try.'[24]

Before they left, Elsie wrote to the *Northern Territory Times* describing the changes that had taken place in the town since they had last visited in 1924:

We went into Alice Springs with our truck and had six days in town. It is a budding city now. Cars and trucks and people everywhere and some beautiful homes. It has improved beyond all recognition since we were here in 1924. The town folk are splendid, I couldn't possibly find words to express my opinion of those big hearted generous and very very hospitable townsfolk and I fell in love with the town itself all over and over again.

She next described her feelings at the prospect of seeing a proper city, Adelaide:

Now we are on our way to Adelaide and expect to have a few weeks in that fair city when our long long trail is traversed and our bullocks sold and delivered. I have never visited a city yet. We went to Darwin 1920 and it was the isle of my young dreams for a week. Then I longed for the bush and my animal pets and play things again. Now I guess Adelaide will be full of thrill, drama, laughter and fun for a week or so and then the lure of the open spaces will ring in our hearts and ears. Dad says I'll never want to leave the city when I get there, but leave that to me.

Then, with the passionate parochialism that characterised many women writers from the Territory, she wrote:

Dear old NT, my country of birth, I pledge to thee love and toil and years to be. Yes, dear friends of the north, be ye sad or happy, old or young, mark my words, I will come back—back to the dear sunny bushland where the open spaces and the big hearts are. And now dear friends and readers I must boil the billy so goodbye one and all...Nay, Aurevoir, for I will come back.

When she and her mother reached Adelaide with the first mob of cattle to be taken on the train between Alice and the South Australian capital, they were hailed as heroines and true daughters of the bush. A year later, with her new city perspective to give her that broader view of life, Elsie passionately expanded on her feelings about being raised in the Territory outback:

When one is brought up among broad-minded frank openhearted people and taught to love and respect everyone else and help each other always they cannot help but love the whole universe of our bush domain. The golden Australian sunshine seems to penetrate its glorious goodness to the hearts of all our men of the bush and it fills the women of the west with a feeling of motherly tenderness and capability that goes a long way towards making their souls pure and bright like the rays of the glorious old sun itself.

In October 1932, Elsie married Fred Harris of McLaren Valley Station at the home of her parents, where they stayed for a few days before going to live at McLaren Valley. Sadly, most of her paper records were lost during a fire at the station a few years later. When Fred died in Adelaide, Elsie married again, and she has lived most of the rest of her life outside the Territory.

Her parents remained on Helen Springs station through the war years, during which her mother experienced one of the problems which arose with thousands of troops stationed in the Territory outback — the lack of women in comparison to men. A group of American soldiers had camped overnight at a military area at Banka Banka station. The next night they detoured into Helen Springs and fired shots into the station roof, demanding that the Aboriginal women on the station be handed over to them. Esther Bohning stood on the verandah with a shotgun and told them that she would shoot if they took another step. They retreated and later faced a court-martial.

The Bohnings later moved to Alice Springs, where Esther died in 1952. The local paper readily acknowledged her contribution to Territory life:

The history of the Northern Territory is the story of the Bohnings and the few remaining pioneers...Those who did not know the story would never have guessed that the frail little woman seen moving quietly about last year had played such an active part in the development of the north of Australia, had taken the first cattle train out of Alice Springs and could once ride and handle cattle with the best. When she passed on...Mrs Bohning left five sons, two daughters and five grandchildren. Each of her children have been part of the story, each was in some way connected with the land.

There were other women drovers who followed in the Bohnings' footsteps, the most well-known probably being Edna Zigenbine, who in 1950 became Australia's first female boss drover when she took charge of a drove from Bedford Downs to the Kimberleys.

Isobel Violet Price was another who became a pioneer of central Australia. She was Isobel Hesketh when she met and married Fred Alfred Price in Darwin in 1898. Both had been in the Territory for many years, Isobel coming from a family who had been on Thursday Island and in the Territory since the 1880s, and Fred, a talented actor and singer, having been appointed a telegraph operator in Darwin in 1891. They took an active role in Top End life and were well regarded by the populace. Isobel was forced to leave Darwin in 1901 when she became seriously ill after being bitten by a red-back spider, one of the many hazards of Top End living. She lived in Adelaide with her children until 1903, when Fred was able to join them by getting a posting there. The family lived there until 1914, when he became postmaster at Marree. Two years later he was transferred to the Overland Telegraph Station in Alice Springs. Their daughter, Pearl (Powell), was six when she, her mother, her two brothers and her sister made the three-day trip by train to Oodnadatta and the two-week journey by horse and buggy to join Fred at the station.

There they lived until 1924 when they decided to take a holiday to Adelaide before returning to retire at their newly purchased property, Harper's Springs station. But in Adelaide Fred Price died. Isobel elected to return to the Territory with her four children and run the property herself.

The family travelled for seven weeks by buggy and dray to reach their new home at Harper's Springs, taking with them three camels, a few goats and horses and 200 head of sheep. When they finally arrived in Alice Springs after an arduous trip overland from Oodnadatta, during which they averaged about twelve miles (19 km) a day, they collected the pets they had left behind before going to Adelaide, and

Isobel Price and her family out riding on their central Australian property. Isobel and her daughters were all excellent horsewomen, as were most women who lived in the Territory outback.
Powell-Price collection, Northern Territory Conservation Commission.

Left:
Territory pioneer Isobel Price and her children at Woolla Downs in the mid-1920s, outside the home they made themselves of boughs strung over a large tent.
Powell-Price collection, Northern Territory Conservation Commission.

headed for their new home. There, with her children as her station hands, Isobel built a bough dwelling and set about establishing the property. Her daughter Pearl described the isolation:

We didn't know much about what was going on beyond our own property because we seldom got any mail and our nearest neighbours were at least forty miles [64 km] away. We would collect our mail about every six weeks from Stirling Station where the post office would send it for us. It was my job to collect it and it used to take me two days and three nights to make the return trip.

When Harper's Springs proved unsuitable for sheep, the family packed up again and moved onto the second block of land Fred and Isobel had bought, adjacent to Harper's Springs. 'Mother named it Woolla Downs because our sheep were the first animals to be taken there as stock,' Pearl recalled. Eventually the sheep herd was built up to 3000 and the family had 700 goats, all of which had to be shepherded by the children. When Pearl married another central Australian, Jim Bird, and started life on Bushy Park station, about sixty miles (96 km) northeast of Alice Springs, she once visited her mother, only to find her still tending the cattle, moving them to a well twelve miles (19 km) from the homestead, walking the herd because her side-saddle was broken and she refused to ride astride. Eventually ill health forced Isobel to leave the running of the station to the children, and she moved to Adelaide, where she died in 1957 and was buried with her husband and their first three children in the cemetery in Payneham. But her memory and pioneering effort in the Territory lives on in a collection of photographs preserved and exhibited in the Alice Springs Telegraph Station.

Doreen Braitling was another pioneering woman pastoralist of central Australia. She arrived in the Alice Springs area from England early in the century, with her parents, Bertha and William Crook. After several years of working in various parts of central Australia, they were given a Territory government job at Wycliff Well, drawing water for travelling stock. As a young girl, Doreen and her sister Kathleen did much of the whipping of the water, a method which drew water from the well either by using a horse, camel or working bullock to pull a long rope which lowered and raised buckets to and from the well.

Bertha Crook was one of the few women to give evidence before the parliamentary standing committee on public works in 1921. She lobbied for improvements to their life, telling the chairman:

It would make life more agreeable for us if we had a railway as it is a long way to go now for medical attention in the case of illness. There is no medical aid nearer than Oodnadatta or Darwin...if there were women here and the men were married they would be much more settled and would stay in the country longer...The climate is quite suitable for a white woman. The mosquitoes and flies are very bad but my daughters and I generally have good health, although I suffer from rheumatism in the winter. It would be much nicer, especially for the girls, if we had some neighbours...The nearest white woman is about 180 to 190 miles [290-306 km] away. Two years ago we saw a white woman passing through here, the wife of a drover who was traveling with him.[25]

Gradually the family accumulated a herd of stock that had been either abandoned or lost by drovers, and with this they established a station at Singleton Downs. Doreen, who married well-known Centralian pastoralist Bill Braitling in 1932 and with him established Mount Doreen Station, later wrote her own account of early station life, describing how stores for six to twelve months had to be ordered months in advance. She used a scale of rations based on twenty-two pounds (10 kilograms) of flour, four and one-half pounds (2 kilograms) of sugar and about one-half pound (.25 kilograms) of tea for one person for two weeks, adding other items such as dried fruit, rice, salt and pepper. She pointed out that many bush settlers went onto pastoral blocks with little more than their personal possessions, a plant of horses, a few goats and if they were very lucky a few cattle to start with.

As they had no way of getting building material they made use of whatever natural resources they did have. Some built mud and pise huts. Some added local stone and used the mud as mortar...Some settlers cut down trees and used the timber, placed upright in the grounds, the cracks plastered over with crushed ant-bed mixed with water into a stiff mud and whole white-washed over. The roof was usually thatched with whatever material could be found. Bullrushes made a good thatch...Another type of home usually temporary, was made of green boughs, gum tree or mulga, the floor being earth. A tarpaulin rigged under it kept out the rain.

A lot of goods were packed in deal boxes in those days. As the boxes became empty they were soon made into cupboards by any one handy with a hammer and a few nails...For a mattress...cow hair curled and boiled, then chopped up into small lengths and teased out made a very good filling.

The earth floor was sprinkled each day with water and swept. Inevitably the broom wore out but mulga forest provided fresh young boughs each day which made an excellent broom. To keep food cool a large metal meat dish and an old towel were sacrificed. A wooden box, its sides removed, made the safe frame; opened out sugar or salt bags were tacked around it, the meat dish placed on the top and filled with water. Strips of towelling, one end in the water, the other hanging down on the bats seeped water down the sides and there was the water cooled safe.[26]

Doreen stressed the resourcefulness of the outback dwellers. 'They were taught cleanliness and honesty and what they did not have they seldom yearned for. They learned to make things themselves, or went without.'

Thelma Hunter was a woman who learned resourcefulness at an early age. She arrived in the Territory from West Melbourne with her parents, Mr and Mrs Charles Dargie, and her six brothers and sisters, in 1913, when the family travelled to take up 500 acres (202 hectares) of virgin land on the Daly River. They were part of the ill-fated Dr John Gilruth's plans for colonising the Top End with agricultural and pastoral settlers.

At sixteen Thelma married well-known Territory buffalo shooter George Hunter, and in the next ten years she gave birth to five children, sometimes walking into Darwin to receive help with the births. All the time, the family was on the move between Marrakai and the Alligator River region, tracking buffalo herds. Thelma, along with a group of Aboriginal women helpers, skinned and packed the hides. Her children travelled with them, living in bough sheds and under mosquito nets. Later she abandoned the buffalo hunting life and turned to smoking fish at Shoal Bay.

While there, she was once shipwrecked off Cape Don and spent three days and nights on a low reef until she was rescued by the crew of trepang lugger. Eventually she tired not so much of the outback life but of the ill treatment she received from her husband, who had a violent temper, and she moved to Darwin, where she was eventually divorced. Later she remarried. Several of her children still reside in the Territory.

Elizabeth Darcy was another woman who reared a large family in isolated surroundings. She and her husband George Darcy established a home at Mallapunya Springs in the Borroloola district where Elizabeth gave birth to all twelve of her children with little or no medical assistance, and educated them herself. In November of 1944 Elizabeth and one of her sons, Michael, disappeared from Anthony's Lagoon in circumstances which were never fully explained. They were never seen again.

Living on an isolated station before the advent of effective means of communication meant particular hardship if any illness arose in the family or any serious accident occurred. One of the northern pioneer women who decided to do something about the situation was Sarah Graham, who for many years during and after the First World War lived on the Territory's largest property, Victoria River Downs, as wife and helpmate of the manager. When fever broke out in the area, Sarah began to lobby politicians and the owners of the station, Vesteys, about the need for a medical centre in the area, particularly for women. Eventually her efforts were rewarded when the Australian Inland Mission built Wimmera Hostel only 300 yards (274 metres) from the Victoria River Downs homestead.

A newspaper reporter of 1924 paid tribute to Sarah's efforts:

The energetic lady who was the moving spirit, set to work collecting subscriptions, and with these and the proceeds of some race meetings organised for the purpose a sum of 1100 pounds was obtained. Some station hands gave ten guineas and one donor gave fifty pounds...A modern airy building has been erected...and two nurses are installed, one a double certificate...Before the home was established expectant mothers were obliged to make a journey of over 200 miles [322 km] over roughest roads to get the necessary attention.[27]

Coping with isolation was part and parcel of living in the remote regions of the Territory. Ellen Margaret Hobley, who was raised in the Roper River country, was eighteen before she saw any life other than that of the outback. At the age of two she arrived in Queensland from England with her father and mother, Mr and Mrs John S. Hobley. Her father, who had been to Australia at the turn of the century and travelled extensively in northwest Australia, decided to take up Territory land in a soldier settlement scheme that followed the First World War. They travelled by horse and dray for nearly three years, with the adventurous Mrs Hobley driving the buckboard, before reaching their destination on the Roper in the early 1920s.

'We had one maple folding table, a sewing machine, linen, oak tool chest, suitcases, harness and camping gear,' Ellen, who was then five, later recalled. 'There was no track to our block, only thirty miles [48 km] of bush to the station which was on the north bank of the Roper. It was a hot, sweltering ride...I was on a packhorse, though none of us had ever ridden before the journey.'[28]

With axe and shovels they selected a house site in four square miles [10 km²] of virgin bush where mails and supplies only reached them every six months. 'We had no financial or technical assistance; learned by trial and error,' Ellen said.

Dad cleared the land himself with one plow and got enough timber for a house. By the end of the second year our house was up, measuring twenty-two by twelve feet [6.7 x 3.7 metres] with a stone and clay fireplace at one end. Mother made curtains of dyed hessian and dad made a double bed for the three of us. We never did get a fridge and the only washing machine we ever had was mother. She boiled clothes in a kerosene tin over fire and made soap from caustic soda and tallow from every scrap of fat she found. Every once in a while another station would send us a bag of meat and suet in exchange for eggs and dairy produce...It was a lonely life for mother...our only real contact with the outside world was with policemen and a few drovers.

In 1924 a cyclonic storm caused the mighty Roper to rise six feet[2 metres] in two hours, gale force winds ripped the roof off their home and the family had to take refuge for two days in one small corner of the room. 'The whole world was wind and water,' Ellen said. When the storm subsided, the family moved to a higher and safer place two miles upstream and spent another six months living in a bough shed and tent until a new house could be constructed. Even then they were not totally secure from the ravages of the unpredictable tropical weather.

One day the river rose fifty feet [15 metres] in just a few hours, with no warning...leaving us marooned on a little island with our goats and other animals with us. When the river finally fell back, there were many miles of grazing country lost...Most of the old pioneers fought a losing battle, not only having nature against them but also time and distance and man.[29]

The Hobleys once visited two of their few neighbours, Harold and Doris Giles of Elsey Station. Doris later remembered the day they arrived:

I heard a loud rattling noise and looked up to see a funny old truck coming up from Roper Bar. Steam was pouring out the radiator, the engine was knocking and we were amazed to see the wheels had no tyres. They had come over a hundred miles [160 km] on rims. Two people got out and introduced themselves...The driver was a bushman who had volunteered to get them up to see us. They had on weird hats they had made out of pandanus palms. Their dresses were two straight pieces with two smaller pieces for sleeves and no shape whatever...We took them into the railway siding and it was fun to hear Ellen's outspoken comments on everything. She had never seen a train except on pictures and had no other companions but her parents. She enjoyed the holiday spent with us.[30]

In 1936 Ellen, then eighteen, and her mother made a trip to Perth. It was Ellen's first taste of real civilisation. Dressed in broad-brimmed hats plaited from grass growing on their farm and long, plain, one-piece dresses, they were conspicuous in the fashion-conscious city. The papers were fascinated by this girl who had lived for more than a decade in the 'wilds' of the Territory and described her bewilderment at 'ships, trains, electric light, glass windows, huge buildings, crowds of people and many other commonplaces of modern civilisation which she knew existed but [had] never seen.'[31]

Despite being homesick for the relative peace and space of the Roper River, Ellen stayed in Perth to study motor mechanics. After completing her motor mechanic certificate the self-taught girl from the bush went on to study aero engineering, aircraft construction and mechanical drawing, topping Australia in her chosen field of study, and eventually went on to fly her own aircraft. She later married another long-term Territorian, Frank Litchfield, and though they made their home in Queensland the Territory remained a big part of them and they have maintained contact with their many Territory friends and relatives.

Ellen's mother returned to the Roper, but when she suffered a broken wrist after a fall the Hobleys decided to move to Darwin. Within days of their arrival in December 1939, they received news of the biggest flood of the century sweeping the gulf country. The flooding Roper had enveloped their home, burying it in seventeen feet (5 metres) of water and destroying all their household treasures, including a library of 2000 books that Mrs Hobley had carefully packed with one hand. All that remained was one kitchen knife.

Doris and Harold Giles' Elsey property was caught in the same flood. Again Doris described the drama:

After Christmas my husband left me at the homestead with only a stockman and a Chinese cook and, of course, the blacks. We had five inches [12.5 cm] the day after he left and a total of twenty inches [50 cm] in five days. The wireless set was out of order...The river was rising and on the fifth day we decided to shift. I kept some of the girls and camp boys back to stack stores out of danger, and took flour, tea and sugar onto high shelves in the loft over the stockman's quarters. The wireless set and the electric light engine we also put away. At two am Jack the stockman came in to report that the river had broken its banks and was almost in the front gate of the homestead. The muddy water was up to my knees by daylight with the possibility of a few crocodiles. The out kitchen went sailing by with a few fowls on the roof and was not seen again.

The trucks were under water, we could not transport anything to the high ground indicated by the blacks, the stools and chairs came floating out of the main kitchen and all round was a raging torrent. Jack made me leave and I packed a small case with money and important papers and left in what I stood up in. Luckily it was hot weather and it did not matter about being wet. I had a boy on each side of me to drag me through the waist deep water.

They built a raft out of boards cut from a tree and clung to it while it swept down the river, past their submerged homestead and trees climbing with snakes and other creatures trying to escape. Finally the rains ceased and the water began to subside almost as fast as it had risen, revealing what was left of the mud-clad homestead.

When Japanese bombs fell on Darwin Doris was evacuated to Brisbane, but she was allowed back a few months later to help look after the many people who called into the station during the war years. As a former AIM nurse, Doris enjoyed the company of the nursing sisters at the nearby military hospitals.

Another woman who remained in the Top End during the war was Olive Underwood, who, with the help of Aboriginal women, built a fine stone homestead at Coolibah Station, near Joe Bradshaw's old haunting ground. The women were also responsible for building stone outhouses, including a fine meat house. Olive gained a well-deserved reputation for being an immaculate and hospitable homemaker in the middle of the Territory's outback.

These are only a few of the countless stories of women's innovations, tragedies and triumphs in the isolated regions of the Territory. There are women today who, although their lives in the outback have been improved greatly by increased communication and transport systems, still live in isolation, carrying on the pioneering tradition of the women of the wayback. Jeannie Gunn's rather stereotyped portrait of outback life has now been challenged by writers such as Melissa McCord in her *Outback Women* and Ann McGrath in her *Born to the Cattle*. In these, station life is depicted as very much a working partnership between black and white and between men and women.

Baldwin Spencer was one who recognised women's unsung contribution to Australian life as early as 1923 when he wrote:

We hear of monuments being erected to pioneer men, but when you have been out in the never never country you begin to feel that in Canberra, Australia's capital, there should be at least one great monument dedicated to the pioneer women of Australia. The women of the backblocks live in a state of almost complete isolation and loneliness and Australia owes to them a great debt.[32]

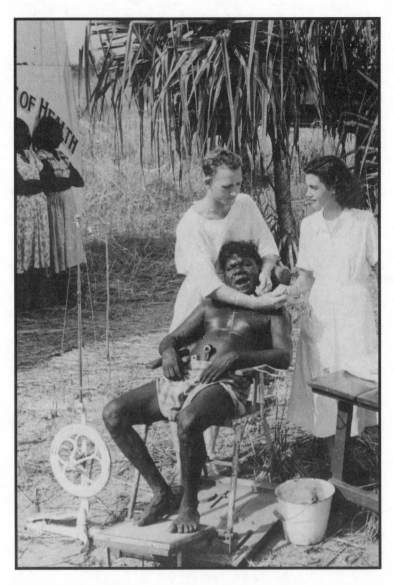

Wendy James, evacuated from Darwin in 1941 with her defiant mother
Poppy Secrett, remembers the immediate post-war Territory with affection, even
though conditions were sometimes primitive. Before her marriage to surveyor
Earl James she worked as a dental assistant with the health department,
travelling to isolated communities to help provide dental care to the people
in those regions. In 1983 Wendy became the inaugural convenor of the
Northern Territory Women's Advisory Council, established to keep the
government in touch with the views of women on various community issues.
Photograph courtesy of Wendy James.
Northern Territory Health Department.

Chapter 12

Post-War Pioneering (1945-1989)

'I believe that the future development of this [Territory] will be determined by the endurance of its pioneering womenfolk for I have always held that in the final analysis, women are the real arbiters of a nation's destiny.'
Mrs Arthur Calwell, 1952

The women who were able to remain in the Territory during the war or chose to return when it was over were no less pioneers than those who had taken part in Territory life a century earlier, for the war had changed the face of the Territory quite dramatically.

Women who returned to Darwin returned to a town still under military occupation and in most cases to homes that had been bombed and looted, and if that hadn't destroyed them, the white ants probably had. Compulsory acquisition of land led to years of dispute with authorities, not to mention the heartache of people being dispossessed of their homes. Adding to the stress was the fact that for months, most people wanting to return to the Top End needed permits to do so — a situation which would be repeated nearly thirty years later when Cyclone Tracy ripped through Darwin.

One of the first women allowed to return to Darwin when hostilities ceased was Poppy Secrett. Poppy had already demonstrated her determination to live in the Territory when she had defied instructions to remain away until the war was over. Poppy and her three young children had been forcibly evacuated to Perth late in 1941 but by early 1943 she had had enough of 'southern life'. She put her two older children in boarding school, bundled up her youngest daughter and returned to the Territory to try to join her husband Stan, who was working with the civil construction corps. Stan met her and smuggled her 'up the track', deceiving army security until they arrived at Dunmarra, about half-way between Darwin and Alice Springs. Here officials agreed to turn a blind eye to her presence and she was allowed to stay, becoming an official 'housekeeper' if anyone asked. She was thus able to see her husband Stan, who worked in the area, reasonably often. When she became pregnant, Stan had to cover her and their young daughter, Lorilee, under blankets and smuggle them back to Alice Springs in a truck, again avoiding army security. In Alice Poppy gave birth to twin sons and arranged for her other two children, Wendy and John, to join them in Alice, where they remained until the armistice was signed and, as Wendy later remembered, 'everyone went berserk'. Even though there was a permit system in force until February 1946, they persuaded authorities to allow them to return to Darwin, and by October of 1945 they were back, one of the first four civilian families in town. Wendy, who, nearly forty years later would become convenor of the Territory's first Women's Advisory Council, remembered it well:

There were Japanese prisoners of war still here and they would whistle and shriek as they were driven in trucks past mum in the street. There were a few shops, like Cashmans, Quongs and Burnetts but it was still a military atmosphere that prevailed. Housing was primitive and I hated washing day. We soaked the clothes overnight with flaked soap, boiled them up next day in a copper and had to lift them out, scalding hot with a stick. Toilet facilities were 'flaming furies' which were set alight in the back yard and were a constant reminder of primitive conditions. Those monstrosities took two days to burn and two days to cool down so we had to work in with our neighbours.

There was no industry in Darwin, only public service, but people came back because they loved the tropical lifestyle. They fought to stay and by staying helped to establish what there is today. I remember as each woman arrived back, mum would make a fuss of them and the women would form a great bonding. They set about developing the social structure. People who returned did not come back because there was any future really, but because they wanted to live here.[1]

Nevertheless the primitive housing conditions, combined with high prices and scarce food commodities — problems that were exacerbated by frequent trouble on the wharf, which sometimes delayed the unloading of essential supplies — caused hardship for many families. Women quickly learned the force of collective action and wasted little time in forming the Darwin Housewives Association, a deceptively innocent-sounding group that undertook several effective lobbying campaigns to improve conditions for women in the war-torn town. A driving force behind the group for many years was Lou Stewart, a self-appointed lobbyist who is often unofficially given credit for being the persistent voice that ensured that a housing commission scheme was finally introduced into the Territory. Lou had arrived in Darwin prior to the war but was evacuated on the *Zealandia* late in 1941. When she first returned after the war, she found the family home had been bombed, and the family was forced to live in squalid conditions for several years, during which Lou designed a prototype low-cost house of aluminium in a successful bid to convince the government that a housing commission scheme could work to alleviate the housing shortage without costing people a small fortune. Lou started her campaign by getting support from other women. She helped form the Housewives Association and, as acting secretary during its initial stages, wrote a poem calling on women to unite:

> Come on girls, what's got in yer? Don't you get riled when you cook that dinner?
> No fresh vegetables, out of spuds. Weevils in flour, no soap for suds.
> The meat's allright, we've still got beef; Kids go to school, hard bread to eat;
> There's hundreds of things we can make better. I don't have to pen them in this letter.
> Come on girls, there's lots to do; Let Dad mind the kids for a night or two.
> We don't want to hear your political view,
> Only your troubles over a cup of brew.
> There's nothing that's needed that we can't do, We'll push heaven and earth
>   to get it through.
> But your cooperation is what we need, The more girls we rally, the better the deed.[2]

The sentiments the poem espoused would be echoed in one form or another by many women's groups in years to come, and they worked. Darwin women rallied in support, marched down the main street to protest over inadequate housing and food prices, and became a force to be reckoned with in the community. Lou did more than her share by writing letters to as many top officials as possible, including the Queen, the Governor-General, the Prime Minister and the Minister for the Territories. By 1951 the government had begun making improvements to accommodation facilities, starting with a hostel on the Esplanade and one for women public servants in the renovated Don Hotel. Finally in 1959 a housing commission scheme was introduced.

Another prominent lobbyist in the Housewives Association was Esther Meaney, who had grown up on Stapleton Station near Batchelor as part of the strong and independent Sargent family, who had arrived in the Territory in 1923. Esther's sometimes violent father had treated his fourteen children as 'slave labour' on the station, so Esther was no stranger to hard work and determination. Because of her background, however, she developed a strong sense of justice and compassion for the oppressed and poor. As president of the Darwin Housewives Association in 1950, she instigated a survey of housing conditions in Darwin's inner suburbs, raising public awareness of the fact that there were 500 people in need of housing. Esther also outlined a programme of action for the association, which included campaigning for increases in wages to cope with the high cost of living in the tropics, for the provision of recreation clubs and swimming pools and for a rest room for women in the shopping area. Like many other women across Australia, Esther also involved herself in the Peace Council and in April 1950 she represented the Territory at the great Melbourne Peace Congress, which was attended by more than 12 000 people. She was selected by the peace committee of the North Australian Workers Union and endorsed by the union executive because of her activities with the housewives association and for her 'brilliant down to earth' speech at a large basic wage rally in Darwin earlier in the year. When Esther returned from the conference, she travelled around the Territory promoting the peace message, a message she was still endorsing in 1988, the year her autobiographical book, *Esther*, was published.

Darwin women also re-formed their pre-war Country Women's Association which became another constructive force for improving conditions in the community. In 1953 the group succeeded in establishing the Darwin Outback Mothers' Hostel, and in 1960 it opened the Darwin branch rest room in the city area, a great boon to mothers in particular.

Other women were instrumental in improving the physical look of Darwin— an essential ingredient for the psychological well-being of residents living in quite barren conditions amongst war-scarred ruins. Two women in particular devoted themselves to the 'greening of Darwin' in the early post-war years—May Fitzpatrick and Nancy Eddy. Nancy and her husband lived in a caravan for sixteen months before they were allocated a four-room house in Mitchell Street, surrounded by thick scrub and rubbish. Nancy spent months clearing the land, leaving a few native trees, and then for the next four years mowed, planted and watered until she finally had a neat lawn of native grass and more than a hundred native trees and plants growing in her yard. She haunted libraries in search of botanical information about their names and care and within a few years she had educated herself so well that she was acknowledged as a local expert and attracted the attention of botanists from all over the world.

Then, when she realised that most of the plants and shrubs in Darwin's Botanical Gardens had no identification, Nancy spent more than a year identifying and making plaques for 1000 botanical specimens, so that others in the community could benefit from her knowledge of tropical gardening. Nancy later went on to make a major contribution to the recording and preservation of Territory history, writing many meticulously researched and illustrated family histories and collecting thousands of books, articles and photographs relevant to the Territory's past.

May Fitzpatrick, an admitted 'leftist' who had been active in establishing work-based creche facilities in suburban Melbourne, came to the Territory in 1943 with her husband, pilot Harry Moss, who had been hired by the Connair management in Alice Springs to help out with the war-time flying operation. After spending the war years in Alice Springs, May and Harry bought a couple of trucks and began making trips to and from Darwin to buy and sell war disposal goods. As it did many others, the tropical weather soon seduced May, and when Harry decided in 1949 that he wanted to live in Alice Springs, the marriage split up and May remained in Darwin, which was her home for the next thirty years. Her first job was bookkeeper-cum-social writer for the union-owned *Northern Standard*, a paper she described as 'damn good; it printed the truth'. She also became secretary for the Darwin Worker's Club and secretary and librarian for the CWA. Her main interest, though, like Nancy Eddy's, became tropical gardening and working towards improving the physical look of Darwin. Like Nancy, she educated herself, mainly by reading South African gardening books and articles, and was soon asked to write a gardening column for the new local newspaper, the *Northern Territory News.* May realised that for her gardening education to have any real effect in changing the face of Darwin, others needed to be involved, so she helped form Darwin's first garden club, where people could exchange plants, seeds and information. Today there are many garden clubs throughout the city and they did much towards beautifying Darwin both after the war and after Cyclone Tracy, and have increased public awareness of the tropical gardening techniques pioneered by women like Nancy and May.

Women have also participated strongly in re-establishing the business and economic life of the town and brought a diversity of backgrounds that reflected Darwin's cosmopolitan make-up. Among the early businesswomen were Italian-born Maria Donatelli who gained a reputation in the early 1950s as being a pioneer in the presentation of good food in the hitherto casual Darwin style of eating houses; Helene Harmanis with her exclusive women's boutique; women of the Haritos family with their general goods stores; Lorna Lim and family with the Hotel Victoria and their Smith Street shop, the first pre-war Chinese-run business in the European section of town; Chrissie Paspalis with the family's restaurant and catering business; Vivian Paspaley and the family's pearling ventures; and Jessie Litchfield with her Roberta Library.

WOMEN IN THE CENTRE

Alice Springs had also been affected by the war, although unlike Darwin many residents had remained in the town, including some Darwin families who had moved to Alice during the war to establish their businesses there. This meant the town had been allowed to steadily progress as the acting administrator Leslie Giles observed in his 1946 report: 'Despite the feverish activity it experienced as an army railhead during the war, it has emerged quite unspoilt and has continued to grow. Unlike

Darwin, which has a very small permanently resident and no rural population, Alice is the centre for cattle and sheep stations, missions, mining and gardens.' As such, Alice increasingly needed services to cater for the surrounding district and its own growing population. Again, it was women who played a major role in obtaining them.

Pre-school work in the Territory had its start in Alice Springs when in 1947 the CWA Hall was lent to the local kindergarten, with Miss Pat Kempt as the first director and Lorna Moss as one of the main driving forces. The pre-school committee was particularly active, and succeeded, through public subscription, in building their own school, which was opened in 1954. It was named after Nathalie Gorey, who had been one of the most enthusiastic members of the pre-school movement.

Women also took an active role in getting the vital School of the Air established — first raising money through school committees and mothers' clubs for school broadcasts through the Flying Doctor base, and then for a fully-fledged School of the Air, which opened during the jubilee year of 1951. Miss Adelaide Miethke, a well-known South Australian who had successfully lobbied for many improvements to education and to female teachers' salaries, was one of the driving forces behind the move which was a world first. She was also an instigator of the Country Women's Association Air Branch, the first of its kind in the world, formed in 1952 and operating from the Alice Springs Flying Doctor Base.

As in Darwin, a woman became Alice Springs' post-war botanical expert. She was Olive Pink, who had already made a name for herself as quite a respected, if eccentric, anthropologist. After the war she moved to a Sidney Williams hut in Alice Springs, where she became more eccentric and more colourful. After a few years, sympathetic authorities gave her an area of land, now known as the Olive Pink Flora and Fauna Reserve, on which she grew and experimented with arid-zone trees and plants. Sometimes her experiments made a political or social statement, as veteran Territory journalist, Jim Bowditch (who knew Miss Pink from the 1950s when he edited the Alice Springs paper) discovered during a visit he made to her shortly before her death in 1975:

Intrigued by a line of shrubs, some very healthy looking, others rather seedy and a few on the point of fading away altogether, I asked Miss Pink about them. She told me these were her people shrubs...each named after somebody she felt strongly about in one way or another. People she considered offended against her principles in attitudes to Aborigines she would not water very much. The goodies were well cared for. I was honoured to find she had named one after me but slightly shaken when I found it to be halfway between sound and thirsty. Olive Pink explained that sometimes I was in her good books for what I wrote and sometimes in her disfavour so the shrub was a shade unstable and a little psycho. There were others in various stages of health and ill-health...rather like a novel form of the old voodoo practice of sticking needles in wax dolls while muttering special words of punishment, even unto death. Eccentric? I suppose it could be seen as such. But she worked hard to survive and poured all her other energies into helping the peoples she believed we, as a race, had abandoned. It says much for the lady and some of the town's seniors that after her death at a rather great age, a quiet little park was named 'Olive Pink Reserve'.[3]

Today that park is signposted to let others know of her work, and of the contribution Aboriginal people have made to the Territory.

Other women brought Alice Springs to national attention in the post-war years. Daphne Campbell brought early fame to the Centre when she starred in the film *The Overlanders* with Chips Rafferty and then fell in love with a young Connellan pilot, Sam Calder, and ended up staying and living in the Territory. A few years later Ngarla Kunoth, a fifteen-year-old Aboriginal girl from St Mary's Children's hostel for outback children in Alice Springs, starred in the film *Jedda*, raising awareness of the Territory in general and its Aboriginal culture in particular. Many years later American actress Meryl Streep would bring attention to the Centre in a much more controversial and sensational movie dealing with the life of Lindy Chamberlain, who was found guilty of the murder of her daughter, Azaria, at Ayers Rock in 1982 and more than five years later had the conviction quashed.

As they had in Darwin, women also worked to improve Alice Springs's cultural and artistic life in the early post-war years, in particular Mona Greatorex and Mona Byrnes. Mona Greatorex was a driving force behind the Alice Springs Theatre Group and Mona Byrnes, who was born in Hermannsburg in 1923, became a foundation member and art adviser to the Alice Springs Art Foundation, which administers the nationally recognised Alice Prize. She also achieved recognition as an accomplished Centralian artist and photographer.

Tourism was and still is one the Centre's most important economic bases and women played no small role in its development. Not long after the war an Alice Springs woman, Dorothy Adamson, who began working with Connellan airways in 1947, was sent to England for the firm to become an overseas travel consultant, interesting people in the Territory. Daisy Underdown, who had been in the Centre since the 1920s, built the first tourist chalets at Ayers Rock and helped her son build the Alice Springs Hotel, with another woman, Mona Minahan, providing competition by building the Riverside Hotel in 1959.

Other women recognised the need for Territorians to have a better understanding of their identity and devoted themselves to interesting Territorians in the Territory. Adele Purvis, who married pioneer pastoralist Bob Purvis, advocated that local historical knowledge was a worthwhile community pursuit. In the 1950s she wrote extensively on central Australian history and, although some of her information was not always strictly correct, it was pioneering work, and she did much to create an interest in preserving central Australian history, including becoming foundation member of the National Trust. In Tennant Creek, Hilda Tuxworth, who arrived in the immediate post-war period and was sister in charge of Peko Mines until 1958, did much the same for that Centralian region. As well as being active in most community organisations, she began conducting oral interviews with old Tennant identities, and in 1978 she published a history of Tennant Creek, one of the few histories of the region. She also helped form the Tennant Creek Historical Society and National Trust and in her eighties was researching and writing the history of the stations surrounding Tennant Creek.

Some women concentrated on setting up much needed Territory medical and social services in the outback areas. Among the quiet achievers in this area was Dorothy Hall, who had come to Darwin in 1937 as a nurse to the AIM hospital at Victoria River Downs and was in Katherine when the Japanese bombed that town. After the war Dorothy went to Pine Creek and took over the nursing community, working unpaid until 1963, when finally she was given forty pounds a month. In Alice Springs, Deaconess Eileen Heath was active in improving life for Aboriginal children. At the request of the diocese of Carpentaria and the Australian Board of Missions she went to Alice Springs in 1946 to establish a hostel for Aboriginal children, later becoming an officer with the welfare branch and a foundation member of the Prisoners Aid and Rehabilitation association. The late Olive O'Keefe, who had married John O'Keefe in Katherine in 1938, returned to the Territory in 1946, bringing with her the Aboriginal children of Melville Island, who had been evacuated during the war. She joined the Alice Springs hospital in 1949, where she established an Aboriginal ward. She lived her latter days in Katherine, where she was nurse not only to people but to dogs, cats and all manner of pets. When she died in 1988 she was hailed for her contribution to community welfare, and her home was restored as a National Trust property.

Another woman who made a major contribution to nursing in the Territory's outback areas was Ellen Kettle, who arrived in the Territory in 1952 as a nurse at Yuendumu, an Aboriginal settlement 185 miles (298 kilometres) west of Alice Springs. She lived in an unlined war-time camouflaged iron hut and in 1954 became the first Rural Survey sister, pioneering mobile health work in isolated areas. In 1967 she wrote of her experiences in a book, *Gone Bush*. Another woman who helped pioneer education in isolated areas, especially for Aborigines, was Margaret Dodd, who arrived in 1949 to visit Mainoru cattle station. In 1957 she opened a small school in an iron hut, and soon many Aboriginal students were attending; their command of English improved dramatically, enabling them to communicate better in the modern world. She also nursed while at the station and devoted much time after her retirement in 1968 to teaching Aboriginal health.

THE STRUGGLES OF ABORIGINAL WOMEN

Perhaps the greatest changes in the post-war Territory occurred for the women of Aboriginal descent. One of the foremost spokeswomen on increasing awareness of Aboriginal culture has been Vai Stanton, grand-daughter of Lucy McGinness of Territory mining fame. Her story is representative of what happened to many women of part-Aboriginal descent in the official post-war shift from a protectionist policy to one of assimilation.

Vai tells the moving story of her mother, who was taken from her mother at the age of six and put in the Darwin Aboriginal compound. 'She told me she used to repeat her name, her skin and her mother's name every night before going to sleep so that one day she could find her mother,' Vai says. 'When we were young, I remember my mother walking up and down the railway looking for her, until finally she found her. Even though all this happened to her, she taught us kids not to be bitter.'[4]

In a 1978 address to the Territory Labor Party Vai graphically described the dilemma and drama many of her people had faced, in comparatively recent times:

Although I am an Aborigine, born in this country we call Australia, I obtained my exemption and was only granted citizenship of this country in June 1950...My mother was a compound girl. She was taken from her mother when she was six years old. My beautiful mother, Kingarli of the Gurinji, institutionalised...I was a very

Aboriginal women on Bathurst Island have developed a successful business enterprise, Bima Wear, using traditional Aboriginal designs screen-printed on colourful materials and sold as fabric lengths or made up into a variety of fashions. In 1988 they staged a highly successful fashion parade at one of Darwin's leading hotels. Photograph by Clive Hyde.
Northern Territory News.

young and immature person when I first learnt the extent of the oppression of the Native Affairs Act on me, and realised that all Aboriginal people were subjected to this degradation in their own country.

In 1947 Vai married a European man, Jim Stanton, who had worked with her father during the war. They were shocked and devastated when they were told in 1950 that in order for them to have Vai's family on their property they had to have official permission and they had to obtain a Certificate of Exemption for Vai, so that she would not be subject to the Aboriginals Ordinance of 1918-1943. The exemption would mean that she did not need the Protector of Aboriginals' permission to live with her husband. Jim was threatened with gaol and a one-hundred-pound fine if he did not comply.

'I was really shocked to find out that I wasn't the person I thought I was. I was reduced to a nobody, I was a ward of the Government...I still remember signs in certain areas of Darwin: Out of bounds to Aboriginals, Chinese and Dogs,' Vai said.

Over the ensuing years they joined in the fight for reform and for 'half-castes' and 'fullbloods' to get the full rights of citizens. Among the most prominent figures was Vai's father, Jack McGinness. Jack left Katherine in 1946 to move to Darwin, so that he could become more effective in his people's struggle, and helped form the Halfcaste Progressive Association in 1950, which ensured a change of policy in 1953 and gave part-Aborigines a say in their own destiny. In the years since, Vai and many other Aboriginal women have taken an increasingly active and vocal role in making public and raising awareness of their own circumstances, with the aim of reducing racist reactions in the community.

Many of them were products of the Retta Dixon Home, established in Darwin in 1953 by Amelia Shankelton, an AIM worker who arrived in July 1940 and set up a small mission house in Parap, before she was asked in 1941 to escort Aboriginal evacuees to Balaclava in South Australia. After the war she returned to establish the Retta Dixon Home for children and single mothers at Bagot. The history of the home, with both its positive and negative aspects, has now been written by Barbara Bartell, the daughter of Nellie Cummings, one of the original six pre-war occupants. This valuable piece of social history indicates that Aboriginal women are increasingly being moved to tell their story in their way.

Many Aboriginal women have gone on to become leaders in their own communities and amongst their people. Some have worked within the political structures, some in the social welfare area and some in commerce. One of the most successful Aboriginal women's business enterprises was Bima Wear on Bathurst Island. The project was the brainchild of Sister Eucharia Pearce, who evacuated children from Melville Island during the war and returned to the Territory in 1945. After spending eighteen years tending to patients at the leprosarium on Channel Island, she returned to Bathurst Island in 1968 and set up a programme training women in sewing and handicrafts using traditional design in screen printing. The results were the highly successful Bima Wear and Tiwi designs, now of worldwide note. Helping to achieve that recognition in the early days was a woman of Aboriginal descent, Shirley Collins, who created outlets in Darwin and organised many fashion parades and publicity to promote the work of the Tiwi women.

TERRITORY WOMEN IN DECISION MAKING

Following Jessie Litchfield's lead in the 1920s, post-war Territory women also began to take an active role in local government. The woman who really pioneered female activity in Territory local government was Lillian Dean who had first arrived in Darwin in 1947 as a travelling photographer. After two years of this nomadic existence she settled in Darwin and established a photographer's shop in an old tin hut in town, where she quickly gained a reputation as a first-class portrait photographer. After years of amusing incidents and hard work in the photographic business and in her other main field of interest, horse racing (she was a member of the Turf Club committee for ten years), Lillian stood for local government.

Shortly after the Darwin City Council was reconstituted in 1957, Lillian won a by-election for the ward of Fannie Bay, campaigning with a simple and direct message: 'The sane, levelheaded expression of opinion of a woman councillor is needed in our progressive Municipal Council. My policy is to interpret your wishes, desires and plans and give voice to them in the deliberations of the council.'[5] She did just that. Her message and her performance appealed, and she won two more elections and a reputation as a practical woman of principle. Most agreed with the assessement of her by her close friends, Mavis and Reg Weston, who described her as 'a wonderful person of strong character; a good Aussie battler'. Dorothea Lyons, another friend who became a popular post-war Darwin mayoress when her colourful lawyer husband 'Tiger' Lyons was elected as mayor, summed up Lillian's pioneering contribution this way: 'She was an outstanding person, a real inspiration to others. She was a very good citizen for Darwin and established a way of life here.'

Women in local government later spread 'down the track'. When the Katherine town management board was constituted in the early 1970s, Cynthia Bader, a director of a local building firm, was the first female to win a seat on the board in a by-election in 1973. She campaigned on the grounds that Katherine must have a woman representative on its board and she won. By 15 February 1978 Katherine town management board accepted the offer of local government for the place and a local woman, Pat Davies, was elected first mayor. Pat, who had moved to Katherine in 1974 and helped instigate such community services as the creche, the senior citizens club, the pensioners association and Katherine Night Shelter, was still mayor in Australia's bicentennial year.

Other women stood for political office, and even though the first few candidates were unsuccessful they paved the way for others. When the Territory was granted a limited legislative council in 1947, an Alice Springs woman was among the contenders for a seat. She was former AIM nurse Olive Donnellan, who campaigned both on her impressive fifteen-year record of community service and on the grounds that a woman's voice was needed in government. In 1951, at the age of sixty-eight, veteran Territory advocate Jessie Litchfield tried her luck as an independent for the federal parliamentary seat on a platform of getting a 'better deal' for the Territory. She hired a taxi and travelled 3000 miles to campaign for her cause, which included advocating that the Territory be divided into northern and central 'states', only this time it should be done properly, giving the locals a say in their own destiny. She lost the election but gained the admiration of most Territorians for her passionate loyalty to and faith in the Territory. In 1957 another Alice Springs woman, Beth Reus, stood for the Australian Labor Party in the legislative council elections claiming that 'as a housewife and small property owner, [she had] a personal interest in all matters concerning the welfare and livelihood of the people of Alice Springs.'

Finally in 1960, sixty-six years after Territory women had first been given the vote, a Territory woman achieved political victory. In that year two women stood for the legislative council—Sylvia Connick, a former *Australian Women's Weekly* journalist who was in Darwin when it was bombed, and Lyn Berlowitz, a Darwin businesswoman. The victor was Lyn, who stood as an independent member for the Darwin suburban seat of Fannie Bay, advocating freehold land and better living conditions for families. She argued that unless women were encouraged to stay in the Territory, men would soon leave too. The newspaper of the day congratulated her for being successful at convincing the voters that it was time a woman 'had a go' and sagely noted that many men, as well as women, must have voted for her. The editor gave full credit to her achievement in the face of substantial odds, however, writing:

The Territory is generally considered to be still very much a man's country. The last

Writer and journalist Jessie Litchfield, who first arrived in the Territory in 1907, became one of its most passionate propagandists. She wrote several books (only one of which was published), and hundreds of articles for newspapers and magazines, and she served as the first and only woman editor of the Northern Territory Times *from 1930 to 1932. Evacuated under protest during the Second World War, Jessie later returned to Darwin to establish the Roberta Library and to resume a long-standing interest in politics, standing for the federal House of Representatives seat in 1951 at the age of sixty-eight.*
Roderick/Litchfield collection, Northern Territory State Reference Library.

official census supports it—4,107 more males than females. This being so she has assumed something of the proportions of a female David bowling over a Goliath in defeating veteran and experienced Labor leader Paddy Carroll.[6]

Lyn retained her seat for only one term. Although it was nearly a decade before another woman was successful, that woman was successful with a vengeance. She was Dawn Lawrie, who successfully stood as an independent member for Nightcliff in the legislative council elections of 1971 and remained in office for the next twelve years. For the first three years she was the only woman in the council, but her

The first woman to be elected to political office in the Territory was
Fannie Bay businesswoman Lyn Berlowitz, who won the Fannie Bay seat in
1960. She is pictured here with her male colleagues.
Northern Territory Parliamentary Library.

articulate and clever participation in debates quickly won her a well-deserved reputation as one of the most effective members, despite the fact that she had been expelled from her Melbourne school at the age of sixteen. Her legislative wins in parliament, which included abortion law reform, prison reform, and repeal of the vagrancy act, served as an inspiration for other women who were increasingly involving themselves in public issues.

By the time the 1974 election rolled around, the Women's Electoral Lobby had become a considerable force in the Top End and all candidates were interviewed as to their stand on issues. Because of a strong anti-Labor backlash resulting largely from the federal Government deciding to acquire thirty-two square miles (82 km²) of semi-rural land near Darwin, no Labor members were elected. However, the Country Liberal Party added a woman to their ranks—Liz Andrews, who soon became Minister for Education and Attorney General in the Goff Letts government, the first fully elected Assembly in the Territory and the forerunner to self-government. During the next three years, Dawn Lawrie became widely regarded as the parliamentary 'opposition', being the only really non-conservative member, although her independent colleague Ron Withnall often supported her arguments.

Dawn Lawrie, who first stood for a seat in the Territory parliament in 1971 and held the seat for twelve years, became one of the most vocal and forceful women in the Territory. Following her political career, she became the Territory's Human Rights and Equal Opportunity Commissioner and in 1988 became the first Territory woman to receive a vice-regal appointment—Administrator of Cocos (Keeling) Island. Photograph courtesy of Gavin Perry.

CYCLONE TRACY AND POST-CYCLONE POLITICS

That election was in October, two months before Australia's greatest civilian disaster was to wreak havoc on Darwin and, to a lesser extent, the entire Territory. Those of us who experienced the terror of Christmas Eve 1974, as Cyclone Tracy slowly moved her intensely violent, screaming mass across the city, are unlikely to forget it. For nearly eight hours thousands of Darwinites scrambled to find safe shelter as their homes were ripped from them, collapsing like card-houses. Possessions, some accumulated over a lifetime, hurtled past, at times moving in almost surrealistic slow motion, as if to make certain we understood the ephemeral quality of material things. Sheltering in the remains of bathrooms, wardrobes, laundries; clinging desperately to totally exposed floorboards, or lying, as we did, sodden and shivering outside, next to a metre-high cyclone fence to protect ourselves from flying debris, many wondered if they would survive the night. Remarkably, most did, though some still suffer the psychological effects of the night and the traumatic aftermath. It changed many lives, exposing both strengths and weaknesses in individuals who had never had to face themselves in such a way before. By dawn, the extent of the destruction became appallingly apparent — Darwin had been destroyed.

Even governments and other Australians had to reassess priorities. The federal Labor government responded swiftly and with extreme generosity as did the people of Australia who dug deep and often into their pockets to help their fellow Australians in a time of great need. All down the track the people of the Territory offered comfort and refuge to the shocked cyclone victims, and scores of individual women in all urban centres made food for the travellers and found the most desperately needed items, usually baby bottles and nappies. In Alice Springs the relatively small population collected $150 000 in just a few hours. Women were at the forefront of organising help and assistance, women such as Alice Quota Club member Margaret Wait who set up a reception area at the airport, and Shirley Brown, who as acting president of the the Alice Red Cross took charge of the Relief Centre at Alice Springs High School. Women were at the head emergency centre at the airport and organised billets for hundreds. By 9 January about 5500 evacuees from Darwin and 2500 cars had passed through the town.

Coincidentally on hand to help with cyclone relief arrangements in Alice Springs was the Territory's first lady, Peg Nelson, whose husband Jock had been the first Territorian appointed as Administrator in 1973. Peg, the daughter of Lew and Lillian Bloomfield, some of the Centre's earliest pioneers, had lived all her life in central Australia and was in Alice Springs for Christmas, thus escaping experiencing the cyclone destruction of Government House in Darwin. Jock (whose father, ironically, had been the man to oust the first commonwealth administrator, Dr Gilruth) returned immediately to Darwin, and Peg, after doing what she could to help cyclone victims in Alice, joined him two weeks later. For more than a year, they experienced the same inconveniences as the rest of Darwin did — leaky roofs, wrecked kitchens and other rooms, and frequent power blackouts.

In Darwin Eileen Cossons, daughter of the pioneering outback family of Ada Gaden, set up a kitchen-cum-mess-hall in the ground floor of the old police headquarters at the corner of Mitchell and Bennett streets and fed hundreds of policemen and families. She also had the foresight to rescue the supreme court judge's wigs and gowns from transient marauders. Eileen was one of many women throughout the devastated town who worked to alleviate the hardships facing almost every resident.

Although the disaster exposed many good human qualities, as always in a time when officialdom must move swiftly, it also exposed insensitivies and mistakes — not the least of which was the decision to evacuate women and children from the town, and then require everyone returning to have permits. The sense of *deja vu* for those who had experienced war-time Darwin was compounded when the government threatened to acquire much land and replan the place.

The experience of one of the Top End's most well-known and longest living pioneers of Aboriginal descent, Nellie Flynn, epitomised the defiance many others felt. For three days after the cyclone the indomitable Nellie, then aged ninety-three, hid under scraps of canvas in her roofless Rapid Creek home to escape being forced to evacuate. Nellie had been born in the 1880s at Powell's Creek, the daughter of Territory pioneer Lindsay Crawford and an Aboriginal woman who died before Nellie knew her. She had weathered nearly a century of Territory life, including defying evacuation orders after the bombing of Darwin in 1942, walking in nearly every post-war *Northern Territory News* walkabout, beginning with the first in

Pioneer Territorian Nellie Flynn lived to celebrate her hundredth birthday and was an active participant in Territory affairs all her life.
Northern Territory State Reference Library.

1961, in which she participated at the age of eighty, walking the whole 25 kilometres. She made headlines around Australia as 'Shotgun Nellie' in 1969 when young boys lit a fire that swept down her creekbed and destroyed her footbridge. Armed with her fifty-nine-year-old rifle she took post beside the ruins and challenged the boys to come back, assuring them they would get 'what for' if they did. With such an independent and resourceful character, Nellie was not about to leave her home after a cyclone. Although she was eventually persuaded to leave her Rapid Creek home for better premises, she won the battle to keep her garden, and understanding Darwin City Council parks and gardens staff helped transplant her trees and shrubs to her new home.

Nellie was not alone in her stance against post-cyclone authority. One of the most outspoken critics of the evacuation and post-cyclone town planning decisions was Dawn Lawrie, who made her views known in many forums:

I worked at the Airport for the duration of the evacuation and the question most often asked of me was 'they'll let me come back, won't they? My answer was 'Of course, this is Australia and there is no law in Australia which could prevent you returning to your home.' How wrong I was! With what I believe to be an act of almost criminal stupidity, the Australian Government and the Northern Territory Legislative Assembly passed an infamous ordinance requiring that citizens of this town evacuated under stress had to have a permit to return. This is something I will neither forget nor forgive and is a shameful page in Australia's history. It deserves to be remembered and discussed so that this mistake will never be repeated.

There were tales in the southern newspapers of Darwin being no place for a woman or children...lies and damned lies. There was no threat to the women left in the town, nor any threat to the children, other than the obvious hazard of debris, broken glass and so forth...For a few weeks Darwin was virtually a town without children and I realized then just what a dreadful act the Pied Piper had perpetrated on Hamlyn. A town without children is a dead town and officialdom nearly accomplished that which Cyclone Tracy could not do, that is to kill Darwin...This was my first real lesson in how stupid, arrogant and how completely out of touch decision making can become but that was but a foretaste of further bureaucratic bunglings on a gigantic scale.

Although the citizens whose lives were to be vitally affected were compulsorily excluded from their city, a barrage of politicians, advisers and consultants descended on poor Darwin like one of the seven plagues of Egypt. There was to be a new Darwin, a new grand plan, decided by experts without having to bother about the opinions of the bothersome citizens...At this stage those left in Darwin were affecting what temporary repairs they could and received a rude shock if they decided to start rebuilding in earnest...many found that what had been their residential block had been re-zoned either as a road, a green space or some other zoning which would not allow them to rebuild on their site.[7]

The result of this was the spontaneous formation of residential action groups, the first organised by Dawn Lawrie for her own electorate of Nightcliff. This was followed by the Fannie Bay Resident Action Group, in which another leading battler was Pam O'Neil, who was about to make her own mark in Territory history. A friend and sympathetic social reformer, Dr Lyn Reid, was the first elected chairperson of the Darwin Citizens Advisory Council. She brought a wealth of understanding and experience to the job, having been a foundation member of the Women's Electoral Lobby, the Family Planning Association, and the Darwin Women's Centre.

It seemed fitting that in May 1975, during the International Year of Women, Dr Ella Stack was elected Darwin's first woman mayor, after serving six years as an alderman on the council. She quickly became a driving force on the Darwin Reconstruction Commission and assumed a high profile around the country, publicising the needs and assets of the cyclone damaged city she headed. She was a controversial, visionary woman, and few would deny that she worked hard towards accomplishing what she believed to be the first priority: 'We have to get our priorities

*From 1977 to 1983 the Territory parliament boasted one of the highest
representations of women members of any Australian parliament, with women
comprising a fifth of the membership. They were Noel Padgham-Purich
(far left, standing), Dawn Lawrie (far left, seated), June D'Rosario
(far right, standing) and Pam O'Neil (far right, seated).*
Northern Territory Parliamentary Library.

right—we must put people back into houses that they can afford and as soon as
possible.'[8] One of her lesser known but significant contributions to post-cyclone
Darwin was her foresight in recording the personal cyclone experiences of more than
a dozen Darwin citizens, the tapes of which are lodged with the National Library in
Canberra. Ella went on to become the first female secretary of a large government
department in the Territory, the Health Department. Other urban centres in the
Territory elected women as their heads of local government and in 1988 Alice
Springs, Katherine and Palmerston all had women mayors.

In the 1977 Legislative Assembly election, Liz Andrews lost her seat, but three
other women were elected — Noel Padgham-Purich for the Country Liberal Party
and Pam O'Neil and June D'Rosario for the Labor Party. When the Territory achieved
self-government the following year, parliament became a forum for many debates on
issues affecting women, with Dawn, Pam and June making a formidable trio, arguing
for reformist views and legislation. Pam, who had been active in many community
organisations and groups affecting women, went on to become deputy leader of the
Labor Party in the Territory, the first woman to hold such a position in a major party
in Australia. June, a particularly articulate, quick-witted, and competent town
planner, became a shadow minister with economics and land management as some
of her portfolio areas. The substance these women gave to parliament was widely
acknowledged, regardless of their political views, and for a while the Territory

Cultural diversity has been a hallmark of the Territory since its earliest days and among the prominent cultural groups represented in the 1980s are the Timorese. Timorese women take a leading role in promoting understanding of their culture and their recent political struggles. Here (from left) Maria Alice Casimiro, Dulcie Munn and Fatima Gusmao take part in a play, Death at Balibo, *which premiered in Darwin in 1988. Photograph by Brenda Yee.*
Darwin Theatre Group.

enjoyed the distinction of having women comprise nearly a fifth of its parliamentary members.

However, in the emotional election of 1983 the then extremely popular Country Liberal Party Chief Minister Paul Everingham convinced the majority of Territorians to register their opposition to the handing over of Ayers Rock to Aboriginal title. Dawn Lawrie, Pam O'Neil and June D'Rosario were casualties of that emotive vote for conservative politics. With their demise, not only the voice of women, but the articulate voice of reasoned and reformist debate, had been dramatically slashed from Territory parliament. The Country Liberal Party's female member, Noel Padgham-Purich, survived, and for a short time became a government minister, but she was later dumped by her own party. Interestingly, she stood against the CLP in the next election and won.

The talents of the other three women did not go unnoticed. Dawn Lawrie became the Commissioner for Equal Opportunity in the Territory and in 1988 became the first Territory woman to be appointed to a vice-regal position when she took office as the Administrator of Cocos (Keeling) Island. June D'Rosario returned to her profession of town planning, and as well as establishing a prospering business, was chosen to serve on several influential standing committees, including the National Capital Planning Committee, the Ulara Katatjuta National Park Board of Management and the National Population Council. Pam O'Neil went on to become Australia's first Sex Discrimination Commissioner. She later voiced her views about the potential for women to achieve in the Territory: 'The Territory is young and fluid and old values aren't so entrenched so there tends to be more opportunity for anyone to have a go.'

LOOKING FORWARD

The Territory in the 1970s and 1980s has become a more 'ordinary' place, although it still enjoys a romantic reputation as one of the world's last frontiers. It has been a place where new communities are still being established and new pioneering ventures undertaken.

As it has at other times in its history, the Territory has also become a new frontier for people from other countries, and the 1970s and 1980s have seen an influx of migrants to the Territory, in particular, refugees from Vietnam and Timor. Many migrant women have been active in helping their people adjust to their new lives. Among the most prominent have been Teng Hoay Murray, Lourdes Pereira, and Alice Casimero. Malaysian-born Teng, fluent in five languages, came to the Territory in 1973 and has been a vital link between people of non-English-speaking backgrounds and the wider community. She survived Cyclone Tracy and has helped Timorese refugees cope with arriving and settling after Indonesia took over their country. She has also engaged in much voluntary work for Vietnamese Chinese immigrants. Lourdes arrived in 1975 and began at once helping with radio monitoring and translation work, giving background to those fighting for an end of Indonesian military rule in Timor. She worked as a hospital helper and has been the driving force behind many cultural events staged by the East Timor Culture Group, a band of artists whose musical and dance performances are dedicated to informing the public about the Timorese response to the Indonesian takeover. Also prominent on the cultural front was Alice Casimero, who co-wrote the original stage play *Death at Balibo*, which deals with the deaths of five Australian journalists covering the war in East Timor and was performed for the first time in Darwin in 1988.

In Alice Springs an Aboriginal sacred sites issue in 1983 highlighted the strengths of Aboriginal women within their own culture. Taking a leading role was Amelia Kunoth, the grand-daughter of an elder of the Aranda tribe, Erruphana, who once controlled all the land around Alice Springs; before anyone could enter the area through Heavitree Gap they needed his permission. The main water supply for the Aborignal people of the region was the original Alice Spring at the Old Telegraph Station where Amelia was born, the daughter of one of Erruphana's daughters and an Englishman. Nearly ninety years later, Amelia was the acknowledged traditional guardian of the site, which was threatened by a proposal to dam the area. During the debate, Amelia went to the site and put her arms around the sacred rock, which would have been covered with water had the dam proposal proceeded, and said: 'They can flood it if they like, but they must never damage this rock.'[9] Amelia died the next year with the site still intact. Her grand-daughter, Rosie Kunoth-Monks, who had played Jedda in the movie of the same name, publicly gave her support by resigning in protest from her new government position.

Another issue of concern to Aboriginal women in the 1980s has been that of 'child brides'—young women promised to Aboriginal men not of their own choosing, a situation which sometimes resulted in incidents of domestic violence. One of the first such cases to be brought to public attention was that of Lorna, an Aboriginal girl from Wattie Creek who sought refuge with sympathetic Territory parliamentarian Dawn Lawrie in 1982, claiming that young girls were being pack raped and attacked with nulla nullas and that many did not want to be married to their promised husbands, often much older than themselves. In 1988 just before taking up her appointment as Cocos Island's administrator, Dawn Lawrie, who had been serving as the Territory's Equal Opportunity and Human Rights Commissioner for two years, said:

I am still receiving representations from Aboriginal women not wishing to have to go through with an arranged marriage. But it is a subject no one wants to know about and therefore a difficult one to address and redress. There is still a deathly silence about the problems facing Aboriginal women who are, in some ways, perhaps the most vulnerable members of society. There is a general lack of awareness about how strong they are, however. I've seen Aboriginal women take very firm decisions about ridding their communities of alcohol and petrol sniffing, for instance. I have the utmost respect for the courage and fortitude of Aboriginal women.

Territory women from a variety of backgrounds and cultures have taken strong stands on other social issues, in particular the peace movement. In 1983 women from around Australia descended on Alice Springs to lodge their protest at Pine Gap and its presumed international military significance. Although their presence was highly controversial, it evoked an awareness among local women which the 1988 Women's Information Officer Di Shanahan believed has been instrumental in motivating other women to become more involved in issues affecting them. June Tuzewski, the Territory Women's Advisory Council convenor from 1985 to 1987, agreed, although she pointed out that many of the local women who gave support to the demonstrations suffered a backlash of public opinion after the demonstrators had left. 'But because of the backlash, we organised a meeting of women to discuss it and that led to further meetings and a decision to try to increase women's representation on local government, which did happen,' June said.

June's time as convenor of the Women's Advisory Council reinforced her view of the many strengths Territory women possess.

There are a lot of strong, quiet achievers out there. I think women in the Territory do show a different kind of strength than women in more populated, less isolated southern regions. Those who come here and choose to stay have to accept the challenge of living in a unique environment where perhaps more self-initiative is required to ensure that quality of life is maintained. In the Territory there is not just the opportunity for women to become more involved in community and political affairs, but often the necessity for them to do so if they want things changed.

One of the major achievements of the council has been the preparation and presentation of a Remote Area Study of the needs of isolated Territory women, highlighting the differing needs of Aboriginal women, women in mining towns such as Jabiru and Nhulunbuy, and women on stations and missions. The study, instigated under the direction of the previous Women's Advisory Council convenor Wendy James, and a member, Ann Rebgetz, has been hailed as an important first in Australia. The concept of tackling the problems faced by women in remote areas had been pushed for some time by Jane Miles, who had been living with her family in Kakadu, where her husband worked as a ranger for twelve years. Jane, who designed the cover of the remote area study, has taken a keen interest in narrowing the communication gap for women in remote areas and has been the driving force behind *Bush Buzz*, a newsletter designed for isolated families.

A few years prior to the study, a group of women from Katherine and the Top End brought about another world first when they formed the Penguins of the Air, a group designed to give women in remote and isolated areas of the Top End confidence and skill in public speaking. One of the inaugural members of the group was Terry Underwood, who came as a bride in 1968 to a pastoral property near Katherine. In 1982 she organised for a play, *The Year of Dimboola*, to be rehearsed by outback people over the airwaves and performed a few weeks later in Katherine. It was a resounding success. Terry has also been a member of the inaugural Women's Advisory Council, active in the Isolated Childrens and Parents Association and secretary of the Territory Cattlemen's Association.

In the bicentennial year, women took steps to recognise the contributions other women had made to the Territory and in a very short time organised a Women's Register 48-88, with nominations and biographies being received from all over the Territory. The register was published after four months of intensive work by the project officer, Territory-born Teresa Lea, and a short time later a poster was produced to be displayed and sold at the bicenentennial travelling exhibition. It depicted artistically and textually the contribution made by eight Territory women, who represented a broad cross-section of women. They were Miriam Hagen, an accomplished artist living in Tennant Creek and grand-daughter of famed Territory publican Katherine O'Shea; Lily Ah Toy, a Territory-born Chinese woman who has been intricately involved in the Territory's business and social life since the 1930s; Bonnie Henderson, one of the world's best aerobatic pilots, who grew up on Bullo River station in charge of cattle, mustering and stockmen and was taught to fly by her American father; Sally Thomas, chief stipendiary magistrate of the Territory and the first woman stipendiary magistrate in Australia, active in many areas of social justice programmes; Margaret Dodd, who pioneered education for Aborigines at Mainoru station and also taught Aboriginal health; Gladys Ah Mat, a part-Aboriginal woman who had been taken from her mother, raised in a compound, evacuated during the war and returned to be matriarch to one of the most wide-spread families in the Territory; Milingimbi-born Dorothy Janke, an accomplished linguist who became the first Aboriginal literacy worker at Milingimbi and the first female member of the Milingimbi town council; and Lorna Moss, who instigated the Territory's first pre-school in Alice Springs in 1947 and has since devoted many years to the provision of children's services in the Centre.

Territory women have come a long way since the first attempts at British settlement in the 1820s. Numerically they have achieved near equality to men, the 1986 census showing 81 501 males and 73 347 females living in the Territory. In some cultural groups — such as the Aboriginal, Indian, Malaysian and Filipino — women in fact outnumbered men. Today women are participating in every facet of Territory life. In the highest echelons they are present, running government departments, heading major businesses, entering public life, achieving significant social reforms and continuing to work towards a more equal society. Of course, they experience setbacks and there have been times of disappointment and loss — legislative, social and political — but that is part of the challenge and the boom-and-bust history of the Territory, and women have increasingly shown they do not give up on issues of real concern to them.

Although many people and publications still perpetuate a macho-male image of the Territory, and although it is still a struggle to break through some of the entrenched public service and party political barriers, there is no doubt that women have made a major impact in all areas of Territory life, just as the Territory has had a significant impact on them. The Territory's small population, vast land mass, and its 'open' and multicultural lifestyle encourage women to discover their full potential if they choose to do so. One Territory social worker has said 'Women are still pioneers in the Territory, the environment challenges them to pioneer themselves, and that is where pioneering should start; it makes for stronger individuals.' Increasingly Territory women are choosing to do just that and are coming out of the shadows to take their rightful place in the headlines, and, more importantly, in the decision-making process. In the interests of a healthy, balanced society, it is essential that they do, and that their contribution be recognised and valued.

They can take heart from the women who have battled before them. A former Alice Springs resident, Cloudy Beale, herself a pioneer, once described the characteristics that she felt set Territory women apart: 'They're a tough individual lot. Maybe you have to be to come up here in the first place. They survived with hard yakka and a good yarn and a lot of determination. I don't know if it was they who made the Territory or the Territory that made them.'[10] It was probably a bit of both.

There is little doubt that, inspired by the example, and sensitive good humour of the pioneer women who have preceded them, the modern women of the Territory will ensure that the words of Elsie Masson are amply illustrated in the future: 'On the woman no less than on the man depends the success of a great venture such as the civilisation and development of the Northern Territory.'[11]

The composition of the 1988 Northern Territory Women's Advisory Committee reflects the Territory's cultural and geographical diversity. Standing, from left, are: Mary Yarmirr, Croker Island; Nerolie Golder, Nhulunbuy; Josephine Stone, Alice Springs; Sue Schmolke, Darwin (convenor); Heather Galvin, the Gulf region; Stephanie Hill, Katherine. Seated, from left, are: Betty Pearce, Alice Springs; Becky Watkins, Jabiru (deputy convenor); Annette Milikens, Darwin; Meg Iles, Tennant Creek; Wendy Whiley, Groote Eylandt; Kathrina Bryen, Yulara; Beryl Mulder, Darwin. Eileen Cummings, Darwin, was absent when the picture was taken. In August 1988 the council was the first group to present a submission to the select committee on constitutional development for the Territory, presenting a women's perspective on matters raised in connection with preparing a draft constitution for Territory statehood.
Northern Territory Office of Women's Affairs.

ENDNOTES

Chapter 1

1 Journal of Allan Cunningham, botanist with King on the *Bathurst*, NSW Archives.

2 P.P.King, *Voyages for the Survey of the Intertropical Coasts of Australia,* facsimile edition, London, 1969.

3 Correspondence to Melville Island 6 August 1827, NSW Archives.

4 *Historical Records of Australia* record that an inquiry was held into the conduct of the officers and female prostitutes during the voyage of the *Friendship* to Australia and that Hicks, as first officer, had to give evidence. He was accused of misbehaviour and of assisting the men in gaining access to the women, but several people testified on his behalf claiming his innocence. It is not clear why Sophia and her brothers and sisters were on this particular ship, unless their mother was also on board, as it was a female transport ship.

5 *HRA* refer later to William Hicks being allowed to go to Timor to collect his remaining child and as there is no record of another birth in New South Wales it seems safe to assume she had a child or a miscarriage while at Fort Dundas.

6 Gold family papers, Mitchell Library, Sydney.

7 *HRA,* in d'Umaresq's reply re. Richardson's request for the promised rations.

8 From convict records in the Society of Australian Genealogist records in Sydney. John, who had been given a ticket of leave following his sojourn on Melville, had had it revoked in 1831 for being intoxicated. He requested the authorities to be lenient with him as he had three small children to look after.

9 *HRA* September 1828, letter from Hartley to MacLeay.

10 MacArthur to Colonel Owen, Deputy Adjutant General, 23 May 1846.

11 *Ibid.*

12 Elsie Masson, *Untamed Territory,* McMillan, London 1915.

13 Alfred Searcy, customs officer in the Territory in the 1880s, had particularly interesting comments to make about her and obviously enjoyed her affection.

14 F. J. Allen, 'Archaeology and the History of Port Essington.' Ph.D. thesis, Australian National University, Canberra, 1969.

Chapter 2

1 One of Darwin's major festivals in recent years has been the Beercan Regatta. Various other drinking competitions occur throughout the Territory.

2 Wendy Birman, *Gregory of Rainworth: a Man in his Time.* University of Western Australia Press, Perth, 1979.

3 *Ibid.*

4 Russell Braddon, *Thomas Baines and the North Australian Expedition,* Collins, Sydney, 1986.

5 Adelaide *Advertiser,* 29 October 1864.

6 A phrase Alfred Searcy, later a customs officer, was fond of using in relation to the nakedness of Aboriginal women.

7 R.H. Edmunds' diary, 27 March 1866, p. 87. Mortlock Library, Adelaide.

8 *Ibid* ., 3 July 1865, p. 38.

9 S. W. Herbert's diary, 1870-72. Mortlock Library, Adelaide.

10 Edmunds, *op cit,* 31 July 1865, p. 43.

11 *South Australian,* 5 February 1867.

12 *Ibid.*

Chapter 3

1 Reynolds, letter to the South Australian government during his Territory visit.

2 Elizabeth Sweet, 'Early Experiences in the Northern Territory - the Pilot of the Roper', SA Public Service Review 1907.

3 Harriet Daly, Digging, Squatting and Pioneering Life in Northern Australia. London, 1887.

4 Government resident correspondence, 10/6 (1870), Adelaide archives.

5 J. M. Gullick quoting Isabella Bird.in 'Bloomfield Douglas, a Biographical Note', JMBRAS ,Vol. 48, p. 51.

6 Diary of trooper Catchlove, 1870-72, Mortlock Library, Adelaide.

7 Sweet, op cit.

8 Daly, op cit.

9 Bogle's diary, 2 October 1875. Michell Library, Sydney.

10 Letter from Packard to the government resident, 4 May 1874. Adelaide Archives.

11 Reminiscences of government resident G. B. Scott. Special collection, Darwin Institute of Technology, Darwin, NT.

12 Letter from Lindsay to J. L. Parsons, minister responsible for the Territory, 12 April 1882. Quoted in P. F. Donovan, 'David Lindsay 1856-1922, Explorer, Surveyor and Northern Territory Apologist,' South Australiana. Vol. 18, No. 2, September 1979.

13 Ibid.

14 Foelsche, op cit .

15 From Gosse's diary in the Mortlock Library, Adelaide. Gosse served in the Northern Territory telegraph department from 1878 to 1902, when he was transferred back to Adelaide.

16 Diary of Emily Creaghe, Mitchell Library, Sydney.

17 'White Versus Black,' Sydney Mail, 30 September 1882.

Chapter 4

1 Original is located in the Mitchell Library, Sydney.

2 Letter from F. R. Finniss to his father, 21 March 1886. No. 473, Adelaide Archives.

3 Published in the Empire Review over several months in 1904.

4 The historic 'Sandfly' had actually arrived in Darwin in December 1886 and begun shunting in May of 1887, but the people waited for the arrival in July of the larger 'Port Darwin' to launch celebrations.

5 NT Times, 17 May 1901.

6 NT Times, 11 June 1895.

7 NT Times, incorporating the North Australian , May 1895.

8 NT Times, 14 January 1910.

9 NT Times, 24 July 1903.

10 Ibid.

11 NT Times , 23 October 1913.

12 Ibid.

13 D. C. S. Sissan, 'Japanese in the Northern Territory 1884-1902', South Australiana, March 1977, pp.3-50.

14 1887 Government Resident Report.

15 Alfred Searcy papers, Mortlock Libarary, Adelaide.

16 From Graham Loughlin's entry on Dashwood in the Australian Dictionary of Biography. The entry also says he had fathered an ex-nuptial son in 1892, but does not indicate whether this was before or after taking his post in the Territory.

17 Searcy, op cit.

18 1899 Government Resident Report

19 A full account of the fight for women's suffrage in South Australia is given in Helen Jones's book In Her Own Name: Women in South Australian History, published in 1986 by Wakefield Press.

20 SA parliamentary debates, 12 September 1893, pp. 1457-58.

21 NT Times, 25 October 1901.

22 NT Times, 14 April 1905.

23 NT Times, January 1911.

Chapter 5

1 Royal Commission of the Northern Territory, Minutes of Evidence, 1920, pp. 298-308.

2 Elsie Masson, Untamed Territory.

3 Ibid.

4 Ibid.

5 Sir George Buchanan, parliamentary report on the Northern Territory, 1925, p. 20.

6 Information for this section is from pp. 85-149 of Apsley's book, Amateur Settlers, London, 1927.

7 Memories written by Doris Giles later in life and loaned to the author by Chief Justice Austion Asche, and Dr Val Asche. Chief Justice Asche's mother was a close friend of Mrs Giles.

8 The original is held by the Northern Territory Conservation Commission in Alice Springs and a copy is held by the Mortlock Library in Adelaide.

9 Masson, op cit.

10 Administrator's Report, 1912.

11 Administrator's Report, 1913.

12 Ibid.

13 Letter from Daisy Bates to Senator George Pearce, 1 August 1920, Australian Archives, CRS A1 35/1066.

14 Letter from Staniforth Smith to Bates, 25 September 1920, Australian Archives CRS a1 35/1066.

15 Adelaide *Register* September 1924.

Chapter 6

1 Melbourne *Herald*, 30 April 1929.

2 SA Archives.

3 Adelaide *Advertiser*, 10 August, 1929.

4 From a series of articles Margot wrote in the *Tennant and District Times* in 1987. Also from personal interviews and talks with the author.

5 In an undated interview with a southern newspaper, held in Pethrick Room, National Library.

6 *Northern Standard*, 19 July 1927.

7 For a detailed account of the Coniston Massacre see John Cribbin's *The Killing Times*, Fontana Books, Sydney, 1984.

8 Letter from J. A. Carrodus to the NT Administration re. employment of Women as Protectors, 23 August 1939, National Archives 38/26959.

9 The quotes are taken from a letter which was kindly loaned to the author by Chief Justice of the Northern Territory, Austin Asche, and his wife Val. Judge Asche is the son of Beryl and Eric and spent much of his boyhood in Darwin.

Chapter 7

1 In an interview with the author, 1987.

2 An interview with the author in 1980, some of which was used in an article in the *Darwin Star* newspaper.

3 Agnes Hannon, 'All Out! The Effects of Evacuation and Land Acquisition on the Darwin Chinese 1941-1954,' BA Hons thesis 1985.

4. This account was written while she was resting at Mt Kosciusko two months after the raid, and was published two for the first time in the *Sydney Morning Herald* in 172.

5 The Melbourne *Age* 23 February 1942.

6 RAAF Nursing Sister Archival notes, Australian War Museum

7 *Red Grew the Harvest: Missionary experiences during the Pacific War as related by Sisters of Our Lady of the Sacred Heart*, Ed. by F.N.D.S.C.

8 'Reflection of Darwin' by Clive Turnbull, Melbourne *Herald* 20 February 1942.

9 Extracts from Winnie Sargent's reminiscences in possession of author.

10 This story is lodged with the State Reference Library of the Northern Territory, along with a photographic collection from Miss Laffer.

11 *Ibid*

12 Edith McQuade White, *Reminiscences of an Army Nurse*, Eager and Lamb, Brisbane, Qld, 1950.

13 *Ibid*

14 Much of the information on the Red Cross comes from the valuable, but so far unpublished, manuscript of E.M. Webb, Melbourne *Herald* correspondent during the war. It is entitled *Australian Red Cross in War 1935-45* and is held with the Red Cross headquarters in Melbourne.

15 AWAS history, archives, Australian War Museum

Chapter 8

1 The quotes from Eliza throughout this chapter are contained in articles in both the *NT Times* and the *Northern Standard* at the time of Eliza's death in Darwin in 1921. They were extracts from reminiscences which she had given to her grandson, Claude Arnold, a few years earlier.

2 *Ibid*.

3 This information is contained in both Eliza's memoirs and in Dudley Kelsey's reminiscences, Mortlock library, Adelaide, SA.

4 About mid to late 1876 when the Commercial Hotel appears to have ceased operating as a hotel.

5 Rev Bogle's diary, Mitchell Library, Sydney, NSW.

6 *Ibid*.

7 *NT Times* 19 February, 1881.

8 13/871, National Archives.

9 The information on Eileen Fitzer comes from many interviews with the author, including one transcribed in 1979 and held

in the NT Archives Oral History section.

10 The material relating to Granny Lum Loy came from an interview conducted with the author in 1980. It was conducted in her own language with her grandson, Ron Chin, acting as interpreter. Although I understood nothing of what she said, she was so expressive in the way she spoke, it was almost possible to know what she was describing, particularly her description of the Darwin bombing.

11 Interview with the author in 1979.

12 The information on Hilda came from an interview with the author in 1980 and at other times.

13 See Chapter 7.

Chapter 9

1 Because of the importance of communication in the settlement, the people attached to the overland and overseas telegraph were amongst the elite of Darwin for many years.

2 Harriet Daly, *Digging, Squatting and Pioneering Life in Australia's Northern Territory*, London, 1887.

3 Dudley Kelsey, 'An Old Man's Legacy' 1939. Mortlock Library, Adelaide.

4 Correspondence in to Government Resident, A 5159, NT Archives.

5 Billy Linklater's papers in the Mitchell Library.

6 Letter from E. Ryan to Government Resident, Dec 31, 1889, NT Archives.

7 *NT Times*, 11 July 1890.

8 *NT Times*, 14 October 1892.

9 *NT Times* 1 January 1896.

10 Kelsey, *op cit.*

11 The full ten stanzas are on display in Ellie's Bar at the Hotel Victoria.

12 Correspondence re. compensation of the Federation Hotel from Byrnes and Fannie Haynes, National Archives 17/1928.

13 This story is told in Ernestine Hill's book, *The Territory*, but it has also been told in various forms by people who knew her and related their own versions to the author.

14 From her obituary in the *Northern Standard*, 31 October 1952.

15 This information came from notes supplied by Lil Lovegrove who told of her

father, Tom Styles, meeting them at the Tanami during this time.

16 Apsley, *op cit*, pages 85-86.

Chapter 10

1 D. Blackwell and D. Lockwood, *Alice on the Line*, Rigby.

2 Robert Frearsons' *Guide to the Arltunga Goldfields*, 1903.

3 This information comes from her death certificate but the spelling of the name Marritt varies considerably and makes accurate genealogical research extremely difficult. Variations of the spelling of the name include Marriott, Marriett, Merriot, etc. It should also be noted that the only birth certificate I found in Tasmanian records which tends to coincide with the information on her death certificate is the birth of Sussanah on 17 September 1843 to Thomas Merrett, a private in the 96th regiment and Elizabeth nee Black.

4 From an interview with the author in 1980. Story printed in the *Darwin Star*.

5 *Ibid.*

6 *Ibid.*

7 *Northern Standard* , 18 April 1935, from *Sun News Pictorial,* 18 March 1935.

8 Papers of Charles Cecil B663 ML MSS 1652 Mitchell Library.

9 E. Hill, *The Territory.*

10 Reminiscences written by Fannie Bell in 1957 and given to the author by her daughter, Heather Harris.

11 *Ibid.*

12 Letter, 3 July 1913, from Jenson to Bevan, NT Archives, Burns file.

13 *NT Times.*

14 Vanda Marshall, *We Helped to Blaze the Track.*

15 *Op cit.*

16 *NT Times*, 1924.

17 *NT Times,* 1921.

18 From an interview with Jaci O'Brien, 1986.

19 CRS item 716/16, National Archives.

Chapter 11

1 Alfred Searcy. *In Australian Tropics.*

George Robertson & Co, London, 1909.

2 The role of the Aboriginal women in the outback is beginning to be recognised in written work, in particular Ann McGrath and Dianne Bell have recorded their contributions and lifestyles.

3 For a full and colourful account of the building and history of Spingvale station, see Peter Forrest's *Springvale Story and Early Years at the Katherine*, Murranji Press, Darwin, 1985.

4 *NT Times* article, 25 March 1930, in an account of their 50th wedding anniversary, when Mrs Giles reminisced over half a century.

5 Phyllis Uren, 'Phoebe Farrar 1868-1960', in *Unsung Heroes and Heroines*, 1988. Phyllis is Phoebe's daughter.

6 Their marriage certificate lists her occupation as musician.

7 30 April 1914.

8 Niemann papers, W. Miles, 1909, NT Archives.

9 Interview with Mrs C. Hennessy, 2 August 1982; interviewer Dallas Cooper, Transcript TS 243, NT Archives, Darwin.

10 Michael, Terry, 'Across the Top of Australia,' article in *People*, 5 May 1965.

11 The information on this trip came from Linklater's notes in the Mitchell Library in Sydney (Al 10/9) and from an article which appeared in the *Sydney Morning Herald* and the *Scone Advocate* in 1943.

12 G. Buchanan, *Packhorse and Waterhole*, Hesperian Press, WA, 1984.

13 Commonwealth Archives correspondence 13/4909.

14 Brisbane *Daily Mail*, 31 October 1920.

15 *Ibid.*

16 *NT Times*, 13 August 1921.

17 *NT Times*, 1 February 1935.

18 *NT Times*, 24 January 1922.

19 *NT Times*, 1 February 1924.

20 *NT Times*, 19 February 1924.

21 *NT Times*, 13 May 1924.

22 *NT Times*, August 1924.

23 *NT Times*, December 1925,

24 Obituary for Mrs Bohning, *Centralian Advocate*, 2 January 1952.

25 Evidence taken at Wycliffe Well, 18 July 1921, pp. 42-43.

26 Val Whalan, *A Fitting Heart, Alice Springs and the Red Centre*. NT Education Department, Darwin, 1984.

27 *Northern Standard*, 5 December 1924. Partly a reprint from the Brisbane *Mail*.

28 Taped interview with Ellen Hobley, courtesy of her family.

29 *Ibid.*

30 Reminiscences written by Doris Giles, loaned to the author by Val Asche of Darwin.

31 *Northern Standard*, 31 January, 1936 (reprint from a Perth paper).

32 Article in Melbourne *Age*, 1923.

Chapter 12

1 Interview with the author, 1988.

2 Reprinted in an interview Lou gave to the *NT News* on 27 November 1982.

3 The Darwin *Advertiser* 24 February 1983.

4 Personal interview with the author.

5 *NT News*, July 1958.

6 *NT News*, February 1960.

7 D. Lawrie, 'The Frustrations of a Civil Population Associated with a Major Reconstruction Scheme,' paper given at 1977 Australian Survey Congress in Darwin.

8 *NT News* , 7 May 1975.

9 *Centralian Advocate*, December 1984, article by Jenny Brands.

10 1964 (no month) interview with Cloudy Beale in the *Australian*, copy in Pethrick room, National Library.

11 *Untamed Territory*.

BIBLIOGRAPHY

ABBOTT, C. L. A. *Australia's Frontier Province,* Sydney, Angus & Robertson, 1950.

ADAMS, DAVID (ed.) *The Letters of Rachel Henning,* Harmondsworth, Middlesex, Penguin 1985.

ADAM-SMITH, PATSY *When We Rode the Rails,* Knoxfield, Vic, J.M. Dent Pty Limited, 1987.

ADAM-SMITH, PATSY *Australian Women at War,* Melbourne, Thomas Nelson,1984.

ALCORTA, F. X. *Darwin Rebellion, 1911-1919,* Darwin, University Planning Authority, 1984.

ALEXANDER, FRED *Australia Since Federation,* Melbourne, Thomas Nelson, 1982.

ALFORD, KATRINA 'The Drover's Wife and her Friends: Women in Rural Society and Primary Production in Australia, 1850-1900', in *Working Papers in Economic History* No. 75, Canberra, Australian National University, 1986.

ALLEN, F.J. 'Archeology and the History of Port Essington', Ph.D. thesis, Australian National University, Canberra, 1969.

ALLEN, JIM and CORRIS, PETER *The Journal of John Sweatman,* Brisbane, University of Queensland Press, 1977.

APSLEY, LORD and LADY *The Amateur Settlers,* London, Hodder & Stoughton Limited, n.d. (c. 1927).

ANONYMOUS (Mrs Charlotte Barton) *A Mother's Offering to her Children [by a Lady Long Resident in New South Wales],* Milton, Qld, Jacaranda Press, 1979 (facsimile edn).

AUSTRALIAN MILITARY FORCES *Khaki and Green,* Canberra, Australian War Memorial, 1943.

BALDWIN, SUZY (ed.) *Unsung Heroes and Heroines of Australia,* Melbourne, Greenhouse Publications, 1988.

BARKER, H. M. *Camels and the Outback,* Adelaide, Rigby, 1977.

BARRETT, CHARLES *Coast of Adventure: Untamed North Australia,* Melbourne, Robertson & Mullens Ltd, 1941.

BARRIE, DOUGLAS R. *The Heart of Rum Jungle,* Batchelor, NT, S & D Barrie 1982.

BEATON, RENE *Feet First, or How I got to have Lunch with the Queen,* Orange NSW, published by the author, 1986.

BELL, DIANE *Daughters of the Dreaming,* Melbourne, McPhee Gribble, 1985.

BELL, DIANE *Generations,* Melbourne, McPhee Gribble/Penguin, 1987.

BIRCH, ALAN and MACMILLAN, DAVID S. (eds) *The Sydney Scene 1788-1960,* Sydney, Hale & Iremonger, 1982.

BIRMAN, WENDY *Gregory of Rainworth: a Man in his Time,* Perth, University of Western Australia Press, 1979.

BLACK, CLEMENTINA (ed.) *Married Women's Work,* London, Virago Press, 1983.

BLACKWELL, DORIS and LOCKWOOD, DOUGLAS *Alice on the Line,* Adelaide, Rigby (Seal Books), 1976.

BLAIKIE, GEORGE *Great Women of History,* Sydney, John Fairfax Marketing, 1984.

BLAZE, B. R. *Genealogy in a Changing Society* (Proceedings of the First Australasian Congress on Genealogy and Heraldry, Melbourne, 1977), Oakleigh, Vic, Australian Institute of Genealogical Studies Incorporated, 1980.

BOOTH, SALLY SMITH *The Women of '76,* New York, Hastings House, 1976.

BOWMAN, BRYAN *The Glen Helen Story* (no publication details).

BROMBY, ROBIN *Rails to the Top End,* Narrabeen, NSW, Cromarty Press, 1987.

BROWN, DEE *The Gentle Tamers: Women of the Old Wild West,* Lincoln, University of Nebraska Press, 1958.

BUCHANAN, G. *Packhorse and Waterhole,* Carlisle, WA, Hesperian Press, 1984 (facsimile edition).

BUCKNALL, GRAEME *Flynn's Mantle of Safety: The Story of Adelaide House,* Alice

Springs, The John Flynn Memorial Book House, 1984.

BURCHILL, ELIZABETH *The Paths I've Trod*, Melbourne, Spectrum, 1984.

CARMENT, DAVID *The Tuxworth Government: A Political History*, (Faculty of Arts Occasional Papers Series No 1), Darwin, University College of the Northern Territory, 1987.

CARROLL, BRIAN *From Barton to Fraser*, Stanmore, NSW, Cassell Australia, 1978.

CARROLL, JOHN (ed.) *Intruders in the Bush: the Australian Quest for Identity*, Melbourne, Oxford University Press, 1985.

CARTER, JAN *Nothing to Spare: Recollections of Australian Pioneering Women*, Ringwood, Vic, Penguin, 1981.

CHAMBERS, CORAL *Lessons for Ladies: a Social History of Girls' Education in Australasia 1870-1900*, Sydney, Hale & Iremonger, 1986.

CLARK, MANNING *A Short History of Australia*, New York, New American Library (Mentor Books), Second Edition, 1980.

CLARKE, HUGH V. *The Long Arm*, Canberra, Roebuck Society, 1974.

CLUNE, FRANK *Overland Telegraph: an Epic of Endurance and Courage*, Sydney, Angus & Robertson, 1955.

CLYNE, ROBERT *Colonial Blue: a History of the South Australian Police Force, 1836-1916*, Netley, SA, Wakefield Press, 1987.

COCKBURN-CAMPBELL, THOMAS *Land of Lots of Time*, Fremantle, Fremantle Arts Centre Press, 1985.

COLE, KEITH *The Aborigines of Arnhem Land*, Adelaide, Rigby, 1979.

COLE, KEITH *Dick Harris, Missionary to the Aborigines*, Bendigo, Vic, Keith Cole Publications, 1980.

COLE, KEITH *Fred Gray of Umbakumba*, Bendigo, Vic, Keith Cole Publications, 1984.

COLE, KEITH *A History of Numbulwar*, Bendigo, Vic, Keith Cole Publications, 1984.

COLE, TOM *Spears and Smoke Signals*, Casuarina, NT, Adventure Publications, 1986.

COURTENAY, P. P. *Northern Australia: Patterns and Problems of Tropical Development in an Advanced Country*, Melbourne, Longman Cheshire Ltd, 1982.

CRAMP, K. R. *A Calendar of Events in Australian History*, Sydney, Royal Australian Historical Society, 1933.

CRAWFORD, EUGENIE *Ladies Didn't:, Recollections of an Edwardian Girlhood [by Eugenie McNeil]*, Ringwood, Vic, Penguin, 1984

CRAWFORD, PATRICIA (ed.) *Exploring Women's Past: Essays in Social History*, Carlton South, Vic Sisters Publishing Ltd, 1983.

CRAWFORD, R. M. et al. *Making History*, Fitzroy, Vic, McPhee Gribble/Penguin, 1985:

CRIBBIN, JOHN *The Killing Times: the Coniston Massacres 1928*, Sydney, Fontana Books, 1984.

CROWLEY, F. K. (ed.) *A New History of Australia*, Melbourne, William Heinemann, 1984.

DALY, MRS DOMINIC *Digging, Squatting and Pioneering Life in the Northern Territory of South Australia*, London, Sampson Low, Marston, Searle & Rivington, 1887.

DANIELS, KAY (ed.) *So Much Hard Work: Women and Prostitution in Australian History*, Sydney, Fontana Books, 1984.

DANIELS, KAY and MURNANE, MARY *Uphill All the Way: a Documentary History of Women in Australia*, St Lucia, University of Queensland Press, 1980.

DAVID, MARY EDGEWORTH *Passages of Time: An Australian Woman 1890-1974*, St Lucia, University of Queensland Press, 1976.

DAVIS, ABE *A Day Before Yesterday: Good old Sydney Town*, Sydney, the author, 1980.

DE VRIES-EVANS, SUSANNA *Pioneer Women Pioneer Land: Yesterday's Tall Poppies*, Sydney, Angus & Robertson, 1987

DICKINSON, JANET *Jessie Litchfield - Grand Old Lady of the Territory*, Blackwater, Queensland, the author, 1983.

DIXSON, MIRIAM *The Real Matilda: Women and Identity in Australia, 1788 to 1975*, Harmondsworth, Middlesex, Penguin, 1978.

DONOVAN, P. F. *A. Land Full of Possibilities: A History of South Australia's Northern Territory*, St Lucia, University of Queensland Press, 1981.

DONOVAN, P. F. *At the Other End of Australia: the Commonwealth and the Northern Territory, 1911-1978*, St Lucia, University of Queensland Press, 1984.

DOWNER, SIDNEY *Patrol Indefinite*, Adelaide, Rigby (Seal Books), 1977

DUNN, MICHAEL *Australia and the Empire, From 1788 to the Present*, Sydney, Fontana Books, 1984.

DURACK, MARY *Kings in Grass Castles*, Condell Park, NSW, Corgi Books, 1985.

ELDER, BRUCE (ed.) *The A to Z of Who is Who in Australia's History*, Brookvale, NSW, Child & Associates Publishing Ltd, 1987.

ELSE-MITCHELL, The Hon Mr Justice *American Influences on Australian Nationhood*, reprinted from the *Journal of the Royal Australian Historical Society*, June 1976.

EUSTIS, NELSON *Australia's Greatest Air Race, England-Australia 1919*, Adelaide, Rigby (Seal Books), 1977.

FENTON, CLYDE *Flying Doctor*, London, Georgian House (third edition), 1952.

FLETCHER, BRIAN *Colonial Australia Before 1850*, West Melbourne, Thomas Nelson (Australia) Ltd, 1976.

FLYNN, FRANK *The Living Heart*, Sydney, F. P. Leonard, 1979.

FORD, MARGARET *End of a Beginning*, Adelaide, Rigby, (Seal Books), 1977.

FORREST, PETER *Springvale's Story and Early Years at the Katherine*, Darwin, Murranji Press, 1985.

FORTY, GEORGE and ANNE *They Also Served: A Pictorial Anthology of Camp Followers through the Ages*, Kent, Midas Books, 1979.

FULLER, BASIL *The Ghan: The Story of the Alice Springs Railway*, Adelaide, Rigby, 1975.

FYSH, HUDSON Sir *Qantas Rising*, Adelaide, Rigby (Seal Books), 1965.

GALE, FAY (ed.) *We Are Bosses Ourselves: the Status and Role of Aboriginal Women Today*, Canberra, Australian Institute of Aboriginal Studies, 1983.

GALE, FAY (ed.) *Woman's Role in Aboriginal Society*, Canberra, Australian Institute of Aboriginal Studies (third edition) 1986.

GOODMAN, RUPERT *Our War Nurses: the History of the Royal Australian Army Nursing Crops 1902-1988*, Brisbane, Boolarong Publication, 1988.

GRIFFITHS, OWEN *Darwin Drama*, Sydney, Bloxham & Chambers Pty Limited, n.d .(c.1945).

GUNN, Mrs AENEAS *We of the Never Never*, Richmond, Vic, Hutchinson Group, 1982.

GUNN, Mrs AENEAS *The Little Black Princess*, London, Angus & Robertson, 1983.

HALL, TIMOTHY *Darwin 1942: Australia's Darkest Hour*, Sydney, Methuen, 1980.

HARNEY, W. E. *North of 23⁰*, Sydney, Australasian Publishing Co. Pty. Ltd, n.d.

HEATLEY, ALISTAIR *A City Grows: a History of the Darwin City Council 1957-1984*, Darwin, Australian National University North Australia Research Unit, 1986.

HENEY, HELEN *Australia's Founding Mothers*, Melbourne, (Thomas Nelson) Australia Ltd, 1978.

HERBERT, XAVIER *Capricornia*, Sydney, Angus & Robertson, 1979.

HERBERT, XAVIER *Poor Fellow My Country*, Sydney, Fontana Books, 1976.

HILL, ERNESTINE *The Territory*, Sydney, Ure Smith (Walkabout Pocketbook), 1970.

HISTORICAL SOCIETY OF THE NORTHERN TERRITORY *Fort Wellington Raffles Bay, North Australia*, Printers and Converters, Singapore, 1971.

HOWARD, ANN *Women in Australia*, Kensington, NSW, Bay Books, 1984.

HUGHES, ROBERT *The Fatal Shore*, London, Collins Harvill, 1987.

HUNT, SUSAN *Spinifex and Hessian: Women in North-West Australia, 1860-1900*, Nedlands, University of Western Australia Press, 1986.

IDRIESS, ION L. *Man Tracks*, Sydney, Angus & Robertson, second edition, 1956.

IDRIESS, ION L. *The Tin Scratchers: the Story of Tin Mining in the far North*, Sydney, Angus & Robertson, (Queensland Classic edn), 1981.

JEANSCH, DEAN and LOVEDAY, PETER *Under One Flag, The 1980 Northern Territory Election*, Sydney, George Allen & Unwin, 1981.

JOHNSON, MARJORIE *Salt of the Earth* Melbourne, Collins Dove, 1988.

JONES, HELEN *In Her Own Name: Women in South Australian History*, Netley, SA, Wakefield Press, 1986.

JONES, TIMOTHY G. *Pegging the Northern Territory: a History of mining in the Northern Territory 1870-1946*, Darwin, Northern Territory Government Printer, 1987.

JOY, WILLIAM *The Aviators: True Adventures of Australian Airmen*, Adelaide, Rigby, (Seal Books), 1978.

KEARNEY, Mr Justice *Murranji Land Claim*, Report by the Aboriginal Land Commissioner No. 25, Canberra, Australian Government Publishing Service, 1987.

KEESING, NANCY *Lily on the Dustbin: Slang of Australian Women and Families*, Ringwood, Vic, Penguin, 1983.

KELSEY, D. E. *The Shackle*, (ed. Ira Nesdale), Blackwood, SA, Lynton Publications, 1975.

KELSEY, D.E. *An Old Man's Legacy*, (unpublished reminiscences) Mortlock Library, Adelaide, 1939.

KENEALLY, THOMAS *Outback*, Sevenoaks, Kent, Hodder & Stoughton, (Coronet Books), 1984.

KENEALLY, THOMAS, ADAM-SMITH, PATSY and DAVIDSON, ROBYN *Australia Beyond the Dreamtime*, Richmond, Vic, William Heinemann Australia (BBC Books), 1987.

KEOGH, E. J. *Locked Away in Fannie Bay: Reminiscences of [a] Prison Officer*, Darwin, Department of Education, 1983.

KERR, MARGARET GOYDER *The Surveyors: the Story of the Founding of Darwin*, Adelaide, Rigby, 1971.

KIMBER, R. G. *Man from Arltunga: Walter Smith, Australian Bushman*, Victoria Park, W A, Hesperian Press, 1986.

KING, P. P. *Voyages for the Survey of the Intertropical Coasts of Australia*, (facsimile edition), London, Libraries Board of South Australia, 1969.

KINGSTON, BEVERLEY *My Wife, Amy Daughter and Poor Mary Ann*, Melbourne, Thomas Nelson (Australia) Pty Ltd, 1980.

KIRKE, WENDY *Handbook of Central Australia*, Alice Springs, Alice Springs Regional Tourist Association Inc., 1986.

LAKE, MARILYN and KELLY, FARLEY (eds), *Double Time: Women in Victoria - 150 years*, Ringwood, Vic, Penguin Books, 1985.

LAMOND, G. H. *Tales of the Overland, Queensland to Kimberley in 1885*, Victoria Park, WA, Hesperian Press, 1986.

LEA, JOHN P. *Government and the Community in Katherine, 1937-78*, Darwin, Australian National University North Australia Research Unit, 1987.

LEGGOE, JOHN *Trying to be Sailors*, Perth, St George Books, 1983.

LEICHHARDT, LUDWIG *Journal of an Overland Expedition in Australia from Moreton Bay to Port Essington*, London, T & W Boone, (facsimile edn) 1847.

LESKE, EVERARD (ed.) *Hermannsburg: a Vision and a Mission*, Adelaide, Lutheran Publishing House, 1977.

LOCKWOOD, DOUGLAS *Australia's Pearl Harbour: Darwin 1942*, Adelaide, Rigby (Seal Books), 1977.

LOCKWOOD, DOUGLAS *The Front Door: Darwin 1869-1969*, Adelaide, Rigby (Seal Books), 1977.

LOWENSTEIN, WENDY and LOH, MORAG *The Immigrants*, Ringwood, Vic, Penguin, 1980.

LUCHETTI, CATHY *Women of the West*, St George, Utah, Antelope Island Press, 1982.

McBURNEY, YVONNE *HMS Buffalo*, Strathfield, Educational Material Aid, 1977.

McCARTHY, DUDLEY *Everyday Life in

Australia: World War I Years, Lane Cove, NSW, Hodder & Stoughton, 1986.

McCORD, MELISSA *Outback Women,* Sydney, Doubleday, 1986.

McGRATH, ANN *Born in the Cattle: Aborigines in Cattle Country,* Sydney, Allen & Unwin, 1987.

McINNIS, R. A. *Diary, 1940-1944,* Darwin, Department of Lands, 1981.

McKENZIE, MAISIE *Flynn's Last Camp,* Brisbane, Boorlarong Publications, 1985.

McKINLAY, BRIAN *The ALP: a Short History of the Australian Labor Party,* Richmond, Vic, Heinemann, 1981.

MACKNIGHT, C. C. *The Voyage to Marege: Macassan trepangers in northern Australia,* Melbourne, Melbourne University Press, 1976.

McLAREN-TURNER, PATRICIA (ed.) *Australian and New Zealand Studies,* British Library Occasional Papers 4, London, The British Library, 1985.

McLAUGHLIN, EVE *Illegitimacy,* (A McLaughlin Guide), West Midlands, Federation of Family History Societies, 1985.

McMURCHY, MEGAN, OLIVER, MARGOT and, THORNLEY, JENI *For Love or Money: a Pictorial History of Women and Work in Australia,* Ringwood, Vic, Penguin, 1983.

McPHEAT, W. SCOTT *Flynn: Vision of the Inland,* Sydney, Hodder & Stoughton, 1977.

McQUEEN, HUMPHREY *Gone Tomorrow: Australia in the 80s,* Sydney, Angus & Robertson, 1982.

McQUEEN, HUMPHREY *Social Sketches of Australia, 1888-1975,* Harmondsworth, Middlesex, Penguin, 1980.

McQUEEN, HUMPHREY *A New Britannia: an Argument concerning the Social Origins of Australian Radicalism and Nationalism,* Ringwood, Vic, Penguin, 1980.

MAFF, WINSOME *Katherine's No Lady,* Katherine, Corporation of the Municipality and the National Trust, n.d.

MAGAREY, SUSAN *Unbridling the Tongues of Women,* Sydney, Hale & Iremonger, 1985.

MARSHALL, VANDA *We Helped to Blaze the Track: Pioneering Experiences in the North,* Townsville, the author, 1980.

MARSHALL-STONEKING, BILLY *Lasseter: The Making of a Legend,* Sydney, George Allen & Unwin, 1985.

MASSON, ELSIE R. *An Untamed Territory: The Northern Territory of Australia,* London, Macmillan & Co., 1915.

MEANEY, ESTHER *The True Life Story of an Australian Country Girl,* Ingham, North Qld, Valu Print, 1988.

MILFORD, R. H. *Australia's Backyards,* Sydney, The Macquarie Head Press, n.d. (c. 1934).

MOSS, JIM *Sound of Trumpets: History of the Labour Movement in South Australia,* Adelaide, Wakefield Press, 1985.

MULVANEY, D. J. and CALABY J. H. *'So Much That is New': Baldwin Spencer 1860-1929,* Melbourne, Melbourne University Press, 1985.

NAKANO, ANN *Japanese Women: a Century of Living History,* Adelaide, Rigby, 1986.

NESDALE, IRA *The Little Missus: Mrs Aeneas Gunn,* Blackwood, Lynton Publications, 1977.

NIEMANN, MARY *Land of the Lotus Eaters,* series published in Melbourne *Leader,* Vic, 1920.

[NORTHERN TERRITORY] *Government House,* Darwin, Northern Territory Government Printer, third edition, 1980.

OGDEN, PEARL *Leg's more Sweeter than Tail,* Darwin, Northern Territory Department of Education, n.d. (c.1982).

PENMAN, ROBYN and STOLK, YVONNE, *Not the Marrying Kind: Single Women in Australia,* Ringwood Vic, Penguin, 1984.

PERROTT, MONICA *A Tolerable Good Success: Economic Opportunities for Women in NSW 1788-1830,* Sydney, Hale & Iremonger, 1983.

PETRICK, JOSE (ed.) *The Renner Diaries,* Darwin, Northern Territory Department of Education, 1983.

PETRICK, JOSE *Street Names History of Alice Springs,* Alice Springs, *Centralian Advocate,*

1980 (includes *Story of the Centralian Advocate* by Robert Watt).

PETERSON, NICOLAS (ed.) *Tribes and Boundaries in Australia*, Canberra, Australian Institute of Aboriginal Studies (Social Anthropology Series No.10), 1976.

PIKE, GLENVILLE *Frontier Territory: the Colourful History of Northern Australia*, Darwin, the author, n.d.

POWELL, ALAN *Far Country: a Short History of the Northern Territory*, Melbourne, Melbourne University Press, 1982.

POWELL, ALAN *The Shadow's Edge: Australia's Northern War*, Melbourne, Melbourne University Press, 1988.

POWNALL, EVE *Australian Pioneer Women*, Currey O'Neil, n.d.

PYE, JOHN *The Tiwi Islands*, Darwin, the author, n.d.

PYE, JOHN *The Daly River Story: a River Unconquered*, Darwin, the author, n.d.

RADI, HEATHER (ed.) *200 Australian Women: a Redress Anthology*, Sydney, Women's Redress Press Inc, 1988.

RAJKOWSKI, PAMELA *In the Tracks of the Camelmen*, North Ryde, Angus & Robertson, 1987.

RAMSLAND, JOHN 'Catherine Helen Spence: writer, public speaker and social and political reformer, 1825-1910' in *South Australiana*, Vol 22, No 1, March 1983.

READ, PETER (ed.) *A Social History of the Northern Territory*, 9 Vols, Darwin, Northern Territory Department of Education, 1979.

REID, RICHARD and JOHNSON, KEITH *The Irish Australians: Selected Articles for Australian and Irish Family Historians*, Sydney, Society of Australian Genealogists, 1984.

REYNOLDS, HENRY *The Other Side of the Frontier: Aboriginal Resistance to the European Invasion of Australia*, Ringwood, Vic, Penguin, 1982.

RICH, JENNY *Gum Leaf and Cow Hide: William Voules Brown, South Australian Pioneer and His Family 1809-1986*, Eastwood, the author, 1986.

RICHARDS, ERIC (ed.) *The Flinders History of South Australia*, Netley, SA, Wakefield Press, 1986.

RICHARDS, MICHAELA and GLEESON, JANE *Mataranka and the Daly: Two Studies in the History of Settlement in the Northern Territory*, Darwin, Australian National University North Australia Research Unit Monograph, 1985.

ROBINSON, PORTIA *The Hatch and Brood of Time: a Study of the First Generation of Native-born White Australians 1788-1828*, Melbourne, Oxford University Press, 1985.

ROSS, NANCY WILSON *Westward the Women*, San Francisco, North Point Press, 1985.

SACHSE, HANS JOACHIM *Darwin Memorials: History in Stone and Bronze*, Darwin, Darwin City Council, n.d.

SAWER, MARIAN and SIMMS, MARIAN *A Woman's Place: Women and Politics in Australia*, Sydney, George Allen & Unwin, 1984.

SEARCY, ALFRED *In Australian Tropics*, London, George Robertson & Co., (second edition), 1909.

SEARCY, ALFRED *In Northern Seas*, Darwin, Northern Territory Department of Education, (facsimile edition), 1984

SEKULESS, PETER *Jessie Street*, St Lucia, University of Queensland Press, 1978.

SHEPHERDSON, I. G. (Ella) *Half a Century in Arnhem Land*, One Tree Hill, SA, the author, 1981.

SKILL, MARJORIE *Sweet Nell of Old Sydney*, North Sydney, Urania Publishing Coy, 1984.

SOWDEN, WILLIAM J. *The Northern Territory As It Is*, Darwin, University Planning Authority, (facsimile edn), n.d.

SPILLETT, PETER *The Discovery of the Relics of HM Colonial Brig 'Lady Nelson' and the schooner 'Stedcombe'*, Darwin, Historical Society of the Northern Territory, 1982.

SPILLETT, PETER *Forsaken Settlement*, Dee Why West, NSW, Landsdowne Press, 1979.

STEVENSON, IAN R. *The Line that Led to Nowhere: the Story of the North Australia Railway*, Adelaide, Rigby, 1979.

BIBLIOGRAPHY

STIRLING, ANNIE LIVINGSTONE *Memories of an Australian Childhood 1880-1900*, East Melbourne, Vic, Schwartz Publishing Group, 1980.

STREHLOW, T. G. H. *Journey to Horseshoe Bend*, Adelaide, Rigby (Seal Books), 1978.

STRINGER, COL *The Way It Was: a Photographic History of the NT*, Darwin, Eagle Publications, n.d.

SUMMERS, ANNE *Damned Whores and God's Police: the Colonization of Women in Australia*, Ringwood, Vic, Penguin, 1977.

TAYLOR, PETER *An End to Silence: the Building of the Overland Telegraph Line from Adelaide to Darwin*, Sydney, Methuen, 1980.

TEALE, RUTH (ed.) *Colonial Eve: Sources on Women in Australia 1788-1914*, Melbourne, Oxford University Press, 1978.

TEECE, C. W. and PIKE, GLENVILLE *Voice of the Wilderness*, Mareeba, Qld, Pinevale Publications, 1982.

THOMAS, ATHOL *Bulls and Boabs: Kimberley People and Places*, Perth, St George Books, 1985.

TRAN, MY-VAN and NELSON, RICHARD D. *A Report on the Settlement of Indo-Chinese Refugees in the Northern Territory*, Darwin, Department of Community Development, n.d.

TUXWORTH, HILDA *Tennant Creek Yesterday and Today*, Tennant Creek, the author, n.d. (c. 1978).

VFX 47777, *A Brief Record of the Australian Army Nursing Service, 1939-45*, List Print, n.d.

WALKER, F. *A Short History of the Legislative Council for the Northern Territory*, Northern Territory Parliamentary Paper No. 1, 1986, Darwin, Government Printer, 1986.

WARBURTON, CARL *Buffaloes*, Sydney, Consolidated Press Limited, 1944.

WARD, RUSSEL *The Australian Legend*, Melbourne, Oxford University Press, (second edition), 1985.

WEBB, E.M. *Australian Red Cross in War 1935-45*, unpublished manuscript held by Red Cross headquarters, Melbourne, Vic, n.d.

WEBSTER, E. M. *An Explorer at Rest: Ludwig Leichhardt at Port Essington and on the Homeward Voyage 1845-1846*, Melbourne, Melbourne University Press, 1986.

WHALAN, VAL *A Fitting Heart: Alice Springs and the Red Centre*, Darwin, Northern Territory Department of Education, 1984.

WHITAKER, J. A. *Borroloola, Isolated and Interesting 1885-1985*, Darwin, Government Printer of the Northern Territory, n.d.

WHITFORD, BOB (text) and MARTIN, COLIN (design) *Red Dust and Distant Horizons*, Darwin, Northern Territory Department of Education, 1988.

WILSON, HELEN J. *The Quality of Life, or A Study on Municipal Functions in the Town of Darwin 1930-1946 and the Effect of the Military Build-Up Therein*, unpublished MA (Qual) thesis, University of Queensland, 1986.

WILSON, HELEN J. and ESTBERGS, ELIZABETH *The Northern Territory Chronicle*, Darwin, Northern Territory University Planning Authority, (second edition), 1984.

WINDSCHUTTLE, ELIZABETH (ed.) *Women, Class and History: Feminist Perspectives on Australia 1788-1978*, Fontana/Collins, 1980.

INDEX